Persuasion:

Understanding, Practice, and Analysis

Persuasion:

Understanding, Practice, and Analysis

Herbert W. Simons
Temple University

ADDISON-WESLEY PUBLISHING COMPANY
Reading, Massachusetts · Menlo Park, California ·
London · Amsterdam · Don Mills, Ontario · Sydney

This book is in the
Addison-Wesley Series in Speech Communication

Consulting Editor:
Frederick W. Haberman

ISBN 0-201-07082-0
CDEFGHIJKL-HC-7987

Preface

As suggested by its title, this book is designed to help readers **understand** the process of persuasion, **practice** persuasion effectively, and **analyze** the persuasive discourse of others.

The first of these functions is considered primary. Thus, although the book focuses on such practical and paradigmatic tasks as speech making and campaign planning, its purview extends to borderline cases of persuasion—an ostensibly scientific report in a psychology journal, a seemingly unintended flicker of an eye at a cocktail party, a pastoral poem, a militant confrontation at a university. Where "how-to-do-it" principles are suggested, they are placed in a research context. Theories are described, studies are cited, and cautionary comments are offered about the limitations of research generalizations.

Theorists of persuasion frequently label themselves as either behaviorally oriented social scientists or as traditionally oriented humanists. Our experience has been that the former tend to ask trivial questions which they answer quite well; the latter ask highly provocative questions but aren't quite sure how to answer them. Hence, although we shall borrow from both, we shall also be critical of both. What one prepublication reader referred to as "Herb's favorite windmills" will be found kicking up dust on various pages of this book. Chapter 2 flails away at various claimants to nonrhetorical status and offers a "map" of persuasion's "domain" that some will undoubtedly regard as downright imperialistic. Chapter 3 takes on just about everybody for failing to deal adequately with situational factors. Chapter 11 debunks the comforting but mistaken notion that the "laws" of logic are none other than the "laws" of thought. Particular attention is called to Chapter 13. Here we argue that the traditionally recommended approach to persuasion (we label it the "co-active" approach) has limited applicability to social conflicts. Combative and expressive alternatives are introduced and compared with the co-active approach as methods of social protest. Other distinctive features of the book include a quasi theory of rhetorical proof that combines Aristotle and dissonance theorist Leon Festinger (Chapter 11), advice to moderates on how to achieve institutional change (Chapter 12), and some pointers on how to detect inobvious meanings, methods, and motives in the discourse of others (Chapter 14).

Immodestly, we believe this book can be read with profit by a variety of students—from sophomores taking persuasion as an elective to beginning graduate students. Our experience is that students benefit most from a multipurpose introductory course, and we have adapted the book to fulfill several different learning objectives:

- Development of a conceptual framework for understanding the psychological dynamics of persuasion;
- Awareness of competing theories and perspectives;
- Sensitivity to persuasion's dimensions and scope;
- Familiarity with findings from the psychological research literature on persuasion;
- Ability to apply findings from research to practice;
- Appreciation of the differences between persuasion in conflict and non-conflict situations;
- Understanding of the role of persuasion in society and culture;
- Improved skill at preparing persuasive messages;
- Improved skill at critically analyzing persuasive messages;
- Consciousness of the ethical choices incumbent upon persuaders.

Depending on which of these objectives he or she expects to emphasize, the instructor might well wish to supplement this book with others (see our list of recommended readings at the end of Chapter 1 and elsewhere) or modify the reading sequence. For example, you may wish to stress the critical function of rhetorical study, and thus require students to read Chapter 14 early on in the course. Or you may have a series of performance assignments, and thus move Chapters 6 through 11 ahead in the reading order.

This book was conceived well before son Michael was conceived. By the time the manuscript was completed, Michael had perfected the phrase, "Daddy workin', workin', workin'." In the meantime, Gayle Simons was patient and kind, thoughtful and thought-provoking; she did more than any husband deserves. Also warranting special thanks are Arthur Bochner, Jesse Delia, and David Swanson who offered first-rate critiques of various drafts, Kenneth Anderson and C. David Mortenson who helped set some early directions, Bev Moulton who typed the manuscript, Chuck Tardy who helped copyedit and prepare the indexes, and Kathy, Madeline, Rachel and Mrs. Stoertz who took turns keeping Michael off Daddy's lap while Daddy was working. Finally, we wish to thank our own students. They convinced us that ideas usually reserved for graduate students can also be internalized and appreciated by undergraduates.

Philadelphia, Pennsylvania   H.W.S.
January 1976

Acknowledgments

In Chapters 5, 8, and 13, we draw substantially from previously published articles and chapters of our own. We wish to thank the publishers for permission to incorporate materials from the following:

Ch. 5 "Psychological theories of persuasion: an auditor's report." *Quarterly Journal of Speech* 57 (1971).

Ch. 5 "Persuasion and attitude change." In Barker, L. L., and Kibler, R. J. (eds.). *Speech-Communication Behavior*, Prentice-Hall, Englewood Cliffs, N.J. (1971).

Ch. 8 "Similarity, credibility and attitude change: a review and a theory." *Psychological Bulletin* 73 (1970) (with R. J. Moyer and N. Berkowitz).

Ch. 13 "The carrot and stick as handmaidens of persuasion in conflict situations." In Miller, G. R., and Simons, H. W. (eds.), *Perspectives on Communication in Social Conflict*, Prentice-Hall, Englewood Cliffs, N.J. (1974).

Ch. 13 "Requirements, problems and strategies: a theory of persuasion for social movements." *Quarterly Journal of Speech* 56 (1970).

Ch. 13 "Confrontation as a pattern of persuasion in university settings." *Central States Speech Journal* 20 (1969).

The author also wishes to acknowledge permission from copyright holders to reprint or quote from the following:

Excerpt (p. 40), from A. J. Weigert, "The immoral rhetoric of scientific sociology," *The American Sociologist* 5 (1970).

Excerpt (p. 50), from P. Watzlawick, J. H. Beavin, and D. D. Jackson, *Pragmatics of Human Communication: A Study of Interaction Patterns, Pathologies and Paradoxes*, W. W. Norton, Inc., New York (1967).

Excerpt (p. 58), from M. Edelman, *The Symbolic Uses of Politics*, University of Chicago Press, Chicago (1967).

Excerpt (p. 62), from L. F. Bitzer, "The rhetorical situation," *Philosophy and Rhetoric* 1 (1968).

Excerpt (p. 116), from S. E. Asch, *Social Psychology*, © 1952, p. 407. By permission of Prentice-Hall, Inc., Englewood Cliffs, N. J.

Chart (p. 119), after D. Katz, "The functional approach to the study of attitudes," *Public Opinion Quarterly* 24 (1960).

Excerpt (p. 154), from R. Roth, "Violent demonstrations bring sorrow to the capitol," *Philadelphia Sunday Bulletin* (May 9, 1971).

Figure (p. 157), after W. Schramm, *The Process and Effects of Mass Communication*, University of Illinois Press, Urbana, Ill. (1960).

Excerpt (p. 157), from W. Schramm, *The Process and Effects of Mass Communication*, University of Illinois Press, Urbana, Ill. (1960).

Excerpts (pp. 172, 173), from L. J. Nebel, "The pitchman," *Harper's Magazine* 222. Copyright © 1961 by *Harper's Magazine*. Reprinted from the May 1961 issue by special permission.

Excerpt (p. 238), from P. G. Zimbardo, "The tactics and ethics of persuasion," *Attitudes, Conflict and Social Change*, Academic Press, New York (1972).

Excerpt (p. 247), from C. U. Larson, *Persuasion: Reception and Responsibility*, Wadsworth Publishing Company, Belmont, Calif. (1973).

Excerpt (pp. 252–3), from W. A. Gamson, *Power and Discontent*, Dorsey Press, Homeward, Ill. (1968).

Excerpts (pp. 263–264), from B. H. Raven and A. W. Kruglanski, "Conflict and power," *The Structure of Conflict*, Academic Press, New York (1970).

Excerpt (pp. 270–1), from P. G. Zimbardo and E. Ebeson, *Influencing Attitudes and Changing Behavior*, Addison-Wesley, Reading, Mass. (1969).

Excerpt (p. 274), from J. H. Skolnik, *The Politics of Protest. Violent Aspects of Protest and Confrontation. A Staff Report to the National Commission on the Causes and Prevention of Violence*, Simon and Schuster, New York (1969).

Excerpt (pp. 297–8), from L. W. Brown, "The image-makers: black rhetoric and white media," *Black Communication: Dimensions of Research and Instruction*, Speech Communication Association, New York (1974).

Excerpts (pp. 302–3), K. K. Campbell, *Critiques of Contemporary Rhetoric*, Wadsworth Publishing Company, Belmont, Calif. (1972).

Excerpt (pp. 307–8), W. Buckley, "Impeach the speech, not the President,"

(May 20, 1973). Copyright © 1973 by The New York Times Company. Reprinted by permission.

Excerpt (p. 315), G. Wills, "The big week in Washington," *The New York Review of Books* 21 (1974).

Excerpt (p. 316), M. H. Nichols, "Lincoln's first inaugural," *American Speeches*, David McKay, New York (1954).

Excerpt (pp. 321–2), from *Fear of Flying* by Erica Jong. Copyright © 1973 by Erica Mann Jong. Reprinted by permission of Holt, Rinehart and Winston, Publishers.

Excerpt (pp. 326–7), K. Burke, *A Rhetoric of Motives*, University of California Press, Berkeley, 1950. Copyright © 1969 by Kenneth Burke. Reprinted by permission of the University of California Press.

Excerpt (pp. 335–7), "Ford's risky plan against slumpflation." Reprinted by permission from *Time*, The Weekly Newsmagazine; Copyright Time Inc. (1975).

Excerpt (pp. 338–42), S. Gearhart, "The lesbian and God-the-Father, or, all the church needs is a good lay—on its side," Copyright 1973, by Sally Gearhart.

Excerpt (pp. 344–5), from P. Hoyt, "Civil Rights. The eyes of the world are upon us," speech delivered to the Arkansas Press Assoc., Little Rock, January 10, 1958, *Vital Speeches of the Day*, City News Publishing Co., Southold, N. Y.

Contents

Part

1

Understanding Persuasion

"Where shall I begin, please your majesty?" asked the White Rabbit.
"Begin at the beginning," the King said gravely, "and go on till you come to the end: then stop."

Lewis Carroll
Alice's Adventures in Wonderland

The
Study
of
Persuasion

For almost as long as people have persuaded, others have written about it. Still referred to as *rhetoric* by many, the study of persuasion goes back to at least the time of the ancient Greeks and probably before. One of the first books in recorded history could be considered a treatise on the subject; it was a handbook on how to flatter the Pharaoh (Gray, 1946). Later, when democratic forms of government replaced the autocratic judgments of Pharaohs, both the practice and study of rhetoric came into full prominence. The ancient Greeks and Romans identified rhetoric with speech-making in the performance of three vital public functions. Citizens in those days argued their own legal cases in the courtroom (*forensic* oratory), presented speeches on ceremonial occasions (*epideictic* oratory), and participated in debates about matters of public policy (*deliberative* oratory). As might be expected, it was not long before rhetoric became a required subject in school. For the Roman citizen, rhetoric was considered an indispensable branch of study, one of the seven liberal arts.

Periodically, the field of persuasion has degenerated and has then had to be regenerated. Systematized by the early Romans; bastardized during the period of Rome's decline; kept relatively dormant during the Middle Ages, except as a vehicle for propagating the faith (note the origin of the word "propaganda"); "rediscovered" during the Renaissance period; it has at times been occupied with noble aims and at times been identified with "making the worse appear the better reason." If terms like "rhetoric," "persuasion," and "propaganda" have negative connotations, it is partly because practitioners of the art have often been flatterers, deceivers, con artists, and exhibitionists. But if rhetoric is sometimes the handmaiden of the unscrupulous, it is also a tool for making the good appear valuable, the true believable, and the beautiful appreciated. It is for these reasons, perhaps, that the study of persuasion has always attracted sinners and saints alike: on the one hand, men like Hitler and Goebbels, but on the other hand, such greats as Aristotle, Plato, Cicero, Quintillian, Augustine, Bacon, Hume, Locke, Mill, and Emerson.

Why Study Persuasion?

A dozen or more business fields have a direct interest in persuasion, as do at least an equal number of academic fields. The "people professions"—law, sales, social work, etc.—could just as well be called "persuasion professions." Within colleges and universities, the interdisciplinary nature of the subject is reflected by the variety of courses in different academic departments that bear upon it: "Public Opinion and Propaganda," "Argumentation and Debate," "Interpretive Writing," "Mass Communication," "Rules of Evidence in Criminal Law," "Homiletics," "Community Organizing," and many others.

Why such widespread interest in persuasion? On a personal level, it may be asked, "What's in it for me?" The study of persuasion may be said to serve three functions: a control function, a consumer protection function, and a knowledge function.

Control Function

Although we may object to the terminology, each of us is a human engineer, involved in the task of constructing messages and manufacturing our own images in ways that are designed to influence others. On a purely personal and private level, we may want to "make it" with a member of the opposite sex, or convince a friend to go with us to the movies, or persuade a parent to "lend" us five dollars. Our interest in persuading may also be professional. We may plan for careers or be involved in careers for which persuasion is a mainstay. Even if we do not think beyond college, let it be remembered that what we do to earn high grades is also a form of persuasion.

Beyond the private and professional levels, many of us are interested in working for social and political betterment. We may be seeking population control, or more funds for cancer research, or racial equality, or greater participation in university governance. What methods are most appropriate for achieving these ends? If we are seeking donations to the American Cancer Society, should we ask potential donors for much more than we expect them to give in the hopes of getting what we bargain for, or would that approach cause rejection? If it is change we are after, should we be moderates and sign petitions or should we be militants and stage confrontations? Should we drop bombs on society or should we drop out of society? Too often, these decisions are made purely on a gut level, without sober analysis of their persuasive consequences.

Consumer Protection Function

A second reason for studying persuasion is that we may thereby become more intelligent, discriminating consumers. Much as we may practice persuasion, most of us spend more time as consumers of persuasive messages. We are literally bombarded by these communications from the moment we are awakened by the clock-radio to the instant we fall asleep before the television set. According to one estimate (cited in Wolin, 1975), average youngsters see 250,000 television commercials by the time they have completed high school! According to another estimate (Fotheringham, 1966), the average American is exposed to 1500 messages per day! There are over 11,000 newspapers, 7,000 magazines, 4,000 radio stations, and 650 television stations in this country. Advertising alone constitutes a 20-billion-dollar-a-year industry, and small wonder. Our medicine cabinets, to cite one example, are replete with items that were sold to us through commercials: this deodorant because it's guaranteed to work for 24 hours; that toothpaste because it's recommended by the Dental Association; those headache pills because they're twice as fast as Brand X; that mouthwash because it tastes like spring. Samuel Becker (1971, p. 26) has provided a remarkably apt account of the communication explosion to which contemporary man has been subjected.

> This man lives in a veritable pressure cooker of communication; everyone and everything is pushing him. The media are pushing him to buy a car and cigarettes and to stop smoking; to use deodorants and to wear an auto seat belt and to vote for the party of his choice and to support our most recent war effort and to parade against war. His children are pushing him to play with them or to give them money for the movies or to buy them a car. And his wife is telling him to mow the lawn and take it easy and fix his tie. And those above him are pushing him to stop making *them* work so hard. And all of this pushing is done through communication. He is pushed by his television set and radios and newspapers and magazines and billboards and handbills and memoranda and even the old-fashioned open mouth which is often so uncomfortably close to his ear. He is attacked not only at the supraliminal levels, but at the barely liminal and even at the subliminal. He cannot escape this barrage of communication, and his wife wonders why he is not more communicative in the evening when she demands, "Talk to me. Why don't you talk to me?"

Although not all communication from others must be guarded against like the plague, quite obviously there is a need for vigilance in the face of unscrupulous persuaders and there is every reason to weigh and evaluate controversial assertions even when they emanate from those we trust. The consumer protection function is served by experts on the subject in two ways. First, they suggest tests of evidence and argument by which competing claims may be evaluated. Second, through critical analysis of communications disseminated for mass consumption they reveal to us how we are manipulated by others. During the fifties, Vance Packard (1958) created a furor by exposing the methods used by *The Hidden Persuaders*, advertising consultants who claim to have found ways to gear products to unconscious strivings. The reception accorded Packard's book was probably equalled by *The Selling of the President, 1968* (McGinniss, 1969), an in-depth study of how Richard M. Nixon employed television to further his Presidential ambitions. Both of these are examples of research in the critical tradition, a tradition that has persisted for hundreds of years.

Knowledge Function

A final reason for studying persuasion has less to do with practical utility than with the insights about humanity and the social order that such

... cure the d.
blame the woman;
embarrassing to detail some
,ptoms of her suffering, even to ...
.mily physician.

It was for this reason that years ago Mrs. Pinkham, at Lynn, Mass., determined to step in and help her sex. Having had considerable experience in treating female ills with her Vegetable Compound, she encouraged the women of America to write to her for advice in regard to their complaints, and being a woman, it was easy for her ailing sisters to pour into her ears every detail of their suffering. * * * * * *

No physician in the world has had such a training, or has such an amount of information at hand to assist in the treatment of all kinds of female ills.

This, therefore, is the reason why Mrs. Pinkham, in her laboratory at Lynn, Mass., is able to do more for the ailing women of America than the family physician. Any woman, therefore, is responsible for her own suffering who will not take the trouble to write to Mrs. Pinkham for advice.

This Advertisement of "Lydia Pinkham's Vegetable Compound" was Printed on June 27, 1905 (About Two Months Ago).

MRS. LYDIA E. PINKHAM'S MONUMENT
In Pine Grove Cemetery, Lynn, Massachusetts.
Mrs. Pinkham Died May 17, 1883 (22 Years Ago).

An early example of the consumer protection function. From Edward Bok, "Pictures that tell their own stories," *Ladies' Home Journal*, September 1905, p. 15. Since passage of the Pure Food and Drug Act in 1906, advertisers have had to be more subtle in their deceptions.

study may provide. The knowledge function may be divided into two categories: knowledge of the role of persuasion in society and knowledge of the psychological dynamics of persuasion.

Paradoxically, we are both creators and products (and often victims) of our culture in a never-ending cycle. The movements and campaigns of persuasion that we wage produce the very structures and processes that govern our thoughts and behaviors. Apart from our own personal roles as persuaders and persuadees, we may be interested in studying the interplay of individuals and the social order—the effects of individuals on the groups, organizations, and institutions with which they affiliate, and the effects these same collectivities have on them.

Of particular interest to a society beset by social problems is the role of persuasion in the creation or reduction of those problems. Some problems in our society are problems of persuasion, while others may be ameliorated by persuasion; but in all cases, a study of persuasive communications provides a mirror image of the political and social issues that we confront and of the means employed to deal with them. Looking back over the sixties, one may recall some of the great issues of the period through a handful of speeches and essays. A president beseeches us to "get this country moving again." A mighty papal doctrine issues from a fragile old man. Glasses in hand, a senator delivers a lecture on the "Arrogance of Power." A vice-president challenges the objectivity of the news media. An Algerian revolutionary recalls Christ's prophecy that "The last shall be first and the first shall be last." Even more compellingly than through speeches and essays, one glimpses the issues confronting a polarized nation through its slogans and nonverbal symbols: "Make love, not war" and "America—Love it or leave it"; peace buttons and bumper stickers, construction helmets and flag decals; the "V for Peace" and the former "V for Victory"; "Black Power," "Student Power," "Chicano Power," "Red Power," and "White Power."

In addition to knowledge of the role of persuasion in society, there is considerable benefit in coming to grips with the psychological dynamics of persuasion. From an examination of persuasion at work, one gets a better understanding of how human beings attend to stimuli, how they order their environment, how thought and emotion interact. Psychological theories of attention, perception, learning, motivation, emotion, etc., have in turn contributed greatly to our understanding of persuasion. Several chapters in this book bring psychological theories to bear upon the subject.

The control function, the consumer protection function, and the knowledge function are closely interrelated. In order to become a discriminating consumer of persuasive messages, it is useful to be aware of the techniques that others may use to influence you. In order to persuade effectively, it is necessary to anticipate how consumers of persuasive messages are likely to respond. And in order to respond discriminatingly or persuade effectively, it helps to have a general understanding of the nature of the persuasive process and the role of persuasion in society. By the same token, our experiences as persuaders and persuadees may help us to understand in small ways how persuasion has shaped human choices and destinies during the major events of history, and we may also come to a better understanding of the contemporary political process. Ultimately, the knowledge function is the highest function, one from which control and criticism can proceed intelligently.

In some respects this text is a handbook. It provides principles by which we may better persuade or more critically react to persuasive communications by others. But on another and perhaps more important level it is designed to provide insights about persuasion, independent of whether these insights lead to effective practices.

Methods of Studying Persuasion

Depending on individual goals, the serious student of persuasion may choose among a wide variety of research methods. Although scholars these days rely heavily on social-scientific methodologies, it should be remembered that for almost all of its long history, the field of persuasion has been the province of the humanities. Drawing on the experiences of those who practiced the art, and on the critical judgments of trained observers, humanists from Aristotle onward fashioned rhetorical principles that have withstood the test of time remarkably well. Many of these principles dealt with techniques of effective persuasion, but others were principles for evaluating the logic and ethics of persuasive discourse. A fundamental tenet of humanists is that persuaders must take moral responsibility for the techniques they employ and for the social consequences of their acts.

For purposes of gaining personal insights about persuasion, the methods traditionally employed by humanists are still of great value. Much can be learned by informal observation of professional practitioners at work or by participant observation in campus, community, and social affairs. We would strongly urge that you attend legislative hearings, interview professional fund-raisers, read sales manuals, and carefully examine appeals in television advertisements and techniques of argumentation at jury trials. Better still, we urge that you get personally involved outside the classroom by running for an elective campus office or attempting to implement a program for institutional change, or that you simply take some time to prepare a diary of when and how you persuade in a typical week.

Besides observing persuasion on the contemporary scene, students of persuasion have been able to learn a great deal from historical studies of public address. Various anthologies (e.g., Graham, 1970; Grover, 1968; Wrage and Baskerville, 1960, 1962) and magazines (e.g., *Vital Speeches*) provide collections of important speeches, and other anthologies (e.g., Auer, 1963; Brigance, 1943; Nichols, 1955) provide interesting historical studies of rhetorically significant events. Still other historical studies (e.g., Baldwin, 1924; Howell, 1956; Kennedy, 1963; Wallace, 1954) survey rhetorical theory and practice over large periods of time, in part to discover how contemporary rhetorical thought has been shaped. A reading of rhetorical history may not always have the direct benefit of helping us to construct persuasive messages, but it should certainly help us to understand more clearly how persuasion functions in society.

Especially useful as sources of insight about persuasion are historical or contemporary studies that utilize one or another method of *rhetorical criticism*. To be a critic of rhetoric is not simply to observe and describe persuasive discourse, but to pass judgment on it or account for it in some way. The aim of rhetorical criticism may be to assess a persuasive work in terms of its enduring significance, or to appraise its artistry or logic, or to reveal its hidden meanings and motives. Oftentimes, the critic is able to shed light, not simply on the items of discourse studied, but also on some larger problem, issue, or theoretical question that happens to be illuminated by that discourse. Rhetorical critical methodologies and examples of applications of these methods are presented in such works as the following: Black (1965), Brandt (1970), Campbell (1972), and Scott and Brock (1972). They should be used to supplement our introduction to rhetorical criticism in Chapter 14.

We come now to what is probably the most dominant approach to scholarly research on persuasion these days, the use of social-scientific methods.[1] Although the contributions of humanists and social scientists are in many ways complementary, important differences may also be noted. First, many of the issues of concern to humanists are outside the pale of scientific inquiry. Questions of ethics, beauty, rhetorical artistry, etc., may be deemed important by social scientists, but they recognize also that such questions are not answerable by scientific methods. Second, whereas humanists retain faith in the subjective impressions of sensitive observers, social scientists attempt to replace personal judgments with impersonal, objective methods. Using what is sometimes referred to as the *behavioral* approach, social scientists subject theories and hypotheses to rigorous empirical tests. Third, humanists tend to regard persuasion as a highly individualized art and tend to be suspicious of extrapolations from scientific research to judgments about how human beings ought to persuade. Scientists, by contrast, insist that their methods yield reliable generalizations which can be used with profit by would-be persuaders.

Behaviorally oriented persuasion scholars utilize polls, surveys, and quantitative methods of content analysis, but for purposes of drawing inferences about factors promoting persuasive effectiveness, their chief tool is the controlled experiment. Recall the Crest toothpaste commercial of recent vintage in which two groups of children were reportedly tested

---

1. During the sixties, according to McGuire (1969), more articles on persuasion appeared in journals of social psychology than on any other subject. One theory alone (Festinger's theory of cognitive dissonance) has generated over 300 studies.

for number of cavities before and after having brushed with either Crest or "another leading toothpaste" over an extended period of time. In the jargon of science, type of toothpaste is known as the *independent variable*, while number of cavities is the *dependent variable*. Each group is a *treatment group*, assigned to an *experimental condition*.

In the well-conducted experiment, *controls* are exercised to ensure that treatment groups are equivalent in all respects except exposure to the independent variable. To ensure initial comparability, the groups are drawn from a common pool of subjects, *randomly assigned* (e.g., by lot) to experimental conditions, and perhaps *matched* on relevant variables. During the course of the experiment, potentially contaminating variables (e.g., methods

---

Readers might well profit from conducting simple experiments of their own. Here are some ideas for research:

1. Request help from strangers under varying conditions. For example, systematically vary arm, hand, and facial cues when hitchhiking. Test for number of rides you got. Or alter your dress when requesting money or directions. (Note: In such situations, it is morally imperative that you debrief subjects afterwards by explaining the nature and purpose of your study).

2. Have a friend stand within earshot of others and then answer a series of survey questions according to your previous instructions. On a controversial issue such as no-fault divorce, the responses should reflect "pro" positions in some cases, "con" positions in others. Also have your friend vary such factors as his or her alleged expertise on the subject or the type of evidence used to support the position taken. Then, in each case, ask bystanders their positions and see if they vary as a function of your friend's responses.

3. Systematically vary your dialect (e.g., "Hippie" vs. "straight") in requesting by phone the opportunity to appear for the same job interviews. Test for number of times you are invited to come down.

4. Make up bogus petitions on a controversial campus issue and show students petition sheets already signed by either a large proportion of professors or a large proportion of students. Test for effects of prestige on willingness to sign.

5. Contact people by phone and ask them to list both the pros and the cons on a controversial issue. As they are responding, murmur "good" or "that's interesting" or "hmm" after either the pro or con statements. Then ask them to indicate their overall positions on the issue and see if they varied as a function of the reinforcing comments you provided.

As you read on in this book, other possibilities for experimental research will no doubt occur to you.

of brushing, food intake) are kept constant or allowed to fluctuate at random. So as to prevent subjects from reacting unusually, the true purpose of the experiment may be concealed or procedures devised such that subjects are not even aware that they are participating in an experiment. Similarly, constraints may be placed on experimenters to ensure that their own biases or expectations do not influence the results. Finally, a statistical procedure is used to determine whether the groups differed on the dependent variable beyond what might be expected by chance. If, in a statistical sense, the Crest users had significantly fewer cavities, and if all the appropriate controls had been applied, the researchers could be reasonably well assured that, at least in this experiment, their hypothesis was confirmed.

Substitute, now, such independent variables as strength of fear appeal, degree of speaker credibility, or other types of persuasive stimuli. Similarly, substitute for number of cavities such dependent variables as degree of attitude change or level of commitment. You now have the persuasion experiment in its most basic form. In more complex experiments, there may be two or more independent or dependent variables, or other nuances of design, but the basic ideas of manipulation and control are still present. Clearly, the method is capable of generating relatively objective findings, and we shall be reporting many of them in this book.[2]

Generalizing From Behavioral Research

A key assumption made by adherents to the behavioral approach to persuasion is, as we have seen, that it is possible to derive valid generalizations from scientific research—generalizations that can be applied by the preacher and the seducer, the technical specialist addressing a group of colleagues and the politician addressing the average voter. Yet, as we should be well aware by now, there are important differences in persuaders, goals, media, contexts, audiences, and subject matter. Does this mean, therefore, that persuasion, like love, is fun to speculate about but impossible to generalize about? An art and not a science? Not quite!

Both the possibilities and the pitfalls inherent in the behavioral approach are nicely illustrated in the accumulated body of findings on the

---

2. Space prohibits a more detailed treatment of experimental designs and procedures. For an excellent introduction to experimental methodology, we recommend Anderson's (1971) *The Psychology Experiment*. For a more comprehensive discussion of experimental and quasi-experimental designs, see Campbell and Stanley (1963). For a simplified digest of findings from persuasion experiments, see Karlins and Abelson (1970). A more thoroughgoing review has been written by McGuire (1969). See Ellul (1965, pp. 259–277) for an excellent critique of experimental research on persuasion.

relative effects of strong versus weak fear appeals. We have chosen this area because it has been especially well researched.

Higbee (1969) has examined 35 studies dealing with fear appeals. If anything, his review underscores the fact of differences with which any seeker after generalizations must necessarily contend. Topics have included dental hygiene, smoking, tetanus, safe driving, fallout shelters, population growth, mental health, cancer, safety belts, roundworms, grades, tuberculosis, syphillis, viewing an eclipse, army life, and donating blood. Media have included printed messages, tape recordings, tapes plus slides, films, and live, oral presentations. Receivers have differed in terms of sex, age, cultural and educational background, and personality characteristics. Sources have ranged from those with extremely high credibility to those with extremely low credibility. Messages have differed in terms of strength of fear appeals (strong, moderate, weak), whether recommendations were given and how specifically, whether reassurances were offered, and whether opportunity was provided to act on recommendations (Higbee, 1969).

By now the research area must certainly seem complex and perhaps bewildering. To further complicate the picture, let us add that combinations of the variables investigated have interactive effects on attitudes and behavior. Still another factor is that reported descriptions of studies may not be entirely comparable. For example, one researcher's "strong" fear appeal may be another's "weak" fear appeal. Finally, the studies often yield contradictory results.

There is indeed a temptation to surrender in the face of such confusion, to terminate all further consideration of the issues with such familiar phrases as "Everything's relative"—"It's all a matter of degree"—"It depends on the situation." Conclusions such as these are perfectly valid, but they are also virtually useless. They are starting points for inquiry, not ending points. What can be done to make better sense of a body of literature such as the research literature on fear appeals? A further look at Higbee's (1969) summary of the literature suggests some useful guidelines.

First, as in most other research areas, simplistic, all-or-none, either-or hypotheses are belied by research. Repeatedly in this book we will qualify generalizations with terms like "generally speaking," "more often than not," and so on. The literature on fear appeals suggests that *more often than not, strong appeals are more effective than weak appeals, but not always.*

Second, expect reversals. For many years it was believed by researchers that strong fear appeals interfered with comprehension of the message and caused defensive avoidance reactions. There is still some evidence for these hypotheses but recent research tends not to support them, except, perhaps, with chronically anxious and other disturbed persons.

Third, view the number and variety of studies as an advantage rather than a disadvantage. Generalizations are more reliable when they are based on a great many studies and when each new study varies in some way from what had been done before.

Fourth, and most important, search for *contingent generalizations*. A contingent generalization is one which states the conditions under which a given level of an alleged causal variable (e.g., strong fear appeals) is likely to affect another variable (e.g., attitude modification) or affect it most intensively. *Although research on persuasion has not yielded very many nontrivial, either-or generalizations, it has unearthed a number of non-trivial, contingent generalizations.* On the basis of Higbee's review, a number of contingent variables *do* appear, reliably, to apply to any number of persons, subjects, and situations. It appears that strong fear appeals are especially effective when presented by highly credible sources; that the specificity and ease of implementation of recommendations for action increases the effectiveness of fear appeals, regardless of level of fear; and that, in addition to employing strong fear appeals (e.g., showing slides of rotted teeth rather than simply describing cavities as harmful), the persuader should also be sure to demonstrate the high likelihood of the unfavorable consequences of inaction (e.g., telling children that unless they brush their teeth properly they are highly likely to get cavities).

From research of this kind, scholars have become better able to understand the dynamics of persuasion and to provide useful advice to persuaders. Still, we would caution readers not to apply behavioral research findings formularistically, the way a cook uses a recipe. Our hope is not only that you will familiarize yourselves with these findings, but that you will also profit from personal practice and observation, from analysis of the communications of others, from reading humanistic studies of rhetorically significant public events, and from an examination of other social science research that may apply more specifically to the particular rhetorical problems you face. (There is, for example, an extensive body of sociological literature on techniques of community organizing, a body of political science research on electoral campaign strategies, and so on.)

Moreover, as you become more familiar with the procedures used in behavioral research on persuasion, we urge that you interpret findings critically. From time to time we have offered our own criticisms, especially of the tendency of behavioral researchers to ignore situational factors.

Finally, we urge once again that you immerse yourselves in the details of the unique situation confronting you, carefully analyzing your own goals, your audience, your subject matter, and the context in which you will be communicating. Behavioral research provides a rough guide to practice, but it is only one means for acquiring rhetorical sensitivity—and a limited one at that.

Fear appeal used in public service advertisement. Although it is impossible, out-side the laboratory, to separate the effects of messages like this from the effects of other message stimuli, we do know that the nation as a whole is smoking more now and enjoying it less. Can it be that the fear appeals used in anti-smoking campaigns have tended to be too mild, or that they have tended to focus too heavily on the problem and too little on providing recommendations for action coupled with reassurances that appropriate action will bring results? (Courtesy of American Cancer Society)

A Preview of Emerging Themes in the Study of Persuasion to be Developed in This Book

In the past several years, a number of developments in the field have served to enrich the study of persuasion. Many of these developments will receive considerable attention here.

Enlargement of Scope

Until relatively recently, the study of persuasion was confined to oral and written communications and their gestural and inflectional accompaniments. Now, in addition to the language of words, gestures, and inflections, attention is being focused on *object language and action language.*

Objects take on linguistic properties when they become identified by others as symbolic extensions of ourselves. As we shall argue in the next chapter, artistic creations such as paintings and sculptures may function rhetorically as symbolic objects. Of and by itself, hair is not a linguistic object, but let it be shaped and groomed in culturally meaningful ways and it becomes a statement by or about its possessor.

Similarly with human actions. Peaceful picketing, for example, is a kind of action language, referred to in legal circles as "symbolic speech." Also in the category of action language are ritual acts such as flag salutes; maneuverings in competitions, such as troop deployments in war; and time-related activities such as showing up late for a party. In Chapter 2 we shall argue that even acts of force and violence may be symbolic in nature.

Fusion of Rationalist and "Irrationalist" Perspectives

From time immemorial, theorists with contrasting views about the nature of man have inevitably derived, from their opposing premises, contrasting views about how persuasion works. Human beings, said the rationalists, are distinguishable from the beasts by dint of their capacity to reason. Logic is their guide, and choice, based on free will, is its outcome. The rational processes may be temporarily distorted by the passions, but ultimately reason prevails.

Psychologists from Sigmund Freud to John Watson, the founder of modern behaviorism, have taken what we call the "irrationalist" position. Depending on the particular theorist, humans are considered victims of irrational, hereditary instincts and emotions or passive organisms waiting to be programmed into action by anyone capable of pushing the right psychological buttons.

Contemporary persuasion theorists may shade toward one or the other extreme perspective, but most of them now acknowledge that the human being is neither a purely logical animal nor a purely illogical animal but something of both. Correspondingly, it is appropriate to speak of "proof" in persuasion but to emphasize that such proof is distinctively rhetorical—adapted not so much to the logician's rules of logical consistency as to the less stringent but often more creative "rules" by which particular audiences judge persuaders' arguments to be logical or illogical.

Our position draws heavily from psychological consistency theories (to be described in detail in Chapter 5). Basically, our thesis is that individuals seek a psychologically consistent view of the world. If that view is logically consistent, so much the better, but often as not, what is factually true or deductively valid is also unpleasant, disturbing, or threatening; hence, psychologically "inconsistent" or "unbalancing." Within limits, we may tolerate psychological inconsistency for the sake of logical consistency. But if the issue is important enough to us—for example, if we are advised by a friend that we are unattractive to the opposite sex—we are likely to seek ways to reduce the imbalance. Among the many "rebalancing" mechanisms available to persuadees, some, like belief or attitude change, are generally sought by persuaders. The job of persuaders is first to create psychological imbalance in the persons they seek to persuade, and then to "close off" undesired rebalancing mechanisms while simultaneously promoting the resolutions they favor.

Interest in Contextual Factors

It is a central thesis of this book that persuasion can best be understood as an ongoing, open system of interactions in which the persuader's rhetorical choices and actions and the receiver's attitudes and behaviors are both influenced by historical, temporal, physical, political, and cultural "givens" in particular situational contexts. Surprisingly, contextual variables were, until the last decade or so, victims of systematic inattention by behaviorally oriented social psychologists, especially those who relied entirely on findings from experiments conducted in classrooms and laboratories. The tendency has abated somewhat,[3] but many psychologically oriented persuasion theorists continue to foster the misimpression that what holds true in the experimental setting will necessarily hold true in "naturalistic" settings. Furthermore, in order to exercise control over "nonessential" variables, they frequently conduct experiments which isolate persuasive messages from contexts that might give them greater meaning and significance. For equally understandable reasons, "performance" courses in public speaking

---

3. Rather than assuming that generalizations from laboratory research apply to real-life settings, more and more researchers are now testing these generalizations in naturalistic, field situations. See, for example, Bickman and Henchy (1970).

and persuasion have often contributed to these misimpressions. Persuasive speaking becomes an academic exercise, to be performed and later dissected as an isolated event by persons lacking a genuinely perceived stake in the issues at hand or any but artificial constraints on what can be said or done. For practical reasons, we too will have to simplify in this book, but we will be placing greater emphasis than most textbooks on such ongoing persuasive interactions as campaigns and movements, and we will periodically underscore the importance of contextual differences that seem to make a difference. The nature and functions of contextual factors are taken up in Chapter 3.

Attention to Situations Involving Reciprocal Influence

Historically, the study of persuasion has focused on situations involving active message senders and passive message receivers. For every speaker, there was an audience. For every writer, there was a reader. Roles were clearly defined.

Within the past decade or so, considerable attention has been given to two-way patterns of communication in which the roles of persuader and persuadee shift abruptly, as in a heated conversation between friends. Particular attention has been given to social conflicts, which almost always involve reciprocal influence. A *social conflict* may be defined as *a clash over incompatible interests in which one party's relative gain is another's relative loss.* In a conflict over wages between management and labor, for example, each side seeks to maximize its interests at the relative expense of the other. The subject of persuasion in social conflicts is discussed at length in Chapter 13.

Search for Alternatives to the "Co-Active" Approach

Concomitant with their interest in social conflicts, persuasion theorists have been exploring alternatives to traditionally recommended strategies of persuasion. From Aristotle onwards, the generally recommended approach has involved a mix of logic and psychology, aimed at modifying beliefs, values, or attitudes as a precondition for changes in behavior. Persuaders have been advised to employ manipulative stratagems, but they have been cautioned to avoid threats or acts of force. Instead, the focus has been on finding common cause with audiences. The customary advice has been to be audience-centered, to protect egos, to adapt to the listeners' frame of reference, to speak their language; in general, to *move toward* the audience psychologically so as to secure audience acceptance in return. Because of its emphasis on joint movement toward a common position, we call this grand strategy "co-active persuasion."

We will be describing co-active stratagems in Chapters 6 to 12 of this book and we will be recommending their use in most rhetorical situations. Like many of today's theorists, however, we no longer regard the co-active way as the only way, or even necessarily the best way, to persuade antagonists and third parties in conflict situations. Alternatives to the co-active approach are discussed in Chapter 13. They include divisive discourse, threats, "forced compliance" techniques, and expressive stratagems.

Toward a Definition of Persuasion

How might we define persuasion and distinguish it from "nonpersuasion"? A useful way to construct a definition is to look for common characteristics in what language specialists refer to as *paradigm cases*—examples from ordinary discourse that almost everyone would agree are instances of persuasion. Probably all of us would agree that the following are paradigm cases:

- a politician presenting a campaign speech to attract votes;
- an advertiser preparing a commercial for presentation on television;
- a legislator urging support for a bill;
- peaceful pickets displaying placards to passers-by;
- a trial lawyer's summation to a jury;
- a parent advising a child to marry a rich boy;
- a college representative recruiting student applicants;
- a missionary proselytizing for religious converts;
- a newspaper editorial complaining about anti-inflationary measures;
- a Casanova attempting to seduce a fair maiden;
- a minister imploring parishioners to respect human dignity;
- an essayist decrying American materialism;
- a student appealing for a make-up exam.

From the foregoing cases it is possible to identify common elements that constitute *defining characteristics* of persuasion.

Human communication. Each of the above cases involves acts of human communication, whether verbal or nonverbal, oral or written, explicit or implicit, face-to-face or via an indirect medium such as television. Occasionally, "persuasion" is used metaphorically to refer to nonhuman acts, as when we say, "The severity of the blizzard persuaded me to go indoors." For the most part, however, the term is restricted to exchanges of messages between human beings.

Attempted influence. To influence another is to alter his or her behavior in preferred ways. At one extreme of *pressure to influence,* an individual's behavior may be modified by unintended messages or by direct experience. At the other extreme, behavior may be changed as a result of raw, physical coercion or other stimuli which trigger automatic, involuntary responses. In a gray area between these two poles—its geography only vaguely mapped—lies the "domain" of persuasion. Persuasion is a manipulative act, but it also leaves receivers with the perception of choice.

All of the paradigm cases given above involved attempted influence. The politician attempted to attract votes; the legislator sought passage of a bill; the student sought permission to take a make-up exam. In some contexts it may be appropriate to refer to "persuasion" as an effect already produced by messages, whether intended or not. For example, we might say, "She persuaded me without even trying." So long as the context is made clear, this deviation from dominant usage need not bother us greatly. Our conception of persuasion remains virtually the same.

Beliefs, Values, or Attitudes. One way to plot the domain of persuasion a bit more exactly is to say that persuasion is aimed at modifying *not only* overt behavior in preferred ways, but also beliefs, values, and/or attitudes. If a robber were to knock you unconscious and take your money, this would alter your behavior but it would not modify your beliefs, values, or attitudes in preferred ways.

Beliefs, values, and attitudes are covert, "in-the-head" phenomena whose existence can only be inferred by outsiders. Admittedly, these are troublesome concepts, mired in ambiguity, which will need considerable clarification in later chapters. For now, let us offer provisional notions of what these terms mean.

To begin with, we can say that attitudes, beliefs, and values are all *judgments* of a kind. Attitudes are judgments about how to act; beliefs are judgments about what is true or probable; values are abstract judgments about such matters as what is moral, important, beautiful, etc.

More precisely, we can say that attitudes *incline* us toward action. They are predispositions to act in particular ways toward particular objects. The politician sought favorable attitudes toward himself as a candidate so that his listeners would vote for him and perhaps contribute to his campaign. The legislator sought favorable attitudes toward the bill she was sponsoring in the hopes that her colleagues would join her in supporting it.

Roughly speaking, the beliefs and values that we hold influence our attitudes and our attitudes influence our actions. In this sense, beliefs and values are *components* of attitudes. If the candidate's listeners believed that he would help lower their property taxes and if they considered lower property taxes important, chances are that they would be more inclined to support him. Any characterization of an object may be considered a *belief* about that object. Any generalized attraction or repulsion bearing on the object or on attributed qualities of the object may be considered a relevant *value*.

We should note that persuasion is not always aimed directly at modifying attitudes or altering overt behavior. On any one occasion, in fact, its aim may be to modify a single belief or value. Thus, the trial lawyer in our example sought to modify beliefs about the defendant's guilt or innocence; the minister focused solely on the value of human dignity.

A Working Definition of Persuasion

On the basis of the foregoing discussion, we may define "persuasion" as *human communication designed to influence others by modifying their beliefs, values, or attitudes.*[4]

For the most part, our use of the term "persuasion" will be confined in this book to paradigm cases. That being so, few should question our use of the term or the definition we assigned to it. The question arises, however, whether paradigm cases constitute the whole of persuasion. Is persuasion practiced solely by advertisers, lawyers, politicians, ministers, and their ilk, or is it also practiced by others who might not ordinarily be thought of as persuaders? Is it appropriate, for example, to refer to the activities of scientists addressing other scientists as "persuasion"? Can our definition be applied to newscasters and educators or to poets and dramatists? And if representatives of professions such as these are labeled as "persuaders," should this demean their status? We turn to questions of this kind in the next chapter.

Summary

Rhetoric, the study of persuasion, has had an uneven past, paralleling the use of the tool by saints and sinners alike. Conceived by the ancient Greeks as the prime instrument of democracy, it has at other times been fashioned for ignoble purposes. Few people are unambivalent in their feelings about persuasion; none can do without it.

The study of persuasion serves three vital functions. First, it informs persuasive practice, enabling would-be persuaders to maximize their oppor-

---

4. The reader may wish to compare our definition with definitions found in other textbooks on persuasion. See, for example, Anderson (1971), Bettinghaus (1973), Fotheringham (1966), Larson (1973), Minnick (1968), and Scheidel (1967). Each of these books is also a valuable resource for your continued study of persuasion.

tunities for *social control*. Second, it enables us to become more intelligent and discriminating *consumers* of persuasive communications. Third, and most important, it adds to our *understanding* about human psychology and the individual's place in society and culture. Although Part 1 of this book roughly corresponds to the understanding function, Part 2 to the control function, and Part 3 to the consumer protection function, the functions are in fact complementary and inseparable. For those interested only in consumer protection, for example, we would still advise a careful reading of Part 2.

Although many rhetoricians continue to study persuasion humanistically, as an art rather than a science, it has, in the last forty years, become an object of great interest among social psychologists and other behaviorally oriented social scientists. Studies of persuasion are now routinely carried on in rigorous field and laboratory experiments, and we shall review a great many of them in this book. Despite shortcomings in individual studies, the behavioral approach has added considerably to our understanding by unearthing nontrivial, contingent generalizations about persuasion. Providing the findings from such research are interpreted critically and applied selectively to cases, we think they can serve as a useful guide to practice and analysis.

Several recent trends in the study of persuasion that will be highlighted in subsequent chapters were previewed here: the considerable broadening of rhetoric's scope; the fusion of rationalist and "irrationalist" perspectives; the emphasis being given today to contextual factors in persuasion; attention to situations involving reciprocal influence, including conflict situations; and the search for alternatives to what we have called the mainstream "co-active" approach.

Finally, a definition of persuasion was culled from an examination of what some philosophers call *paradigm* cases of the term. We defined persuasion as human communication designed to influence others by modifying their beliefs, values, or attitudes.

Getting Started: Ten Most Recommended Readings

Note: The books and articles listed here are not necessarily the best on the subject, but each in its own way is an excellent supplement to this one and each can be read relatively quickly and with interest by the beginning student of persuasion. Scattered throughout this book are notes referring to other recommended readings on particular topics.

1. Bem, Daryl J. (1970). *Beliefs, Attitudes and Human Affairs*. Belmont, Cal.: Brooks/Cole Publishing Co.

Our students love this book and we can understand why. Bem makes the psychology of persuasion come alive in this brief, funny, boldly opinionated treatment of the foundations of beliefs, values, and attitudes.

2. Berger, Peter L. (1963). *Invitation to Sociology—A Humanistic Perspective.* Garden City, N.Y.: Anchor Books.

   This is a beautifully written little book that should be required reading for anyone interested in the role of persuasion in society. Berger's perspective on social interactions is in many ways identical to the perspective we offer in Chapter 2.

3. Bryant, Donald C. (1953). Rhetoric: its functions and its scope. *Quarterly Journal of Speech* 39: 15–37.

   This is a seminal article on the nature and scope of persuasion which has greatly influenced humanistically minded rhetorical scholars. Although Bryant's conception of rhetoric differs from ours in important ways, his is nevertheless an excellent definitional statement that should help you to see the humanistic study of persuasion as a living tradition.

4. Campbell, Karlyn K. (1972). *Critiques of Contemporary Rhetoric.* Belmont, Cal: Wadsworth.

   This is one among many introductions to rhetorical criticism. After telling us how to be a rhetorical critic, Professor Campbell then offers a number of message-centered critiques of contemporary discourse. Campbell brings passion and verve to her analyses, and she invites us to be as critical of her work as she is of the work of others.

5. Jones, Edward E. (1954). *Ingratiation: A Social Psychological Analysis.* New York: Appleton-Century-Crofts.

   Jones and his colleagues have conducted an intriguing set of experiments on this fascinating subject, many of which can be replicated easily by readers. The studies provide, as a byproduct, an excellent introduction to behavioral research methods in persuasion.

6. Mehrabian, Albert. (1971). *Silent Messages.* Belmont, Cal.: Wadsworth.

   No one has performed more experiments on the influence of nonverbal messages than Albert Mehrabian. Here the author summarizes his research and the research of others in highly readable form.

7. Nimmo, Dan. (1970). *The Political Persuaders: Techniques of Modern Election Campaigns.* Englewood Cliffs, N.J.: Prentice-Hall.

   In this book, Nimmo looks at political campaigning from the framework of communication theory. Particular attention is given to methods and effects of the mass media in electoral contests.

8. Novak, Michael. (1974). *Choosing Our King.* New York: MacMillan.

   Social scientists often forget that political values are always embedded in symbols. Novak does not. In this book on the symbols that we attach to the

American Presidency and to the men who aspire to it every four years, Novak brings a distinctively rhetorical stance to his analysis of presidential campaigns.

9. Schiller, Herbert. (1973). *The Mind Managers*. Boston: Beacon Press.

Schiller takes a hard, cynical look at some of the institutionalized rhetorical practices in our society: advertising, the electronic media, psychological warfare, and others. Many of his criticisms cannot be dismissed.

10. Zimbardo, Philip, and Ebbeson, Ebbe. (1969). *Influencing Attitudes and Changing Behavior*. Reading, Mass: Addison-Wesley.

This is another behaviorally oriented text on persuasion which is highly popular with students. The book is addressed to a number of socially relevant issues and brings interesting research to bear upon them. Readers will also find here an excellent summary of methods of attitude measurement and research design.

The Status, Ethics, and Scope of Persuasion: a Perspective

Consistent with our desire to help readers not only practice persuasion but also understand persuasion, we offer here a series of related premises that, together, constitute a perspective on its status, ethics, and scope. The need for a statement of perspective seems all the more urgent in light of the curious place of persuasion in our culture. Criticized by some for being too manipulative, it is assailed by others for not being manipulative enough. Along with such roughly synonymous terms as "rhetoric" and "propaganda," it is in many contexts a "devil" word, a term of disapproval. Reporters, educators, and scientists deny that they practice it; poets, dramatists, and composers insist that it gets in the way of their art. Some economists and political scientists tend to minimize its importance in the overall scheme of things, believing that it is money and power that really do the talking in society. In the process of defending their subject matter, rhetoricians (i.e., persuasion theorists) have attempted to make it palatable by acting as though the co-active approach to persuasion (briefly introduced in Chapter 1) is the only approach. They have done so despite the inappropriateness of co-active persuasion for many conflict situations.

We should warn the reader that our perspective on the status, ethics, and scope of persuasion sets this book apart in some ways from other treatments of the subject. In particular, we call the reader's attention to our "map" of persuasion's domain on page 44, in which we distinguish between "paradigm" and "peripheral" cases of persuasion.

Premise One: One Cannot Talk About Persuasion for Very Long Without Reflecting Cultural Values.

In any culture, certain symbols function as "god" words or "devil" words (Weaver, 1953)—symbols of approval or derision, of group identification or disidentification. That this is so in our own culture is easily apparent for such "god" words as "freedom," "democracy," and "capitalism" and for such "devil" words as "slavery," "totalitarianism," and "communism." Words of this kind tend to be defined, illustrated, and differentiated from other terms in ways that preserve and reinforce the prevailing values of a society or those of its ruling elites. In service of these ends, the culture provides what Stevenson (1945) has called "persuasive definitions," definitions consistent with the mythical beliefs of a society rather than its harsher realities. When examples of "god" words and "devil" words are offered, they also tend to be one-sided. "Freedom," for example, is identified with "capitalistic" nations such as the United States. Distinctions between terms tend to be rockbound and rigid; there is no middle ground. In conventional parlance, for example, a nation is either "democratic" or "totalitarian"—it cannot be neither or some of both. The net effect of these verbal treatments is persuasive indeed. "God" words and "devil" words tend to become *reified* —regarded not simply as symbols but as *things* with magical powers. When a society strongly identifies with its "god" words and strongly "disidenti-fies" with its "devil" words, its values become highly resistant to change because they are no longer even regarded as values. They become as real and as solid as the ground beneath our feet.

As we hope to show in subsequent sections, the term "persuasion" tends to be defined, illustrated, and differentiated from other terms in ways that support prevailing values. Like it or not, "persuasion" is frequently not a neutral term. Along with such roughly synonymous terms as "rheto-ric," "propaganda," and "indoctrination," it reflects political and cultural values. Compared to such words as "expression," "education," "informa-tion," "art," "description," and "scientific proof," it is a "devil" term. The conventional wisdom holds that *our* nation exports "documentary" films abroad while our enemies distribute "propaganda" films. Our schools are said to "educate" or "acculturate," but school teachers do not claim to "persuade" or "indoctrinate." Employers "orient" or "train" but never "brainwash" their employees. Poets and dramatists "express" themselves or create "art" but never purport to indulge in "mere rhetoric." Situation comedies and football games "entertain" us but do not "persuade" us. Scientists and philosophers "describe," "explain," "reason," or "prove" but they never employ "rhetoric" or "persuasive appeals." When "persua-sion," "propaganda," and "rhetoric" *are* used in references to artists, scien-tists, newscasters, etc., they are almost always terms of derision; ways of indicating the language-user's belief that artists, scientists, or other profes-sionals have pretended to be what they are not; that they have somehow violated principles held in high esteem by their professions. In these con-texts, the terms have come to mean "deception" or "impurity," something that the language-user wishes to expose. No wonder that "persuasion," "propaganda," and "rhetoric" are often preceded by such adjectives as "mere," "just," and "only"; worse yet, by such expletives as "malicious," "devious," and "dishonest." In popular discourse we might say, "I wish my teacher would stick to the facts and stop trying to persuade us." Or, "His rhetoric stood in the way of his art." Or, "The argument that males are inherently stronger than females isn't scientific, it's male chauvinist propaganda." [1]

---

1. These examples of "rhetoric about rhetoric" may be viewed as but instances of a more widespread phenomenon, the use of persuasion to maintain social order and stability and to preserve or enhance the status, power, and wealth of priv-ileged groups within society. For a general introduction to this perspective, we recommend Hugh Duncan (1968), *Communication and Social Order*. Duncan is a disciple and systematizer of Kenneth Burke (1950, 1969) whose writings are more difficult but immensely profitable to the patient reader. Also quite useful from a slightly different perspective is Weaver's (1953) *The Ethics of Rhetoric*. Of course, persuasion may also be used to attack governing societal arrangements, and the authors we have recommended are alive to these possibilities too.

Only in relationship to such words as "coercion," "force," and "power" is "persuasion" ever a "god" word, and there it seems to depend on whether we are opposed to particular users of force or for them. For example, we say, "I wish the demonstrators would try to persuade us rather than try to shove their program down our throats." But we also say, "I wish the President would stop talking about civil rights (giving persuasive speeches) and start doing something about it (forcing change)." Generally speaking, "persuasion" is contrasted favorably with "coercion" in our culture, and we tend to associate it in relation to coercion with acts and persons we approve.

It should be clear by now that in a great many contexts, "persuasion" and its near synonyms are emotionally loaded terms. There is a range of cases in which our culture regards "persuasion" neutrally or as a necessary evil, but that range is limited. Largely, the range is restricted to paradigm cases of persuasion, such as those we cited in Chapter 1: a politician presenting a campaign speech, a trial lawyer's summation to a jury, a legislator urging passage of a bill, and so on. Even here, it may be noted, a negative onus is attached to the activities of such prototypical persuaders as the politician, the salesperson, the advertiser, and the public relations consultant. This may be one reason why poets, dramatists, scientists, etc., are loath to think of themselves as persuaders.

Premise Two: Distinctions Between Persuasion and Nonpersuasion Tend to be Overdrawn In Our Culture. Practically All Human Acts and Artifacts Have a Rhetorical Dimension.

Because "persuasion" is treated as a "god" word or a "devil" word in relationship to its alleged alternatives, it should not surprise us that distinctions between "persuasion" and "nonpersuasion" tend to be sharply drawn in our culture. We think they are not only sharply drawn but overdrawn, particularly as regards such disciplines as news reporting, education, art, and entertainment.

Consider, for example, the distinctions commonly drawn between persuasion and newscasting or education. Such distinctions are based on the notion that the reporter and teacher are, or ought to be, accurate, objective, and complete in giving information. Presumably, it is possible to provide descriptions of the real world without bias, inference, selection, judgment, etc. The "facts speak for themselves." By implication, persuaders are extra-factual or false to facts. They render value judgments or interpretations, and they are subjective and one-sided.

The story goes that three umpires disagreed about the task of calling balls and strikes. The first one said, "I calls them as they is." The second one said, "I calls them as I sees them." The third and cleverest umpire said, "They ain't nothin' 'till I calls them."

The point of the story is, of course, that "man is the measure of all things." A strike is a strike only in terms of arbitrary standards set up by baseball authorities and applied to the real world by umpires. In a strict sense, facts themselves are subjective statements, as Poincaré (1929) put it some time ago.

> For a fact is not a thing or event, it is a statement about a thing or event, and it is impossible, or nearly so, to make a statement without implying some theory of events—what is "important" for instance. Thus every statement of fact is an abstraction. It refers to some aspect only of events.

If even facts are subjective in a technical sense, when does a statement describe and when does it persuade? Some hard-nosed theorists (e.g., Berlo, 1960) have insisted that all informative discourse is persuasive, but we do not wish to push our point to that extent. We would call discourse "purely descriptive" when it "sticks to the facts;" specifically: (1) when there are generally agreed upon standards for calling something a fact; (2) when the standards can be applied consistently to the real world; (3) when the language-user can be trusted to apply these standards competently; and (4) when the language-user does not venture beyond the facts. We would call discourse "persuasive" when it departs from these standards, especially when it ventures beyond the facts to include judgments, inferences, suggestions, or interpretations. When a carpenter describes a piece of lumber as a "two by four" or when a student tells us he goes to college at Ambler, Vermont, we generally conclude that these are statements of fact, whether they are true or false (there is always the possibility of error). The statements are subjective in Poincaré's sense, but they are nevertheless statements of fact.

Seldom, however, are matters so clearcut. We may ordinarily trust reporters to report a football score accurately, but we would be wise to question the factual character of their reports on the Arab-Israeli conflict. As this is written, militants on the Left are chastising educational institutions for giving biased support to antiquated values and beliefs. At the same time, conservatives are accusing the "Eastern press establishment" of a liberal or leftist bias in its reports about Republicans. We think both are right. It is precisely in borderline cases such as these that we might speak of "informational rhetoric." In still other instances that we call paradigm cases (admittedly, the differences are of degree) a superficial guise of objectivity should not blind us to obvious persuasive intentions.

Although those who specialize in disseminating factual information (newscasters, historians, descriptive anthropologists, etc.) have come to the position reluctantly, many now recognize that "objective" reporting is generally neither possible nor desirable. Fortunately, we have moved from the days when history books reported little more than names, dates, and places. Many news media analysts now speak of the "fairness test" rather than the test of objectivity as the basic criterion by which news reports should be judged (Friendly, 1971). They maintain that if the news is to have meaning and significance it must be "dramatized," "interpreted," "placed in perspective"—in other words, it must contain rhetorical elements. Such a position necessarily raises many more questions than it answers. Basically, what is "fair" reporting? When does dramatic coverage become yellow journalism? Are "fair" interpretations of the facts always "balanced" interpretations or are there times when only "extreme" judgments "follow" from the facts? These are difficult questions about the *rhetoric* of news reporting, but they are infinitely more realistic than those which presuppose the possibility of reporting on controversial matters objectively.

And what of art and entertainment? If we are to believe some experts, "true" artists are somehow "above" persuasion. Their job is not to preach to us but to express their feelings aesthetically. In textbook terms, their acts are consummatory, not instrumental; they are ends in themselves, not means to an end (Berlo, 1960). Similarly with entertainers. Their job is to make us laugh or forget; to involve us in the nonserious affairs of life. If we are responsive to the artist and entertainer, we react by evincing consummatory interest but not by modifying our attitudes and behavior. The latter are considered to be unnecessary and perhaps accidental byproducts of the receiver's experience.

Once again, we find it impossible to draw hard and fast distinctions. Moreover, we are not always inclined to think less of an artist or entertainer just because he or she has persuasive intent. Corbett (1971) has argued that the young protestors of the sixties were influenced more by films, TV shows, and popular music than by such conventional persuasive instruments as speeches and essays. Clearly, some of these offerings were consciously rhetorical while remaining among the best in art and entertainment available: films like *Dr. Strangelove* and *Easy Rider*, for example; situation comedies like *All in the Family*; the protest songs of Bob Dylan and the rebellious rock of the Rolling Stones.

Our list of rhetorical art and entertainment forms has barely scratched the surface. Historically, one can find counterparts for rock's rebellious message in the poetry that blossomed in Russia just prior to the revolution or in the jazz of the twenties and thirties which, incidentally, Russia prohibited from being aired. Art and entertainment for popular consumption occasionally mock prevailing values, as in the satire of Jonathan Swift. More often than not, however, they are used to reinforce these values. The Greeks staged the Olympic games to affirm communal values and insisted that drama serve the state. Today's college football spectacle provides a clear example of similar reinforcement through entertainment. The game is not complete without the singing of the national anthem, the patriotic half-time show, and the pretty cheerleaders invoking the gods to bless dear old U.

Evidence of persuasive intent in art and entertainment is not always clearcut since the desire to persuade, when present, may be secondary, unconscious, or even deliberately masked. Whatever its intent, however, it can at the very least be said that much popular art and entertainment *functions* persuasively for the receiver.

Consider, for example, the nature of most escapist fare over the mass media. Klapper (1960) has argued that the profit motive compels the commercial mass media to support popularly held values and, hence, to give these values a "monopoly propaganda" position in our society. In reflecting these values, the media tend to intensify them. Whatever the intent of its creators, it is clear that daytime soap operas, comic strips, Western movies, and the like have tended, until recently at least, to present characters and plots stereotypically, in ways that supported the wish-fulfillment needs of others. The old-fashioned Western was a classic example. As Elkin (1950) says, it presented a hero who never lost his temper, fought fair, and always won out in the end. Arnheim (1944) found a similar projection of satisfying values in his study of radio serials. Many people tend to identify vicariously with the characters in escapist materials (Katz and Lazarsfeld, 1955), to discuss them with others as archetypes of real-life situations (Bogart, 1955), and, in the case of soap operas, to glean advice from them (Herzog, 1944).

Regular viewers of daytime television will recognize that soap operas now deal much more explicitly with controversial themes than in the tepid days of *Life Can be Beautiful* and *Our Gal, Sunday* on radio. Life is not nearly as beautiful on today's "soaps," as one character after another experiences nervous breakdowns, tumors, unwanted pregnancies, cancers, divorce, rape, and even incest.

Yet, as Marjorie Perloff (May 10, 1975) has observed in *The New Republic*, daytime soap operas continue to be pitched to the fantasies of the housewives who view them, despite these surface manifestations of social realism. With incredible sameness, they portray sophisticated, Waspish protagonists who reside in attractive suburban towns within safe distance from the Big City, and who live out their days snaring handsome men from each other, or performing miraculous operations between affairs (80 percent of the males are doctors), or sipping lunchtime cocktails at French restaurants, or sneaking idyllic weekends at Far Away Places. People now confront obstacles in "Anytown, USA," and some get hurt, but a post-operative cocktail at Pierre's with Dr. Jerry Kane provides proof to Mrs. Average Housewife that life can be beautiful after all.

It should be apparent by now that persuasion is not confined to speech-making and essay-writing. Art and entertainment, news reporting and formal education may in some cases be all the more persuasive because the intent to persuade is not obvious. That their so-called "true" or "higher" purpose may be something other than persuasion is really beside the point. For example, one may judge a work of art as effective or ineffective persuasion while simultaneously making a separate judgment about its aesthetic qualities. Much aesthetically pleasing art has also served highly regarded rhetorical ends (the plays of Sophocles, for example) and can thus be appreciated on both levels.[2] Wayne Booth (1971, pp. 101–2) has argued along similar lines:

> If all good art has no rhetorical dimension, as so many have argued, then the rhetoric is left to those who will use it for the devil's purposes. . . . How much better it would be if we could develop an understanding of how great literature and drama does in fact work rhetorically to build and strengthen communities.

Let us now turn to other areas in which alleged distinctions between persuasion and nonpersuasion have been overdrawn.

Premise Three: Even the Scientist Is a Persuader of Sorts.

If we are to place trust in the conventional wisdom, not only are there ways of describing the world objectively, there are also ways of *drawing conclusions* objectively. Salespersons and politicians offer facts and reasons to their audiences, but their presentations are always "extra-factual" and "extra-logical"; audience acceptance rests on something *more than* or *other than* the evidence or logical arguments that they present. By contrast, the scientist and the philosopher offer "proofs" that are free of extra-factual and extra-logical factors. Whereas persuasion begins from premises that are acceptable to a particular audience (whether true or not), logical proof begins from premises that are indubitably and universally *true*. Whereas the persuader's arguments are value-laden, the scientist's or philosopher's arguments are value-free. Whereas the persuader is partial, the scientist and philosopher are impartial. Hence, according to the conventional wisdom, persuasion leads us at best to judgments of subjective prob-

---

2. Several essays in Douglas Ehninger's (1972) anthology deal with this issue and with other issues raised in this chapter. On the relationship between rhetoric and literary art, we especially recommend the article in Ehninger by Bigelow.

ability; those who offer "logical proof" lead us to judgments of objective certainty or near certainty.

A popular model of logical proof is the output produced by scientific research. So ingrained, in fact, is the public's faith in the accuracy of scientific claims that to challenge those claims is tantamount to committing a heresy. At the risk of opening up a Pandora's box of questions about how "scientific rhetoric" should be evaluated, let us consider in what respects the scientist is a persuader, summarizing briefly the arguments put forth by a number of responsible advocates of this position.

First, whether we like it or not, the believability of a scientific claim is often affected by the reputation of the authors, the prestige of the journal in which their work appears, and the number of eminent authorities they cite in support of their thesis. Persuasion theorists refer to these as *source credibility* factors. The same article on ESP would stand a greater chance of being accepted by scientists if it appeared in the *Journal of Experimental Psychology*, for example, than if it appeared in *Playboy*.

Second, scientists persuade in part by the language they use. The style of scientific reports is almost always marked by the appearance of impersonal detachment and passivity, as if to convey the impression that scientific procedures and data have an "out-there" existence.

Third, on some issues at least, scientists are bound to reflect value biases, even as they deal with what are alleged to be questions of fact. According to some critics (Szasz, 1970; Louch, 1969), scientists are likely to use terms that have been politically defined, reject unpleasant findings, or raise their standards for acceptance of these findings. Should a given scientist be personally opposed to the use of marijuana, for example, he or she is more likely to "discover" that it is harmful to health than is another colleague who favors its use. To the first scientist, the "high" produced by marijuana may be judged to be "reality-distorting." To the second scientist, it may be judged as "mind-expanding." How shall we label scientific discourse on issues such as these? As purely logical discourse or as persuasive discourse?

Fourth, in acting as though science is purely logical, the scientific community as a whole has helped to reinforce the popular myth of science as omniscient and omnipotent, a sort of God-substitute. One effect of the scientific mystique is the worship of technology and technological solutions. Concomitantly, we tend to have less faith in "human" solutions— preferring the "cold logic" of computers over the "subjective" judgments of people. A related effect is the *legitimation* of controversial positions as "fact." Many social scientists not only treat values as facts; in so doing, they tend to convey the impression that value issues are purely scientific matters, the "answers" to which are resolvable by empirical research.

Homosexuality, for example, becomes a disease rather than a choice. Military planning becomes a scientific problem for the "experts" rather than a human problem requiring political solutions.[3]

It could be maintained that the foregoing claims do not apply to all scientific discourse, or at least to "good" scientific discourse, but there is another class of arguments that cannot so easily be dismissed. Here it is argued that science (and scientific discourse) *cannot* be what it has been familiarly depicted as being; that "good" science relies on extra-factual and extra-logical considerations. Koch (1964) has asserted, for example, that "the scientific process is in principle, and at all stages, *underdetermined by rule*" (p. 21). Perelman (1971) has argued that persuasive elements are "unavoidable in every philosophical argument, in every discussion which is not restricted to mere calculation or seeks to justify its elaboration or its application, and in every consideration of the principles of any discipline whatever, even in the programming of a computer" (p. 119). Others (Kaplan, 1964; Bridgeman, 1959; Polyani, 1958) have insisted that the first premises of scientific theories are unprovable; that "good" theories suggest hypotheses that are not logically deducible from their premises; that theories gain acceptance by being intuitively or at least subjectively satisfying; that the rules of induction are imprecise; that the ultimate test of "objectivity" in the sciences is subjective agreement among scientists at a particular time, and in a particular culture.

How, in the light of these comments, shall we evaluate the contributions of a giant such as Einstein? Thomas Kuhn (1970) has argued that men like Einstein have ushered in scientific revolutions. In every such revolution, says Kuhn, the scientist is not simply extra-factual or extra-logical. By dint of his contribution he transforms what other scientists *mean* by fact and logic; he makes them think in a fundamentally new way. According to Kuhn, the scientific revolutionary induces "conversion." He employs "techniques of persuasion . . . in a situation in which there can be no proof . . ." (p. 151). If we are to believe Thomas Kuhn, was Einstein a persuader? [4]

We are not prepared to argue that scientific or philosophical discourse

---

3. For a fascinating account of how social scientists influence, and are influenced by cultural and political values, see Cronbach's (1975) brief history of the intelligence-testing controversy as it has moved from scholarly journals to the public arena. Says Cronbach (p. 12), "Our scholars chose to play advocate when they went before the public, and they abandoned scholarly consistency." In fairness to the scholars referred to by Cronbach (Herrnstein, Jensen, Terman, and others), it should be pointed out that the mass media encouraged them to treat policy matters as scientific issues and to exaggerate their scientific claims.

4. In fairness, we must also recommend Israel Scheffler's (1967) excellent critique of Kuhn's position.

is extra-logical to the same degree that advertising copy typically is, and before we leave this section, we should probably note some differences. Scientists invoke source credibility factors, but they generally *are* more credible than advertisers and so are the journals in which their work appears. Like advertisers, scientists adapt to an audience, selecting appeals and arguments which are designed to win belief. Scientists recognize that they have a highly critical audience, however, and that the case they make must be more compelling than that of the advertiser. The advertiser may blandly assert that "Nine out of ten doctors smoke Camels" without revealing the basis for this claim. The scientist is obligated to reveal the nature and size of samples cited, the questions asked to elicit such data, and so on. Whereas advertisers are obligated to sell a product, scientists are only obligated to discover and disseminate truth. If they distort or mislead, they stand a good chance of being exposed.

John Stuart Mill (1859) observed long ago that the best test of truth was its capacity to survive in a competitive marketplace of ideas. Toward that end, he urged that all competing views be given the fullest and most capable expression, that they be subject to revision in light of new ideas, and that audiences be critical but open to views which challenged their own. Mill intended his essay as a defense of democratic government but we see it as a more accurate depiction of the scientific enterprise. Their pretensions aside, scientists can lay claim to employing Mill's procedure for arriving at truth. They are distinguished not so much by their particular brand of logic as by their willingness to engage in honest and open dialogue with other scientists.

Premise Four: The "Sophisticated" Person Cannot Help but Be Manipulative, or, if You Will, a Persuader.

From a number of quarters these days, persuasion is under severe attack for being a manipulative activity. Its harshest critics equate not just some persuasion, but all persuasion, with dealing in appearances and images, deception and role-playing, domination and exploitation. Hence, it is not just when persuasion appears in the guise of information-giving, art, entertainment, or science that it is subject to scorn; according to these critics, in fact, persuasion is most reprehensible when it is applied to ordinary, day-to-day relationships. Maintaining that manipulation by persuasion is unnecessary, unhealthy, and immoral, the more extreme critics urge us to cleanse ourselves of manipulative intent through sensitivity training, nondirective therapy, encounter sessions, and the like.

The proposed alternative to persuasion is sold under a variety of labels: "dialogic communication," the "I-thou relationship," the "helping relationship," "communion with others," and "therapeutic communication." Because of its emphasis on direct, open, spontaneous expression of feelings, we choose to call it the *Expressivist* alternative. Its most ardent supporters (including many serious devotees of the Hippie movement) insist that it need not be restricted to close friends and relatives but, indeed, can be a way of life applicable to most interpersonal relationships. Here are some excerpts from Richard Johannesen's (1971, p. 376) able summary of the proposed life style:

> One is direct, honest and straightforward. One imparts himself as he really is and avoids facade, stratagem, or projecting an image. The communication filters formed by roles, conventions, and artifice can be overcome. . . . Things are seen from the other's viewpoint . . . as well as from one's own side. . . . The other is valued for his worth and integrity as a human. The spirit of mutual trust is promoted. . . . The participants themselves view each other as persons, not as objects to be manipulated or exploited. Participants aid each other in making responsible decisions regardless whether the decision is favorable or unfavorable to the particular view presented. . . . One allows free expression, seeks understanding, and avoids value judgments that stifle.

What are we to make of the indictment of persuasion by the more ardent enthusiasts of the Expressivist position? Is all persuasion manipulative? If so, is attempting to persuade others necessarily evil? Equally important, can Expressivism be extended beyond close friendship or kinship circles to more distant social relationships?

Our position is as follows. Much as we might prefer to soft-pedal manipulative aspects of persuasion, there is no denying that it involves purposeful attempts at controlling others through various techniques of audience adaptation. Viewed in this light, manipulation is central to persuasion; a defining characteristic, in fact. We do not concede, however, that persuasion must therefore be evil or that the Expressivist alternative can, or ought to be, a way of life for responsible individuals. In support of our position we offer the following arguments.

First, we unabashedly admit that persuasion deals in appearances. This may simply mean, however, that persuasion takes place on the receiver's terms, according to his or her way of looking at things. Put another way, it is the received message that counts, not the message conceived by the communicator. Strictly speaking, the teacher has not communicated that "two plus two equals four" if Johnny hears "Lou and Sue are sore." In the same way, logic does little good unless it appears logical to others. Certainly, not all persuasion should be roundly condemned for dealing in appearances since, as Bryant (1953, p. 409) has argued:

> . . . Even honest rhetoric is fundamentally concerned with appearances, not to the disregard of realities as Plato and his successors have industriously charged, but to the enforcement of realities. Rhetoric at the command of

honest men strives that what is desirable shall appear desirable, that what is vicious shall appear vicious. It intends that the true or probably true shall seem so, that the false or doubtful shall be vividly realized for what it is.

Our second argument, related to the first, is that while persuasion does indeed involve role-playing and deception of a kind, this too is not necessarily evil. To take on roles in life (as father, husband, etc.) is to fulfill the needs and expectations of others, sometimes out of self-interest, admittedly, but at other times for the sake of others. Moreover, one may behave one way on the job and another way at home without necessarily becoming a chameleon. Mature individuals have a consistent core of personality that they exhibit in all of their many roles. As for deception, we grant that there is great danger in certain kinds of deception, especially when it is used for questionable purposes. But deception may simply mean putting one's best foot forward, citing those arguments that appear most convincing and filtering out those which, for whatever reasons, would not win belief.

Third, we acknowledge that persuasion may be used to dominate or exploit, but this is not necessarily the case. To persuade may simply mean to give advice or to suggest an alternative way of looking at an issue. Moreover, terms like "domination" and "exploitation" are frequently used by one party to a dispute in order to denigrate a rival who is simply seeking to protect his or her own interests. Certainly, the pursuit of individual interests should not be condemned out of hand. Don't we all have interests that deserve to be protected?

Fourth, while we deeply appreciate the spirit that motivates the Expressivist position, we believe that in its extreme form it is a grossly irresponsible position. To those who truly value other persons, we suggest that there are gross injustices in this world which will persist unless good people stand up to denounce them and take steps to alleviate their causes. Not to persuade is to leave the field wide open for those who perpetrate these injustices. To be sure, not all Expressivists view persuasion as intrinsically evil (see, for example, Buber, 1958) and for our part we would concede that among those we most dearly value and trust, we should attempt to approach the Expressivist ideal. In the political arena, however, and especially in social conflicts, the Expressivist alternative may be hopelessly unrealistic (see Chapter 13).

Finally, we believe that in disclaiming any intent to persuade others, the Expressivists may themselves be practicing deception, perhaps self-deception. There is something wonderfully childlike about the Expressivist ideal, but to the extent that all of us have reached adulthood, it may also be a naïve and impossible dream. Webster defines "sophisticated" as "deprived of original simplicity" and made "worldly-wise." It is of more than passing interest that "sophisticated" derives from the word "sophist," and that in ancient Greece a "sophist" was a teacher or practitioner of persuasion. The point of our philological excursion is that to the degree to which all of us have become sophisticated, we cannot help but be persuaders. The best we can achieve, perhaps, is control over our own tendencies to control others in situations where openness would be more appropriate.[5]

Assuredly, most of us are not so controlled and controlling that we are totally incapable of behaving spontaneously. Quite apart from any intended effects upon others, we growl when angry, shriek when afraid, babble out of sheer pleasure, coo and cluck at our children, and strut and prance before our mates. Even children, however, learn to put these instinctive emotional expressions to use—to laugh seductively, for example, or to employ tears as a device.

It is ironic that even when Expressivism is carried to a full-fledged life style, the Expressivist cannot help but function as a persuader. Paradoxically, the Expressivist is *attempting to persuade us not to persuade*. And if he or she should say nothing and simply act as a model for others to imitate, the Expressivist should well know that modeling is itself a powerful form of persuasion.

Perhaps the difficulty with the extreme version of the Expressivist position is that, like other positions that we have considered in this chapter, it sets up a false dichotomy. Rather than viewing expression and persuasion as mutually exclusive, it might be more accurate to regard Expressivism as a philosophy of life as well as a *strategy* of persuasion. In this way, we might be better able to make sense of such movements as the Hippie movement which, while thoroughly committed to Expressivism, also sought to utilize it for persuasive purposes. For example, we might better interpret Nicola Chiaromonte's (1968, p. 26) prescription to young dissenters to engage "nonrhetorically" in fomenting a social revolution . . . "without shouting or riots, indeed in silence and secrecy; not alone but in groups, in real 'societies' that will create, as far as possible, a life that is independent and wise. . . ."

Premise Five: In Making Ethical Judgments, the Persuader or Recipient of Persuasion Should Consider Means, Ends, and Circumstances.

Lest our defense of persuasion in the preceding pages be interpreted as an invitation to employ any and all means of manipulation, in whatever circumstances, toward whatever ends, we would assure the reader that this is not our position at all. Rather than striving always to win at all costs,

---

5. Our position on the issues discussed in this section closely coincides with the essay written by Hart and Burks (1972). A recent critique of that essay, however, (Sillars, 1974) has also left its mark. Is the question simply one of degree?

the responsible individual might occasionally prefer the position of "honest loser," if for no other reason than that, on pragmatic grounds, the gains in terms of primary objectives are outweighed by negative secondary effects on self, audience, or the society as a whole (*cf.* Chapter 7, pp. 147 to 149). Other things being equal, it is more ethical to speak truthfully and sincerely rather than to traffic in deliberate falsehoods, distortions, or ambiguities; to encourage rational choice rather than to subvert reason; to appeal to the best motives in people rather than to their worst impulses.

Seldom, of course, are things perfectly equal. On the face of it, a lie designed to save another from unnecessary pain is more justified than a lie intended to expand the size of one's bank account. A dubious tactic used to advance equality or freedom of thought is likewise more defensible than the same tactic used to promote inequality or thought control. And circumstances may alter the balance as well. Few would deny, for example, that governmental secrecy is less objectionable in time of war than during periods of peace or that militant protest tactics are more justified as last resorts than as initial invitations to dialogue.

So we come down, essentially, to a situational ethic (*cf.* Fletcher, 1966), one in which the persuader is advised to weigh means against ends, ends against means, and both in the light of circumstances. Admittedly, a situational ethic leads either to trivial prescriptions like "Always tell the truth when you can," or to highly complex assessments of how to balance means and ends in specific contexts—something we continuously struggle with in daily living but regard as fundamentally beyond the scope of this book.

Premise Six: The Intellectual Leaders of Our Society Have a Special Responsibility to Acknowledge Their Rhetorical Identities.

Consistent with the overall tenor of discussion in this chapter, there is one admonition we would emphasize here: that those in the so-called "learned" professions—among them, the very same educators and scientists whose rhetorical practices we illustrated earlier—are especially obligated to reveal the extent to which their discourse is extra-factual or extra-logical. The learned professionals, after all, have historically made special demands on their audiences, insisting on a credulity commensurate with their claims to objectivity. Unless they can better justify those claims, they had better retreat to more defensible and more responsible grounds for belief, arguing in terms of the quality of their rhetoric, rather than denying their practice of it. Otherwise they stand vulnerable to a charge particularly serious for those who purport to discover and disseminate knowledge: misrepresentation of self.

In an article entitled "The Immoral Rhetoric of Scientific Sociology," Andrew Weigert (1970) makes essentially this point as applied to behaviorally oriented sociologists. Their theory and method, he argues (p. 112), "should be understood not merely as objective science, but as a symbolic communication whose principal form is inter-subjective and principal function is rhetorical." Its functions, he maintains, are to recruit and indoctrinate potential initiates and to convince outsiders that scientific sociology is indispensable for solving society's problems. In the introductory college course, for example, students are presented with an idealized version of sociology as a cumulative discipline. In later courses they are led erroneously to believe that strict observance of methodological rules guarantees answers to the research questions being addressed, and that no serious gap exists between the language of research practice and the language of theoretical generalization. (We confess that behaviorally oriented persuasion theorists and researchers are equally guilty of these proselytizing tendencies.)

But why are deceptions by social scientists or other intellectual leaders any worse than deceptions by ordinary persuaders? Here Weigert proposes a "dramaturgical ethic" (p. 111) which we find quite compelling:

> Morality, in the dramaturgical sense, is a question of identity and identity management.... The radical moral demand (duty) on a person is that he actually be that which he presents himself as being. Reciprocally, this same person imposes a radical moral obligation (his right, which is now your duty) on his audience that they believe and accept him for what he announces himself to be....
>
> A scientist, in order to retain his identity, must announce himself as a carrier of unbiased "truth" buttressed by intersubjective evidence of the stated condition or reality.... He possesses a privileged mode of knowing. A rhetorician [i.e., persuader], on the other hand, announces himself as a carrier of biased "truth" armed with logical and emotional symbolic weapons aimed at persuading another person that he should think or act differently. He possesses a privileged mode of persuasion and identification....
>
> If a sociologist practices rhetoric, but identifies himself (to self and/or others) as a scientist, he renders his rhetoric immoral, the immoral rhetoric of identity deception.

Premise Seven: "Mere Rhetoric" Is a Powerful Force in Society.

Earlier, we suggested that while some persons assail persuasion for being too manipulative, others maintain that it is not manipulative enough. The latter is a frequently voiced cry of the angry and the impatient. They are joined by hard-nosed political scientists and economists for whom power and money are what "really" talk in society. Both groups belittle persuasion as "mere rhetoric," "talk rather than substance," the offer of "symbolic" or "psychological" satisfactions rather than "real" rewards or "real" punishments. Hence the use of such expressions as "talk is cheap"; "(Persuaders) sell the sizzle and not the steak"; "(His speech was) nothing but rhetoric"; "Money talks"; and "Power is the name of the game."

Although we are tempted to reject the "mere rhetoric" put-down entirely, there is something to be said for it. Rhetoricians like ourselves tend to seek explanations for historic events solely in terms of public speeches by important figures or other acts of persuasion. The economist reminds us that it is money which elects presidents, as much as, if not more than, the quality of their rhetoric. The political scientist cautions us that behind the fancy words of political leaders is the desire to achieve and maintain power. When evidence is presented to the effect that the number of lynchings of blacks in the South per year occurred in inverse proportion to the success of the cotton crop, we are chastened a bit, and rightly so. Our inclination would have been to attribute the lynchings solely to the persuasive power of racist agitators.

There is, moreover, a sense in which the distinction between the real and the rhetorical is quite appropriate. When politicians or other power figures use talk as a way of avoiding responsible action, or when they traffic in deliberate ambiguities and evasions, it is fair to say they are dealing in "mere rhetoric."

Still, we are uncomfortable with the "mere rhetoric" put-down, especially when it is used to belittle all persuasion. In its noblest sense, persuasion is the means by which ideas are tested, differences resolved, reforms set in motion, communities solidified, and so on. Neither money nor power are any more substantive than good reasons, ably stated, in behalf of a worthy cause.

Furthermore, there is another sense in which even the emptiest phrases and most specious arguments may be of great significance. Much has been made these days of the depths to which advertisers and political campaigners have sunk, and we are equally critical. Yet, however much we may disapprove of their rhetoric, the fact is that it sells their soap and helps elect them. Buyers or voters may have been persuaded on the basis of myths, falsehoods, and illusions, but from their standpoint they were quite real. It is in this sense that distinctions between the real and the rhetorical or the real and the symbolic or the real and the psychological break down entirely. What is "real" is in the eye of the beholder, and it is on the basis of his or her perceptions that society is shaped and history written.

Finally, let us add that persuasion is not restricted to "friendly" verbal discourse with others. It is often the handmaiden of force. We turn to this point next.

Premise Eight: Some Acts of Force and Violence Are Rhetorical in Nature; They Constitute a Type of "Symbolic Speech."

We have already seen that the scope of persuasion extends beyond verbal discourse to include gestures, inflections, artifacts such as artistic creations, and symbolic acts such as saluting the flag or the staging of the Greek Olympics.

But what about such seemingly violent acts as the desecration of the flag by militants or the use of force by Arab guerrillas during the Munich Olympics? Congresswoman Green of Oregon epitomized the views of most Americans when she said of one such act: "That's not persuasion; it's coercion, pure and simple." Not surprisingly, most textbooks on persuasion have echoed this view, for here, finally, "persuasion" becomes a "god" word and its alleged alternative becomes a "devil" word.

Unfortunately, it is not easy to define "symbolic act," let alone to specify criteria by which to distinguish symbolic and nonsymbolic acts of force or violence. The story goes that at one psychoanalytically oriented school of social work, students were considered hostile if they came to class late, anxious if they came early, and compulsive if they came at the appointed hour. Each act was a symbolic act, independent of the student's intentions, and independent of factors he or she might not have been able to control.

If this psychoanalytic view goes too far in one direction, the notion of a persuasion—coercion dichotomy as applied to acts of force or violence goes too far in the other direction. Intuitively, one senses that it obscures as much as it clarifies.

Consider the difference, for example, between guerrilla warfare and an act such as the use of napalm by protestors to destroy draft board files. In the Vietnam war, it was not uncommon for the National Liberation Front to assassinate district officials as a way of eroding the opposition's control of the territory, establishing their own capacity to control it, and generally intimidating the Saigon regime. These acts communicated quite well, but the messages were primarily about the guerrillas' *power to constrain* and were thus rhetorical in only the most minimal sense of the term. In the second case, the protestors were dramatically proferring a *moral claim*, rather than attempting to frighten the adversary through a show of force. The use of napalm to burn draft board records was quite clearly a kind of "symbolic speech," revealed as such by the fact that, in terms of power, the protestors were clearly no match for their adversaries.

Indissoluble mixtures of persuasive and coercive elements are almost always found in confrontational acts, such as campus building seizures, prison riots, and street blockades. In Chapter 13 we shall argue that, as in many other cases of "forced compliance," these acts of force may lead compliers to modify their attitudes so as to make them more consistent with their behaviors. Here we should like to note that the confrontational act of force is inherently symbolic in nature. Not only do the confronters use the act to signal their willingness and capacity to employ greater force in the future; they also seek, by their acts, to dramatize the essential fairness of their position.

Premise Nine: It Is Useful to Distinguish Between Paradigm Cases of Persuasion, Peripheral Cases of Persuasion, and Cases of Nonpersuasion; Concomitantly, to Speak of Co-active Persuasion as the Paradigm Strategy and to Distinguish It from Peripheral Strategies of Persuasion.

It should be clear by now that our culture sharply delimits the scope of persuasion, reserving for its "domain" such paradigm cases as those listed in Chapter 1: a political campaign speech, a commercial in behalf of a product, a minister's sermon, and so on. We hope we have shown in this chapter that traditional distinctions between persuasion and nonpersuasion are grossly overdrawn and unjustifiably invidious. At the same time, we hope we have not given the impression that everything a person says or does is persuasion or that there are essentially no differences between what such prototypical persuaders as advertisers and politicians do and the persuasion characteristically practiced by poets, scientists, or others of their ilk.

Recall that we defined persuasion as human communication designed to influence others by modifying beliefs, values, or attitudes. Recall, too, that we acknowledged that persuasion involved manipulation of sorts and that it was extra-factual and extra-logical. By these definitional criteria, a great deal of what people say or do cannot be classified as persuasion even though it might function persuasively for others. Some artists neither consciously nor unconsciously seek to persuade. Some entertainers do just that and nothing more. Some information-giving does not venture beyond the facts. Mathematical discourse, for instance, might well be considered purely logical. An infant's birth cry is certainly a case of pure expression. Some coercion neither allows choice nor modifies attitudes (e.g., robbers who come up to their victims from behind and knock them unconscious before taking their money). Although conventional distinctions are overdrawn, clearly there are cases of nonpersuasion.

By way of clarifying our position, we think it useful to introduce the concept of *peripheral cases* as a companion term to the notion of paradigm cases, introduced earlier. A peripheral case is a fuzzy, borderline instance of a phenomenon. As applied to persuasion, it is neither a paradigm example of persuasion nor a "pure" case of nonpersuasion. To speak of peripheral cases in this context is to reject either-or dichotomies, to admit of the possibility that there may be ambiguity or overlap between persuasion and nonpersuasion. Among the peripheral cases are those that have been the focus of this chapter: The rhetoric of educators and news reporters, rhetorical art and entertainment, scientific rhetoric, expressive persuasion, and coercive rhetoric. When consciously and deliberately employed to influence others, we think it makes sense to think of them as *strategies* of persuasion. Co-active persuasion may be viewed as the primary or paradigm strategy, these others as secondary or peripheral strategies.

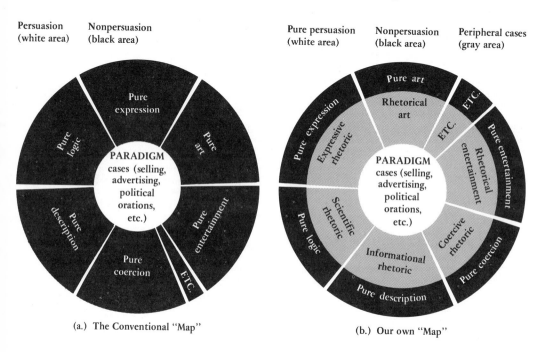

Fig. 2.1 Two conceptual "maps" of persuasion's domain (a) The conventional "map" (b) Our own "map"

With the concept of peripheral cases in hand, we may construct a conceptual "map" of persuasion that better reflects the "territory" than the map represented by the conventional wisdom. Note that what distinguishes the two maps in Fig. 2.1 is the addition of peripheral cases to our map as "outlying areas" within the "boundaries" of persuasion.

About This Book

Despite their obvious significance, the areas at the periphery of persuasion's domain have received scant attention from scholars in the field. We think they are areas, indeed, complete with their own characteristic persuaders, persuadees, strategies, tactics, and message forms. It will not do to pretend that they are cases of nonpersuasion or that because "good" newscasters, poets, scientists, or what have you, are somehow supposed to function nonrhetorically, their rhetoric should not be studied.

Still, we would be remiss in a textbook of this kind if we so focused on peripheral cases that we ignored those paradigm cases with which persuasion is conventionally identified. When we refer to the term "persuasion" in this text, we shall ordinarily have paradigm cases in mind. This book is primarily about orating and essay-writing, campaigning and sermonizing, and other acts that can be considered clearcut cases of persuasion. In keeping with that focus, we shall generally be discussing variations on the co-active approach to persuasion.

At the same time, we shall devote a rather large chapter to a discussion of alternatives to the co-active approach. Moreover, in Part 3, we shall be looking at ways of analyzing peripheral cases. Finally, we shall have more to say in Chapters 7, 8, and 11 about the ethics of persuasion.

Summary

In our culture, "persuasion," "rhetoric," and other allied terms are often used as though they referred to "enemy territory." Rigid distinctions are commonly drawn between persuasion and pure expression, pure art, pure description, pure logic, pure entertainment, and pure coercion. For all but the last distinction, persuasion is treated as a "devil" word, a reflection of the language-user's belief that someone (an educator, a newscaster, a poet, a scientist, or whomever) has appeared to be what he or she is not; that this individual has violated a "purity principle" associated with his or her craft or culturally prescribed role. Given this state of affairs, educators, artists, scientists, and others have been understandably loath to label themselves as persuaders.

We have attempted to show that while conventional distinctions between "persuasion" and "nonpersuasion" enable us to further clarify the nature of the persuasive domain, they seriously underrepresent its scope, reflect erroneous assumptions about persuasion's alleged alternatives, and unjustifiably undermine the status of persuasion. Apart from paradigm cases of persuasion such as those listed in Chapter 1, we have held that there are many *peripheral cases* involving ambiguity or overlap between persuasion and nonpersuasion. Not only do politicians, ministers, salespeople, advertisers (and other stereotypical persuaders) persuade; there is a rhetorical dimension in the discourse of poets and scientists, newscasters and entertainers, law enforcers and law violators. On a typical issue such as legalization of marijuana, our attitudes may be formed or modified by a great variety of messages. Some will undoubtedly be paradigm instances of persuasion: a minister imploring us to avoid using marijuana, a friend suggesting we "turn on" together; a television commercial picturing the consequences of driving under its influence. Other messages will not appear as conspicuously rhetorical in their intent, substance, or effects; but, at the same time, they will not appear to be pure instances of nonpersuasion either. These are peripheral cases and they may include such messages as the following: the psychedelic sounds of the Rolling Stones, a L'il Abner serial on a pot-pusher, a selectively evidenced article on marijuana in a scientific journal, a news report on a raid by police of a pot party, surprise encounters with friends smoking marijuana in public, a parental threat of punishment for smoking, and a sit-in at the office of a dean who suspended a student for possession of the weed.

As for the ethics of particular persuasive practices, we proposed that while some means of persuasion are, in general, more unethical than others, no device should be condemned out of hand without regard to ends and circumstances. Another premise having to do with ethics bore on the discourse of so-called "learned" professionals. They, in particular, we argued, had an ethical obligation to acknowledge their roles as persuaders.

One purpose of this chapter has been to provoke examination of questions. If "good" art may be both aesthetic and rhetorical, is it ever appropriate to criticize art for being rhetorical? If the test of "objectivity" in news reporting must be replaced by the "fairness" test, what constitutes "fair" reporting? If scientists are not purely logical, by what standards should we evaluate their discourse? If as "sophisticated" persons, we cannot help but be manipulators of sorts, are some forms and uses of manipulation more ethical than others? If persuasion deals only in symbolic satisfactions, is it any the less powerful a force in society than "real" rewards and "real" punishments? Although we are mindful of the ill consequences that may result from one or another practice of persuasion, we are by no means inclined to regard persuasion as primarily a "devil" word. In any event, we invite readers to address these issues themselves.

3

Persuasion as a Communication Process

When a persuasive communication succeeds spectacularly, we readily explain its effectiveness by pointing to sensational elements—a brilliant and memorable slogan, perhaps, or a unique style of delivery. In reality, its effectiveness is always a product of a complex mix of communication factors—what Wrage and Baskerville (1962) have called an alchemy. The persuader as alchemist must blend available materials in ways that are adapted to the audience. From conception to reception of the message, any number of things can go wrong.

To communicate means literally to make common. When we stop to think about it, the fact that one person is able to understand another—let alone be persuaded by him—must seem nothing short of miraculous. Somehow, communicators must bridge space and time, and even more significantly, they must bridge the psychological gaps which separate one human being from another. That attempts at communication often fail should not surprise us.

This chapter provides an introduction to persuasion as a communication process and to the nature of language as the essential tool of that process. What are the major components of communication and language? What role is played in communication by contextual factors? Through what stages do messages pass? We shall attempt to answer these questions here, beginning with a look at rather simple patterns of communication and then moving to more complex patterns.[1]

Components of Communication

Communication always involves at least one *message*, transmitted by a *source*, via a *medium*, to a *receiver*, within a *situational context*. In more complex situations, there may also be *channels* intervening between the initial source of a message and its final destination.

Message

In a narrow sense, the "message" refers to what is said or implied by communicators through words, gestures, and inflections. It includes the positions they take, the arguments and appeals they use to defend a position, the order and arrangement of their materials, and, at a more micro-

---

1. Readers wishing to explore these issues further should have no difficulty locating source materials. A still useful introductory text is Berlo's (1960) *The Process of Communication*. Mortenson (1972) offers a comprehensive treatment of communication theory and research in textbook form. Watzlawick, Beavin, and Jackson (1967) is among the most provocative books we have read on the subject, and is especially useful for understanding communication in ongoing, dyadic relationships such as marriage. Barnlund (1968) has compiled an excellent anthology of articles on communication theory and research.

"Do the protestors cause the authorities to take punitive countermeasures or does the recalcitrance of the authorities constitute the reason for the protest in the first place?" (Photo by David Speace, courtesy of *Temple News*)

scopic level, the individual word choices and nonverbal cues that together constitute their presentation. In the broadest sense, the message is any-thing to which the receiver may attach meaning. In addition to what is said by words, gestures, and inflections, it includes the receiver's reactions to the context, to the medium, to the source as a person, and to any and all actions (or inaction) he or she might take of a public nature. Although we will ordinarily refer to the message in its narrow sense, at times (made clear, we hope, by context) we will switch to its broader meaning. Often, it is impossible to separate these effects.

A message is always as much a response as it is a stimulus. Ordinarily, we think of persuaders as active, receivers as passive, but these designa-tions are in some ways arbitrary. Persuaders respond to perceived characteristics of the receiver, to internal cues, and to contextual stimuli. Where exposure to a message is voluntary, it often makes sense to think of receivers as persons who persuade themselves and to regard the communicator strictly as an intermediary. In a sense, the electorate tells politicians what they must say to them in order to be elected. In the same way, parishioners select a minister who will tell them what they want to hear. The seducer is as much a persuadee as the seduced, the leader as much a follower as those who are led. Viewed in this way, it becomes difficult to assign causes and effects in persuasion, especially in ongoing relationships. Do the protestors cause the authorities to take punitive countermeasures or does the recalcitrance of the authorities constitute the reason for the protest in the first place? Does the domineering wife cause the henpecked husband to be docile or is his docility the cause of her aggressiveness? Once again, persuasion is an ongoing system of interacting events, not a mechanical push-button process.

Persuasion is primarily concerned with intentionally transmitted messages but it should be kept in mind that in any relationship joined by the dimensions of space and time, we cannot *not* communicate. Watzlawick, Beavin, and Jackson (1967, p. 49) have put it this way:

> Activity or inactivity, words or silence, all have message value: they influence others and these others, in turn, cannot *not* respond to these communications and are thus themselves communicating. It should be clearly understood that the mere absence of talking or of taking notice of each other is no exception to what has just been asserted. The man at a crowded lunch counter who looks straight ahead, or the airplane passenger who sits with his eyes closed, are both communicating that they do not want to speak to anybody or be spoken to, and their neighbors usually "get the message" and respond appropriately by leaving them alone. This, obviously, is just as much an interchange of communication as an animated discussion.

Source

The *primary source* of a message is the communicator who transmits that message, but any number of *secondary sources* may be associated with its transmission. These may include the sponsor of a meeting, the chairman, persons or groups referred to by the communicator, or persons who helped construct the message.

Receivers are as much dependent on judgments about the source as on the arguments and appeals contained in the message. Especially when we feel incompetent to evaluate arguments and appeals on their own merits, we tend to rest our judgments of a message on the company it keeps.

In a real sense, source and message are indistinguishable. From an audience's standpoint, the prior reputations of the persuaders constitute part of their message, as do their physical characteristics should they appear in person. From that point on, the interaction of person and content is even more manifest. An apparently insincere compliment may confirm a suspicion that the persuader is not to be trusted. Or a particularly strong assemblage of evidence on a given point may produce confidence in the persuader's expertise.[2]

It is the audience's image of the source that influences beliefs or attitudes, not what the source is really like. Psychologically oriented persuasion theorists speak of *respect* (perceived competence or expertise), *trust* (perceived reliability or trustworthiness), and *attraction* (perceived dynamism and good will) as clusters of attributes most associated with source credibility. Included within these broad categories are such perceived attributes as knowledge of subject, impartiality, sincerity, honesty, prestige, warmth, enthusiasm, interest in and liking for the audience, and physical attractiveness. In conflict situations, especially, credibility is also affected by a source's perceived power to reward or punish his audience.

Medium

A medium is a carrier of messages, a means through which they may be expressed. Broadly speaking, media may be oral or written, verbal or nonverbal, direct or indirect, but within those general categories communicators may select from among a wide variety of message forms. An advertiser may choose among newspapers, magazines, word of mouth, or television. An executive may elect to convey the same message by telephone, memo, bulletin board, platform speech, conference, loudspeaker, informal conversation, company newspaper. The modern protestor may be credited with having invented any number of message forms: be-ins, sit-ins, lie-ins, swim-ins, rock festivals and festivals of life, building occupations, and guerrilla theater.

The media differ, quite obviously, in terms of their technical capabilities, but they also differ in terms of feelings generated toward them. McLuhan (1964) has described radio as a "hot" medium, television as a "cool" medium. Print is generally regarded as most trustworthy, but in relation to memos, bulletin boards, telephone, and other media, Dahle (1954) and others have found that direct, face-to-face communication is perceived as warmer, more personal, and except for highly technical information, more accurate.

Receiver

Receivers are a factor of communication in their own right, as is illustrated in this personal anecdote. Some time ago, we ran into a perfect example of

---

2. Theory and research on source credibility is presented in several chapters of this book, especially Chapters 4, 5, 8, and 11. A more compact summary of the research literature is found in McGuire (1969, pp. 182–200).

The Peter Principle, the rule of organizations that sooner or later all employees are promoted beyond their level of competence. Our acquaintance had been a top-notch engineer but now he was sales manager for the computer division of a large electronics firm and he was doing miserably.

"I can't understand why my company isn't selling computers as effectively as IBM," he said. "We have the best computers in the world. What's more, I've written out a sales spiel for my men that's dynamite. All they have to do is memorize it and say it smoothly. Our products should do the rest."

We asked our friend how IBM achieved its success. "Oh well, you see they use a different type of salesman than we do. Our salesmen are all former engineers; what we care about is our products and our men know them inside and out. IBM hires these 'personality boys' who sit down with the customer and get real chatty with him. The fact is, they spend more time listening to the customer yak about his problems than on selling their products. It's a waste of time to me, but I have to admit that it works."

What the sales manager failed to realize, of course, is that by "wasting time" listening to the customer's problems, IBM's salesmen were accomplishing a great deal. Besides showing interest in the customer as a human being—a factor of no small consequence in itself—they were learning first hand how to *tailor* their messages so as to achieve their intended effects. IBM's approach might be characterized as receiver-oriented. The approach contrasts quite favorably with the source-oriented approach of IBM's competitor. Here are the essential differences between the two approaches.

Source-Oriented	*Receiver-Oriented*
Assumes that all receivers are alike;	Assumes that all receivers are unique, or, at the very least, that some differences make a difference;
Decides *for* the receivers what they need, want, know, value, etc.;	Learns from the receivers, if possible, what they need, want, know, value, etc.;
Selects specific persuasive goals for any one occasion on the basis of his or her own timetable;	Selects specific persuasive goals for any one occasion on the basis of the receivers' *readiness* to be persuaded;
Communicates *at* the receivers by means of a "canned" presentation;	Communicates *with* the receivers by adapting the message on the basis of a mutual interchange if at all possible;
Promotes solutions on the basis of their supposed intrinsic merits.	Promotes solutions on the basis of their capacity to resolve or reduce the receivers' special problems.

Situational Context

Surely the least studied force in persuasion is that vast but ineluctable array of "atmospheric" factors we call the situational context. The context is like the background and physical setting for the action in a play. Less eye-catching than the action itself, contextual factors nevertheless make the speeches and responses of the actors understandable and constitute message stimuli in their own right. One may read a *Hamlet* soliloquy from the printed page, but how much more meaningful it becomes when we know what has transpired beforehand, when we are aware of the immediate occasion for his utterance, when we can see him alone in a darkened chamber, when we are made aware of what is impending and what is occurring simultaneously, and when the intricate network of social roles, norms, and relationships is revealed to us.

In "real life" these same contextual factors are at work. The *historical context* may include prior interactions between source and receiver as well as experiences unique to each of them. The immediate *occasion* may be a Fourth of July celebration, a Presidential inaugural, or a bull session among friends. *Temporal-physical* factors may include such items as the time of day, the temperature of a room, or the number of mosquitos competing for an audience's attention at an outdoor rally. The context for a speech at a protest rally may also include such *contemporaneous events* as newspaper reports about the object of protest, demonstrations and counterdemonstrations in other cities, and so on. *Impending events* may include an election about to be held or an imminent final examination period. Finally, the context includes *sociocultural norms* that each party brings to a situation as a result of group, organizational, societal, and cultural affiliations. These, in turn, help to define authority, power and status relationships, influence judgments about what behavior is appropriate in the situation, and contribute to perceptions about the possibilities for compatibility and cooperation or incompatibility and conflict. We shall say more about the context shortly.

Channel

A channel is an intermediary, a receiver and retransmitter of messages from an initial source to a final destination. One potential disadvantage of going through channels is that messages may be distorted by the intermediary or never retransmitted, but there are also advantages. The use of channels permits a source to reach many different persons through informal, face-to-face communication who could otherwise be reached only by more formal means. The intermediary may also be in a better position to restate the message persuasively to those with whom he or she habitually has contact.

The persuader as disseminator of new ideas. Young Indian couples being taught family planning and welfare. (Courtesy of United Nations/ILO)

The concept of a channel is best illustrated in formal organizations since at least the prescribed channels of communication are identifiable by examination of the organization chart. In a mammoth organization such as General Motors, there may be scores of channels intervening between the company president and the lowliest employee. In any organization, there are also informal channels, such as grapevines, that often compensate for the rigidity of formal communication systems. Not only may the informal network be faster; it may also, for some purposes at least, be regarded as more authentic.

The study of how messages get diffused is relatively recent, but it has been richly rewarding. One finding of special importance is that the mass media often persuade indirectly, through persons known as *opinion leaders*. These are respected members of any subcommunity, in many respects similar to the persons they influence, who serve as channels of information and opinion.

Supporting the notion that successful mass campaigns are often accomplished through indirect means is research on how new ideas or innovations get adopted. Becker (1971) reported a study on the dissemination of birth control advice in Formosa. Three out of four acceptors of the advocated method of birth control had had no contact with the official communicators or field workers and, after a year of the campaign, one-fourth of the acceptors came from areas not even being reached by the campaign.

The Language of Communication: Some Useful Distinctions[3]

Signals and Symbols

Signals are the primitive tools of communication, shared by humans and nonhumans alike. An ape signals the approach of an enemy with a loud cry; the human does likewise. The response to the environment is immediate, automatic, and tied concretely to events taking place in the here and now. Similarly, the response *to* the animal's signal is triggered: it is either instinctual or learned through basic conditioning. Humans react signally to both environmental stimuli and social stimuli. The familiar clatter of wheels on a track may signal the arrival of a train; a contorted facial expression may signal another's anger. Signals announce their objects.

A *symbol* is something that stands for something else, whether an object referent, an abstract idea, or an internal state of the organism. Symbols stand in an arbitrary relationship to their referents. There is no intrinsic reason that my dog is called "dog" in English and "chien" in French; no intrinsic reason, again, that the sequence "my dog" makes more sense than "dog my," except that through cultural conditioning we have learned to associate rightness with one sequence and wrongness with another.

The miracle of the human's symbol-using ability is often taken too much for granted. Other animals use language to send and receive highly stereotyped signals, but few animals have even rudimentary symbol systems. Given our symbol-using capacities, we can form and combine sounds into words, phrases, sentences, paragraphs. Through symbols we can learn from past generations and we can pass on our knowledge. We can talk about the not-here and the not-now; refer to unicorns and magic mountains, to yesterdays and tomorrows. Able to speak concretely, we can refer to the who, what, when, where, how, and why of an event. Able to speak

---

3. For an excellent anthology of theory and research on language, see DeVito (1973).

and think abstractly, we can deal with cause and effect, take roles, make predictions, give and get feedback, and invent concepts. No other creature can make that statement!

Literal Language and Figurative Language

At the poles of a continuum from the literal to the figurative, one may plot the language of the technician and the language of the poet. Somewhere towards the middle of that scale we may locate the language of the persuader. Literal language is dry and precise; it is designed to be taken at face value. Figurative or metaphorical language is alive and picturesque, but in some ways playful; it is the language of the imagination. Insofar as persuasion deals with the practical and the mundane, it demands a kind of literal discourse—the language of hard fact and cold logic. Insofar as persuasion plays on feelings and deals with uncertainties, it requires the language of metaphor.

A metaphor is an implied comparison between things which are essentially unlike each other. Ordinary discourse is infused with metaphor: "the face of a clock," "the flow of ideas," "the heart of the matter." Initially these figurative references must have seemed odd to their hearers, but as Turbayne (1962) has observed, metaphors move through historical changes: they begin as apparent violations of appropriate usage, then take their place as appropriate figures of speech, and finally become so embedded in ordinary discourse that they cease to function as implied comparisons. No longer, for example, do we compare the "leg" of a table to the leg of a person; no longer do we think of "grasping" an idea (as one would a stick) as odd or even metaphorical. These terms come to have their own literal meanings.

Metaphors enable us to see one thing in terms of another. As rhetorical devices, they help persuaders to shape a receiver's view of a phenomenon that is susceptible to varying interpretations. The figure chosen quite obviously makes a difference. Thus, within the social sciences, a given theorist may evoke an image of the human being as a stimulus-response machine; or as a more complex machine, such as a calculator or computer; or as a swirling sea of only partially channeled energies; or as a mental acrobat seeking to retain or restore psychological balance (see Chapter 5). Similarly, in the realm of public affairs, it is commonplace to use organismic metaphors in referring to the "body politic," or to describe political conflicts as "games," or to refer to secular philosophies in religious or medical terms. Overarching metaphors of this kind function as *myths;* they guide our thinking on a variety of issues. Should the metaphor as myth be repeated and reinforced often enough, it may, like other metaphors, come to be understood literally.

A popular metaphor of the seventies. (Courtesy of Association for Voluntary Sterilization)

Denotative Meanings and Connotative Meanings

Name something, put it in a class, and separate it from all other members of that class, and you will have defined that something in denotative terms. Describe that something further by referring to its physical characteristics and you will still be operating at a denotative level. But now think about what that something means to you personally, in terms of your evaluative or emotional associations, and you will be getting at its connotative meanings. A Cadillac is a large, self-propelled passenger vehicle, but it is also, for many people, a symbol of power and status.

Seldom do we separate the denotative and connotative meanings that symbols have for us, and apart from such obviously loaded words as "spik," "commie," and "crazy," seldom are we aware of the many nuances of connotative meaning that ordinary words have for us. According to motivational analyst Ernest Dichter (1960), many seemingly neutral objects evoke strong emotional, if unconscious, reactions. Dichter has made a fortune specializing in the study of the connotative meanings of advertised products. Here are some of his findings:

- Wood is "living, throbbing warmth" (p. 99).
- Glass is mysterious and dangerous, yet tantalizing and strangely pleasurable (p. 100).
- Compared to the grapefruit, the orange is sunnier, younger, faster, and friendlier, but it is also less cool, less reserved, and less intellectual (p. 102).

Form and Substance

Attention to the meanings of words (or other symbolic elements) in persuasive discourse is not enough; meaning is also conveyed by the *form* that communication takes. Edelman (1967), for example, identifies *hortatory language* as a *form* of political communication.

> Hortatory language is especially conspicuous in appeals to particular audiences for policy support. . . . More directly than any other, this language style is directed at the mass public.
>
> It is worth noting first that the stable meanings of form associated with this language style are all the more significant because the denotations of its content are so notoriously unstable and ambiguous. Popular semantic analysis concentrated on the terms commonly employed in hortatory language, such as "democracy," "communism," "justice," and "the public interest," and nothing is easier than to show that people read different meanings into them. But a style employed so fervently, formally and informally, by everyone involved in political processes must have social and political functions other than the dissemination of semantic confusion. . . .
>
> Whether or not people agree with a particular appeal, and in spite of the almost total ambiguity of the terms employed, each instance of the use of

this language style in our culture is accepted as evidence of the need for widespread support of public policy. Those to whom appeals are made must be influential. The premises of the reasoning may be disputed, but the assumption that the appeal is necessary and that the public response will in fact influence policy is taken for granted and is strengthened by every serious response. Both denial and support of the soundness of a particular argument bolster the assumption equally effectively. [Thus] if the *content* of hortatory political language draws out different responses from different groups, its *form*, for reasons already suggested, calls out the same responses from the mass audience exposed to it. By reinforcing their confidence in the reality of public participation in policy-making and in the central role of reason, it promotes their acceptance of policy (pp. 134–138).

Information About Content and Information About Relationships

Messages are simultaneously substantive and interpersonal. They convey information about content and also about the relationship between source and receiver (Watzlawick, Beavin, and Jacobson, 1967). At the same time that we may be telling a waiter how we like our eggs (the substantive aspect) we also may be telling him something about how we see ourselves, how we see him, how we see him seeing us, and so on (the interpersonal aspect). Information about content is best transmitted verbally, whereas communication about relationships generally takes place nonverbally and without conscious awareness. Oftentimes, of course, the verbal, substantive message is *about* the relationship, as when a candidate promotes her own qualifications. At these times, especially, the nonverbal message may belie the verbal message. The campaigner may think she is saying, "I'm as sincere as they come," but nonverbally she may inadvertently be telling us how insincere she is. Differences in wording may also contribute to understandings about relationships. Compare, for example: "I'd like my eggs over light" with a customer who says: "Tell your cook to flip them before he murders them." The waiter would probably not be too mistaken if he interpreted the second customer as saying not only how he wanted his eggs but that he viewed himself as a very important person, that he viewed the cook and waiter as incompetent flunkies, and that he viewed them viewing him as someone with superior status.

Meaning and Constraint in Communication: The Importance of the Situational Context

As was suggested earlier, meaning is always contextual. The individual words of an utterance take on meaning from their linguistic contexts; the entire utterance takes on meaning from its situational context. If we are to communicate effectively, we must successfully anticipate the receiver's sense of the "logic" of the situation. Likewise, as receivers, we may make better sense of the communicator's message by placing it in a situational context.

But if contexts add meaning, if they have a kind of "logic," they also, for this same reason, place constraints on what communicators can say and on how receivers can act in light of what they hear. Let us deal more specifically with these functions of the situational context.

The Interpretive Function

Contextual rules provide grounds for interpreting ambiguous message stimuli. Divorced from situational contexts, verbal messages are often ambiguous and frequently indecipherable. This is especially true of messages that cannot be taken literally. Not long ago, we read of a member of the Indian parliament who became infuriated by a report that the United States was about to help Pakistan launch a takeover of India. It turns out that the legislator had taken a satirical Art Buchwald column at face value.

More often than not, we recognize a contextual rule only when it is broken. Passing an acquaintance on the street, we shout out, "How ya doin'?" and we are literally stopped and told—for fifteen minutes! Ceremonial exchanges such as this one was supposed to have been are examples of *ritual behaviors,* forms of "frozen language" in which each actor is expected to perform in a certain way. By definition, they cannot be interpreted literally although the animating spirit that motivates them may be real enough. The ceremonial " 'How ya doin', 'I'm fine' " ritual may reflect feelings of genuine warmth and respect.

Most public exchanges have ritual aspects although they are so commonplace that we do not think about them. Among the most commonly recognized rituals are religious rituals of sacrifice, obedience, and respect, and secular rituals of friendship, courtship, dominance-submission, and social cohesion. Rituals such as these may serve important functions. The ritual confrontations between East and West at the U.N., for example, are often a verbal substitute for more lethal physical encounters. The various rituals associated with homage to the English monarch have offered continuity to Britain's social order over the centuries.

Related to ritual behavior is what Boorstin (1962) has called the pseudo-event. A pseudo-event is a contrived exchange that is staged as though it were a spontaneous happening, often through collusion between the parties to the exchange. A group of demonstrators escalate their shouting at the behest of the television camera crew. Behind the scenes of a "live" talk show, a political candidate's staff screens potentially damaging phone calls while the candidate gives the impression that no controls are being exercised. In many cases, the audience for a pseudo-event knows that it is staged but gets satisfaction from it anyway. Commercials on television are essentially pseudo-events. So are the shouting matches at labor-management contract negotiations. Pseudo-events have become a dominant part of the American scene.

The context also provides grounds for interpreting gestures, inflections, and other such expressions of self. When the job interviewer suddenly sits forward in his or her chair, is this a sign of interest in the interviewee's remarks, or of gastric distress, or of a desire for termination of the interview? Is the fainting spell an indication of severe emotional distress, or an unconsciously expressed wish for dependency, or, as might have been the case in Victorian England, a sign of an ill-fitting corset? A crewcut may be worn to convey an image of oneness with Middle America, but mightn't it also be worn because it feels cool in summer or offers aesthetic pleasure?

Although the same act may be biologically necessitated, or motivated by whim, or constitute an innocent expression of taste, psychologists are more and more disposed to find conscious or unconscious rhetorical intent in seemingly innocuous behaviors. The subject of nonverbal behavior has spawned numerous studies of how space is used rhetorically in social interactions (*proxemics*) and other specialized investigations of body movement (*kinesics*). These studies underscore both the importance of sociocultural norms as regulators of nonverbal behavior (Birdwhistell, 1970; Hall, 1959; Mehrabian, 1971), and our earlier point that one cannot *not* communicate.

Contextual clues also provide grounds for interpreting action language as discourse. Rhetoricians often miss the truth in the familiar saying that actions speak louder than words. The commitment to a cause may be expressed by verbalizing about it or by nonverbal gesticulations, but it is most clearly conveyed by the overt actions one takes with respect to it. Foreign policy experts have learned to read military actions as though they were a language. A classic example of communication through action was the Cuban missile crisis in which both sides staged a war of nerves through military moves and countermoves. Note that these actions were not unambiguous. Indeed, it is often the point of such actions to keep the opposition guessing. To decipher the actions of others, one must pay close attention to the historical context, to the words that accompany them, and to other contextual factors such as cultural norms and contemporaneous events. Finally, the physical characteristics of the immediate situation may convey messages in their own right. To a sensitive observer of physical settings, the architecture of a building or the decor of a room may communicate as much as the words that are spoken within it. The friendly architecture of the modern bank building stands in sharp contrast to the formidable pillars of old-fashioned bank architecture. Within the bank, one may glean information about the relative importance of a bank employee from *status symbols:* such cues as size of the desk, quality of the wastepaper basket, and possession of a key to the executive washroom.

The Prescriptive Function

The same "rules" of context that may enable us to decipher the words and actions of others also may guide our own thoughts and behavior. Few persons like to think of themselves as conformists, but the truth is that all of us are, and in many more ways than we think. Through the powerful process of socialization we learn to take roles, respond to social definitions of problems and events, observe cultural sanctions and taboos and other more formalized constraints. Within more specific social contexts, we learn to observe definitions of "a fair day's work for a fair day's pay," rules of the bargaining "game," informal codes of dress, punctuality, and so on. Finally, the immediate situation places additional demands upon us. Lloyd Bitzer (1968, p. 8) speaks here of the situational context as prescribing a fitting response:

> Rhetorical discourse is called into existence by situation; the situation which the rhetor perceives amounts to an invitation to create and present discourse. The clearest instances of rhetorical speaking and writing are strongly invited—often required. The situation generated by the assassination of President Kennedy was so highly structured and compelling that one could predict with near certainty the types and themes of forthcoming discourse. With the first reports of the assassination, there immediately developed a most urgent need for information; in response, reporters created hundreds of messages. Later, as the situation altered, other exigencies arose: the fantastic events in Dallas had to be explained; it was necessary to eulogize the dead President; the public needed to be assured that the transfer of government to new hands would be orderly. . . .

One way to appreciate the role of contextual imperatives is to compare the way we communicate with each other today with communication patterns of bygone eras. Although we might regard the following turn-of-the-century advertisement as "camp," persons reading it then were probably quite taken by it.

BEHOLD!

A HAPPY HOME, THE HUSBAND LAUGHS AGAIN,

O'ER THE WIFE'S FEATURES PLAYS A PLEASANT SMILE.

THE CHILDREN TOO IN ROSY HEALTH ARE SEEN,

THAT MODEL HOME IS HAPPY ALL THE WHILE.

THOUSANDS OF HOUSEHOLDS KNOW THIS WONDER STRANGE.

TO *TARRANTS' SELTZER* OWE THIS MIGHTY CHANGE.

N.B. NO HOME SAFE WITHOUT IT.

If today's contextual imperatives are unlike those of decades past, neither are our own imperatives like those of other peoples. In one African culture, obesity in women is considered a mark of great beauty. Among some peoples, the deflowering of a virgin is felt to be so repugnant that it is performed by a hireling as menial labor. In sharp contrast to our own culture, many Eastern peoples wear white at funerals and smile to express grief.

Still another way of "reading" contextual mandates is to look at our own culture as though we were a primitive people being "discovered" by a cultural anthropologist. Using the jargon of the professional anthropologist, Horace Miner (1956) has provided a remarkably incisive description of the toilet habits of the Nacirema people, a culture that might seem strangely familiar to ours because, in fact, it is our own (try spelling Nacirema backwards).

According to Miner, the Nacirema are preoccupied with health, and hence have one or more "shrines" in their homes in which they engage in private rituals and ceremonies designed to ward off debility and disease. The shrine contains, among other things, a "charm-box," built into the wall, which houses various "magical potions." These are prescribed by "medicine men" and purchased from "herbalists." For every real or imagined malady, the medicine man prescribes a different potion, "in an ancient and secretive language."

The Nacirema are horrified and at the same time fascinated with the mouth. "Were it not for the rituals of the mouth, they believe that their teeth would fall out, their gums bleed, their jaws shrink, their friends desert them, and their lovers reject them" (p. 504). Yet the "mouth-rite" involves a rather grotesque practice: "It was reported to me that the ritual consists of inserting a small bundle of hog hairs into the mouth, along with certain magical powders, and then moving the bundle in a highly formalized series of gestures" (p. 504).

The foregoing discussion has stressed the "rule-like" character of the situational context. Recall that we have talked of the context as "prescribing" a fitting response and that we have referred to the "logic" of the situation.

These points are worth stressing, but they should not be overstressed. As was noted earlier, the communicator has freedom to improvise within the framework of situational constraints. The range of viable options is restricted, but in most cases there remains considerable room for rhetorical invention. Moreover, the "logic" of the situation may itself be ambiguous and therefore susceptible to a variety of interpretations. In a marital context, for example, the husband may decide that it is "logical" for the wife to answer the phone because she is nearer to it. The wife may interpret the "logic" of the situation quite differently, believing that since the husband is "only" watching a football game on television, he should answer it. We shall examine other problems of this kind in the next section.

Persuasion in Stages: A Simplified Communication Model

Thus far we have talked of the message as a fixed entity, almost as though it were a gift package containing an idea that a source (*A*) could hand to a receiver (*B*). In actual fact, the message is a constantly changing energy form that passes through stages in *A*, is modified further as it travels through a medium, and is changed again as it passes through corresponding stages in *B*. In this section we look at how the message is molded by *A* and remolded by *B*. A central theme of the section might be stated as follows: *persuasion takes place through a communication chain, the chain no stronger than its weakest link.*

As with any ongoing process, it is never possible to fix a true beginning or ending to a communication flow or to mark off stages of the process without being oversimplified and arbitrary. Moreover, unlike purely physical processes, much of the communication process cannot be observed directly; we can only theorize about the internal flow within *A* and *B*. What we do know suggests that the message-processing system is far more intricate than that of any computer and certainly more complex than any flow charts we can construct to represent the process.[4]

For our purposes, it is useful to begin with the source conceiving the message and to chart the internal flow in roughly parallel stages for *A* and *B:* (1) a *conceiving stage,* at which *A* selects from among competing alternatives a set of ideas and feelings that he would like to convey; (2) an *encoding stage,* at which the message is linguistically formed and then converted into physical stimuli that can travel through space; (3) a *decoding stage,* at which *B* reconverts physical stimuli into semantically recognizable forms; and (4) an *evaluation stage,* at which *B* wrestles with any discrepancies between the message she has just received and what she has previously thought and felt. In addition to these stages, it is helpful to plot the *inputs* for *A* and the corresponding *outputs* for *B*. The source's inputs are past and present experiences which together have led him to develop a set of predispositions that now impel his communication behavior.

The receiver's *outputs* are, similarly, a set of modified attitudes, beliefs, values, and behaviors that were produced by *A*'s message in conjunction with previous interactions with the outside world.

---

4. Several theorists have developed models of stages in the communication process. For an excellent summary, see the chapter by Ronald L. Smith in Barker and Kibler (1971).

A simplified model of the basic process of persuasion is presented in Fig. 3.1. Note that the main flow of communication (represented by gray arrows) is from *A* to *B*, but note, too, a series of black arrows moving in the opposite direction. These are intended to represent *monitoring functions* that *A* and *B* each perform, both in the processing of incoming information and in the transmitting of new messages.

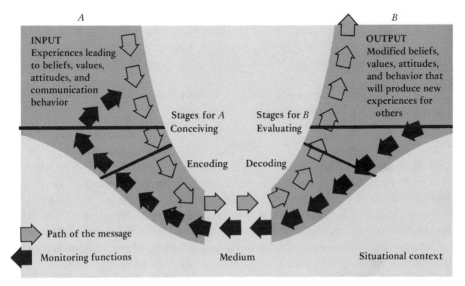

Fig. 3.1   A simplified model of stages in persuasion

A useful way to envision these monitoring functions is to picture *A* and *B* as big-time executives, each having two mental secretaries. The first mental secretary selects and orders the information that will be placed in the executive's In Box. Like any capable secretary, it screens out the junk mail, modifies or discards information that might be too disturbing or too complex, searches for information that the boss would like to have, and assigns priorities of importance to the final collection of mail. The second mental secretary provides the executive with second thoughts about whether the messages he is in process of transmitting actually fulfill his intentions. Its job is to provide *internal feedback* about messages, to suggest needed correctives before they are placed in his Out Box, or to suggest the need for additional messages in cases where the initial message has already been transmitted and appears to contain errors. Although we have spoken of these monitoring functions metaphorically, they are fairly well confirmed by psychological and physiological research. People selectively expose themselves and attend to competing messages, and selectively perceive, store, recall, and utilize the information they attend to. At the transmitting end they have the gift of foresight, a limited but nevertheless important capacity to empathize with the receiver and to anticipate the reactions their messages will receive. Given this capacity, people are able to revise initially conceived messages through internal feedback about expected audience reactions. Should an individual be physically and psychologically open to the actual responses of others, he or she may be able to modify future outputs through an analogous process known as *external feedback*. In the unidirectional model we have presented, there is no provision for external feedback, but in two-way communication, as in interviews or informal conversations, each party is constantly adjusting to the reactions of the others.

By now it should be clear that the communication flow is monitored from the moment A experiences incoming stimuli to the point at which B modifies her attitudes. Let us look more closely at the stages intervening between initial inputs and final outputs.

Conceiving the message. To borrow a phrase coined by Walter Lippmann, A and B each have "pictures in their heads," images formed from past experiences that together constitute their respective frames of reference. Among these psychological maps are images of themselves, of others, of the world "out there," and, because of human self-consciousness, images of images. For our purposes, the most important of these images are the beliefs, values, and attitudes that bear on any given communication transaction. It is on the basis of the images A has of the subject at hand, of the demands of the situation, of the receiver, of the available media, and of his own goals, that A transmits to B.

Encoding the message. It would be nice, perhaps, if by osmosis or surgery, A could simply transplant his images in B. Unfortunately, his vaguely formed thoughts and dispositions do not communicate directly. Although many of A's images will already be in linguistic form (it is virtually impossible to think abstractly without language), they will need to be arranged and adapted into an ordered sequence of signs (symbols or signals) that have meaning for B, and transformed further into physical stimuli that B can pick up on her sensory antennae and reconvert into equivalent linguistic forms. Encoding is the process of converting the pictures in our heads into verbal or nonverbal stimuli capable of being sensed and understood by others.

Earlier we spoke of the "miracle" of language, but language also has its pitfalls, even among those who share a common tongue. In an age of specialization and polarization, failure to "speak the same language" exacerbates cleavages among professions, generations, races, and subcultures. But even among relatively homogeneous groups, there are problems. How does one convey the pain of a toothache or a feeling of rapturous love, or

Like the donkey in the photo above, we may hear but not listen, listen but not understand, or understand but remain unmoved. (Photo courtesy of Miles Orvell.)

describe any other internal state? How does one define terms like "freedom" and "justice," words that not only have widely varying usage in our culture, but that are loaded with surplus emotional meanings? How does one disentangle the many meanings for "simple" words like "is," "may," "ought," "must"?

Even more dangerous are the misuses of language to which all of us are prone: a tendency to compartmentalize ongoing processes linguistically and then assume that the dichotomies and trichotomies we establish exist in the real world; a tendency to assume that all members of a category are alike because they have one name; a tendency to treat inferences and value judgments as though they objectively described events, rather than as our own interpretations of those events. Because the pictures in our heads are largely verbal, deficiencies in language and in language use affect not only the way we encode messages to others; they also affect the way we talk to ourselves.

Decoding the message. Just as *A* monitors the incoming experiences that will form his constellation of images, *B* calls upon a "mental secretary" to screen *A*'s messages. In many cases, *B* can choose whether or not to be physically exposed to a message. She can decide whether to watch a given movie or read a particular pamphlet. But even when physically exposed, *B* can fail to attend to some or all of the message. She may be incapable of hearing or seeing the stimulus, either because of competing external stimuli (called *channel noise* by some theorists), or because of *psychological noise* within her own system. Oftentimes, *A* and *B* give the appearance of talking to each other but are really engaged in a process of *psychological bypassing,* as in this example:

A: "What a day I had at the office! The receptionist was hung over and——"
B: "Joey was a rotten little menace all day. I don't know what to do——"
A: "Yeah. So, in the middle of all this, the boss collars me——"
B: "Well, anyway, I locked him in his room after he knocked over the jar of jelly."

Even in the absence of competing stimuli, *B* may get a different message than that intended by *A*. When the message stimulus reaches *B*'s eyes or ears (or other senses), it is no more than a series of sound waves or light waves of varying frequencies and intensities. Small wonder, therefore, that the decoding process should be imperfect.

Stuart Chase described a terrifying episode toward the close of World War II. Having dropped an A-bomb on Hiroshima and having decimated the Japanese fleet in the Pacific, the U.S. high command sent a note to the Japanese demanding unconditional surrender. The word in their reply was "*Makusatsu*," an ambiguous term meaning either "no comment at this time" or "not worthy of comment." Although there is now considerable evidence that the Japanese intended the former meaning, our interpreter assumed the message had the latter meaning. The U.S. dropped a second A-bomb, this time on Nagasaki, and thousands were killed, perhaps unnecessarily.

The evaluative stage. Recall that *B* also has a frame of reference consisting of beliefs, values, and attitudes that were formed prior to *A*'s message. Again, for the purpose of analyzing a given communication event, the most important of the elements in *B*'s picture world are her images of the subject at hand, of the source, of the medium and situational context, and of her own needs, goals, and aspirations. Together, these images will determine how *B* decodes *A*'s message and, more importantly, how she will evaluate its contents in relation to other thoughts and feelings. Although these images may well be modified in the course of A's presentation, we call them *antecedent factors* since they exist in B prior to A's message.

It is at the evaluative stage that the communication chain is most vulnerable to breakage. In conflict situations especially, the images B holds are likely to be at sharp variance from those held by A. Even if B should allow disturbing or threatening messages to be decoded accurately, there is little guarantee that the effects intended by A will be the effects secured. Rather than accepting A's recommendations, B may decide that A is a fool, or that the issue really isn't very important, or that the recommendations don't really apply to her personally. And as we shall emphasize in Chapter 4, even if B should modify her attitudes, she may continue to behave as she did before.

More Complex Patterns of Communication

The focus of the last section was on the relatively simple case of unidirectional, face-to-face communication by a single source to a single receiver. This may be diagrammed as follows:

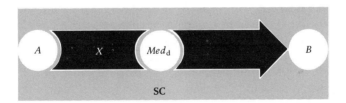

Here, as before, A refers to the source, B to the receiver. X is the message. Med_d means that the medium in this case is direct (face-to-face). The arrow indicates the direction of the message. SC refers to the situational context.

In this section we shall present and discuss briefly diagrams of more complex communication patterns. We can readily see that communication can get exceedingly complex with the addition of components, as when there are two or more sources or messages or receivers, or where communication takes place through an indirect medium such as television, or where attempts at influence are reciprocal, or where there are intervening channels. Note that the patterns to be presented in these diagrams are themselves highly simplified by comparison to some patterns in our daily experience. For example, a televised press conference during a political campaign would involve all of the additions of components to be presented here and still others not presented.

1. Two Receivers or More

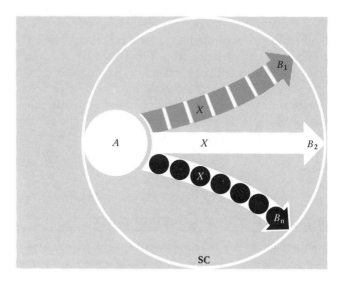

In all cases, the letter n indicates that there may be more than one or two of a given component; for example, a single speaker may address thousands. Note that we have not made reference here to the medium (med). This will be included in other diagrams only where relevant.

When a communicator must deliver the same message to more than one receiver, the problems of audience adaptation are enormously magnified. One receiver may be hostile, another sympathetic. One may be ignorant of the issues, another well informed. Imagine the problems of adaptation faced by a Presidential candidate giving a nationwide address. Instead of an audience of one, the audience may be millions of people scattered across the globe. The immediate audience for the address may be a convention of unionists, but directly and indirectly, it may be carried to countless others. What pleases liberals may displease conservatives. What turns on blacks, urbanites, and Western allies may turn off whites, suburbanites, and Eastern allies.

A second effect of having more than one receiver is that there is almost always communication within an audience. Some communicators may turn this to their advantage. An angry crowd may be stirred as much by *social contagion*, the spread of emotional intensity within an audience, as by the speaker. Some professional communicators—religious revivalists, political agitators and superpatriots among them—have also learned to manipulate the physical and social environment in such a way as to facilitate a concentration of audience attention on the communicator. The room may be large, hot, and crowded, the seats uncomfortable and close together, the audience interspersed with a claque of noisy supporters, the main speaker preceded by a musical program involving audience participation. On a platform high above the audience, surrounded by symbols of identification, the speaker's job may be easy indeed. In the same setting, of course, a speaker with a position discrepant from that of the audience would find it impossible to make headway.

2. Two or More Messages

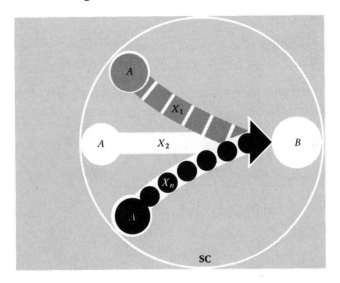

Just as it has been easier for students of persuasion to study passive audiences, it is also much easier to study each individual message transmitted to a receiver in isolation from prior and subsequent messages. From a receiver's standpoint, however, the totality of messages received on a given topic during a given period may form a unique and indivisible mosaic. For any one of us, for example, the message unit or composite on the question of whether to purchase a Sony tape recorder may be formed from an advertisement that we saw in a magazine, a few exchanges with friends, an overheard conversation, and a classroom speech on the benefits of tape recorders for improving communication skills. The series of messages that form a composite single message for a receiver is, as Becker (1971, p. 31) puts it, "scattered through time and space, disorganized, has large gaps; he is exposed to parts of it again and again; and there is great variance with the message to which other receivers are exposed."

Although it is often convenient to view a single speech or essay as a message unit, such an orientation is of limited value for purposes of analyzing campaigns or movements. Such long-term activities are always designed to have cumulative impact. Campaigns and movements have the distinct advantage of presenting one idea at a time or of moving the audience one increment at a time, and in each case applying the principle of repetition with variation. In successive advertisements, campaigners for the Volkswagen "bug" may variously emphasize its ease of handling, its durability, its tradeability, its popularity, and each time play on the theme that the VW is a good buy for the money. The leaders of a protest group may launch their movement by working only for interest and attention. Later they may seek to delegitimize their opponents. Only then may they seek seriously to sell their program for change.

3. Two or More Sources as Communicators of the Same Message

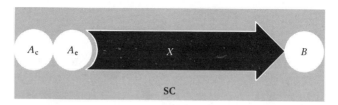

The foregoing diagram involved two or more messages, each from a different source. In this diagram there is only one message, but it is conceived by one person (A_c) and encoded by another (A_e).

The encoder of a message is usually the person who conceives its contents, but not always. Drafts of an important Presidential address, for example, may pass through several hands before a finished product is adopted. In the same vein, the narrator of a documentary on television may have far less to do with its contents than persons known in the business as "gatekeepers": editors, scriptwriters, and the like, whose job it is to screen the plethora of material from which the documentary is made.

4. Reciprocal Influence

As was suggested in Chapter 1, most of what we know with confidence about persuasion comes from situations involving inert, passive audiences that function primarily as receivers and do not attempt to persuade in return. Yet in employment interviews, bargaining sessions, business conferences, and many other situations, the roles of persuader and persuadee are interchangeable. In these situations the communicator cannot simply prepare a set message and communicate it unaltered. Genuine two-way communication requires that each party pattern planned remarks flexibly, listen carefully and critically, and adjust responses to the messages of

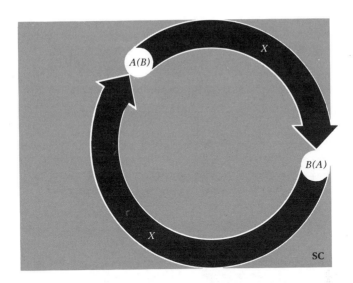

others. Even in situational contexts where the communicator is expected to deliver a unidirectional message, the seasoned persuader often converts the situation into one in which there is ample opportunity for give and take.

5. Reciprocal Influence Through Delegative Channels

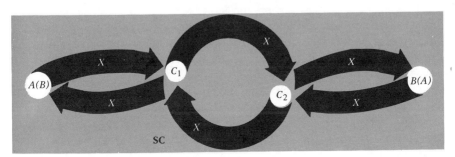

In the above diagram, C_1 and C_2 are channels of influence, respectively, for A and B. Each channel, of course, may also have personal persuasive goals.

Those who followed the career of Adlai Stevenson as United Nations Ambassador under Kennedy and Johnson were often surprised—as he at first was surprised—by discrepancies between what he believed and what he was compelled to say publicly. Where twice he had been the Presidential nominee of his party, Stevenson now found that he was not a free agent; indeed, that he was often compelled by his superiors to advocate policies that he himself abhorred. Such is the nature of what might be called *delegative* communication.

Delegative communication is most clearly seen in bargaining or negotiation situations involving organizations or governments. The negotiators for unions, for example, are instruments of their unions and may frequently be obliged to ask for recesses in bargaining sessions so as to receive advice from the unions' membership. At the same time, of course, they should be entrusted representatives, free within limits to exercise their own discretion, and free, too, to counsel the unions on how to counsel them. Once again, the delegative relationship is considerably more complex than the simple, unidirectional, two-person situation that we examined earlier.

6. Use of An Indirect Medium

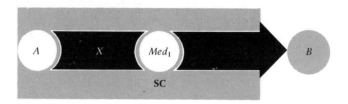

It is difficult to convey the impact of the mass media on contemporary society. Trautmann (1970) has pointed out that not until the middle of the nineteenth century was there mass literacy and means for dissemination of identical content. Until that time, therefore, there could be no truly mass media persuasion. Public proclamations and pageants, yes, but only for those who could hear or see them. Posters and leaflets, but only for those who could read.

With the electronic media, it is possible to convey messages more quickly, more vividly, and to much larger numbers of people. Dramatic events in remote corners of the globe and beyond have been brought visually into our living rooms while other events here at home have been "staged" for the TV cameras. With the advent of satellite television, persuaders may reach across the globe directly and may reach millions more indirectly. A major happening like the shooting of President Kennedy may be known by two-thirds of the American public within 30 minutes and by over 90 percent of the public within two hours (Becker, 1971). At the same time, persuaders may be stuck with unintended listeners or, worse still, with overexposed listeners, as in the case of a public that was hardened to horrors by several years of TV film clips of the Vietnam war.

The impact of the electronic mass media may be exaggerated by some, and they may be inferior to face-to-face communication for certain persuasive purposes, but there is considerable evidence that they are about the only means of reaching—let alone persuading—large segments of the population. Robinson and Swinehart (1968) have compiled some astounding data on mass media exposure among different population strata. Among those the authors call the "mass majority," comprising over half the population, less than ten percent had read any nonfiction books in a sample year, read a news or opinion magazine, read national or international news first in the newspaper, or sought out additional news. Yet most persons in this same population segment used television and radio daily and preferred to get news from TV rather than from any other medium. Even among college graduates, 30 percent had read a nonfiction book in a sample year while only ten percent had read opinion magazines such as *Harper's* or *The New Republic*.[5]

Still, it is all too easy to overestimate the persuasive effects of the electronic media. If we are to believe writers like Marshall McLuhan, the under-thirties of our society are products of the new communication technologies, radically different as a result from their elders. For McLuhan, presentational forms are more important than content. Values, taste, perception itself, are all presumably determined by the media to which we are oriented. Just as judgments of source credibility merge with judgments of a message, we can agree that the effects of message and medium tend to become indistinguishable. We cannot agree, however, that what is said counts for little next to the vehicle by which it is conveyed.

Comparing Simple and Complex Communication Situations

A recurring theme of the last two sections of this chapter has been that no single account of the persuasive process is likely to do justice to the variety of persuasive communication situations we are exposed to and to the complexities found in some of them. As might be expected, scholars have focused on relatively simple situations. Except where differences in situations manifestly make a difference (as between one-way and two-way communications, for example), it seems a reasonable assumption that what holds true of the simple situation should hold true of more complex situations. At the same time, there is a clear need for theories of a more specialized nature: theories of campaigns, theories of delegative communication, and so on. Two illustrations of situations only barely discussed until now should help to clarify this point.

We have suggested that inherent in formal organizations are formal and informal channels of communication. In addition, all formal organiza-

---

5. The best reference work that we know of on mass media research is Pool and Schramm (1973), *Handbook of Communication*. We shall be discussing the political effects of the electronic media in Chapter 12.

tions have certain structural characteristics (hierarchy, division of labor), and certain functional requirements. As a consequence of these inherent conditions, persuasion in formal organizations is different than in other situations. Within an organization, for example, in addition to knowing *who* communicators are, it is helpful to know *what* they are (their job specialty) and *where* they are (in the hierarchy). As Paul Pigors (1949) has suggested, who they are tells us their *point* of view, what they are tells us their *angle* of view, and where they are tells us their *scope* of view. Together, these tell us a great deal about how they will persuade and how they will react to the persuasive communications of others. Variables of this kind might provide basic elements for a theory about persuasion that is specifically geared to formal organizations.

A qualitatively different set of communication factors from those found in simple communication situations or within formal organizations is confronted by those who lead protest movements, especially militant movements. By its very nature, a movement is at odds with the system, the values, the laws, or the authorities that it challenges. At the same time, it cannot purchase internal support from its members in the same way that formal organizations like General Motors can. Movements by their nature involve several sources transmitting several messages. Given their structural and functional characteristics, certain patterns of persuasive communication are again predictable.

In general, we will not differentiate among different communication situations in ensuing chapters. We will assume, except where specifically noted, that what holds true of one situation holds true of another. From time to time, however, we will suggest differences, and in Chapter 13, we will theorize in some detail on the nature of persuasion in conflict situations.

Summary

A recurring theme of this chapter has been that persuasive messages cannot be viewed as though they were simply discrete, self-contained, intrinsically meaningful stimuli, operating like magical potions to produce pushbutton effects on receivers. First, as a process, communication has no real beginning or end; in fact, the message is as much a response as it is a stimulus. Second, it is often impossible to disentangle what is said (the message in its narrow sense) from the impact of source, medium, and context. Broadly speaking, we cannot *not* communicate. Third, even purely verbal discourse evokes connotative meanings, not just denotative meanings; figurative interpretations, not just literal interpretations. Fourth, the form of a message communicates quite independently of its semantic content, and in communicating that content we also—often inadvertently—transmit information about interpersonal relationships. Finally, meaning is ultimately, and most significantly, in receivers. The effective persuader is receiver-oriented, not source-oriented.

Nor is it accurate to think of the message as a fixed entity. In reality, the message is a constantly changing energy form that travels through stages within source and receiver. Even in the simplest cases—those involving unidirectional influence by a source to a single receiver, without the interposition of channels or indirect media—there are several links in the communication chain, the chain itself no stronger than its weakest link. For our purposes, we may speak of a conceiving stage, an encoding stage, a decoding stage, and an evaluative stage—just within source and receiver—with corresponding inputs and outputs for each. Problems of communication may occur at any of those stages. In more complex situations, such as those briefly examined in the last section of this chapter, the addition of communication components may greatly magnify the difficulties of the communicator's task.

Considerable emphasis was given in this chapter to the importance of the situational context. Recall that the context was likened to the background and physical setting for a play. As in a play, any one "scene" takes on meaning from what has gone on before as well as from the props and furnishings that appear on stage. In "real-life" dramas, too, there is a "logic" of the immediate situation which narrows the actor's range of sensible options while better enabling the audience to interpret these actions.

There are differences, however, and they provide a fitting, if pessimistic, conclusion for this chapter. As actors on a "living" stage, we perform in dramas that have no beginning and no end. The stage itself is but part of a larger stage which is part of still another; it is not bounded by a proscenium arch. In life, moreover, we are often cast in roles or placed in situations that are not of our own choosing. We are free to improvise, to be sure, but only within limits set by our culture and by the institutions and groups with which we are affiliated. And we also cannot improvise too freely because our actions have real consequences; we cannot walk out of the theater.

4

The Receiver: Variables and Possible Effects

We have repeatedly emphasized in this book that persuasion deals in appearances, that it takes place on the recipient's terms, that it is the received message that counts and not the message conceived by the communicator, and that the receiver is by no means a passive entity. It is high time, therefore, that we identify those receiver variables which bear most directly on persuasion. The first three sections of this chapter identify factors of special importance in formulating strategies of audience adaptation. In the first section, particularly, we attempt to lay some conceptual groundwork by relating the concepts of attitude, belief, value, and overt behavior to each other. We move then to a rather extensive catalogue of possible persuasive effects, some of them intended, others unintended, but all of them important in formulating goals and subgoals. Next we review evidence on determinants of accurate audience analysis. And, finally, in the summary section of this chapter, we present a list of questions that persuaders may utilize in constructing their own audience-analysis inventories.

In discussing receivers we shall draw heavily on concepts used by other authorities. Unfortunately, the terms most familiarly used by the experts—terms like attitude, behavior, belief, opinion, and so on—are mired in ambiguity through inconsistent usage. As early as 1935, Gordon Allport (1935) found as many as 14 definitions of the term "attitude" in his review of the literature. Attitudes have been variously defined as perceptual or cognitive properties, as affective or emotive characteristics, and as forms of behavior or action. So great is the conceptual confusion surrounding the term that several authorities have all but abandoned the task of defining it. After reviewing the numerous and often conflicting distinctions drawn between attitudes and opinions, it has occurred to McGuire (1969) that they may be "names in search of distinctions" (p. 152). Berelson and Steiner (1964) gave up their attempt to distinguish opinions, attitudes, and beliefs and settled for a single composite term, "OAB," to designate all three. It should be clear that the definitions which follow cannot possibly reflect the many ways they are used by others. Whenever possible, however, we have attempted to offer definitions that suggest useful distinctions and that are consistent with dominant usage among social scientists.

The Key Factors: Attitudes, Attitude Components, and Overt Behaviors

Attitudes

An attitude is defined as a relatively enduring predisposition to respond favorably or unfavorably toward an attitude object. The various parts of the definition deserve further comment.

First, as a predisposition, an attitude is an "in-the-head" variable; its presence must be inferred and cannot be observed directly. Individuals may *say* they favor legalizing marijuana but their verbalized statements, sometimes called *opinions*, may not reflect their true attitude. To infer people's attitudes, the outside observer has several options available.[1] The simplest way is to ask them, as in a Gallup poll. Another way is to observe them in action, especially when they do not know they are being observed. Still another method involves the administration of tests and scales that psychologists have specifically devised for purposes of attitude measurement. These include direct measures such as rating scales and indirect,

---

A widely used, and fairly typical attitude-scaling technique is the semantic differential, a flexible, multipurpose instrument used to tap connotative meanings of concepts. To tap attitudes toward concepts (one type of connotative meaning), the investigator asks subjects to react to the concept (e.g., war, Gerald Ford, solar heating) on a number of evaluative, bipolar scales, such as the following:

Gerald Ford								
Good	+3	+2	+1	0	−1	−2	−3	Bad
Beautiful	+3	+2	+1	0	−1	−2	−3	Ugly
Desirable	+3	+2	+1	0	−1	−2	−3	Undesirable
Worthy	+3	+2	+1	0	−1	−2	−3	Unworthy
Moral	+3	+2	+1	0	−1	−2	−3	Immoral

The zero position represents neutrality or no opinion and 1, 2, and 3 represent mild, moderate, and extreme degrees of intensity, respectively, in either direction from the midpoint. A simple means of scoring is to average or summate individual scale ratings for any given concept. For a detailed discussion of the rationale and development of the semantic differential, see Osgood, Suci, and Tannenbaum (1957). We will be referring to the method again in Chapter 5 in our discussion of congruity theory.

---

unobtrusive measures such as free-association tests. If an individual repeatedly associates sex objects with "mother," we may make bets on the person he most desires. Still another way to infer attitudes—admittedly a dangerous method, but sometimes the only one—is to glean them from knowledge of an individual's demographic characteristics: her age, occupation, race, etc.

A second point warranting attention is that attitudes vary in terms of

---

1. For an introduction to methods of attitude measurement, see Kiesler, Collins and Miller (1969), pp. 9–22. The book, *Unobtrusive Measures*, by Webb, *et al.* (1966), provides a number of interesting, indirect measures of attitudes. For a look at a number of topic-specific attitude measures, see Shaw and Wright (1967).

direction (for or against) and *degree* or *intensity* (mildly for, strongly against, etc.). There is a world of difference between lip-service commitment to a proposition and whole-hearted commitment.

Third, an attitude is a relatively *enduring* predisposition. Implicit here is the notion of consistency across time. If an individual claims to be a pacifist one day and proposes war the next, we cannot safely infer this person's attitude.

Fourth, an attitude is a response *to* something: a proposal, an event, a person, etc. All of us hold attitudes toward ourselves, toward other people, toward the various mass media, and—of special importance—toward policies recommended by persuaders. When we refer to attitudes in this book, we shall generally have in mind the receiver's attitude toward the persuader's *proposition of policy.*

A proposition is a debatable assertion and a proposition of policy is an assertion that suggests an action proposal. It suggests that a receiver should or should not engage in some action or be in favor of or opposed to some action. An advocated proposition of policy may be quite general (e.g., "The government should do something about pollution") or quite specific (e.g., "City Council should pass Bill 239876 to regulate industrial waste disposal"). It may be positive (e.g., "Buy American!") or negative (e.g., "Let's not let patriotism determine purchases"). It may be important (e.g., "Please marry me") or unimportant (e.g., "Let's serve duck, not chicken"). It may be explicit (e.g., "Don't go to school at Princeton") or implicit (e.g., "Princeton students are snobs and you don't want to be a snob, do you?").

Attitude Components: Beliefs and Values

Chances are that if you are anywhere near as opinionated as this writer, your attitudes are based on a number of strongly held beliefs and values. If you are a supporter of intercollegiate athletics, for example, one such belief might be that intercollegiate athletics encourage a spirit of competition; a corresponding value would be that a spirit of competition is good. As Jones and Gerard (1967, p. 159) have put it, an attitude is "the implication of combining a belief with a relevant value."

Recall that in Chapter 1, we referred to *beliefs* as characterizations of objects. (In the previous example, intercollegiate athletics was the object and it was characterized as promoting a spirit of competition.) Beliefs may be about the past ("The world was created in seven days"), the present ("It is raining outside"), or the future ("It will remain cold tomorrow"). They may be expressions of purely conceptual relationships ("$3^2 \times 4^2 = 5^2$"), descriptions of the real world ("The resources of this country are being depleted"), or causal inferences ("The oil squeeze is causing world-wide inflation"). They may be about objects in the environment ("Chickens lay eggs"), about other people ("The speaker thinks there will be a depression") or about ourselves ("My intuition tells me I'm in love with Gayle"). Finally, they may be beliefs about the *credibility* of the *sources* of our beliefs (e.g., "My senses tell me true;" "The speaker knows what he's talking about;" "The authority quoted by the speaker is competent;" "The majority is usually right;" "I can trust my intuitions;" "Since I've told Gayle that I love her, it must be so").

Beliefs exist on a *probability dimension* (Fishbein, 1963). With respect to capital punishment, for example, we may believe it *probable* that capital punishment does not deter crime, that it discriminates against the poor, and that it violates the Constitution. This is illustrated in Fig. 4.1. Note that we have worded the items in Fig. 4.1 so that someone opposing capital punishment would assign only "plus" ratings. Technically speaking, we hold beliefs ("plus" ratings) and disbeliefs ("minus" ratings). When a belief or disbelief approaches a $+3$ or -3 on the probability scale, it becomes, in our minds, an item of knowledge or fact. As it approaches the zero point on the scale, it becomes a speculation.

Rokeach (1973, p. 3) offers five assumptions about *generalized* values with which we agree: "(1) the total number of values that a person possesses is relatively small; (2) all men everywhere possess the same values to different degrees; (3) values are organized into value systems; (4) the antecedents of human values can be traced to culture, society and its institutions, and personality; (5) the consequences of human values will be manifested in virtually all phenomena that social scientists might consider worth investigating and understanding."

Whereas beliefs exist on a probability dimension, *values* exist on an *affective* (i.e., emotion-laden) dimension, the midpoint of the scale constituting indifference or neutrality. We might think of values as *generalized attractions and repulsions;* they are general or abstract in the sense that the same value can be applied to a variety of attitude objects or characterizations of those objects. Indeed, when linked to objects or object characterizations by way of *value assertions,* they help to direct our feelings toward attitude objects.[2] Among our values are those derived from our biological or genetic inheritance (e.g., survival, safety, sleep, etc.), from

---

2. The best social-scientific treatment of values that we have read is Rokeach (1973). We shall be amplifying on our concept of values by several references to his book in subsequent footnotes.

cultural and substructural influences (e.g., in our culture, progress, success, bigness, freedom of opportunity, etc.), those derived from identification with the norms of the groups with which we are affiliated (e.g., a particular work group's definition of a fair day's work), and uniquely personal idiosyncratic values (e.g., a given individual's food tastes).

At the risk of inviting charges of ambiguity, we shall be using the term "value" to do considerable conceptual work for us. Thus, depending on the context, we may refer to values as residing in people (e.g., the abstract value of self-fulfillment) or in objects (e.g., murder as intrinsically unethical); in ends (i.e., terminal values) and in means toward a given end (i.e., instrumental values). Jones and Gerard's (1967, pp. 158–159) use of the term is quite similar.

> In our usage value refers to a wide variety of motivational phenomena. Any singular state or object for which the individual strives, or approaches, or extols, embraces, voluntarily consumes, or incurs expense to acquire, is a positive value. Anything that the individual avoids, escapes from, deplores, rejects, or attacks is a negative value.

We are now in a better position to see how beliefs and values constitute the cognitive and affective *components* of attitudes. With respect to major cognitive categories in belief statements about capital punishment, for example, a given individual might assign high values to crime deterrence and nondiscrimination against the poor and only a slightly high affective rating to the value of constitutionality. This is also illustrated in Fig. 4.1. To a significant degree, *our attitudes should be a joint product of the probabilities we assign to relevant belief statements about the topic and the affective ratings we assign to key value terms in those statements.*

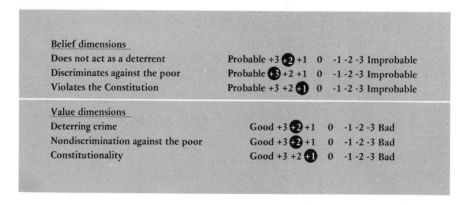

Fig. 4.1 Cognitive and affective components: a hypothetical illustration of some beliefs and values that may contribute to an individual's negative attitude toward capital punishment

Is there a formula by which, if we knew all the beliefs and values which an individual perceived as relevant to his or her attitude, we could predict that attitude? We think not. Nevertheless, a knowledge of the receiver's most salient beliefs and values should help you greatly in your efforts to mould or change his or her attitudes. To understand more clearly the relationship between attitudes toward policy propositions, attitude components, and persuasive discourse, let us imagine a typical receiver— we shall call her Joan—who is opposed to capital punishment.

Joan's attitude might well have been *formed* from hearing persuaders voice their opposition. In defense of the *proposition of policy* that capital punishment should be abolished, the persuader might have presented a number of relevant *belief* and *value assertions*, organized in logical fashion, as follows:

Capital punishment does not deter crime (belief)
Deterring crime is important (value)

Capital punishment discriminates against the poor (belief)
Discrimination against the poor is evil (value)

Capital punishment laws are unconstitutional (belief)
Obeying the constitution is necessary (value)

Therefore (by implication), we should be opposed to capital punishment (attitude).

These assertions are themselves debatable; they constitute *subpropositions* of belief and value. Sometimes, in fact, any one belief or value assertion may serve as the focus for an entire speech or essay. Rather than directing a frontal assault at an overall attitude, the persuader may argue only that capital punishment is unconstitutional or that obeying the Constitution is necessary. In these cases, the assertions take on the status of *propositions* of belief or value, rather than just *subpropositions*.

We should by no means regard belief and value modification in their own right as less consequential. Indeed, altering certain beliefs and values may be a more significant feat than modifying attitudes; for example: convincing an agnostic that there is a God (belief); reducing adherence to the Puritan ethic among persons reared to accept traditional folkways (value). When belief or value questions are of intrinsic importance, the persuader might well address them without worrying about whether, or how, belief or value commitments will be translated into overt behavior.

No doubt the persuaders who influenced Joan found it necessary to defend some of their belief and value assertions by reference to still other assertions, as shown in the following arguments.

The Constitution is the highest law in the land (belief)
If states routinely ignore constitutional requirements when framing laws, there will be anarchy (belief)
Anarchy is highly undesirable (value)

Therefore, obeying the Constitution is necessary (subproposition of value).

Joan may accept other subpropositions on the basis of the persuader's perceived credibility. Even here, supporting belief and value judgments are implicit:

Smith says capital punishment doesn't deter crime (belief)
Crime ought to be deterred (value)
Smith is trustworthy (belief)
Trustworthiness is important (value)

Therefore, capital punishment doesn't deter crime (subproposition of belief)

Just as belief and value assertions were used to *form* Joan's attitude toward capital punishment, so these same types of assertion may be used to *change* her attitude:

Capital punishment is defended in the Bible (belief)
The Bible contains God's laws (belief)
God is just (value)

Therefore (by implication), we should be in favor of capital punishment.[3]

Or they may be used to *intensify* her unfavorable attitude:

Because capital offenders have rarely been executed, capital punishment actually encourages capital crimes (belief)
Encouraging crimes is even worse than not deterring them (value)

Therefore (by implication), we should be even more opposed to capital punishment than we were before (intensification of unfavorable attitude)

By now it should be clear why beliefs and values constitute highly significant components of attitudes. We should point out, however, that an

---

3. The reader may be wondering at this point whether it is really possible to alter values that serve as bases for attitudes. Suppose the receiver couldn't care less about the rule of constitutional law. Suppose, even more fundamentally, that he or she valued racial discrimination; in fact, was an out and out bigot. We shall be taking up this issue more fully in Chapters 8 and 11. For now let us note that persuaders generally appeal to *agreed-upon* values when they seek to modify attitudes. However, should basic value differences arise, there are still means for dealing with them, the most fundamental of which is to compel receivers to examine the consequences of a given value in light of other values that they hold. Using this technique, Rokeach (1973, Chapter 9) has been able to induce, experimentally, long-term changes in values that ultimately affected the overt behavior of his subjects.

attitude is always something *more* than the sum of its cognitive and affective parts. In changing cognitive or affective components we are likely to change the attitude, but attitude change is not *guaranteed*. The receivers may not see the change in an attitude component as relevant to their attitudes or, as we shall point out in Chapter 5, they may tolerate the psychological inconsistency between their attitudes and one or more attitude components.

Relationship Between Attitudes and Overt Behavior

If an attitude is a predisposition toward something, presumably individuals should act toward that something in ways consistent with their attitudes. Compared to relatively unprejudiced persons, those who score high on measures of prejudice toward blacks should also be found to be more discriminatory toward blacks. Workers who assign relatively high ratings to their jobs should also perform more effectively on their jobs. Students who express disapproval of cheating should also be less likely to cheat when given the opportunity. And if any of these persons should modify their attitudes, their behavior should presumably be modified as well.

So, at least, psychologists have thought. The presumption of attitude-behavior consistency has, in fact, been a cornerstone of persuasion theory over the centuries.

Surprisingly, the attitude-behavior consistency hypothesis has not been confirmed by research, or at least not to the same degree that psychologists had anticipated. On the basis of a review of 15 studies, Vroom (1964) found that job attitudes and job performance were only slightly and insignificantly correlated. Wicker (1969) summarized research on the relationship between attitudes and a large variety of behaviors: civil rights participation, cheating, labor union attendance, petition-signing, voting in student elections, providing public accommodations to minority group members, and many others. He concluded that, on the whole, attitudes were only slightly related to actions, if they were related at all. Although there have been comparatively few studies on the relationship between changes in attitude and changes in behavior, the studies that have been reported have revealed similar findings (Festinger, 1964; Greenwald, 1965, 1966). To be sure, not all studies have found insignificant correlations between attitudes and behavior or between attitude change and behavior change. In most circumstances, for example, election surveys are extremely accurate predictors of how people actually vote. Changes in attitudes toward candidates are similarly reflected at the polls. It is a safe bet that persons who join groups like the Women's Christian Temperance Union are not adamant enthusiasts of drinking parties; that Legionnaires are rarely pacifists, and so on. Still, the preponderance of evidence has failed to confirm commonsense expectations.

What are we to make of the findings that attitudes and behaviors are often poorly correlated? Since all we can ever measure directly are publicly observable behaviors (recall that attitudes are always inferred and can never be measured directly), should we abandon the notion of attitude entirely and content ourselves with talking about only that which we can observe? The approach is tempting, but intuitively we know that there is such a thing as a private attitude and that it is not always the same thing as what we say in public. If we abandoned the notion of attitude, how would we ever distinguish between voluntary changes in behavior (those produced by persuasion) and involuntary changes in behavior (those produced by pure coercion)?

Perhaps we should retain the notion of attitude but abandon the expectation that attitudes are in some way related to behavior. This approach is also tempting, but it once again violates our intuitive knowledge that the two variables are related in some way. Is there a third alternative?

A number of theorists (Rokeach, 1968; Fishbein, 1967; Kiesler, Collins and Miller, 1969; Burhans, 1971) have, indeed, proposed a third alternative, one that underscores the thesis we developed in Chapter 3 about the importance of the situational context. All of them agree that attitude-behavior discrepancies can be understood or explained away without either abandoning the notion of attitude entirely or concluding that attitudes and behavior are unrelated. There are some differences in their positions but we shall focus on similarities.

First, as Rokeach (1968) has emphasized, researchers have often done a poor job of measuring attitudes. Since an attitude is a relatively enduring and consistent predisposition, we should not be content with a single measure of an attitude (the typical procedure in research on attitudes) but should utilize, instead, a procedure in which we measure the attitude across time and in a variety of situational contexts. Suppose, for example, that an individual asked for a draft deferment during the war in Vietnam on grounds that he was opposed to war. Quite obviously, the selective service examiner would have had grounds for suspicion, but should the individual have been a known Quaker and should he have volunteered for alternative service in a hospital ward serving patients with contagious diseases, the examiner might have reasonably inferred that pacifism was a genuinely held attitude in that case.

Second, any given behavioral act seems to be a product of not one but several attitudes. Whether we sign a petition to save the California redwoods, for example, may be determined not only by our attitude toward the redwoods, but also by our attitude toward the act of signing petitions and toward the person who solicits our signature. When researchers or practitioners fail to find strong relationships between attitudes and behavior, it is frequently because they have not adequately or comprehensively assessed all of the relevant attitudes.

Third, when measures of attitude and measures of behavior are not correlated, it is often because the situational contexts are different. Concomitantly, attitudes measured in typical testing situations are not the same attitudes as those brought to bear in "real-life" situations. In two studies of the relationship between prejudice and discrimination, for example, (La-Piere, 1934; Kutner, Wilkins and Yarrow, 1952) managers of restaurants and hotels were first asked in the abstract whether they would serve "a Chinese couple" or "a Negro." Many refused. When these same subjects were confronted with a "real-live" Chinese couple or a "real-live" Negro, they served them. The discrepancy may be explained, however, when it is recognized that stereotypical attitudes toward a given group and attitudes toward specific members of that group are not necessarily the same, especially when, as in both studies, the latter were well-dressed, polite, charming, etc.

A fourth point, related to the third, is that factors in the situational context may constrain individuals from acting on their attitudes. We may be convinced of the proposition that our boss should be tarred and feathered but be realistically loath to act on it. In the protective atmosphere of the classroom, it may be easy to agree with a student who decries reports of onlookers standing around helplessly while innocent persons are being attacked. It is another thing, however, to go to a stranger's defense, especially when there is imminent danger to self.

In these cases, the constraints on behavior involved the possibility of economic or physical punishment, but there are other, less tangible, situational pressures that may be equally constraining. As we indicated in Chapter 3, all of us conform in one degree or another to various cultural, subcultural, institutional and group norms of "appropriate" behavior. Sometimes we obey these norms because we have internalized them; at other times, because disobedience carries with it the threat of direct punishment. We obey at other times, however, out of a fear of censure, embarrassment, loss of face, or out of a positive sense of identification or attraction toward groups with which we are affiliated. When pressures such as these have been found to be present in psychological experiments on persuasion, some critics have viewed them as artifacts which confound and distort the results. In a sense they do, but as Rokeach (1968) has insightfully observed, all "real-life" situations carry such "demand characteristics" with them, at least to some degree. This has prompted him to suggest that behavior is always a function of at least two attitudes, an attitude-toward-object (A_o) and an attitude-toward-situation (A_s). In relatively free-choice situations, the A_o may be expected to determine behavior; in relatively restricted choice situations, the latter may be expected to dominate. As Rokeach (1968) puts it:

> A given attitude-toward-object, whenever activated, need not always be behaviorally manifested or expressed in the same way or in the same degree.

Its expression will vary adaptively as the attitude activated by the situation varies, with attitude-toward-situation facilitating or inhibiting the expression of attitude-toward-object, and vice versa.

Among the situational factors that influence one's A_s is the factor of accountability. This is illustrated in an experiment (Linn, 1965) where many of the same subjects who had indicated on an attitude scale that they would be willing to be photographed with Negroes refused when actually approached to do so and when asked to sign a release for public distribution of the photos. Typical responses were: "I didn't know if I should sign or not. I really couldn't visualize the consequences," "I don't know how I feel until I'm actually confronted with the situation," "In the questionnaire I wasn't faced with the real thing."

Rokeach's distinction between attitude-toward-object and attitude-toward-situation appears to us to make a good deal of sense, although we would prefer another term than attitude-toward-situation. The term does not adequately reflect the idea of the situational context as something that exerts pressure upon us to behave "appropriately." Moreover, we would rather reserve the term "attitude" for a single class of phenomena, rather than always having to qualify our usage by indicating whether it is an attitude-toward-object we are thinking about or an attitude-toward-situation. As an alternative, we will be speaking of behaviors as a joint function of attitudes (by which we mean "attitudes-toward-object") and situational pressures (what Rokeach calls "attitude-toward-situation").

By way of summarizing what we have said so far, let us picture a housewife who has been asked to donate to the Red Cross by a neighbor in the apartment building. Weighing on the decision about whether to give and how much to give will be such factors as the prospective donor's attitude toward charities, toward the idea of being solicited, and toward the Red Cross in particular. In a relatively free-choice situation, these attitude factors would be decisive, but it is quite conceivable that in this situation, the housewife might also be saying to herself: "I'd better give or she'd think I'm cheap and spread the word around the building . . . Maybe I'd better give a dollar since that's what the others are probably giving . . . Since I have a baby coming, I'd better not give more than a dollar . . ." More than likely, these situational pressures would cause an otherwise reluctant housewife to even *want* to give, at least her "fair share." The situational context would not only influence her behavior but would also influence her attitude toward the object.

There are undoubtedly a number of additional factors that help us to understand why changes in attitudes are not always accompanied by changes in behavior. One often-neglected factor militating against behavior change is inertia, especially when people are asked to give up old habits. Another reason that behavior does not always change is that people do not always know *how* to act in the face of their new attitudes unless they are given explicit directions. What does it mean in behavioral terms, for example, to become a religious mystic? Finally, new attitudinal commitments may be sufficiently satisfying in themselves so that action becomes psychologically unnecessary. The conviction that we have come to see the spiritual light of day, for example, may be just the excuse we need to maintain our old behaviors.

All things considered, the concept of attitude is still quite useful. As Kelman (1974, p. 112) has put it, "the low correlations between attitude and action found by many of the studies in this genre, though pointing to the limitations of the attitude concept, do not demonstrate its invalidity." On the contrary, he implies, the studies merely point up the many things persuaders must consider when they seek to analyze a receiver's current attitudes, and the many things they can do when they seek to modify those attitudes.

Rather than taking one single measure of an attitude, says Kelman, the serious practitioner should probably take several measures of each of the many attitudes that may bear on a recommended action. Consistent with the previous discussion, he argues that attempts should be made to discover both the motivational and situational determinants of present attitudes. Especially important in this regard is investigation of the audience's past *actions* as they bear on their attitudes. As he puts it, "The nature and the consequences of the action bring to the fore challenging insights, role expectations, social supports, or direct experiences, which are the stuff out of which attitudes emerge" (p. 314). Also important is consideration of the perceived range of future action alternatives. How do people order alternatives in terms of preference? Are there any actions they might be prepared to take, and even wish to take, if the right circumstances arose? Rarely, says Kelman, are we committed to just one action from a range of possible choices, although, clearly, there may be one preferred action that characterizes our present behavior.[4] In general, says Kelman (p. 316):

> Attitude and action are linked in a continuing reciprocal process, each generating the other in an endless chain. Action is the ground on which attitudes are formed, tested, modified and abandoned.

---

4. The notion of a range of endorsable commitments is quite similar to the concept of latitude of acceptance in a theory we will be taking up in Chapter 5 (Sherif, Sherif, and Nebergall, 1965); the difference is that the former refers to actions, the latter to judgments.

In general, we are quite taken with Kelman's article and strongly recommend it to readers. While Kelman's ideas are not sufficiently developed or tested to earn the status of a formal theory, they do a splendid job of reconciling differences in other theories, in synthesizing prior research on attitudes, and in provoking readers into reexamining the attitude-action relationship.

As for modifying the receivers' attitudes and subsequent behaviors, the implications from the foregoing discussion are many. Rather than simply attempting to modify attitudes in the abstract, persuaders can help to make a modified attitude *salient* to a situational context. They can provide specific instructions on *how* to act. They can help the receivers *interpret* the context, including the context of their own past actions, so that it appears conducive to favorable action. They can encourage receivers to *expand* their perceived range of endorsable action preferences and perhaps alter the *ordering* of those preferences. They can cause the receivers to view the recommended action as *expected* or even *inevitable.* Finally, they can *alter* the context itself so that different situational pressures or more intensified situational pressures are brought to bear upon receivers.

Other Receiver Variables

Knowledge of Subject

Despite the welter of information available on most matters affecting our lives, it is a reasonably safe conjecture that the educated among us tend to overestimate knowledge levels of the general populace and also tend to hold inflated views of their own degrees of knowledge. Opinion polls repeatedly bear out this observation. In one survey, a national sample was asked this trick question: "Do you believe that incest is good for the economy?" About 70 percent said yes! Other evidence suggests that in voter primaries, the electorate tends to vote the name rather than the issues. A Kennedy was elected to major office in Massachusetts, for example, despite the fact that he was not previously known to the electorate and was unrelated to the Kennedy family of national fame. Media coverage of a candidate evidently attracts support for a candidate, but does not necessarily lead to knowledge of the candidate's stands on issues. In the 1968 primary, for example, many New Hampshire residents voted for Senator Eugene McCarthy because they thought he was a "hawk" on Vietnam rather than a "dove."

College students have fared little better on information surveys. At the time Dean Rusk was Secretary of State, about half the students at one midwestern college suggested, in response to a poll, that he was dean of their college. Just after four students were killed by National Guardsmen at Kent State University, Tompkins and Anderson (1971) questioned students and faculty to determine what communication factors might have contributed to the tragedy. Their report squares with surveys of other campuses. Not only did students and faculty not know what rules and regulations they were supposed to obey during the crisis period; practically all students, and many faculty, could not name one of the four divisions of the university or any of its vice-presidents.

If knowledge is what is missing, it would seem to follow that knowledge is what persuaders must provide to their audiences, and, in some cases, this is undoubtedly true. Critical audiences, and especially audiences with a vital stake in the issues, must be provided with details of the advocate's proposal and evidence and arguments to support it. Paradoxically, however, those who know least about a given issue tend to be influenced least by information campaigns (Katz, 1960). Some persons are generally disinclined to acquire new information; others lack the wherewithall to acquire it. We shall return to this point in our discussion of personality factors.

Interest in Subject

It is generally true that persons who are uninformed also tend to be apathetic and that persons who are apathetic tend to lack information about the issues. Both tend to be "fence-sitters" on public issues and in political elections they frequently fail to vote. Still, they constitute an important segment of potential voters and campaigners frequently make special efforts to entice them to the polls. The fact that political campaigns are often pitched to this segment of the electorate is one reason that they are often reduced to verbal pablum and camouflaged as entertainment.

The polar point at the opposite end of the spectrum from apathy has been variously described as *involvement, perceived importance of the issues, attitudinal commitment,* and *behavioral commitment.* In some respects, they are conceptually distinct.

As used by Sherif, Sherif and Nebergall (1965), involved persons are those who have an ego-investment in the positions they take on a given issue. As Sherif (1965), puts it:

> It is one thing to change from one brand of soap to another. It is quite another thing to change a person's stand toward persons, objects, groups, and institutions that he accepts or rejects as related to himself.

Somewhat distinct from involvement in a position is perceived importance of the issues themselves (Freedman, 1964). For example, it is quite possible to regard the conflict between Catholics and Protestants in Northern Ireland as an important conflict without necessarily having a personal stake in the matter.

Finally, one may regard an issue as important, be more or less ego-involved, and still not express a behavioral commitment toward it. The greater the degree of behavioral commitment, the more likely we are to bolster attitudinal commitments and to resist attempts at counterpersuasion. McGuire (1969) distinguishes among private decisions, public announcements of belief, and active participation on the basis of the belief. The latter would probably serve to strengthen attitudinal commitments the most. On the other hand, persuaders may seek to secure conversions by inducing receivers to express unfelt behavioral commitments on the assumption that in actively "role-playing" a position, one learns to develop a private commitment to it.

Although the above distinctions have theoretical significance, it is not always easy or important to separate them in practice. From the persuader's standpoint, probably the most important observations that we can make now are: (1) some degree of interest in an issue (involvement) is necessary before receivers will actively decode messages; (2) degree of attitudinal commitment, extremity of position and ego-involvement tend to be highly correlated and inversely related to susceptibility to change; (3) behavioral commitments, especially active and effortful behavioral commitments, tend to bolster attitudinal commitments.

Persuasibility Factors

Some persons tend to display susceptibility to persuasive communications as a general trait while others are consistently receptive to certain kinds of appeals or arguments or to certain types of topics. The former has been labeled *communication-free persuasibility;* the latter, *communication-bound persuasibility* (Janis and Hovland, 1959). What are some of the factors associated with persuasibility?

1. *Age and Sex.* Children's Liberation and Women's Liberation take note! The preponderance of available evidence suggests that children and women are, on the average, more persuasible than their adult male counterparts. (Cronkhite, 1969; Janis and Fields, 1959). These variables are among the few, in fact, that are fairly straightforward in their relationship to persuasibility.[5]

2. *Intelligence and Level of Education.* These factors illustrate the complexity of relationships ordinarily found between receiver variables and persuasibility. On the one hand, brighter, more educated persons should

---

5. This is not to suggest, of course, that women are innately more persuasible; rather, that socialization processes have given truth to the stereotype of the malleable kitten. As Rosenfield and Christie (1974, p. 247) put it, "By instilling 'feminine' qualities and deemphasizing 'human' qualities, society had effectively cast her ballot for her." These authors also find some experimental evidence that "women are gradually growing away from the 'traditional' dependence upon others and acquiring more confidence in their own judgments" (p. 253). For a comprehensive review of the psychological literature on sex differences, see Maccoby and Jacklin (1974).

presumably be critical as receivers—unwilling to accept a proposition until they have carefully weighed and measured what has been said. On the other hand, they also should be more able to decode persuasive communications. Because of these offsetting tendencies, persons of average intelligence and education are probably most persuasible (McGuire, 1969).

3. *Self-Esteem.* As with the variable of intelligence, persons with average self-esteem are probably most persuasible. Those with low self-esteem are probably most persuasible with regard to propositions that do not threaten their egos and least persuasible toward ego-involving propositions (McGuire, 1969). An underlying assumption of many theories of persuasion (to be reviewed) is that most persons tend to hold favorable views of themselves and to protect themselves from ego-threats. This would mean that if, for example, we tolerated unfavorable views of ourselves, we would probably remain unpersuaded when presented with evidence that we were inconsistent or dishonest or illogical or unintelligent. Although the assumption would appear tenable, it is belied by clinical evidence that many persons are self-rejecting. Compounding the problem of analyzing relationships between self-esteem and persuasibility is the difficult task of measuring self-esteem. Those who proclaim most loudly that they are self-satisfied are often, but not always, least satisfied with themselves. On the other hand, those with secure egos need not boast about them and may therefore appear to be self-rejecting when they are not.

4. *Authoritarianism and Dogmatism.* Dogmatic and authoritarian individuals tend to maintain rigid, either-or belief systems, are intolerant of ambiguities, and tend to be highly defensive (Rokeach, 1960). Dogmatic persons tend to regard positions similar to their own as the same as their own while regarding propositions somewhat discrepant from their own as extremely discrepant. Other evidence suggests that they tend to lean on images rather than issues, and, compared to most persons, are more easily reinforced but less easily converted on ego-involving issues (McGuire, 1969).

5. *Attitude Structure.* Is a given attitude based on a large or small number of beliefs and values, and to what extent are these beliefs and values logically tied together and consciously connected to the attitude in question? Once again, the relationship between attitude structure and persuasibility is complex but, in general, the simpler the attitude structure the easier it is to change.

6. *Cognitive Clarity.* A personality variable which predisposes persons to have complex or undifferentiated attitude structures is known as *need for cognitive clarity* (Cohen, 1964). Cognitive clarifiers are persons who characteristically react to ambiguous situations by seeking more information; cognitive simplifiers are persons who react to ambiguity by seeking

simple solutions that may not do justice to the complexity of the situation and may lead them to reject proposals that do justice to its complexity.

7. *Coping-Avoiding.* Also related to attitude structures is what Goldstein (1959) has called the *coping-avoiding* variable. Like clarifiers and simplifiers, copers and avoiders display characteristic patterns of dealing with ambiguity, complexity, and inconsistency—copers being, in general, more resistant to threatening communications than avoiders.

Undoubtedly there are many other personality variables associated with persuasibility but they are probably even more complexly related than those we have named. By way of summary, sex and age seem to be factors associated with communication-free susceptibility. Dogmatism, low self-esteem, and similar variables, are factors that inhibit change on complex topics or toward positions that are ego-threatening. These and most others that we have considered are communication-bound factors.

In terms of developing a capacity to adapt effectively to the outside world, all of us should probably strive to be neither consistently persuasible nor consistently rejecting of influence attempts. The *ideally critical* receiver is probably one who has genuinely high self-esteem, is intelligent and well-educated, is tolerant of ambiguity, is a cognitive clarifier, has highly differentiated and logically integrated attitude structures, and copes with problems rather than avoiding them. Such a receiver probably bases judgments more on what is said than on who says it, and is not so defensive that he or she is unable to accept criticism.

Related Beliefs and Values

Besides the receiver's attitude toward the persuader's proposition of policy and his or her beliefs and values with respect to that policy, there are a number of other attitude components that bear on persuasion on any given topic.

1. *Beliefs about the primary source.* Does the receiver regard the source as competent? Trustworthy? Attractive? Dynamic? Powerful? A person of good will?

2. *Beliefs about secondary sources.* The same questions as were just raised about primary sources also apply to sponsors, quoted authorities, and other secondary sources with whom a persuasive communication is linked.

3. *Valued persons, media, and reference groups.* Who are the receiver's primary opinion leaders, preferred media sources for news and opinions, and primary reference groups? The latter are groups that each of us turns to for confirmation or disconfirmation of "correct" beliefs, values, and at-

titudes. Persuaders may capitalize on knowledge of each of the above by linking them to their proposition as secondary sources. Receivers are especially susceptible when their favored reference groups offer conflicting advice or when they find themselves in role conflicts.

4. *Valued styles of language and delivery.* How does the receiver feel about colloquialisms or obscenities, for example? Will the receiver prefer a dramatic, robust presentation of material or a low-keyed presentation? An extemporaneous oral presentation or a more formal presentation?

5. *Belief and value hierarchies.* With respect to any given proposition of policy, receivers are likely to view certain values as more central than others and certain beliefs as more germane. The persuader may also anticipate individual differences in this regard. One receiver may view the Arab–Israeli conflict in financial terms, another from a humanitarian angle. One may regard the refugee issue as most germane, another the issue of territorial boundaries. These differences obviously make a difference in terms of the specific arguments and appeals upon which the persuader may most profitably focus. Demographic variables such as age, race, economic class, etc., are often good indicators of belief and value hierarchies.

6. *Tangential beliefs and values.* Many beliefs and values, while not logically related to a given proposition, may nevertheless be psychologically related for a given receiver. In some cases, these associations are incidental and idiosyncratic, but in others they are shared by a great many persons. We especially have in mind here such associations as between product preferences and colors or names—the kinds of associations that lead motivational analysts to agonize over whether a bottle of aspirin should be packaged in a green or a brown bottle.

Receivers and Audiences

Although we generally use the terms "receiver" and "audience" interchangeably, it is appropriate here to identify characteristics associated with "audience" as a term referring to a group of persons. What are some of the more important factors of audience composition?

Homogeneity. To what extent is the audience composed of like-minded individuals? To what extent are they highly differentiated in terms of attitudes, beliefs, values, and other relevant characteristics? As we indicated in Chapter 3, the presence of a mixed audience seriously compounds the persuader's problems. Goals, strategies, and specific appeals and arguments must be selected with intra-audience differences kept clearly in mind.

Opportunities for interaction. The commercial mass media publics are groups in name only. They have little or no contact with each other and certainly have no reciprocal awareness of each other as members of the same audience. At the other extreme are face-to-face work groups that meet and interact continuously over an extended period of time. Between these two extremes are such groups as the following: (1) the *pedestrian audience,* persons who happen to pass a soap box orator, for example (Hollingworth, 1935); (2) the *passive, occasional audience,* persons who come to hear a noted lecturer in a large auditorium, for example; (3) the *active, occasional audience,* persons who meet only on specific occasions but actively interact when they do meet.

Social cohesion. Through interaction over a period of time, groups such as families and work teams generally develop common purposes, norms of reciprocity, friendship ties, and shared attitudes toward outgroups. From a perceptual standpoint, the group becomes one. Other associations among individuals tend to be casual and fragmented. Indeed the *norm,* at many large apartment house complexes may be one of courteous distance, all the more so because of the opportunities for contact and interaction.

Leader-follower relationships. Within any given ongoing group, various leader-follower relationships are apt to emerge, some based on earned or assigned status, others on the leader's capacity to reward or punish, still others on the basis of perceived expertise, trustworthiness, or attractiveness. As in persuasion through the mass media, the persuader must work especially hard at winning over or neutralizing these opinion leaders.

Generally speaking, the audience composition factors that we have just noted tend to be mutually related. Interaction leads to social cohesion, cohesion to uniformity of opinion and established leader-follower relationships. The equation can of course be reversed: leadership influence leading to homogeneity, homogeneity to cohesion, cohesion to further interaction (Festinger, 1950). Especially in ongoing groups, it behooves the persuader to map out the "sociometry" of the group, neither treating each member as separate and apart from the others nor assuming that all are alike.

Receivers and Effects: A Catalogue

The end products of persuasive communications are effects on the attitudes and behaviors of receivers. In this section of the chapter, we attempt to classify the many different types of effect that may occur.

Intended Effects

An intended effect may be defined as change in a receiver that is consistent with a persuader's goals. *Any* increment of change, however small, may be considered at least partially successful and may be the most that a persuader can achieve on any one occasion. So as to underscore this point, let us imagine a continuum from total opposition to total support of a persuader's proposition of policy:

Total Opposition				"On the Fence"				Total Support
−4	−3	−2	−1	0	+1	+2	+3	+4

Now let us conceive of the many goals or subgoals that a persuader might work toward achieving with a given audience. The following list is representative:

1. *Reduce overt opposition.* For example, a persuader may seek only to reduce on subsequent occasions the volume of catcalls and hisses being received on this occasion.

2. *Reduce private opposition.* The persuader may seek to create doubts in the minds of hostile receivers about the wisdom of their attitudes.

3. *Secure discontinuance of opposition and create genuine indecision.* With receivers who are initially in opposition, creating ambivalence may be a highly satisfactory goal.

4. *Convert disbelievers.*

5. *Convert the uninformed and apathetic.*

6. *Convert the conflicted.* Among the persons on the above continuum whom we classify as "on the fence" are persons who lack information or interest and others who have so much information and interest that they cannot make up their minds. In addition to getting some receivers to "hurdle the fence," the persuader may convert others by getting them "off the fence."

7. *Reinforce favorable attitudes.* Minimally, the persuader may offer confirmation to the receiver that he or she has the "right" attitude.

8. *Activate favorable attitudes.* Here the receiver is moved from a position of private support to one of overt behavioral commitment.

9. *Increase behavioral commitments.* For example, a campaign manager may try to get volunteers to double their output of doorbells rung per day. Or a protest leader may attempt to move followers from participation in acts of peaceful picketing to acts of civil disobedience.

10. *Maintain high levels of attitudinal and behavioral commitment.* A common but frequently overlooked goal of persuaders is continuance of commitments. Here the persuader seeks to discourage backsliding and to maintain behavioral support for his or her proposals.

Several observations can be made about our list of goals.

First, the list of ten may be grouped into general goals of *hostility-reduction* (1–3 above), *conversion* (4–6 above), and *intensification* (7–10 above).

Second, we may roughly identify different *types of receivers* as suitable targets for different intended effects. Goals 1–3 are appropriate for initially *hostile* receivers. Goals 4 and 6 are appropriate for *critical* receivers. By a critical receiver, we mean one who will carefully weigh and measure what is said. These persons are usually either undecided or in disagreement with the source, but are not so opposed that their hostility prevents them from receiving messages openly. Goal 5 is appropriate for *uninformed* receivers and for *apathetic* receivers. Goals 7–10 are appropriate for *sympathetic* receivers.

Third, contrary to commonplace stereotypes about persuasion, not all the goals have to do with securing conversions or getting persons to adopt advocated propositions. In keeping with what we have said, Katz (1960) speaks of *attitude change* (what we have called conversion of disbelievers), *attitude formation* (equivalent to goals 5 and 6 in our list), and *arousal of attitudes* (equivalent to goals 7–8 in our list). Fotheringham (1966) classifies goals in terms of policy propositions. In addition to *adoption*, he speaks of *continuance* (roughly equivalent to goals 7–8 in our list), *deterrence* (roughly equivalent to goal 10), and *discontinuance* (roughly equivalent to goals 1–3). In successive stages, an advertiser may attempt to get receivers to discontinue past habits of hair grooming, adopt his advertised product, continue to use it, and be deterred from trying other, substitute products.

Fourth, depending on whether the persuader's communication is a "one-shot" effort or is part of a long-range campaign or movement, we may classify any single intended effect as a *primary effect* or a *preliminary effect*. For example, the goal of creating indecision among previously hostile receivers may be viewed as an intended primary effect for a single speech or essay, or it may be viewed as a first preliminary step in a long-range campaign to make them ardent supporters.

Fifth, although our list of goals focuses on attitude modification toward policy propositions, we should be reminded that the *relationship* aspect of persuasion is often as important or more important than the *content* aspect. Hence, in addition to the above list of primary goals, we should also be able to conceive of a parallel list of goals having to do with modifications of attitudes toward the communicator, again ranging from reduced overt hostility to continued enthusiastic support.

Sixth, even within the context of a "one-shot" effort, it is possible to speak of effects as *preliminary* to successful accomplishment on that one occasion. Getting attention, for example, is a preliminary step even in attempts at reducing hostility. Several theorists have suggested lists of preliminary effects. Minnick (1957, p. 35) suggests, for example, that persuasive communications will be effective if, and only if:

- They are attended.
- They are accurately perceived.
- They are considered credible.
- They are relevant to the listener's needs.
- They are attainable by means consistent with the listener's personal values.
- They are feasible in the existing circumstances.

Other writers have suggested steps or sequences of persuasion. These lists are similar in many ways:

Monroe's (1949) Motivated Sequence	Brembeck and Howell's (1952) List	Hollingworth's (1935) List
Attention	Gaining and maintaining attention	Catch attention Hold Attention
Need	Arousing desires useful for the persuader's purpose	Impress
Satisfaction (of need)	Demonstrating how desires can be satisfied	Convince
Visualization (of the future)		
Action	Producing the specific response desired	Direct

Seventh, it is useful to distinguish between intended effects that are of *primary* interest to persuaders and those which are of *secondary* interest. Assuming that a persuader's primary interest is in modifying attitudes toward the proposition of policy he or she advocates, here are some secondary intended effects that may still be of great importance:

- Reinforcing the values in terms of which the persuader is defending proposed policies;
- Winning acceptance of subpropositions of belief;
- Increasing perceived competence, trust, attraction, or other aspects of source credibility;
- Inducing appreciation of language and style in communication;
- Serving as an exemplar of ethical behavior whom others may imitate;
- Bolstering the receiver's sense of self-esteem;
- Encouraging exposure to messages from the same or similar channels or media.

Eighth, it is useful to distinguish between immediate effects and de-layed effects. An emotionally charged speech, for example, may have the immediate effect of producing dramatic conversions, but over a period of time its effects are likely to diminish considerably. On the other hand, reformers who are ahead of their time may live to see their initially re-jected proposals come to fruition at a later period.

Finally, we should observe that different intended effects call for dif-ferent persuasive tactics. A hostile audience would be antagonized by the kinds of appeals that are appropriate for sympathetic receivers.

We will amplify on many of these briefly noted concepts and princi-ples in later chapters. For now we would simply advise would-be persuad-ers to delimit their goals in relationship to prior audience attitudes, being careful to differentiate among primary intended effects, preliminary effects for a one-shot effort, secondary effects, immediate effects, and delayed effects.

Unintended Effects

For each of the ten intended effects that we listed above, we may conceive of several unintended effects that could occur, not all of them unfavorable. Rather than becoming a convert to a communicator's proposition of policy, for example, a disbeliever may remain skeptical or become increasingly opposed. Any increments of change in directions opposite to those in-tended are known as *boomerang effects*. Less frequently, a persuader may secure *over-adoption* of a goal. For example, a protest leader seeking to activate the commitments of fellow protestors may find that his bombastic rhetoric has rendered them uncontrollable. Finally, as many persuaders have learned, there are often unexpected benefits to be derived from ac-tively taking a stand on issues. A demonstration fails to terminate campus curfew regulations but, unexpectedly, the university liberalizes its policies on drinking in dormitories. A group of truckers protesting gasoline prices find that they have opened the way for renegotiated contracts with the trucking industry.

In the last example, the effects of the message were unexpected be-cause it reached *unintended receivers*. Frequently this is the case. When the mass media pick up a story or when a speech provokes word-of-mouth reports, the persuader can be sure of reaching many more persons than he or she could possibly have identified in advance. Walster and Festinger (1962) have provided experimental evidence that persuasive messages have greater impact when receivers perceive them to be overheard. On the other hand, a message may be overheard by spies for the opposition, by previ-ously sympathetic receivers who upon overhearing a speaker learn that this speaker suits his or her position to the audience, and by previously opposed receivers who are made more hostile by overhearing messages aimed at supporters (Brock and Becker, 1965).

The study of persuasion has traditionally been focused on messages intentionally transmitted to predesignated receivers. The test of success has been whether the intended effect was achieved. In many respects this orientation is quite serviceable. We now recognize, however, that much of what actually persuades others is planned in only the loosest sense. Broadly speaking, as we have indicated, the message is anything to which the receiver (any receiver!) may attach meaning. Just as we cannot *not* communicate, so we cannot *not* have effects upon others, including unintended others. Persuaders should continue to focus on the strategies and tactics by which intended effects may be achieved. But critics and theorists of persuasion might well broaden their inquiry to include unplanned messages that nevertheless have suasory impact.

Determinants of Accurate Audience Analysis

It should be abundantly clear at this point that knowledge of one's audience is prerequisite to the realistic setting of goals and to the development of strategies and tactics for realizing one's objectives. The nagging question remains, however: Is it possible to assess reliably the attitudes, beliefs, values, knowledge, and interest of another person or persons? Although conflicting research evidence has prevented psychologists from answering this question unequivocally, there seems no doubt but that certain combined characteristics of the predictor, the receiver, and the context increase the reliability of predictions (Tagiuri, 1969).

1. Reliability is increased when the predictor has knowledge of both the person being judged and the context. By superimposing the same photograph of one of his actors on pictures of three different settings, Einsenstein, the great Russian film director, was able to evoke enthusiastic admiration of the actor's capacity to communicate joy, anger, or suffering, depending on the context in which the receiver saw it. A grimace may obviously mean one thing for someone at a funeral; another for someone in a track meet. Similarly, knowledge of context may be insufficient. Although we may reliably infer a stranger's feelings from knowledge that his best friend has just died, reliability is increased if the object of judgment is someone we know. "Taken separately," Tagiuri concludes (1969, p. 421), "either the person or the situation allows nonrandom, but indeterminate, judgments. Jointly they yield highly determinate judgments."

2. Judgments about groups are more accurate, generally, than judgments about specific individuals. In estimating average group characteristics there is a kind of "law of sufficient mistakes" operating, a tendency to make

compensating errors. Value-laden judgments about groups are subject to great error, however, especially when predictions are based on unrepresentative samples. Readers might be surprised at one expert's characterization of the "generation gap" of the late sixties as "overblown, oversimplified, sentimentalized" (Adelson, 1970, p. 10). Although a gap did exist on such issues as marijuana use, it was in some respects quite mythical if we are to believe the survey data Adelson compiled from an impressive number of studies. About four out of five college students surveyed reported that they had generally close and friendly relationships with their parents. On political issues, three out of four tended to vote the same way as their parents and to internalize their values. On these issues the young themselves seemed divided, with greater proportions of them represented at both ends of the political spectrum than was true of the total population. The notion of a generation gap was often based on a comparison between the characteristically more vocal liberal arts students at "elite" campuses and "typical" older persons. According to Adelson, however, about 80 percent of all college-age students either did not attend college or pursued vocational goals. These young people were in most respects quite similar to "typical" elders, on matters ranging from sex to politics.[6]

3. The reliability of our perceptions about people increases with added knowledge of an individual's group characteristics. Knowledge that Jones (or a group of Joneses) is from New York City tells us something about him but not enough to gear a persuasive message to him on most subjects. Knowledge that he is 70 years old, that he is widowed, that he lives in a nursing home, tells us a great deal more. Of course each bit of knowledge is drawn from a stereotype. Still, and this is vital for purposes of persuasion, although any one datum may provide an unreliable basis for pre-

---

6. Recent evidence suggests, however, that "Working-class young people in the United States are taking on many of the attitudes on sex, politics, patriotism, religion, the family, morals and life-style that marked college student thinking of five years ago." (Richard Severo, *Philadelphia Bulletin*, May 27, 1974, p. 10). For example, 25 percent more noncollege youth in 1973 than in 1969 (47 percent from 22 percent) would welcome more acceptance of sexual freedom, which puts them statistically about where college students were on the issue in 1969. Less than half oppose relations between consenting homosexuals whereas almost 75 percent disapproved in 1969. College students also shifted in a liberal direction but less dramatically. The data are based on a massive survey of 3500 young people by Daniel Yankelovitch, Inc. They suggest that the mythical "generation gap" of the sixties may be quite real in the seventies. More significantly, they provide some evidence, admittedly inconclusive, that messages which initially generate negative reactions can have "sleeper effects" on self-rejecting audiences —a point to be taken up in Chapters 8 and 13.

dicting attitudes, values, or beliefs, the composite tends to form a highly reliable whole.

4. Some predictors are characteristically more accurate than others. No one knows quite how it is that accurate assessments of another are made—whether it is a process of inference and analogy, or empathy, or directly perceiving qualities of another that are innately knowable, or some combination. It does appear, however, that characteristics of the "good judge" include broad personal experience, self-insight, social skill, and detachment; furthermore, some persons are distinctly adept at sizing up strangers while others display unusual sensitivity only toward persons familiar to them. One somewhat surprising characteristic of "good judges" is that they tend to be "average" or "conventional" in other ways. The reason for their reliable judgments is that, like most persons, they tend to assume that others are like themselves. Unconventional people tend to make mistakes when they act on this premise; conventional persons do not. That people tend to assume others to be similar to themselves was borne out by a study we conducted (Simons, 1966). We found that predictors used themselves as standards for deriving estimates of the "open-mindedness" of others, independent of whether the yardstick led to accurate or inaccurate predictions.

5. Accurate predictions may be made not only of others' feelings, but also of their judgments about our judgments about their judgments, and so on, in an endless chain. Schelling (1960) has pointed out that such capacities are essential to well-managed interpersonal conflicts. That accurate predictions of this kind can be made is supported by several informal classroom experiments, conducted by Schelling, that readers might well wish to try themselves. In each "study" two persons who are perfect strangers must make the same independent prediction if each is to "win." For example, they must guess "heads" or "tails" or they must think of the same playing card from a list of thirteen or the same monetary figure from a list of six, given no other information. Schelling's students did far better than would be predicted by chance. Note that here, too, the predictor draws inferences from perceptions of demographic characteristics of other group affiliations.

The foregoing has important implications for persuaders. The research seems to suggest that accurate audience analysis is possible; that it should focus on characteristics of both the receiver and the social context; that social sensitivity can be improved with experience and self-insight; and that persuaders may utilize known group characteristics to draw inferences about attitudes, beliefs, or values, provided that they use enough of them in combination, and provided that they check out their own value-laden stereotypes. It stands to reason, of course, that persuaders need not rely on stereotypical knowledge if they have access to more direct data. Before doing a systematic audience analysis inventory it is highly advisable to poll selected members of an audience, to chat informally with a group's spokesman, or, in give-and-take situations, to listen emphatically before forming judgments about a receiver.

Summary

Before goals can be delimited or effective strategies devised, the persuader must carefully analyze the audience. The key concept in any discussion of receivers is *attitudes*. An "attitude" was defined as a relatively enduring predisposition to respond favorably or unfavorably to an attitude object. Every attitude is composed of belief and value components and is more or less consistently linked to other attitudes. Of fundamental concern to persuaders is the receiver's attitude toward the persuader's proposition of policy; that is, the action proposal.

Measures of attitude or attitude change are not always highly correlated with measures of behavior or behavior change. The gap between the two is once again reflective of the importance of the situational context. Attitudes and behaviors do not always seem consistent because they are measured in different contexts and because situational pressures inhibit or facilitate overt action on private attitudes.

Whatever else they do, persuaders should delimit goals for any one occasion in terms of where the receivers stand on a continuum from total opposition to total support of their policy recommendations. So as to underscore the importance of careful goal-setting, we have listed as many as ten possible goals, ranging from reducing overt opposition to maintaining high levels of attitudinal and behavioral commitment. Contrary to commonplace notions, persuasion is by no means confined to securing changes in attitudes or getting receivers to adopt proposals. Equally as important as conversions are hostility-reduction and intensification. Persuaders should also keep in mind that any one message is likely to have a multitude of effects in addition to immediate, primary effects. Some of these will be secondary, others will be delayed, and many will be unintended.

Accuracy in analyses of audiences is possible. It is improved with knowledge of persons as well as contexts, with experience and self-awareness, and by checking out stereotypes through questioning representative members of the audience in advance.

We can think of no better way to conclude this chapter than to provide a list of questions that persuaders may draw upon in constructing their own audience analysis inventories. This basic list should be supplemented by questions about the situational context and by other questions that will undoubtedly apply to specific audiences.

1. What is the degree and direction of the receiver's attitude toward the persuader's proposition of policy?

2. What beliefs and values influence the receiver's attitude? What is their intensity?

3. What is the receiver's attitude toward the source? Toward secondary sources?

4. What relevant knowledge does he or she have, and how accurate is it?

5. How interested or involved is the receiver in his or her own position and in the issues themselves?

6. What behavioral commitments has the receiver manifested? To what extent are they consistent with his or her attitudes? What are their motivational determinants?

7. What demographic and personality factors influence the receiver's degree of communication-free and communication-bound persuasibility? For example, is the receiver dogmatic or undogmatic, a coper or an avoider?

8. What beliefs, values, and attitudes does the receiver hold with respect to related issues?

9. What coincidental associations does the receiver have with respect to the proposition or subpropositions in question?

10. Who and what opinion leaders, media, and reference groups influence the receiver?

11. What styles of language and delivery does he or she value most?

12. If messages are being directed at a group, how is that group composed? Is it homogenous? Cohesive? Is there much opportunity for group interaction? What are its leader-follower relationships?

5

Behavioral Theories of Persuasion

A theory is like a funnel. Into the funnel come findings about phenomena which the theory attempts to summarize and explain. Out of the funnel come deduced hypotheses which, when tested, add new grist for the theoretical mill. The heart of the theory—the narrow part of the funnel—is a set of assumptions, basic concepts, definitions of those concepts, and explanatory statements or theorems which relate the concepts to each other.

Behavioral theories of persuasion are developed from experimental research on how attitudes are formed and modified by communications. They include *general* theories which attempt explanations of a broad range of rhetorical phenomena and *miniature* theories about such specific phenomena as the nature of source credibility, the effects of fear appeals, and the consequences of counterattitudinal advocacy.

Although we may not be as rigorous or as systematic as the professional social scientist, most of us are persuasion theorists of a sort, and our "theories" probably influence our practice of persuasion as well. Like the social scientist, we have all gathered evidence about persuasion—informally in most cases—which we have attempted to organize, summarize, and interpret. And like the social scientist, our "theories" of persuasion are probably rooted in assumptions about the nature of man.

Whether our theories are useful or not is another matter. Ideally, a theory should be clear, consistent, capable of being tested, and able to yield valid predictions, provocative in that it stimulates new research, and comprehensive, yet elegant, in the sense of explaining a great deal by means of a minimum number of working principles. If we are to use theory as a guide to persuasive practice, it may be that we can learn from one or more of the theories to be described in this chapter.

Behavioral research on persuasion has spawned a great many general theories which can be roughly categorized as learning theories of persuasion, perception theories, functional theories, and "balance" or "consistency" theories. We will provide a sampling of each type, giving special attention to the perception theory of Sherif, *et al.* (1965) and to two balance theories, Osgood and Tannenbaum's (1955) congruity model and our own favorite, Festinger's (1957; 1964) theory of cognitive dissonance. As was indicated in Chapter 1, the balance theories attempt a reconciliation of the age-old "rationality-irrationality" controversy. Borrowing heavily from Festinger, we will present a picture of the dynamics of persuasion as involving the "unbalancing" of psychological elements and subsequent "rebalancing" of those same elements. Our own conception will serve as a framework for theoretical discussion in Part 2 and will be elaborated upon in several of the chapters in that unit.[1]

---

1. Note that in Chapters 3 and 4 we presented bits and pieces of theoretical formulations, including our own (e.g., our treatment of relations between atti-

---

Some Examples of Prestige Suggestions

... when the Confederate General Basil Duke arrived in New York at the end of the Civil War "Old Crow quite naturally would be served."

"George Washington warned against entangling foreign alliances. Invited on all sides to internationalist adventures, we should remember the wisdom of the Father of our country."

"Eminent minds have come to the conclusion that in our civilized world the evil in man prevails over the good. As Hobbes put it, 'The life of man is solitary, poor, nasty, brutish, and short.' If I am accused of pessimism, all I can say is that I have lots of company and famous company, too."

A leading entertainment figure says: "*Relax* tablets relieved my headache. You can help your headache troubles too!"

For purposes of illustration, we have chosen to compare each of the general theories to be summarized here in terms of the miniature theories they have generated about a phenomenon known as "prestige suggestion." Prestige suggestion is alleged to occur when a prestige source such as a sports hero is linked to an advocated proposition. In its purest sense, it occurs in the absence of any other information! Presumably, attitude modification occurs automatically, without critical thought by the persuadee.

---

tudes, attitude components, and overt behavior in Chapter 4). Whether one chooses to call them "theories" or not hinges on how strictly one wishes to define the term. The same holds true for several of the theory-like constructions presented in Part 2. Although the "theories" to be presented in this chapter are more fully developed than others to be presented in this book, some would argue that they, too, fall short of being true scientific theories; indeed, that social psychology remains in a pretheoretical stage. However one labels them, they should be of interest to readers because each paints a different and provocative picture of the why and how of attitude-modification, and some of them have yielded nonobvious predictions, confirmed by research, that suggest important stratagems for practitioners. Readers interested in exploring these theories further might begin with such introductory texts as Insko (1967) and Kiesler, Collins, and Miller (1969).

We should add that our survey of general theories is in some ways unrepresentative. First, we have omitted two paradigms that have had great impact on rhetorical thought, the Freudian and the Skinnerian. Unfortunately, neither of these has been systematically developed into a theory of persuasion per se. Second, all of the theories presented here assume a source who acts and a receiver who reacts; none of them are very appropriate for conflict situations involving reciprocal influence. Psychologists in recent years have begun to develop theories of reciprocal influence (e.g., Gergen, 1969), and although none of these deal uniquely with persuasion and attitude-change, we shall have occasion to refer to them in Chapter 13.

Does it? Quite obviously, this is an important test of the "irrationalist's" claim that the human is an essentially uncritical animal. We shall see that each of the general theories approaches this issue somewhat differently. We shall also see illustrated an excellent example of a critique of behavioral research.

Learning Theories of Persuasion

Persuasion may be viewed as a form of learning. Just as a caged rat in a laboratory may learn to approach some stimuli and avoid others, so may a human being learn that Nationalist China is "good," Communist China is "bad." And just as rats may modify their behavior as a result of the experimenter's "messages," so may humans modify their attitudinal responses toward the two Chinas on the basis of persuasive communications. Learning theorists have developed principles governing the acquisition of responses to new stimuli, their transfer to new situations, their extinction, and so on. Theoretically, at least, these same principles should be applicable to persuasion.

Learning theories of persuasion range from S-R (Stimulus-Response) models which view the human as a passive entity to S-O-R (Stimulus-Organism-Response) models which view persuasive learning as a joint product of the messages an individual receives and the mediating forces within the individual which act upon those messages to determine persuasive outcomes (e.g., Weiss, 1968). S-R theories attempt to predict behavior strictly from a knowledge of observable stimuli and responses. S-O-R theorists find it necessary to hypothesize the existence of mediating forces within the organism, directly linkable to external stimuli and responses, which help to predict behavior.

Among the S-R learning theories which are applicable to persuasion, several hold that attitudinal responses may be modified through classical conditioning (e.g., Staats and Staats, 1963). We can presumably be conditioned not just by characteristics of a message, but also by associations between a source and the position he or she advocates. Pavlov's dog, you will remember, was classically conditioned to salivate at the sound of a bell after the bell was linked to the presence of meat powder. In the same way, a listener might be conditioned to respond to an advertised product after the product is linked to a prestige source. The already favorable source might be akin to the meat powder, the more neutral product analogous to the bell. The process of *prestige suggestion*, illustrated in this case, can thus be viewed as an instance of classical conditioning.

If the S-R account seems unsatisfactory, it may be because it says nothing about the internal state of the receiver at the time he or she is persuaded. What prompts the receiver to listen to the commercial in the first place? Why does he or she want the product at all, let alone the brand being advertised? What, in short, are the motivational bases for the receiver's behavior?

At a minimum, S-O-R learning theories posit some internal state of motivation which must be "triggered" in order for persuasion to take place (e.g., Hovland, Janis, and Kelley, 1953). The motivational state is generally described as painful or unpleasant; it *drives* the organism to seek relief from his discomfort. Biological drives such as hunger and thirst are said to be *primary* and quite powerful. Others, such as curiosity, social approval, and acquisition are believed by some learning theorists to be *secondary* or acquired drives, learned by association with primary drives. Why might viewers want a given product, such as tea or ginger ale? Because their thirst drive has been activated? Why might they want Lipton's or Canada Dry in particular? Perhaps because they are driven to seek the approval of the source who has been linked to the brand name.

Readers familiar with conditioning theories might wish, for comparison's sake, to contrast the classical-conditioning model, applied to prestige suggestions, with the operant or instrumental-conditioning model presented by B. F. Skinner. In the latter case, the persuadee might first be asked his or her opinion of the advertised product. If the response was favorable, it could be strengthened by positive reinforcers such as "good" or a friendly nod of the head by the prestige source. If it was unfavorable, the source could scowl or withdraw affection (forms of punishment), apply irritants or other aversive stimuli to the persuadee until the persuadee reversed his or her position (known as negative reinforcement), or reinforce successive approximations of the ultimately desired response until the response itself was forthcoming (shaping). The paradigm suggests the importance of engaging persuadees in dialogue rather than simply communicating *at* listeners, as in the typical platform speech. It also underscores the importance of offering incentives to persuadees, either in the form of direct rewards or escape from punishment. Although we have elsewhere expressed dissatisfaction with Skinnerian paradigms applied to persuasion (see Simons, 1971), we very much appreciate his emphasis on the hedonic pleasure/pain principle.

As evidence has accumulated to challenge the simple "trigger-action" theories of drive reduction, other S-O-R theories have been developed which say a good deal more about internal states of attention and comprehension and which introduce new and more complex accounts of motivational processes. Note that the communication model presented in Chapter 3 (see Fig. 3.1) reflects a mediational, S-O-R view of persuasion.

Perception Theories of Persuasion

Whereas S-R theories focus on external inputs and outputs, theories of perception are primarily concerned with the world of inner experience, the way the world looks to the individual doing the perceiving. Attitudes are not so much behavioral responses as they are "pictures in our heads," evaluative frames of reference which may *predispose* us toward behavioral responses. Persuasion is viewed as a process of reordering perceptual categories based on organized cues from the environment and on internal needs and values. Even the listener seated in a large auditorium is viewed as an active entity, forever seeking to give meaning to his or her experiences.

Far from picturing prestige suggestion as an automatic conditioning process, perception theorists such as Soloman Asch (1952) have held that some linkages between prestige sources and the positions they advance are not at all persuasive; moreover, those that do have impact are persuasive precisely because they lead receivers to restructure their perceptions of the attitude object. Thomas Jefferson's plea for "revolution every twenty years" would have quite another meaning to a receiver if the utterance were attributed to Karl Marx.

Other perception theorists are similarly critical of accounts which treat prestige suggestion as relatively automatic and predictable. Robert Merton (1946) has theorized that, to be maximally effective, sources must appear to have *symbolic fitness;* what they represent to the audience as persons must somehow mesh well (form a "'good gestalt'") with the product they advertise.

Still another theory, proposed by C. Sherif, M. Sherif, and Nebergall (1965), would challenge the ability of persuaders to sell all products equally well. Because of the importance of this theory, we will describe it in some detail.

The problem posed by the authors might be stated as follows: How do persuaders perceive an advocated proposition that is discrepant from their own? According to the theorists, there are, for each of us, a range of propositions we can accept, another range of possible statements toward which we would be noncommital, and a range or latitude of rejected statements.

The size of each range is highly dependent on the individual's degree of ego-involvement on a given issue. If we are highly ego-involved, we are likely to have extremely small latitudes of acceptance and noncommitment and a large latitude of rejection. For example, if we are died-in-the-wool Republicans, we are likely to accept only such statements as the following from a list of nine (A to I):

A. The election of the Republican presidential and vice-presidential candidates in November is absolutely essential from all angles in the country's interest.

B. On the whole the interests of the country will be served best by the election of the Republican candidates.

C. It seems that the country's interests would be better served if the candidates of the Republican Party were elected in November.

Not only will we reject statements favoring the Democrats (G to I), but even such moderately "pro" statements as the following one are likely to be rejected or regarded noncommittally:

D. Although it is hard to decide, it is probably true that the country's interests would be better served if the candidates of the Republican Party are elected in November.

The subjective category system of a typical, ego-involved Republican may be diagrammed as follows:

Position:	A	B	C	D	E	F	G	H	I
Category	+	+	+	O	–	–	–	–	–

where + = acceptance, O = noncommitment, – = rejection, and ——— = range.

On the other hand, if we are uninvolved on an issue—for example, if we lack familiarity with it—our categories of acceptance, noncommitment, and rejection are likely to be rather undifferentiated.

Crucial to the success of a persuader's efforts is how his or her proposition is subjectively categorized by the recipient. Propositions falling within our latitudes of acceptance tend to be *assimilated;* i.e., perceived as more similar to our own than they really are. Propositions falling within our latitudes of rejection tend to be *contrasted;* i.e., seen as more unlike our own than they really are. Moreover, as the authors point out:

> ... when a communication opposed to a subject's position is displaced away from his stand, it is dubbed *at the same time* as unreasonable, false, propagandistic, and even obnoxious, depending on the degree of displacement. Correspondingly, when a communication is assimilated closer to the bounds of acceptability, it is found more truthful, more factual, less biased, and tolerable. . . . (p. 227).

The skill and *ethos* of the persuader figure most prominently when we are relatively uninvolved and thus have large latitudes of noncommitment. Here the wording of a speech, or its logic, or the prestige of a speaker may be decisive in securing acceptance of the proposition. Thus, should a moderately prestigious source attempt to sell uninvolved listeners on the merits of "the pill," he might be fairly successful. On the other hand, should even a highly prestigious physician attempt to sell a conservative Roman Catholic audience on the advisability of using birth control pills, his effort might well boomerang.

To illustrate at least one perception theorist's critique of prestige-suggestion research from an S-R framework, we may turn to Asch's review (1952) of some early studies. In such studies the subjects typically were asked for their evaluations of an attitude object before and after being exposed to the views of a prestige source. If there were differences between evaluations on the "pre-test" and the "post-test," the differences were attributed to the influence of the prestige source. No other information was provided; the purpose of the learning theorist was to demonstrate that the prestige suggestion effect can be produced automatically and uncritically. The task might have been to evaluate the beauty of various Christmas cards or to judge which of two statements is more grammatical or to appraise a series of ethical claims. In studies of this kind (Moore, 1921; Thorndike, 1935), sharp differences between pre- and post-tests were reported.

Asch begins his critique by asking that we put ourselves in the place of the subjects. In similar situations, would we be willing to change our notions about the good, the true, and the beautiful quite so readily? Did the observed changes correspond to any change of conviction? Here, Asch notes that we are left in the dark.

> We do not know whether the tasks touched off any conviction or whether they were taken seriously or in an off-hand way. It is possible that the latter occurred, since the judgments called for were artificial and often ambiguous (p. 450.)

Referring to a similar experiment, Asch suggests other possibilities:

> Possibly because the social setting constrained them by placing them under the necessity of arriving at a judgment, the subjects tried to make the best of it and in the process fell into the experimental trap. Is it necessary to conclude that they did so by altering their evaluation? Elsewhere the writer has suggested another possibility. Once the subject has accepted the task he feels the need to arrive at a judgment. Not having a clear basis to go on he leans on the clues the experimenter has placed in his path. But his concern may no longer be that of reaching a clear conclusion but to respond in a way to escape censure or ridicule. The result may be that his expressions of judgment do not carry conviction to himself and no longer represent actual evaluations (p. 407).

In his critical comments on the prestige-suggestion experiments, Asch has anticipated the flavor of two related variants of perception theory: *attribution* theory (Jones, *et al.*, 1971) and *self-perception* theory (Bem, 1965). Both raise questions that have not been dealt with adequately by the theories we have examined thus far. Moreover, both show promise of becoming dominant theories in social psychology (not just persuasion) in the years ahead.

As described by Kelley (1971), attribution theory is concerned with how an observer assigns causation to the actions of another. According to the attribution theorists, all of us function as amateur psychologists when confronted with this routine task. On the basis of whatever limited information we have at our disposal, we attempt to make reasonable inferences about the intentions, motivations, and competencies of others, and we use these inferences to evaluate them and to decide on actions based on what they have said or done.

Chief among the questions we ask ourselves is whether the other's actions are *internally* caused or *externally* caused. In the case of a message by a prestige source, for example (or a message about a prestige source by an experimenter) we are more likely to discount the message as untrustworthy if we perceive it to be dictated by such external factors as social pressure (Jones, Davis, and Gergen, 1961), status or power deprivation (Thibaut and Rieckin, 1955), or opportunity for personal gain (Walster, Aronson, and Abrahams, 1966).

Although serious question has been raised whether the methods used by the attribution theorists permit the interpretations they have drawn from their experiments, they nevertheless have helped us to understand the processes by which receivers assign high credibility ratings to some sources, low credibility ratings to others. Correspondingly, that same understanding by practitioners of persuasion can help them to manipulate attributions by receivers; they can learn, for example, to employ ingratiation techniques sparingly, so that they do not give the impression of pleasing others for the sake of personal gain (Jones, Gergen, and Jones, 1963).

Whereas attribution theory is concerned with explaining the behavior of others, self-perception theory is concerned with how we explain our own behavior. Bem (1965) maintains that the same attributional processes used to interpret the behaviors of others are also used to interpret our own behavior. In situations perceived to be relatively free of external constraints, we commonly examine our behavior to "discover" our attitudes. (Did I say that? I must have meant it! Did I do that? I guess I must be that kind of person.) Where external circumstances are perceived to be controlling (recall Asch's supposition about the early prestige-suggestion experiments), our actions or expressions of judgments do not carry conviction to ourselves.

Although other explanations have been offered to account for the data, there seems to be no doubt at this point that we often infer our beliefs, values, and attitudes from a retrospective look at what we have said or done. The observation is an important one since common sense tells us that the reverse process is by far the more typical one—i.e., deciding what to say or do on the basis of our attitudes or attitude components. Self-perception theorists have provided impressive evidence that we are frequently unaware of why we have acted until we have acted, and then we lean on external cues to infer inner states (e.g., Schachter and Singer, 1962; Valins, 1966). Later in this chapter we shall look at dissonance theory explanations of discrepancies between attitudes and behavior, and in Chapter 13 we shall summarize a good deal of research bearing on the issue.

Looking back, we can see that all of the theorists reviewed in this section offer conjectures about what goes on in the private world of another. In doing so, they take the risk of making claims that they may not be able to support. By contrast, for example, S-R and S-O-R drive theorists can claim that they are dealing primarily with directly observable phenomena. Nevertheless, if they do nothing else, perception theorists perform a valuable service by reminding us that it is the receiver's *psychological* reality which counts in persuasion, not the physical reality of sounds and light waves emitted by the persuader. No matter how well-intentioned the source may be, no matter how reasonable the message, it is the receiver's perceptions of these qualities which affect his or her attitudes.

Functional Theories of Persuasion

There are a number of functional theories (Kelman, 1961; Smith, Bruner and White, 1956) but we shall focus here on one developed by Daniel Katz (1960).

Katz takes a conciliatory position in the rationality-irrationality controversy existing between the learning theorists and the perception theorists. Like the rabbi confronted with an irate husband and an equally irate wife, he argues that both are right, but each under certain conditions. According to Katz, appropriate strategies of persuasion cannot be developed until one knows whether a particular attitude held by a receiver serves an adjustment, an ego-defensive, a value-expression, or a knowledge function, or some combination thereof. An ego-defensive listener, for example, will not be persuaded by arguments which link adoption of a given proposal with appeals to his self-interests. Nor will he be persuaded by group pressures or by "information campaigns" of the kind often employed in extolling the virtues of brotherhood. As Katz's chart on page 119 suggests, it is a lot easier to reinforce prejudiced attitudes than it is to change them. Whereas attitudes serving an adjustment function may be modified by picturing the rewarding consequences of adopting a given position or the unpleasant consequences of nonadoption, ego-defensive attitudes can only be changed through a process akin to psychotherapy. (See Table 5.1.)

Katz provides a useful reconciliation of learning and perception theories and he even finds a place for psychoanalytic formulations about ego-defensiveness. One wishes it were easier, however, to identify the function or functions which a given attitude serves for an individual. Katz provides

Table 5.1 Determinants of attitude formation, arousal, and change in relation to type of function

Function	Origin and Dynamics	Arousal Conditions	Change Conditions
Adjustment	Utility of attitudinal object in need satisfaction. Maximizing external rewards and minimizing punishments	1. Activation of needs 2. Salience of cues associated with need satisfaction	1. Need deprivation 2. Creation of new needs and new levels of aspiration 3. Shifting rewards and punishments 4. Emphasis on new and better paths for need satisfaction
Ego defense	Protecting against internal conflicts and external dangers	1. Posing of threats 2. Appeals to hatred and repressed impulses 3. Rise in frustrations 4. Use of authoritarian suggestion	1. Removal of threats 2. Catharsis 3. Development of self-insight
Value expression	Maintaining self-identity; enhancing favorable self-image; self-expression and self-determination	1. Salience of cues associated with values 2. Appeals to individual to reassert self-image 3. Ambiguities which threaten self-concept	1. Some degree of dissatisfaction with self 2. Greater appropriateness of new attitude for the self 3. Control of all environmental supports to undermine old values
Knowledge	Need for understanding, for meaningful cognitive organization, for consistency and clarity	1. Reinstatement of cues associated with old problem or of old problem itself	1. Ambiguity created by new information or change in environment 2. More meaningful information about problems

few clues and, except for ego-defensiveness, it is often impossible to distinguish the functions operationally.

Balance Theories of Persuasion

The assumption that we seek a psychologically consistent view of the world—first articulated by perception theorists—serves as the major premise for a number of "balance" theories, some referred to by that name (Heider,

1958; Cartwright and Harary, 1956), others referred to variously as "consistency" theories (Abelson and Rosenberg, 1958), or "dissonance" theories (Festinger, 1957; Brehm and Cohen, 1962). Like S-R learning theorists, some balance theorists (e.g., Osgood and Tannenbaum, 1955) maintain that reactions to communications are automatic and predictable. For most balance theorists, in fact, the need for psychological consistency is a basic drive, although Festinger and others would not agree that the drive is automatic or that the response to a message is entirely predictable.

Recall that in Chapter 1 we hinted at our appreciation of balance theories and our sense of balance, imbalance, and rebalancing as central to the persuasive process. Also, recall from Chapter 3 that we pictured the receiver as an active processor of incoming message stimuli. These stimuli include not only *what* is said (the "message" in a narrow sense) but also perceived characteristics of the source, the medium, and the context. On the basis of a number of *antecedent factors* (i.e., his or her existing "frame of reference") the receiver selectively *decodes* these message inputs. The decoded message is then carried to an *evaluative* stage. If the message is persuasive it *unbalances* the receiver's frame of reference but also suggests ways that it can be *rebalanced*. The *output* of the process is *attitude modification*, a change in the receiver's frame of reference that may lead to changes in *overt behavior* as well. Table 5.2 provides a summary of our admittedly oversimplified depiction of the process.

Table 5.2 Major variables and stages in our model of persuasion as a communication process

Antecedent Factors	Input Factors	Internal Stages		Intended Outputs
		Decoding	Evaluation	
Prior beliefs, values, and attitudes	Source Message Medium Context	Attention Comprehension	Unbalancing and Rebalancing	Belief, value, attitude, and/or behavior modification

All balance theories have at least three principles in common: (1) that psychological imbalance (i.e., dissonance, incongruity, etc.) is unpleasant or uncomfortable; (2) that we are therefore driven to reduce or eliminate the imbalance, and (3) that one way we can achieve balance or at least reduce imbalance is by modifying our attitudes in directions intended by a communicator. Individual theorists have added other principles, some of which we shall discuss shortly.

Intuitively, we can grasp the concepts of balance and imbalance through innumerable examples from our own experience. For the most part, our inner world is balanced or consistent. If we are registered as Democrats, we generally vote for Democratic candidates. If we call ourselves "conservatives," we generally support programs that reflect a conservative position. If we have recently purchased a new Ford, we generally do not tell our friends that it is better to buy Chevrolets. If we respect another person's judgments, it is generally because those judgments correspond with our judgments.

In some respects, however, we are likely to experience psychological inconsistencies. Some imbalances are qualitative, while others are a matter of degree. An esteemed friend may hate a movie that we loved, or like it but not nearly as much as we liked it. We may despise city life and find ourselves living in the city, or we may simply prefer the country to the city and still find ourselves living in the city. If we are conscious of these imbalances, we are likely to find them unpleasant.

Thus far we have stressed similarities among balance theories. Now, let us discuss in some detail two quite different theories, illustrating the differences, once again, by focusing on linkages between a source and an advocated position.

1. Osgood and Tannenbaum's Congruity Theory

Let us imagine that a highly admired source such as the Reverend Billy Graham tells us that he likes Kellogg's Corn Flakes. Like the S-R learning theorists, Osgood and Tannenbaum would treat this as a relatively predictable instance of prestige suggestion. Unlike most S-R theorists, however, they would foresee changes in our evaluations of Graham as well as the proposition he advocated.

The congruity model is not confined to cases of prestige suggestion. It is designed to handle all cases, in fact, in which a source (S) and a concept (C) are linked positively (p) or negatively (n) by an evaluative assertion. A unique feature of their theory is its attempt to quantify the predicted effects of incongruity.

The first step in quantifying predictions is to determine whether an assertion is positive (e.g., S likes C) or negative (e.g., S is opposed to C) and to assess receiver evaluations of S and C. To secure these evaluations, Osgood and Tannenbaum utilized a series of semantic differential scales (see Osgood, Suci, and Tannenbaum, 1957), similar to those represented below:

Billy Graham   Bad -3 -2 -1 0 $+1$ $+2$ $+3$ Good

Let us suppose that we initially regard Billy Graham as a $+2$ and Kellogg's Corn Flakes as a -1. The theory predicts that, having heard the minister applaud the cereal, we would experience incongruity. It further specifies that our evaluations of both will move to a balanced or congruous position, but not in equal amounts. Technically speaking, the movement toward congruity of S and C will be in inverse relation to their respective degrees of polarity. What this means is that Graham, a +2 (the ultimate in polarization is 3, whether + or −), will move less toward the middle than Kellogg's Corn Flakes, a −1. By means of the following formula, the theory predicts that Graham (S) will go down in value, but we will have become converts to Kellogg's Corn Flakes (C); specifically, that S and C will balance at a +1 position.

$$\text{The Formula: } \underset{\text{for } C}{\text{Change}} = \frac{|S|}{|C| + |S|} P \qquad \underset{\text{for } S}{\text{Change}} = \frac{|C|}{|C| + |S|} P$$

Where $|S|$ and $|C|$ = the absolute degree of polarization of the evaluator's attitude toward S and C, respectively (in this case $|S| = 2$ and $|C| = -1$); and where P = the algebraic difference in evaluations of S and C for positive statements and, for negative statements, the amount of change necessary for the evaluator's attitude toward the source to be equidistant from zero. (In this case $P = 3$. Had Graham said that he hated Kellogg's Corn Flakes, P would have equalled 1, S would have moved 1/3 to +1.67, and C would have moved 2/3 to −1.67.)

There are, of course, many possible combinations of evaluative assertions linking a source and a concept. In order to provide a sense of the predictions made by the theory, Fig. 5.1 presents illustrations of predicted congruity outcomes for a hypothetical receiver reacting to a series of hypothetical assertions. The predictions are not identical to those which Osgood and Tannenbaum would make since the theorists have added two correction factors to their model that are somewhat beyond this discussion. These correction factors include a "correction for incredulity" (when an assertion is so incongruous that it is not believable) and an "assertion constant" (an empirically derived correction of ±.17 that is subtracted from the amount that the source moves in the original formula and added to the amount that the concept moves). Basically, the predictions are as we have given them. Note that some relationships between psychological elements are balanced from the start. Note, too, that the theory allows for imbalances of degree and not just of kind. Note, finally, that for positive statements, balance occurs at the same point for S and C whereas, for negative statements, balance occurs at points equidistant from zero.

One can find much to criticize in the congruity theory. In looking at examples, it is not always possible to identify who the source is or what the concept is or whether an assertion is positive, negative, or neutral. When the President of the United States toasts the Russian ambassador at a formal dinner, is either the source or the concept the man, his office, or

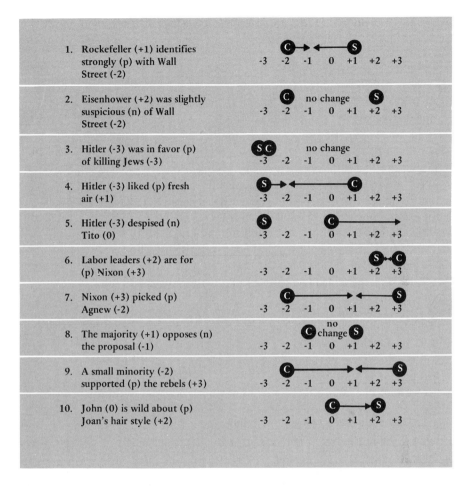

Fig. 5.1 Some predictions of congruity between source (S) and concept (C) for a hypothetical receiver reacting to a series of hypothetical assertions

the country he represents? Is the toast a neutral assertion because of its formality or is it a genuinely positive assertion? Still other problems stem from the fact that the theory makes no provision for differences in the intensity of a positive or negative assertion. Independent of whether Graham loved the cereal or merely liked it, the same prediction would be made by the theory. Another problem is that the theory offers only three ways of balancing psychological elements, either by reevaluating the source, the concept, or both. We shall see that there are probably many other ways. Finally, some examples make the theory appear ludicrous. Take the assertion, "Horses like to eat oats." We would personally rate horses as +2 and oats as −2, but our belief that horses like oats causes us no special fits of discomfort, certainly no automatic urge to eat oats for dinner. The problem here is that the theory makes no provision for differences in the relevance of an assertion to a receiver.

Despite the many valid criticisms that can be leveled at the theory, the general directions of change that it predicts (as opposed to its specific quantified predictions) have been confirmed by research (Osgood and Tannenbaum, 1955; Tannenbaum, 1966). Another virtue of the theory is its relative clarity. Moreover, some predictions are not at all obvious, as when it is estimated that a person we admire moderately (a +2) can pull a hero of ours (a +3) down simply by saying something positive about him.

To understand the power of congruity theory it is necessary to view source-concept linkages within the context of a long series of events. Consider the meteoric rise to fame of Spiro T. Agnew. A "nobody" before he was picked as Richard Nixon's running mate in 1968, Agnew was jokingly referred to as "Spiro Who?". Not long afterward, he was rated the third most popular figure in America, according to a national poll. Imagine yourself as a fairly typical American reading this sampling of headlines from the period and finding your estimate of Spiro Agnew gradually going up: (a) Nixon (+1) Picks Agnew (−2) for Veep; (b) Agnew (by now a −1) Defends Law and Order (+2); (c) Agnew (by now no worse than a −.5) Scorns Hecklers (−3); (d) Hecklers Attack Agnew (by now at least a +.5); (e) Voters (+2) Elect Agnew (now at +1); (f) Agnew (+1) Hails Silent Majority (+3); etc.

Generally speaking, the source does not simply rely on his prior reputation. To enhance his own credibility before doing battle on a controversial proposition, he will usually align himself with beliefs, values, and other attitudes that the audience already shares with him. Consider, once again, the case of Spiro Agnew. Before offering criticisms of the news media, of our liberalized policy toward Communist China, and of "effete intellectual snobs" in universities, Agnew carefully cultivated a favorable image. From his lofty position as a +2 or a +3, Agnew could risk attacking these controversial concepts, admittedly with the possibility that his own credibility would slip a little. As this is written Agnew's popularity has indeed slipped (he was forced to resign from office) but not before he made a dent in the lives of most Americans.

2. Festinger's Theory of Cognitive Dissonance

In sharp contrast to the congruity model is Festinger's (1957; 1964) theory of cognitive dissonance. Whereas Osgood and Tannenbaum offer specific, quantified predictions, Festinger's theory is only loosely predictive. Whereas the congruity model focuses on evaluative assertions linking a source and a concept, dissonance theory converges on a wide range of phenomena. Whereas Osgood and Tannebaum specify only two ways of resolving incongruity, Festinger lists several ways that dissonance may be reduced. Whereas, in Osgood and Tannenbaum's theory, rebalancing is automatic, in Festinger's theory it is not. In general, the congruity model has more in common with mechanistic, S-O-R learning theories whereas Festinger's approach has more in common with the perception theories.

According to Festinger, cognitions or clusters of cognitions (the term "cognition" is used loosely to include any item of organized experience) may be mutually *dissonant,* mutually *consonant,* or mutually *irrelevant.* Whether *logically* inconsistent with each other or *psychologically* inconsistent, dissonant cognitions create pressures to reduce the resulting discomfort.

Taking liberties with Festinger's theory, somewhat, we identify three types of discrepancy, each of which may create cognitive dissonance.

1. *Behavior-attitude* discrepancies are typified by the worker who hates his boss but whose job requires that he be nice to her. Or by the individual who purchases one product but still recalls many advantages of a competing product. Or by the individual who knows that he smokes and also that smoking is bad for his health.

More realistically, as Kiesler, Collins, and Miller (1969) have observed, there are not just two cognitions but two clusters of cognitions involved in these examples. We associate many factors with smoking (lighting of matches, movement of arms, ingestion of nicotine, etc.) and many other factors with health (keeping trim, physically relaxed, free from disease, etc.). Some smoking factors are irrelevant to some health factors, some are compatible, and some are incompatible. What Festinger really means by a dissonant relationship in this case is that the elements we consider *most important* in the cluster of factors that make up smoking are *fundamentally* incompatible with the aspects of health that we value most. Put another way, the drive to reduce dissonance increases in relative proportion to the number and importance of dissonant versus consonant relations between *clusters* of cognitions.

This same principle can also be understood at a higher level of abstraction, to explain how it is that, *in general,* we feel comfortable or uncomfortable with our smoking habit. The knowledge that we smoke is not only linked to the perception that it is fundamentally harmful to our health, but also to perceptions that smoking is a costly habit, that it relieves boredom, that it is enjoyable after meals, and so on. Again, these relations may be fundamentally consonant, dissonant, or irrelevant and, again, our general "dissonance index" with respect to smoking is proportionate to the number and importance of dissonant to consonant relations between elements.

2. *Source-Proposition* discrepancies are of the kind generated by prestige suggestions or by the pressures exerted on a deviant group member by

other members of his group or by knowledge that a cognition we hold is discrepant from even so vague a reference group as "the academic community." Knowledge that our favorite newspaper columnist prefers our choice of political candidates is cognitively consonant (and probably reinforcing, though Festinger does not discuss this). Knowledge that he disagrees with us on the candidate is cognitively dissonant. Unless we also value him as a football expert, knowledge that he disagrees with us on the merits of the Green Bay Packers is likely to be cognitively irrelevant. Here, let us note a difference between dissonance theory and congruity theory; the latter makes no provision for irrelevant relationships.

3. *Attitude Component* discrepancies are inconsistencies between any two attitudes and/or the beliefs and values that bear upon them. (Recall our discussion of attitude components in Chapter 4.) If we regard ourselves as liberals, it is cognitively consonant to promote the reelection of an incumbent governor on grounds that he has run a liberal administration. Should we become convinced, however, that our *beliefs* about his past record are ill-founded or that we err in *valuing* liberal administrations, a state of cognitive dissonance would probably now exist.

Festinger emphasizes that attitude modifications do not automatically follow experiences of cognitive dissonance. Pressures to reduce dissonance are increased as the number and/or importance of dissonant cognitive elements increase. All of us manage to live with some dissonance, however. Moreover, attitude shifts are only one means of relieving dissonance; dissonance-reduction may occur through various forms of *psychological fight* or *flight*. In the case (once again) of a prestige source urging a position discrepant from our own, we may: (1) derogate the source; (2) decide that our disagreement is not very important, or rationalize in some other way; (3) seek social support or supportive evidence for our own viewpoint; (4) misperceive the source's position; (5) compartmentalize (ignore or forget that the cognitions are discrepant); (6) attempt to convince the source (if available) of his or her error; (7) modify our own attitudes.

What happens when a disliked candidate maintains a position consistent with our own? For many "doves" and others who were hostile toward Richard Nixon in 1968, perhaps a state of dissonance was created as they heard Nixon campaigning for election on a Vietnamization platform to "bring American boys home." The campaign was designed to improve Nixon's image, but from Festinger's theory it would follow that "doves" could have reduced dissonance in other ways: by misperceiving Nixon's position, by rationalizing, by compartmentalizing, etc.

Festinger's theory has been criticized on grounds that its basic terms (cognitions, dissonance, etc.) are vaguely defined. Critics have also charged that the theory is imprecise with respect to predicting dissonance-reducing outcomes. Because there are so many outcomes, it is difficult to know which of them will be employed by an individual in a given case.

Problems of this kind present something of a dilemma for persuasion theorists in general. On the one hand, explanations which seem to do justice to persuasion's complexity invariably require terms that are difficult to operationalize. On the other hand, those terms which seem capable of being indexed behaviorally never seem to add up to a picture of the persuasive process. Festinger has opted for a richly provocative theory, but one which is loosely predictive and which calls upon us to exercise our intuitive judgments about the meanings and applications of his basic concepts. At this stage of scholarship in the field, Festinger seems to us to have made an intelligent decision.

In particular, we are pleased that dissonance theory acknowledges the possibility that individuals will at times choose to live with their dissonance rather than attempt to reduce it. In this respect, the theory is consistent with evidence that Robert White (1959) has accumulated on *competence motivation*. Competence motives include the need to explore, to be active, to master problems, and to satisfy curiosities. Human beings and other animals evidently engage in competence-increasing activities, not simply to gain food or shelter or to reduce anxiety or pain or psychological imbalance, but often in *spite* of these needs. White's impressive summary of research includes evidence of apes that try to solve complex problems simply to be able to look out of a window; of rats that choose the longer of two otherwise equivalent paths to food; of children who, within limits, prefer novelty to familiarity; and of animals that endure electric shock, simply to be able to explore a new environment. The point of this evidence, for our purposes, is that we are not static entities. Sometimes we seek self-protection, but we may tolerate dissonance and other forms of psychological pain when they accompany opportunities for growth and development.

We are also pleased that dissonance theory includes a large number of dissonance-reducing alternatives, even if this impairs its predictiveness. The theory serves as a reminder that persuaders must do more than "unbalance" cognitions by creating dissonance. They must also "rebalance" them by directing the receiver in specified ways and by closing off alternative methods of reducing dissonance. Except in rare circumstances, for example, a prestige source cannot simply attach his name to a proposal that is repugnant to receivers. He must show them that it has elements which are consonant with their cognitions, that it satisfies cherished values, that it has social support from other persons whom they hold in high esteem, and that it meets objections which they or others might raise. The point is illustrated by the failure of so many bond issues at election time. In New York, for example, a highway bond issue failed despite support from virtually every leader of state and city government.

Dissonance theory as well as other balance theories have come under increasing criticism for failing to consider the subject's own self-perceptions as elements of cognition. To a woman who considers herself quite feminine, for example, the cognition that she smokes Lucky Strikes and that Luckies are not "feminine" may produce dissonance. For another woman who does not consider herself especially feminine, the two cognitions may be irrelevant to each other. We will consider the role of self-perceptions in Chapter 8.

Still other criticisms have been leveled at experiments conducted within a dissonance theory framework (e.g., Chapanis and Chapanis, 1964), yet even the loudest critics have conceded that the theory has suggested a number of inobvious hypotheses, many of them confirmed by research. In particular, the theory has spawned a highly interesting set of hypotheses about "forced compliance," a subject we will take up in detail in Chapter 13.

Summary

A theory is a systematized set of concepts, definitions, and statements of relationship between concepts. Behavioral theories of persuasion may be general or specific. In this chapter we have briefly examined several general theories, comparing, for purposes of illustration, their positions on the issue of prestige suggestion.

Each of the theories reviewed has distinct limitations (we have deliberately omitted consideration of some of the more sophisticated theories and theoretical revisions), yet each has made important contributions. S-R theories have advanced our understanding of relationships between external inputs and outputs and have clarified key concepts by assigning them operational definitions. S-O-R theories have shown us how organismic variables may be related to external stimuli and responses, especially when the theories have included internal factors of attention and comprehension, along with motivational factors. Albeit with admittedly fuzzy concepts like "symbolic fitness," perception theorists have led us into the inner world of the receiver and have shown us how decoding processes may affect persuasion. The theory of Sherif *et al.* is especially well developed. Katz and other functional theorists have convinced us that persuasion should ideally begin with an analysis of the functions attitudes perform for a given audience in a given situational context. The balance theorists have tickled our imaginations by suggesting inobvious hypotheses and miniature theories. Osgood and Tannenbaum, for example, have shown us how the "kiss of death" effect can work, even when endorsements come from those we value. Festinger has pointed to the many ways that dissonance may be reduced.

The foregoing suggests a set of basic principles of persuasion which, together with principles enunciated earlier, may serve as a conceptual framework for our consideration of strategies of persuasion in Part 2. Consistent with our biases, this summary emphasizes the concept of psychological balance, but we have avoided the specific language of congruity and dissonance theory.

I. Persuasion is a communication process.
   A. It is the received message that counts, not the sent message.
   B. We cannot *not* communicate.
   C. Every message has a substantive and an interpersonal aspect.
   D. A message is always as much a response as it is a stimulus.
   E. Persuasion takes place through stages, the chain of stages being no stronger than its weakest link.

II. Persuasion is a learning process.
   A. Attitudes, beliefs, and values are learned and they can therefore be unlearned.
      1. Learning may take place through conditioning or through more complex information-processing activities.
      2. Learning of a desired attitudinal response is facilitated when the response is rewarded or when the persuadee believes that it will be rewarded.
   B. At one level, messages are learned when they are decoded; i.e., when they are attended to and comprehended. However, decoding does not necessarily lead to attitude change and attitude change does not necessarily lead to behavior change.

III. Persuasion is a perceptual process.
   A. The human being is a meaning-seeking animal who monitors incoming stimuli.
   B. What humans perceive is a function of both external factors and of their needs, wants, values, expectations, etc.
   C. Among peoples' most important perceptions are their attributions of causation.
      1. People tend to discount the trustworthiness of persuaders when they attribute their messages to external causes.
      2. People tend to infer their attitudes, beliefs, and values from their own actions when they have reason to believe that their actions are not attributable to external causes.

IV. Persuasion is an adaptive process.
   A. Messages designed to modify attitudes toward propositions of policy must be geared to levels of audience receptivity.
      1. Receivers include those who are hostile, in disagreement, "on the fence" (including those who are either apathetic, uninformed, or ambivalent), in agreement, or committed to favorable action.

      2. Concomitantly, persuaders may seek to reduce hostility, convert those in disagreement as well as those who are "on the fence," or intensify favorable commitments.

  B. Beliefs and values constitute the cognitive and affective components of attitudes, respectively.

      1. An attitude is largely but not entirely a joint function of the probabilities assigned to relevant beliefs and to the feelings generated toward relevant values.

      2. Propositions of belief and value support propositions of policy but persuaders may focus on defending a single belief or value in any one persuasive effort.

V. Persuasion is an unbalancing and rebalancing process.

  A. People strive to maintain psychological balance (consistency).

      1. Psychological elements (cognitions, evaluations of source and advocated proposition, etc.) may be mutually balanced, imbalanced, or irrelevant to each other.

      2. Inconsistencies between psychological elements may be logical or psychological.

      3. Imbalances are of three kinds:

        (a) behavior-attitude discrepancies,

        (b) source-proposition discrepancies,

        (c) attitude component discrepancies

      4. Imbalances may be of kind or of degree.

  B. Psychological imbalance is unpleasant or uncomfortable to the individual.

  C. The drive to reduce imbalance is not automatic. Individuals can tolerate low levels of imbalance and *must* if they are to grow and develop.

  D. The drive to reduce imbalance increases in relative proportion to the number and importance of unbalanced (versus balanced) relations between clusters of psychological elements.

  E. Imbalances may be reduced or rebalanced in several ways, only one of which is attitude- or behavior-modification in directions intended by the communicator.

      1. Rebalancing may occur through *changes* of psychological elements (including intended changes as well as derogations of the source and "boomerang" effects).

      2. Rebalancing may occur through various forms of *psychological fight* (seeking new information or social support, for example).

      3. Rebalancing may occur through various forms of *psychological flight* (compartmentalization and rationalization, for example).

  F. The persuader must not only create imbalance; he must also *close off* undesired forms of rebalancing.

Part 2

Practicing Persuasion: The Co-active Approach

Politicians have a deep contempt for the art of conveying thought. Quite a few make speeches over a lifetime without ever learning to make, write or even read a speech. Lecture-circuit impresarios are worse; all feel that nothing so impresses an audience (and justifies their fee) as a suffocating recital of the commonplace, combined with a deeply condescending manner. Social scientists, although perhaps improving, have their special instinct for fraternal obscurity. But there is no doubt that business executives are the worst of all. Theirs is the egregiously optimistic belief that people will believe anything, however improbable, if it is said with emphasis and solemnity by the head of a big company. With the ultimate promotion comes the right to proclaim truth.

John Kenneth Galbraith
New York Review of Books,
September 15, 1974, p. 7

The
Co-active
Approach
to Persuasion

This unit of the book is written primarily for those with a pragmatic interest in persuading others, although, inevitably, it will provide instruction for those only interested in understanding how persuasion works or in becoming more discriminating consumers of persuasive communications. Chapters 7 through 12 of the unit focus on the traditionally recommended approach to persuasive practice which we have labeled "co-active" persuasion. In Chapter 13 we shall be comparing the co-active approach with two others which we have termed "combative" persuasion and "expressive" persuasion. All three labels might be viewed as umbrella terms that encompass a variety of more specific (and, in some cases, quite different) strategies. Combative strategies have in common the idea of *moving against* receivers, through verbal discourse and/or symbolic action. The essence of the expressive approach is attempted *nonmanipulation*. Paradoxically, it is a kind of "antirhetorical" rhetoric, one which eschews rhetorical strategizing, either for ethical or expediential reasons. The approach was introduced in Chapter 2 and will be examined again briefly in Chapter 13 as a strategy of persuasion for protest movements. Like combative persuasion, co-active persuasion is manipulative in nature, but it *moves toward* receivers psychologically rather than moving against them. In this brief chapter we shall attempt to explicate the idea of co-active persuasion and identify the essential ingredients of the approach.

What Is Co-Active Persuasion?

So that we may better appreciate the notion of *moving toward* receivers, let us recall that the task of persuasion may be conceived as one of *bridging psychological distances*. Persuasion begins, as Kenneth Burke (1969) has observed, with the dual recognition of the fact of human differences and of the need, somehow, to span the interpersonal divide so as to secure preferred outcomes.

In the face of these differences, there are, as we have noted, certain prerequisites for all persuaders that will be discussed in various chapters of this unit. First, no matter what approach to persuasion is taken, the persuader must gain and maintain the receiver's attention. Attention is a necessary condition for persuasion.

Second, the persuader must work for at least a minimal degree of understanding of the message. The receiver needs to get the right impressions, or perhaps the right misimpressions.

Third, the persuader must work within the framework of the receiver's psycho-logic. As we shall see, even combative strategies require adaptation to the receiver.

Finally, the persuader must create *intra*personal discrepancies in the receiver if *inter*personal discrepancies are to be reduced. Put another way, the persuader cannot say *only* what the receiver believes or feels; that will have achieved nothing. As was pointed out in Chapter Four, even the reinforcement of existing beliefs, values, or attitudes involves an attempt to reduce present or anticipated interpersonal discrepancies by increasing intrapersonal discrepancies. The persuader may seek a greater level of commitment by the receiver or seek to maintain a level of commitment in anticipation that the receiver's ardor would otherwise diminish. Hence, the persuader creates, if possible, intrapersonal discrepancies—gaps between what the receiver "should" feel or think and what he or she does feel or think.

Now, to accomplish these tasks, there may be a temptation to *move against* those with whom we differ by vilifying them, ridiculing them, threatening them, or even pressuring them into actions that compel them to reassess their attitudes. These combative modes of persuasion may sometimes be appropriate, especially in conflict situations, but they also involve great risks. Even assuming the persuader succeeds in unbalancing psychological elements (to use the language of psychological consistency theory), there is the danger that the receiver will rebalance his or her cognitions by various forms of fight or flight.

Rather than moving against receivers or disdaining manipulation, as in the expressive approach, co-active persuaders take pains to build rapport and fashion their image in ways that will commend them to the receiver. Step by step, they then construct a case that is built on what the receiver is led to believe are *shared premises.* If necessary, they plead or entreat, and never do they willfully antagonize or assault egos. In this way, co-active persuaders *move toward* the receiver psychologically on matters related in the receiver's mind to the issue in question. If successful, there is reciprocal movement on the receiver's part toward acceptance of the persuaders' proposition. Ideally, to use St. Augustine's characterization of fully successful persuasion, the receiver now

> likes what you promise, fears what you say is imminent, hates what you censure, embraces what you command, regrets whatever you built up as regrettable, rejoices at whatever you say is cause for rejoicing, sympathizes with those whose wretchedness your words bring before his very eyes, shuns those whom you admonish him to shun . . . and in whatever other ways your high eloquence can affect the minds of your hearers, bringing them not merely to know what should be done, but to do what they know should be done (quoted in Burke, 1969 p. 50).

Major Ingredients of the Co-Active Approach

We should emphasize that while, in its noblest form, co-active persuasion is the oil of democratic decision-making and the means by which truth can be made to prevail, it may also be viewed by morally indifferent per-

A good example of co-active persuasion in a situation where threats of punishment are more generally employed. By his three signs the owner of the parking space entreats rather than demands; he metacommunicates pleasantness and equality rather than power. We would not park in his spot. (Photo courtesy of Miles Orvell.)

suaders as a set of disarming techniques by which they may snow their audiences and sell their snake oil. What counts, from a purely expediential framework, is not whether persuaders *actually* move toward the receivers in any substantive sense but whether they are *perceived* by receivers as psychologically proximate. Thus, much of Ovid's playful advice to would-be Casanovas would fall within the heading of co-active persuasion.

> On deceiving in the name of friendship; feigning just enough drunkenness to be winsome; on astute use of praise and promises; inducement value of belief in the gods; deceiving deceivers; the utility of tears; the need to guard against the risk that entreaties may merely feed the woman's vanity; inducement value of pallor, which is the proper color of love; advisability of shift in methods, as she who resisted the well-bred may yield to the crude; ways to subdue by yielding; the controlled use of compliments; become a

habit with her; enjoy others too, but in stealth, and deny if you are found out; give each of her faults the name of the good quality most like it (quoted in Burke, 1969, p. 160).

Here, in summary, are the ingredients we regard as essentials of the co-active approach. We shall see in Chapter 13 that for each of these ostensibly cooperative measures, there is a combative counterpart.

1. *Rhetoric of Identification.* Co-active persuaders seek *common ground* with the receiver. By words, gestures, clothing, grooming, and so on, persuaders indicate that they and their audiences share a great many demographic similarities as well as common interests and values. Shared values are also affirmed through symbolic acts such as saluting the flag. Should the audience be hostile initially, the persuader moves from areas of agreement to areas of disagreement. In no case does the persuader pretend to be a mirror-image of the receiver; differences contributing to perceptions of expertise, trustworthiness, and attractiveness may in fact be emphasized, but only because these qualities are valued by receivers.

2. *Avoidance of Threats or Acts of Force.* Co-active persuaders offer *emotional appeals,* including fear appeals, but they do not threaten to be the agents of punishment for noncompliance with their recommendations. Threat-making is part of the rhetoric of combative persuasion.

3. *Seemingly Rational Persuasion.* Co-active persuasion is rational persuasion in the sense that it appeals to the receiver's need for logical consistency. However much they may actually deceive or distort, however much they may fail to meet the logician's own standards of candor and logical consistency, co-active persuaders strive to *appear* reasonable and rational. Verbally and nonverbally, they attempt to present themselves as persons who respect and trust the audience and who warrant respect and trust in return.

4. *Attitudes to Action.* Co-active persuaders change attitudes or attitude components as a *precondition* for changes in behavior. Receivers are brought to the point where their beliefs, values, and attitudes are modified. From that point on, it is up to them to modify their behavior.

5. *Equal Access.* Ideally speaking, co-active persuaders seek *no special advantage* over those with whom they disagree other than that which accrues from the persuasiveness of their arguments and appeals. They may actually take great pains to insure that debate opponents have equal access to media, channels, and other such instrumentalities of persuasion.

These five characteristics help to define the co-active approach and to differentiate it, especially, from combative strategies of persuasion. Within the framework of this overall approach, a variety of more specific strategies are available. For example, the persuader may elect to use strong fear appeals or weak appeals or no fear appeals; none of these options are ruled out.

The first five chapters following this one are not arranged in terms of any particular order of preparation or presentation. In fact, there is no natural starting point for preparation, even for a single occasion, let alone a campaign or movement. If forced to choose, we would recommend a sequence along the lines of the following:

1. Formulate goals for the occasion in light of your overall, ultimate objectives.

2. Analyze your audience and the situational context in which you will be operating. See Chapter 4.

3. Revise your goals in light of that analysis. Your analysis will generally reveal the need for a more modest set of goals.

4. Reanalyze audience and context, this time with an eye to the rhetorical problems (resistances, dilemmas, objections) you can expect to face and the strategies that seem most appropriate for dealing with those problems.

5. Formulate a public statement of position and think about when, or even if, you want to express it.

6. Organize the body of your presentation for maximum psychological impact. If you work on an introduction first, expect that you will have to discard it later.

7. Gather evidence and other supporting materials.

8. Formulate arguments and appeals for each of your propositions and subpropositions.

9. Encode your message. If it is a speech, work on your delivery.

10. Begin again from the beginning. A revision almost always helps.

Summary

By way of introduction to this unit on co-active persuasion, we have attempted to clarify the concept and to identify its major ingredients.

Co-active persuasion is the traditionally recommended approach to persuasion. It is a global approach in the sense of embodying many more specific possible strategies. More manipulative than the expressive approach, less divisive than the combative approach, it works at psychological convergence between source and receiver. This is accomplished through a rhetoric of identification, through emotional appeals that fall short of threatening another, and through arguments designed to appear rational. Persuaders aim at belief, value, or attitude change as a precondition for behavior-change, and they do so, ideally at least, in a spirit of give and take.

Formulating
Goals
and
Position
Statements

Whether preparing for negotiations with adversaries or for a speech to sympathetic listeners, persuaders should make a distinction between what they ask for publicly on any one occasion and what they expect to achieve. As we saw in Chapter 4, the goal-setting task involves attention not only to intended primary effects, but also to secondary effects. We begin this chapter with some advice on formulating primary objectives for a specific occasion. Next, we examine research evidence on the when, how, and where of public statements of position. Finally, we offer cautionary comments on possible secondary effects of persuasion.

Formulating Primary Goals

There is a tendency in our culture to assume that some persons—advertisers, propagandists, Philadelphia lawyers—have magical powers of persuasion while the rest of us wallow in the mud of our own impotence. The truth is that professionals and amateurs are much alike in their capacity to influence others. What, then, are the differences? First, we frequently don't know what we want from our audiences on any one occasion. Second, even when we do know what we want, we often expect the impossible. We assume that we can change fundamental attitudes in unconducive social contexts through a single transaction. Then we lament that we have not succeeded.

Setting Highly Specific Goals

Oftentimes, we have a sense of our own convictions, some idea about the audience's convictions, but little sense of what we can expect from the audience in the way of specific covert or overt responses following the reception of our message. Broadly speaking, are we seeking hostility-reduction, conversion, or intensification? Are we attempting to mould attitudes, to change them, to arouse them, or to create indecision? And within those broad goal categories, what specific goals are we seeking to accomplish?

Assume for a moment that we will be addressing a student audience that is mildly sympathetic to our position in favor of welfare reform, and that we are seeking, in a general way, to intensify their attitudes. Beginning speakers are often content with such vague goal statements, but there is considerable value in specifying them further. Let us note that the following, more specific, statements of purpose would lead to quite different approaches to the audience:

- arousing the audience's anger at welfare officials to the point where they are willing to stage a sit-in at the local welfare office;
- providing a better intellectual appreciation of the nationwide scope of the problem;

- instilling an intense emotional sense of what it's like to be totally dependent upon welfare;
- crystallizing favorable attitudes around a specific plan of action.

Generally speaking, persuaders should settle on a single specific purpose for any one audience or audience segment. Even with a highly heterogeneous audience, persuaders may speak on a single, abstract theme, hoping that a pleasing demeanor or ambiguous appeals to cultural truisms will carry the day. Or they may virtually ignore some segments of the audience —admittedly, at the risk of offending them—in the hopes of appealing to other segments. In some cases, communicators may aim at only a small minority of their listeners, as when a representative of the Marine Corps attempts to recruit college students. In other cases, they may aim their messages at the majority (still ignoring some), as when a presidential candidate attempts to forge a winning constituency.

Ideally, of course, persuaders should consider all audience members in framing a specific purpose and they may well have different purposes in mind for different segments of the audience. Such was the case, we suspect, when Stewart Udall, former Secretary of the Interior, and a prominent conservationist, presented a rather unusual testimonial on television in behalf of a Sears product. That it was unusual for a major political figure to endorse a commercial product was acknowledged by Udall himself, but he pointed out that the product was also unique. It was, he said, a new, nonphosphate detergent which, unlike other detergents then in use, did not pollute rivers and streams. Udall emphasized, moreover, that his earnings from performance of the testimonial had been donated to a worthy charity.

Ironically, the substitute ingredients used in nonphosphate detergents have since been found to have polluting effects also, but, disregarding this parenthetical tidbit of information, let us ask what goals Udall hoped to accomplish from doing the advertisement. It seems a reasonable estimate that he had different goals in mind for different audience segments. Among those who were already conservation-minded, Udall undoubtedly sought to change buying patterns and to spark a word-of-mouth campaign in which others would be led to purchase nonphosphate detergents as well. Among those who were indifferent or uninformed about conservation issues or about phosphates in particular, Udall probably hoped to provide the beginnings of an education and to stimulate further thought. Udall's protestations notwithstanding, he might also have attempted to enhance his own image in the public eye. Finally, Udall may have given special thought to a small but highly influential audience segment, the manufacturers of other detergents. By promoting a non-phosphate, the conservationist probably sought to pressure these manufacturers into following Sears' example.

Setting Realistic Goals

Despite contrary evidence from experimental research on persuasion, it is probably unwise to expect sweeping changes in attitudes or behavior on any one occasion. The typical classroom or laboratory experiment utilizes uninvolving issues, captive audiences, and, as we noted earlier, settings that frequently place the subject under unusual pressure to comply (at least publicly) with the position advocated in the message.

The evidence of sweeping changes from research in laboratories and classrooms has not been confirmed by research on mass communications in more naturalistic settings (Hovland, 1959). There are remarkably few instances, in fact, in which a single message, by itself, has produced wholesale conversions of mass audiences. When claims of this kind are made, they are usually exaggerated. More often than not, seemingly spectacular successes at persuasion serve *triggering* or *catalytic* functions; the message initiates or crystallizes concern about an issue but depends on other causal forces to facilitate its effects. A good example of a triggering message is Ralph Nader's *Unsafe at Any Speed* (1965). In 1970 a New York Times headline characterized it as "One Book That Shook the Business World." Indeed, it did, but it would probably have had considerably less influence had Nader not been invited subsequently to address a Senate subcommittee on traffic safety, had General Motors not been publicly exposed for harassing him, and had Nader himself not engaged in strenuous followup efforts. Examples of catalytic messages are the mass rallies and demonstrations of the sixties which "doves" and "hawks" alike have credited with being enormously influential. Undoubtedly they were, but according to the Skolnick Report (1969), the rallies and demonstrations were as much an *outcome* as a cause of antiwar sentiment. Complementary contextual factors included the government's failure to live up to its promises or to justify its claims, the threat of the draft, the crisis of racial conflict, poverty and inflation at home, and the daily reports via the media on American and South Vietnamese conduct of the war, including widespread atrocities. Significantly, as American soldiers were withdrawn from the war, and as the threat of the draft diminished, it became increasingly difficult to stage effective mass protests.

Probably persuaders should only expect small increments of change at any one time unless they are operating within a highly conducive social climate (such as the climate for protest during the sixties), unless they are dealing with initially predisposed audiences, or unless they have had opportunity for repeated contact with the receiver. When receivers are in disagreement, especially when there is a clash over basic values, a whole set of defenses are likely to come into play with the distinct possibility that persuasive attempts may "boomerang." Defenses may also be raised when receivers are asked to adopt new values, beliefs, or attitudes. One reason for the much-heralded success of the advertiser and the propagandist is that they seldom challenge deeply held views. When they do, they employ a gradual approach involving a number of messages over an extended period of time.

Should persuaders strike out for highly ambitious goals despite the odds, they should certainly not be judged or judge themselves by either-or standards. All of us can contribute our own lists of magnificent failures: men like Martin Luther King, Jr., and Malcolm X, perhaps, who accomplished considerably less than they attempted, but only because they dared to reach out for the impossible; defeated presidential aspirants like Norman Thomas and Adlai Stevenson whose losses at the polls were more than matched by less measurable victories in the battle for men's minds. Persuasive efforts should be judged in light of the difficulty of the task to be accomplished, and in terms of tangible as well as seemingly intangible effects.

Formulating Public Statements of Position

Considerable experimental research has been undertaken on the issues of *whether* persuaders should reveal intent to persuade; on *when*, in a speech or essay, they should disclose their position; and on *how discrepant* that position should be from the audience's initial position in order to be maximally effective. Here we shall briefly review some of the evidence bearing on these issues.[1]

Concealing or Revealing Intent to Persuade

As we indicated in Chapter 2, persuaders may disguise intent in a number of different ways. Pretending to "educate" us, they may say, directly: "I'm not here to persuade you." And they might add: "I'd rather let the facts speak for themselves." With somewhat greater subtlety, they may let drop that they don't really care what the audience thinks. Or, feigning interest in learning from the audience, they may characterize the occasion as a "give-and-take discussion." If they persuade through film, they may label the film a "documentary." If they persuade through writing, they may label the essay a "scientific report." The purpose of all these approaches is to allay suspicions about manipulative intent by casting the source in an objective guise.

---

1. Several excellent reviews of the experimental literature on these issues are found in Beisecker and Parson (1972). See chapters in that book by Sherif, Sherif, and Nebergall (pp. 104–121), Papageorgis (pp. 180–196), McGuire (pp. 197–218), and Whitaker (pp. 376–392).

Where the motives of the persuader evoke suspicion from the very start, or where the audience is known to be hostile toward the source's position, there is obviously some reason to conceal intent to persuade. Let us note, however, that these same audiences might be doubly resentful of a source who feigns objectivity and is then found out. Furthermore, the guise of objectivity may also be interpreted as indifference toward the audience. Compare "I have no interest in persuading you" with "I very much want to persuade you because I care about what you think."

Whatever the theoretical grounds for disguising or disclosing intent, the available experimental evidence suggests that revelation of intent to persuade seldom impairs communication acceptance in any significant way and often enhances it (Papageorgis, 1968; McGuire, 1969). Disclosure of intent is especially effective, it would seem, if persuaders couple it with expressed liking for the audience (Mills, 1966) or if, in other ways, they appear attractive (Mills and Aronson, 1965). Disclosure of intent to persuade impedes effectiveness when expressions of intent take place in what Papageorgis (1968) calls a "negative persuasion context"; for example, when the message labeled as persuasive is described as using "scare tactics" and "biased statistics" (Rosenblatt and Hicks, 1966), or when the source of an avowedly persuasive article is purported to be a book on techniques of persuasion (Kiesler and Kiesler, 1964). As we suggested in Chapter 2, persuasion is a "god" word in some contexts, a "devil" word in others.

In view of the ethical presumption in favor of being open and honest with receivers, we would ordinarily recommend that intent to persuade be disclosed, especially since the evidence is, at worst, inconclusive. This does not mean that the *specific* purpose of a speech or the ultimate objectives for a campaign or movement must be disclosed.

Timing of Position Statements

Assuming that persuasive intent should be disclosed, the next logical question is when, if at all, the persuader's actual position should be expressed. Leaving the position implicit has the theoretical advantage of preventing defenses from being raised. In addition, there is evidence from clinical settings that receivers are more effectively persuaded when, through nondirective therapeutic methods, they are compelled to state the repugnant conclusion for themselves. The implicit approach has an important theoretical disadvantage, however: the receivers may not know what the persuader is driving at. In this respect, the therapeutic situation is probably atypical since the receivers presumably have more time and greater motivation to deduce the appropriate conclusion (McGuire, 1969).

One of the earliest experimental studies on this issue was conducted by Hovland and Mandell (1952). An unusually bright sample of college students was led to believe that they were hearing a tape recording of a radio broadcast on the topic of devaluation of currency. A tape recording presented to two equivalent subsamples was identical except that the speaker's conclusions were stated explicitly to one group and omitted from the speech heard by the other group. Even with this exceptionally intelligent sample, the implicit approach evidently created confusion. Overall, the explicit approach was more effective.

The findings of Hovland and Mandell (1952) have generally been confirmed by other research on this issue (Fine, 1957; Irwin and Brockhaus, 1963; Thistlethwaite, de Haan and Kamenetzky, 1955; Weiss and Steinback, 1965). Since a major advantage of the explicit approach is its greater clarity, it would seem to follow that stating the position (i.e., the conclusion) early in the speech or essay would further facilitate decoding of the message. McGuire (1969, p. 186) has suggested still another reason for explicitly stating the position from the outset. Based on the assumption that people prefer to think of themselves as able to resist persuasive influence, he offers the intriguing hypothesis that this preference

> ... produces the tendency for subjects who are forewarned of the source's persuasive intent to yield in advance, even before the source's arguments, pretending to themselves that they actually already agreed with the position for which the source is about to argue.

Where the persuader's position is likely to be highly unpopular, it might be advisable to avoid disclosing it until the very end. Another alternative is to state part of the position at the outset and withhold the remainder. For example, the persuader may intimate at the beginning that her sole purpose is to demonstrate the seriousness of a certain problem. Then, having dramatized the problem, she might reveal her unpopular position regarding the solution.

In any event, the persuader should probably not utilize an implicit approach unless: (1) receivers are highly intelligent; (2) they oppose his or her position but are interested in hearing the issues; (3) the persuader's arguments follow a clear logical progression to an easily deducible conclusion. We shall say more in Chapters 8 and 11 about techniques of reasoning to conclusions with audiences.

The Magnitude of Discrepancy Controversy

Explicitly or implicitly, the persuader always communicates a position that is more or less *discrepant* from the position initially endorsed by the audience. Perhaps he or she is an advocate of a six percent sales tax addressing those who believe only a three percent tax is needed, or a fund raiser for a charity whose audience is sympathetic to the cause but not as committed to it. In any case, the persuader must "guesstimate" when the discrepancy between the proposition and the attitude of the audience will be too great to gain acceptance. Should the tax advocate suggest the need for an eight percent sales tax in order to get the audience to compromise on a six percent tax, or would it be better to ask for only four percent the first time around in the hopes of getting at least some attitude shift? Let us note once again that the question of what to ask for is somewhat different from the question raised earlier of what to expect to achieve.

Persuasion theorists have taken conflicting positions on the issue we have just raised. Festinger (1957), Anderson and Hovland (1957) and others have argued that if we ask for the moon, we are at least likely to get a sizable chunk of it; Sherif, Sherif, and Nebergall (1965) have held that in asking for the moon we may only get a piece of green cheese. The controversy has sparked considerable research and the results are not entirely consistent. Confounding the issue are other variables: the communicator's credibility, the audience's degree of ego-involvement, and the communicator's chances of getting a fair hearing from the audience on subsequent occasions. Typically, the effects of a particular variable like magnitude of discrepancy are confounded with the effects of other variables.

Although the findings from research in naturalistic settings would suggest the need to exercise some caution, the experimental research literature generally supports the conclusion that up to extremely large magnitudes of discrepancy, the more persuaders ask for, the more they are likely to get (Karlins and Abelson, 1970; McGuire, 1969). Persuaders are not likely to get *as much* shift of position as they ask for (see, for example, Bochner and Insko, 1966), but, particularly if they are perceived as highly credible (Aronson, Turner and Carlsmith, 1963; Bergin, 1962; Bochner and Insko, 1966) and if the issue is perceived to be important (Zimbardo, 1960), greater attitude change will occur than if a less extreme position is espoused. On the other hand, several investigators (Freedman, 1964; Greenwald, 1964; Miller, 1964) have provided support for the theory proferred by Sherif, et al. (1965) that when an advocated position falls within the receiver's latitude of rejection (see Chapter 5), it is perceived as more extreme than it really is, thus leading to rejection of the position and possible boomerang effects. Rejection of extreme positions is especially likely when receivers are ego-involved in the sense that they are highly committed to the correctness of their initial positions. (Recall the distinction between issue importance and ego-involvement that was offered in Chapter 4.)

By way of summarizing this complex issue, we would advise persuaders to ask for more than they expect to get, but we would also suggest that they attempt, where possible, to avoid arousing defensive reactions. Issues can be made to seem important without threatening egos. Under these circumstances, and particularly if the source is respected, more extreme positions can then be stated with some degree of safety.

Programming Secondary Effects

It has been said of John F. Kennedy that his concrete accomplishments as President were far outstripped by a contagious spirit and style. Through Kennedy's leadership, the early sixties became a period of revitalized ambitions, a Kennedy dream transformed into an American dream. Through his manner of speech and action, others were prompted to find eloquence, wisdom, and courage in themselves. Although Kennedy was not as adept as his successor at pushing programs through Congress, the Kennedy legacy still endures through a concatenation of these secondary effects.

Secondary effects are the consequences of the means we employ to attain our primary objectives. These means include the arguments we use to support a case and the way these arguments are organized; the appeals we use to secure adoption of proposals and the language in which those appeals are couched. The manner in which persuaders seek to achieve primary objectives may shape a receiver's language habits, basic values, thought patterns, general predispositions to trust or be suspicious of communicators, and so on. When advertisements for sleeping pills are repeatedly premised on the notion that drugs are a suitable escape from problems, the advertiser is selling not only the sleeping pill but its underlying premise. When an essayist oversimplifies to win acceptance of a proposition, this invites others to do likewise, not only on the subject in question, but as a recurrent pattern of thought. Some persuaders are quite scrupulous about the means they employ. Oftentimes, however, secondary influences are overlooked or are sacrificed for the sake of primary objectives. In these cases, the effects of the persuaders' actions may rebound to their disadvantage in the long run. Although initial appeals to a questionable value or a mythical belief may have negligible effect, each repeated use tends to strengthen it. Ultimately, through reinforcement by many persons over a prolonged period, the belief or value may take on what Klapper (1960) calls a "monopoly propaganda" position in a culture. Woe unto the persuader who assails it or even to the persuader who fails to pay homage to it, even in defending proposals that are only tangentially relevant to the belief or value in question.

There is perhaps no more tragic lesson from the history of the war in Vietnam than the fact that Americans were victimized by their own symbols—myths and values that might once have been serviceable if appreciated within a limited framework, but that now, after repeated and extended use, had become overgeneralized notions that entrapped governments and publics alike into commitments they did not want at prices they could not afford.

As presented in the government's own Pentagon Papers, the record is a sorry one indeed: of continued bombings despite all intelligence reports that they were unproductive; of deceptions uttered and deceptions denied; of an unwillingness among government leaders to consider in depth the moral issues raised by American participation in the war. Leslie Gelb, the director of the Pentagon Project, has suggested (*Philadelphia Bulletin,* June 27, 1971) that it was not ignorance that perpetuated unsound and seemingly immoral practices. Rather, it was a kind of basic malaise that made it imperative for each successive administration to act in the name of symbols made into shibboleths by former administrations. These symbols were of two kinds: "god" symbols and "devil" symbols. Following upon World War II, Americans were led to believe that we were an invincible nation, that we were responsible for the well-being of the "Free World," and that we could do no wrong. At the same time, we became convinced that there was a monolithic Red menace, a devil incarnate in the form of creeping communism. Although there was some truth value in these premises during the fifties, they took on a monopoly propaganda position to a point where misapplications and overextensions of these principles could no longer be challenged. Vietnam became a "testing ground for America's will power," a "domino" in the "battle with monolithic communism" over Southeast Asia. Privately, as it turned out, many governmental leaders no longer saw these premises as relevant to prolongation or escalation of the war. Publicly, however, they felt they had no choice but to affirm and simultaneously reinforce them. Domestic political considerations seemed to demand affirmation; an indoctrinated America could not tolerate the notion of moral or military humiliation. Even within government councils, however, it became necessary to affirm these premises as a mark of the bureaucrat's "loyalty," "realism," and "sanity." Hence, those critics within government who sought to challenge Vietnam policies had to do so within the framework of a reinterpretation of the consequences of faulty premises rather than through a direct attack on those premises. As in the story of the "Emperor's New Clothes," intragovernmental pressures to conform prevented private doubts from being expressed or tolerated. The ground rules for discussion were such that debate over first premises was foreclosed. From his own experience in government, Norman Cousins (1971) has offered insights into the "kind of atmosphere or ambience in which government strategists operate" (p. 18).

> There is first of all a pervasive sense of gamesmanship. The world becomes a vast chessboard; each piece is assessed for its maneuverability and potential power. In such a game it is almost embarrassing to speak of truth or moral purpose. The highest value is not truth but sophistication (p. 18).

What should persuaders do in the face of audiences that will only accept proposals on grounds that they themselves find repugnant? Our intention in this extended case study has not been to moralize in behalf of unswerving honesty. We have tried to emphasize, however, that winning audience acceptance may entail unacceptable costs to those who seek to persuade. At the very least, they should be acutely aware of the consequences of their acts when they set out to sell good proposals for bad reasons. If they decide to deceive others, they should do so without deceiving themselves.

Beyond that, persuaders might seek to effect compromises between achieving primary effects and achieving secondary effects. They may, for example, present arguments at so abstract a level that they are acceptable to themselves *and* to their audiences. Or they may present a balance of arguments that they find personally compelling and other arguments that they expect the audience will find compelling. Or they may candidly acknowledge to the audience that the position they espouse can be supported for a variety of reasons, and that the arguments they will be presenting are not necessarily those most salient to them personally. Or they may speak forthrightly on the issues, hoping against hope that sound but temporarily unpopular arguments will ultimately produce audience adherence for the right reasons.

Quite apart from the specific arguments used, persuaders can achieve desirable secondary effects by such factors as the quality of their reasoning, the eloquence of their language, and the dignity they accord the audience. In formulating intended effects, we urge that you not overlook these factors as well.

Summary

We have seen in this chapter that persuaders often face difficult choices when formulating private goals and public goals and public statements of position on any one occasion. What persuaders *say* they want, what they *really* want, and what they *expect to achieve* may all be at variance. Moreover, the accomplishment of primary goals may be at the price of undesired secondary effects. What to do? On the basis of case studies and experimental research evidence, we have offered the following advice:

1. Formulate goals with your own values uppermost in mind, but with attention directed also to the nature of the audience and the exigencies of the situational context.

2. Formulate a single, specific statement of primary purpose for any one audience segment on any one occasion.

3. Set realistic goals. In most cases, goals should be revised downwards for "one-shot" rhetorical situations. Expect that on any one occasion your message will at best have triggering or catalytic effects.

4. Seldom is it necessary to conceal intent to persuade, although, with a hostile or opposed audience, it may be necessary to delay specifying your exact position on a controversial issue.

5. Rarely should your position be left implicit. If your stand on an issue is likely to be unpopular, move from areas of agreement to areas of disagreement, stating your position in a general and uncontroversial way at the outset, and identifying the more troublesome aspects of your position later in the presentation.

6. Ask for more than you expect to get, especially if you enjoy high credibility with your audience and if the audience is not highly ego-involved on the issue. Where possible, however, do not advocate positions which, to borrow the terminology of Sherif, et al., fall within the receiver's latitude of rejection.

7. Be aware that winning audience acceptance of your position may entail undesired secondary effects. It may sometimes be desirable on ethical grounds to delay or forego the accomplishment of primary goals for the sake of secondary gains.

Establishing
Common
Ground

In one guise or another, the concept—and, more significantly, the doctrine —of common ground has appeared in the writings of persuasion theorists since time immemorial. As a purely descriptive term, common ground simply refers to the existence of areas of real or perceived similarity between a source and a receiver. As a doctrine, it has been something more than that: an injunction to persuaders to manifest and emphasize interpersonal similarities as a precondition for bridging differences (e.g., Chase, 1949). Taken to its extreme, the doctrine holds that the similarities that unite people are more basic than the differences that divide them. Hence, if people would only recognize these similarities, interpersonal conflicts would disappear, and wars, strikes, riots, and so on, would become unnecessary.

Although we cannot endorse the extreme version of the common ground doctrine, we can and have subscribed to the principle that emphasizing at least certain types of interpersonal similarities is a necessary starting point for co-active persuasion. If persuaders are to create imbalance in receivers by churning up psychological waves, they should ordinarily appear at first as persons with whom the receivers can identify.

Types of Interpersonal Similarities

Technically speaking, there are as many similarities or dissimilarities between people as there are points of comparison. For purposes of discussion, we may identify (1) *dispositional* similarities or dissimilarities, and (2) *membership group* similarities or dissimilarities. Each of these categories may be broken down further in terms of whether the similarity or dissimilarity is (a) *logically relevant* to the proposition being advocated or (b) *logically irrelevant*. Thus we arrive at the following fourfold table into which the most significant similarities or dissimilarities can be placed:

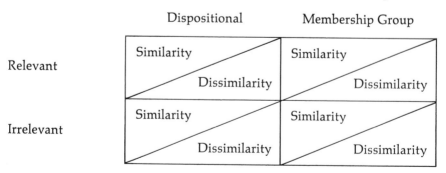

Dispositional Similarities: Shared Beliefs, Values, or Attitudes

References to shared attitudes or attitude components are especially potent when they are *logically relevant* to the proposition being advocated. When a door-to-door vacuum cleaner salesman says he admires his customer's garden, this logically *irrelevant* similarity does no more than enhance his image. When the same salesperson says that he shares the customer's annoyance at vacuum cleaners that are forever getting clogged up, he is doing more than enhancing his image; he is using the assertion as a first premise on which logically derivable conclusions may be anchored.[1] In the same way, another persuader may use the premise that "All of us want truth from our government" as the basis for a reasoned condemnation of the government's credibility gap. Note that in both cases the persuader is attempting to create imbalance in the receiver without appearing as the source of the receiver's discomfort.

Three techniques for emphasizing dispositional common ground deserve special comment.[2] They are (1) the "yes-yes" approach, (2) the "yes-but" approach, and (3) the "assumed we."

The "yes-yes" and the "yes-but" approaches are variants of the same technique (Minnick, 1957). In both cases, little or no hint of any disagreement with the audience is expressed until after a whole string of assertions is communicated about which agreement is sure. The object is to establish a habit of assent, to get receivers nodding "Yes," "That's right," "You said it," either aloud or to themselves. Once this is done the audience will presumably be receptive to more controversial assertions.

Using the "yes-yes" approach, the persuader lays the groundwork for his or her case by identifying a number of acceptable principles or criteria in terms of which the case will later be supported. In our example of the vacuum cleaner salesman, given earlier, he might continue as follows:

> If you're like most of the people I meet, you also want a vacuum that really cleans, one that picks up the ashes and the threads and the crumbs that hide in the corners. I'd guess too that in these days of galloping inflation you don't feel like getting stuck with big bills. . . . Well, okay, I know just what you mean. . . . Here's our new kind of vacuum cleaner and it fits your specifications exactly.

Using the "yes-but" approach, persuaders begin by noting those arguments of the opposition with which they can agree, and then, having shown how fair-minded they are, they offer a series of "buts" that consti-

---

1. We are not saying, of course, that expressions of admiration for the customer's garden are *psychologically* irrelevant. Indeed, expressions of liking for receivers and for acts and attributes associated with them have been found, quite consistently, to be potent forces in persuasion (McGuire 1969). The potential advantage, however, of the salesman's more reasoned appeal is that it is both psychologically relevant and logically relevant. As we shall indicate more clearly in Chapter 10, receivers may even tolerate psychological inconsistency for the sake of logical consistency.

2. For a discussion of other techniques, see Jones (1954).

tute the heart of their case. An extension of our earlier example on the "credibility gap" might go something as follows. It would be particularly appropriate for a hostile or critical audience:

> Look, I'm not one of these people who'll tell you that our government has got to tell all; that it's got to conduct diplomacy in a fish bowl; that it's got to give away secrets that are vital to national security; that it's got to make its wildest contingency plans public. These are valid reasons for keeping things under covers, BUT...

The pronoun "we" may be used in various ways: as a reference to identifiable persons, as an editorial writing style, or as a reference to some vague collectivity that is assumed to include the audience being addressed. It is this latter usage that we have in mind in referring to the "assumed we." In the following excerpt from a news commentary by Robert Roth (1971), the "assumed we" is used again and again to refer, ambiguously, to "those who watched and lived with the antiwar demonstrations" (held during the Spring, 1971 in Washington, D.C.). Whether Roth has the credentials to act as spokesman for a nation or even a city is open to doubt. Still the "assumed we" is effective, for it places source and receiver in the same "right thinking" in-group and invites joint opposition to an equally overgeneralized "they."

> It is imposible to look back on the last three weeks in Washington with anything but mixed emotions. In the first weeks of protest activity, we were proud of those young people who came here to show their government that the peace movement was not dead.... We were particularly proud on the final day of that first week when uncounted thousands gathered to voice a massive demand for peace now.
>
> We were proud of the protesters. They were orderly, decent, well-behaved.
>
> We were proud of our police. They handled a difficult situation with a minimum of fuss.
>
> And we were proud of ourselves. We had put up with the inconveniences, inevitably caused by the presence of the demonstrators, in a spirit of tolerance which was shared even by those who disagreed with the protesters' goal.
>
> We felt pretty good about it.
>
> But then, after a week of uneasy anticipation, came a new wave of demonstrators, and everything changed.
>
> Those who made up this new contingent were anything but decent and orderly and nonviolent. They were deliberately and outrageously disorderly, disruptive, destructive and provocative.
>
> First we were indignant and then we were angry and then we were just plain mad at these antiwar demonstrators whom we now lumped all together.

Who, we asked, did these kids think they were? Why, having made their point in the first demonstration, and made it well, didn't they go home? What right had they to interfere with honest people who had work to do and families to feed?

We were glad when they were arrested and were hit with heavy fines. Perhaps it would teach them the value of money—for which of them had ever earned an honest dime? We were glad when some of them got a taste of the nightstick. Perhaps if more of them had got more of that when they were younger they would have learned how to behave.

All that nice, warm feeling we had had for them that first quiet, impressive week was gone.

Membership Group Similarities

According to Minnick (1957), persuaders may effect attitude change not only by explicitly asserting that they share beliefs, values, and attitudes with the audience, but also by manifesting and/or emphasizing "similarity or identity in origin and parentage; schooling and upbringing; religious training, work experiences, economic class or condition. . ." (p. 126). Unlike assertions of dispositional similarity, Minnick's list of references to shared demography, background, or class membership contains assertions which are relatively verifiable, in some cases referring to readily observable characteristics. Whether apparent to the receiver or not, persuaders are likely to call attention to certain of these membership group similarities for purposes of emphasis.[3]

One function of membership group similarities, we suspect, is in serving as a form of indirect suggestion. Audiences may infer dispositional similarities from evidence of membership group similarities (e.g., "since the speaker and I are both farmers, we must share a concern about . . ."). Even more indirectly, the persuader may *imply* membership group similarities by choice of language, dress, dialect, and so on. Among our professional colleagues we are accustomed to using the jargon of the field and, within limits, to dress and act as others do at professional meetings. In general, subcultures tend to nurture and covet their own distinctive idioms. Among ghetto blacks, for example, Kochman (1969) has identified several different idiomatic forms: "rapping," "shucking," "jiving," "running it down," "gripping," "copping a plea," "signifying," and "sounding." Among Jews, it is quite "kosher" to "schmaltz" sentences in English with yiddish terms or expressions.

---

3. For a discussion of how persuaders identify with their audiences in quite subtle ways, see Burke (1969). Burke's treatment of identification is particularly interesting because he sees it not simply as a set of self-serving techniques, but also, in the more exalted sense, as the means by which human beings may discover their ultimate oneness.

Consistent with the principle that persuasion deals in appearances, we should emphasize here that it is perceived similarities that persuade, not objective similarities. The "weekend Hippies"—so common during the sixties and early seventies—may not have shared the deep-seated feelings of those with whom they sought to identify, but their long hair, languid walk, allusions to "tripping," being "ripped off," "offing the Pig," requests for a place to "crash," age—all of these in combination often made them indistinguishable from "genuine freaks," even to other "freaks."

Whether manifested, implied, or stated, whether genuine or inauthentic, membership-group similarities may be designed to increase perceived attractiveness, trustworthiness, or in-group feelings, and in so doing, increase the chances of gaining acceptance for a proposition. Allusions to similar status may take various forms. In the film, *All The Kings Men*, Huey Long (given the name Willie Stark in the movie) is supposed to have launched his fantastic political career by use of the "plain folks" device. The scene was a local carnival, the audience a group of farmers standing with straws in their mouths at the back of a tent.

> You're all a bunch of hicks. That's right. Hicks! You're hicks and I'm a hick and us hicks are gonna run the state legislature.

Contrasting with the "plain folks" device is the "snob appeal." David Ogilvy, a leader in the advertising field, has suggested that it pays to give most products an "image of quality"—what he calls "a first-class ticket." Products such as Pepperidge Farm, Hathaway, Mercedes-Benz, Schweppes, and Dove are often marketed by means of in-group appeals to persons of real or imagined high status.

Another dimension of membership group similarity, in addition to those we have named, is relevance. As with dispositional similarities, persuaders may emphasize similarities of class, demography, origin, etc., that logically have little to do with the proposition being advocated. Whether irrelevant similarities contribute to persuasive effectiveness is an issue we will take up shortly.

Finally, we should point out that the presumed power of interpersonal similarities has affected not only the selection of message content but the selection of sources themselves in mass media campaigns. Advertisers have made repeated use of the testimonial by persons allegedly similar to the audiences they have sought to influence. On television, for example, the advocate for a brand-name detergent is often the neighbor next door, apron and all. In other campaigns, as we have indicated, persuaders make deliberate use of "opinion leaders" who in many respects are similar to their audiences.

The Case for Establishing Common Ground

There are many good reasons for establishing common ground and we have already hinted at some of them. Let us look here at the evidence and arguments in support of the common ground doctrine and, in the next section, provide grounds for restricting and qualifying the doctrine.

Facilitating Decoding

Quite apart from whether interpersonal similarities are emphasized or remain unemphasized, the fact is that mutual understanding is increased when two people share many similar experiences, speak the same language, and hold many beliefs, values, and attitudes in common. Vick and Wood (1969) have found, for example, that similarity of experience is an excellent predictor of effectiveness at the game of Password. Using the terms "homophily" and "heterophily" for similarity and dissimilarity, respectively, Rogers and Bhowmik (1970–71) have suggested that heterophilic interaction is likely to involve greater effort, cause message distortion, delayed transmission, and restriction of communication channels. They suggest these as some of the reasons that in a free-choice situation interaction is more likely to take place between homophilous individuals. Schramm (1960, p. 6) has underscored the point using a simple communication model, represented below:

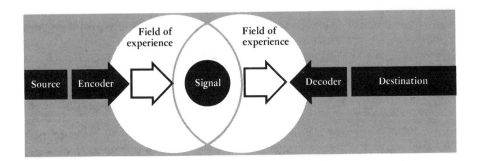

Think of these circles as the accumulated experience of the two individuals trying to communicate. The source can encode, and the destination [i.e., the receiver] can decode, only in terms of the experience each has had. If we have never learned any Russian, we can neither code nor decode in that language. If an African tribesman has never seen or heard of an airplane, he can only decode the sight of a plane in terms of whatever experience he has had. The plane may seem to him to be a bird, and the aviator a god borne on wings. If the circles have a large area in common, then communication is easy. If the circles do not meet—if there has been no common experience—then communication is impossible. If the circles have only a small area in common—that is, if the experiences of source and destination have been strikingly unlike—then it is going to be very difficult to get an intended meaning across from one to the other.

The source, then, tries to encode in such a way as to make it easy for the destination to tune in the message—to relate it to parts of experience which are much like those of the source.

Premise Building

There seems little doubt but that *relevant* dispositional similarities are potent forces in persuasion. Our guess is that they are effective primarily because they serve as shared premises in deductive reasoning. If our assumption is valid, we should find that dispositional similarities have less effect on attitudes toward a proposition of policy when they are logically *irrelevant* to the position being advocated.

Berscheid's two-part experiment (1966) was concerned with irrelevant as well as relevant dispositional similarities and dissimilarities. Presuming that the relationship between similarity-dissimilarity and attitude change was mediated by degree of attraction to the source, she attempted to control for attraction by having a communicator depict himself as similar to the subject on one issue and dissimilar on another. In one experiment, a confederate either expressed agreement with the subject on an underlying value issue relevant to the object of judgment, and disagreement on an irrelevant issue, or the reverse. The communicator then attempted to influence the subject on one of the two issues. Relevant similarity was found to contribute to attitude-change; irrelevant similarity did not. In the other experiment, a "relevant-dissimilar" communicator and an "irrelevant-dissimilar" communicator took the same position as the subject on the object of judgment. Under the former condition the subjects *shifted away* from the position expressed by the communicator; in the latter condition shifts were not significant.

Increasing Attraction Toward the Source

As we have indicated, the relationship between similarity and attitude toward an advocated proposition is alleged to be mediated by attraction to, trust in, and respect for a source. Along with Moyer and Berkowitz (1970), we reviewed a large number of studies bearing on these credibility factors as mediators of the relationship between similarity and attitude change.[4]

---

4. We should point out that these mediating factors are not entirely distinct in the receiver's mind. As Asch (1952) observed long ago, impressions of the attributes of another tend to have spillover effects.

So far as attraction is concerned, there seems no question but that we tend to like and want to be with persons who are dispositionally similar although the evidence on membership-group similarities is less clearcut. In over thirty studies, Byrne and his associates (1971) have found that attraction of a subject to a bogus stranger increases as the proportion of the stranger's reported attitudinal similarities to the subject increases. *In general, we tend to gravitate toward dispositionally similar others, to assume that similar others like us, to exaggerate the degree to which beliefs, values, and attitudes are shared, and as a result of these interacting and complementary factors, to solidify our attraction to them.* Other things being equal, attraction does in turn seem to contribute to attitude change.

Several studies have compared the relative effects of dispositional versus membership group similarities on attraction. For example, are white people generally more attracted to a dispositionally dissimilar white person or to a dispositionally similar black person? Our conclusion from reviewing an admittedly ambiguous body of research findings on the "race versus belief" controversy is that for white subjects who are low in prejudice, race does not affect attraction; for white subjects who are high in prejudice, race exerts a greater effect than attitudinal similarity except where the degree of similarity is complete or virtually complete.

Increasing Respect and Trust Toward a Source

Attraction is one ingredient in a receiver's attitude toward a source; respect and trust are others; and from all accounts they are more significant determinants of attitude-change than attraction. Put another way, disagreement with someone we *like* (but do not necessarily trust or respect) should cause some *imbalance*, but disagreement with someone we *trust and respect* (but do not necessarily like) should cause a great deal more imbalance. Kelman (1961) has suggested that we are likely to *conform* with the recommendations of attractive sources so long as they remain objects of identification; we are more likely to *internalize* the arguments of apparently competent and trustworthy sources, however, and internalization involves a deeper level of attitudinal commitment than conformity.

In general, there seems to be a weak but positive relationship between attitudinal similarity and the factors of respect and trust and a still less dependable relationship between membership-group similarities and these same factors. Utilizing such indices of respect and trust as ratings of a stranger's intelligence, his or her knowledge of current events, and his or her morality, Byrne and his coworkers have not found attitudinal similarity to be related to respect and trust with anywhere near the consistency that they obtained for the similarity-attraction relationship. As Byrne put it in a letter to us (July 2, 1968):

As a general answer, the results are confusing. In some studies all [credibility] items are related to similarity and, in some, only the two attraction measures are.

Although no measures were taken of respect or trust, Brock's (1965) field experiment strongly suggests that these factors may be affected by similarity of experience, and that in some cases, at least, perceptions of shared experience may cause receivers to be persuaded. In Brock's study, paint store clerks were purported to have had experiences in the use of a product similar or dissimilar to the experience anticipated by a customer. After the customer had signaled his decision to purchase, the clerk either recommended a higher- or a lower-priced product of the same type, based on that personal experience. Although the study would have been more impressive had each of the clerks been required to employ both strategies alternately, all other potentially confounding factors seemed adequately controlled. Regardless of price, the clerk whose experience was similar produced significantly greater shifts in purchasing decisions.

Several researchers have directly investigated the relationship between membership-group similarities and the factors of respect and trust, and, in these studies, the common ground doctrine has faired weakly at best. In one study (Lambert, et al., 1960), French and English Canadians concurred in judging the readers of a passage in English as more intelligent and more dependable than the same communicators reading the passage in French. In another study (Anisfeld, et al., 1962), Jewish and Gentile subjects were led to believe, on the basis of dialectical cues, that the same passage was being read to them by either a Jewish or Gentile speaker. The subjects then rated the speakers on such traits as dependability, leadership, intelligence, etc. Gentile subjects tended to give higher ratings to the speaker they assumed was a member of their own group, while the overall ratings by Jewish subjects tended to present a balanced profile, reflecting neither higher nor lower in-group estimates. In one phase of still another study, Haiman (1949) compared ratings of a graduate versus an undergraduate student speaker on such dimensions of respect and trust as sincerity, fairness, and competence. Differences tended to favor the dissimilar, but presumably more prestigious, graduate-student speaker.

Common Ground and Source Credibility: Some Grounds for Questioning or Limiting The Common Ground Doctrine

So widely accepted is the principle of emphasizing common ground that exceptions to it may be of greater interest than the principle itself. Despite its widespread acceptance, it is by no means obvious that emphasis on communicator-receiver similarities will necessarily work to the advantage of the communicator. A distinguished professor of economics, speaking to a lay audience on the subject of international trade, might do well to stress differences between himself or herself and the audience. With the same audience and subject, a lay speaker who admitted sharing the audience's lack of expertise might well be graded high on candor, but not believed. This is but one example of an exception to the common ground principle. Now that we have made a case for establishing common ground, let us use our previously recommended "yes-but" technique to qualify and limit the generality of the doctrine. *Yes*, dispositional similarities increase attraction and have some effect on respect and trust. *Yes*, they serve as first premises when they are logically relevant, and this is important. *Yes*, it's true, similarity of experience does facilitate decoding and may increase credibility. *Yes*, membership group similarities often increase attraction. BUT . . .

The Source as a "Super-Representative"

A careful reading of our case for establishing common ground should suggest some reasons for qualifying the principle, at least as applied to membership-group similarities. Recall that a dissimilar graduate-student speaker was regarded as more competent and trustworthy than a similar undergraduate and that French Canadians evinced greater respect and trust toward an English Canadian speaker. Many other studies support the generalization that some perceived differences work to the advantage of the persuader. Bonchek (1967) found that a professional clinician influenced the sexual identification ratings of students to a greater degree than another student. Haiman (1949) reported that a speech attributed to the Surgeon General of the United States on socialized medicine exerted significantly greater influence on students than one given by a sophomore or by the Secretary General of the Communist Party. Differences between the latter two sources were not significant. Paulson (1954) found that, for male auditors, a dissimilar but more prestigious source was more persuasive. A similar finding was obtained by Aronson, Turner, and Carlsmith (1963), using T.S. Elliot as the dissimilar source.

What is the explanation for these discrepant findings? Note that effective nonmembers of a group tended to be different in the direction of greater competence, expertise, fairness, honesty, etc.; they all evinced greater respect and trust. Put this together now with the general rule that respect and trust are more significant determinants of attitude-change than attraction. The inescapable conclusion is that while similarities may lead to attraction, the relationship between membership group similarity and image of the source *is strongest for those source components least significantly related to attitude change. Put another way, it would appear that sponsorship by similar sources or emphasis on membership group similarities may not always have persuasive value and, in certain cases, may even be dis-advantageous. The persuader might do well to stress differences in the di-rection of greater status, expertise, objectivity, and so on.*

Does this mean that organizations seeking to effect persuasion should necessarily employ highly competent, trustworthy sources, no matter how distant they may appear to the receiver? Does it mean that individual per-suaders should always work to create psychological distance? Studies in which peers or slightly older children were found to be more convincing than adults (Berenda, 1950; Duncker, 1938) would seem to suggest that the "uncommon ground" principle can also be taken too far. Commenting on these studies, Hovland, et al. (1953, p. 50) speculated on the possibility that the term "expert" should be "broadened to include persons who have found adequate solutions to the problem an individual faces, even though in other respects, they may be no more experienced than he and very much like him." Their judgment is strongly supported by research on opinion leaders. These shapers of mass opinion have consistently been found to share dispositional and membership group similarities with the persons they influence. According to Katz (1957, p. 73), they are "in a certain sense the most conformist members of their groups—upholding whatever norms and values are central to their groups." Frequently they share mem-bership in the same primary groups with those whom they persuade. Sim-ilarities of age, occupation, and socioeconomic status have also been noted. Consistent with the experimental findings we have reviewed, the differ-ences tend in the direction of greater credibility. Klapper (1960, p. 34) has aptly described the opinion leader "as a kind of super-representative of his own group." Whether on matters of widespread interest or on issues of concern only to a specialized group, opinion leaders are generally more competent than their peers, more interested, better informed, more gre-garious, and have access to wider sources of information (Lazarsfeld and Menzel, 1963). Generally of the same class as those they influence on pub-lic affairs issues, they nevertheless tend to belong to higher levels of that class (Katz, 1957). People may be influenced by their elders, by persons of higher economic status, or by members of ethnic groups culturally stereo-typed as more prestigious, but the reverse is seldom true (Katz, 1957).

What emerges from this review is that persuaders should be similar to the audience, yes, but they should also be different in ways that in-crease their credibility. By what they say and do they should appear as superrepresentatives of the persons they are attempting to persuade.

Dissimilarities and the Self-Rejecting Audience

Along with many theories of psychological consistency, the common ground doctrine is predicated on the assumption that receivers will entertain a reasonably high estimate of themselves and of the groups with which they are affiliated. This is not always a valid assumption. Rightly or wrongly, many receivers are likely to be self-rejecting, if not as a general predisposition, at least as applied to specific topics and to *relative* differences between themselves and other groups. This may be why French Canadians rated English Canadians as more intelligent and more dependable. In the absence of cultural consensus or an objective basis for choosing between members and nonmembers, in-group identification would probably lead members to regard other members as more credible, but in this case a long history of second-class status had been internalized and confirmed by the French Canadians. An abundance of evidence suggests that other groups also tend to be self-rejecting. Bettleheim (1943) has vividly described the plight of some inmates in German concentration camps who, having been stripped of their egos, began to identify strongly with the norms and behaviors of their brutal guards. In this and in other cases, self-rejection may lead not only to greater trust and respect for out-groups, but to greater attraction as well. McGuire (1969) has assembled evidence from a variety of studies: of anti-Semitism among Jews; of greater hostility toward immigrants expressed by new than by old Americans; of the adoption of white stereotypes regarding Negroes by black college students.

Except among those who defend against feelings of unworthiness by consciously or unconsciously denying them, we would expect that self-rejecting individuals would be more receptive than most persons to a source who manifests and emphasizes dissimilarities. Blacks who exhibit racial pride should find black communicators both more attractive and more worthy of respect and trust. Blacks lacking such pride, however, should be more attracted to a black speaker but more influenced by a white communicator.

The phenomenon of self-rejection should by no means be confined to groups that have traditionally been accorded second-class status, at least on some topics. Topic-related self-rejection appears to be the psychological dynamic behind effective appeals to guilt and envy. The potential for eliciting feelings of guilt has been a powerful weapon in the hands of nonviolent civil rights groups, as when Martin Luther King appealed to the consciences of America from a stance of moral superiority. Affluent white liberals have been especially susceptible to these appeals. Oftentimes, the response to guilt or fear appeals is defensive. Overreactions—for example, to "promiscuity" among Hippies—may be a clear indication that receivers would secretly be glad to change places with the persons they castigate and may signal the possibility for conversion over an extended period of time. In these cases, at least, emphasizing guilt-producing or envy-producing dissimilarities may ultimately work to the advantage of the persuader, even though the receiver's initial response may be one of hostility.

Inauthentic Similarities

We understand that among upperclass youth in Great Britain, it was fashionable for a time to speak in a Cockney accent. The trend paralleled a tendency, begun here during the Beat generation and continued by Hippies, to emulate the colloquial style of blacks in the United States. How should parents have spoken to these young people? How should teachers have addressed them and politicians appealed to them? Shortly after he had been widely criticized for being callously indifferent to activist young people, Richard Nixon let drop that he could "dig" the opposition of many young people to the war in Indochina. Should Nixon have used the colloquial term, even though it was not characteristically a part of his vocabulary? Let us push the issue a bit further. Workers who become supervisers often become objects of suspicion in the eyes of their peers. One's promotion to a "boss" position is often regarded as a kind of treason. How should the person in such a position relate to these resentful former coworkers? As a boss or by acting like "one of the gang"?

Let us also consider the other side of the coin. Is it advisable to manifest or emphasize inauthentic similarities in order to impress persons in positions of authority? Sam Rayburn, the late Speaker of the House of Representatives, is said to have advised fledgling Congressmen to "go along" if they want to "get along." In this same spirit, should aspiring executives also follow that advice? Many new immigrant groups have been pressured to disguise distinctive linguistic, gestural, and dialectal patterns in the name of "assimilation," and now a similar movement is afoot to provide "dialect remediation" for the children of the black ghettos, as a device for making them more employable. To what extent should movements of this kind be encouraged?

Would that we had answers to all of these questions. We have raised them here only to suggest that emphasizing inauthentic similarities *may not always* be advisable, either on pragmatic grounds, or because of ethical considerations. As a practical matter, emphasizing inauthentic similarities may be unnecessary, especially as we have pointed out, if they are logically irrelevant to the proposition being advocated. Moreover, they may invite suspicions of ingratiation, manipulativeness, and condescension that may cause "boomerang effects" for the persuader. There is some evidence, for example, that workers tend to resent supervisors who attempt to be "one of the gang" and other evidence that at least some authority figures respect differences between themselves and their subordinates (e.g., Davis, 1962). This brings us to an ethical question—ultimately a pragmatic question as well—whether the gains on primary objectives from emphasizing inauthentic similarities are worth the negative *secondary effects*. Here we would only point out that by repeatedly emphasizing inauthentic similarities persuaders contribute to making conformity an end in itself and to an ultimately self-defeating end for themselves within their own society. Rather than searching for inauthentic common ground, persuaders might well stress genuinely shared similarities and then be sufficiently tolerant of differences with their receivers that the receivers may be led to do likewise in turn.

Still we should point out that we can be too suspicious of inauthentic similarities. The parent's use of a phrase distinctive to young people may be a way of saying that he or she likes them and cares enough about them to be willing to bridge differences, even to the point of becoming vulnerable to the charge of hypocrisy. The parent (or other communicator) may also be signaling a desire to grow, to change, to learn from his or her offspring. In this respect, many of us are so busy protecting ourselves against the charge of being phony or inconsistent that we fail to recall that the "genuine self" is not something we were born with but something we developed through learning and adaptation over a lifetime and therefore something we can change and improve in the future. *If emphasizing inauthentic similarities means betraying a personal facade that one no longer countenances, then we are all for it. If emphasizing inauthentic similarities means creating a facade to hide one's real dispositions, then we would have serious question about it unless it is absolutely justified by ends and circumstances.*

The Recalcitrant Receiver

Finally we should say something about the extreme version of the common ground doctrine, the position that all interpersonal conflicts would be reconciled if only men would recognize and emphasize the many basic similarities that bind them together. So apparently innocent and well-intentioned is this position that we are reluctant to attack it, yet beneath its guise of innocence there lurks a set of not so innocent assumptions and implications that require exposure. Underlying the position is the assumption that when people strike for better pay or riot because they have been disenfranchised, they do so because of "breakdowns in communication," failures to recognize that the interests of labor and management or of ruler and ruled are ultimately one and the same. In this sense there are no *real* problems between people, only *communication* problems. The implication is that a "co-active" strategy built on manifesting and emphasizing similarities will ultimately resolve these problems. The customary advice is then one of reason, civility, and decorum, of never threatening, harassing, cajoling, embarrassing, coercing, and so on, since threats to persons or property "only make things worse." What this often boils down to is an injunction to persuaders to emphasize commonalities, not only as a basis for winning acceptance of a proposition, but also to agree on the issue under contention—in short, to surrender. Surely, this is not what we have meant by common ground.

In place of the assumptions underlying the extreme version of the common ground doctrine, let us offer two assumptions of our own: (1) that people in positions of power do not always surrender that power willingly, even in the face of good arguments; and (2) that some interpersonal conflicts are *real* conflicts, not simply problems of communication. Put another way, no amount of emphasized similarities is likely to change the behaviors of some hostile receivers, and in the face of their resistance, persuaders may be justified in fighting for their rights. In our judgment, the extreme position that emphasizing similarities is a *necessary* and often *sufficient* condition for persuasion (rather than simply a *contributing* factor in most circumstances) reflects an "Establishment" bias. It tends to conceal or deny the existence of real problems experienced by "outs" and "have-nots," and adds insult to injury by leaving them open to criticism each time they protest, strike, demonstrate, etc., on grounds that they are communicating unethically or ineffectively. The real culprit here is often the person in a position of power who remains unscathed by the charge of poor communication.[5]

Given recalcitrant receivers, real problems, and impatience with slower processes, the persuader may well be justified in resorting to what we have called combative strategies of persuasion. Whether these strategies will necessarily be more *effective* than "co-active" stratagems is another matter. The important point for our purposes here is that in striking a combative stance, the persuader may well appear quite dissimilar from the audience and will have abandoned the common ground approach in many respects. We will be saying a good deal more about these issues in Chapter 13.

Summary

A major underpinning of the co-active approach to persuasion has been the doctrine of common ground. Rhetoricians for thousands of years have urged persuaders to emphasize commonalities as a precondition for bridging differences. These include dispositional similarities as well as membership-group similarities. In this chapter, we have examined the merits of the common ground doctrine while also expressing some reservations as regards its scope of application.

In offering a series of reservations, we have attempted to delimit the doctrine but not to discredit it. Nothing that we have said invalidates the principle that emphasizing interpersonal similarities generally contributes

---

5. For a more full-blown development of this position, see Simons (1972).

to persuasion. So far as authentic, relevant, dispositional similarities are concerned, our endorsement has been unqualified. In particular, we have suggested that persuaders appear not as ordinary members of the group, but as super-representatives; that on ethical as well as practical grounds they should be wary of emphasizing inauthentic similarities; that stressing membership group similarities may be especially ineffective with self-rejecting audiences; and that, in any event, establishing common ground is not a panacea for resolving genuine interpersonal conflicts.

How does the doctrine of common ground tie in with the theories of psychological balance that we presented in Chapter 5? We see a persuader's emphasis on common ground functioning in two ways with respect to psychological consistency: (1) as a wedge that can permit imbalance-producing ideas to "pass through" the receiver's defenses, and (2) as a means of aligning the source with imbalances that the receiver already experiences. In the first case, the persuader must create imbalance among receivers who are psychologically comfortable. Here, by appearing as one of them, at the same time emphasizing those similarities (or in some cases dissimilarities) that beget trust and respect, he or she may promote acceptance of positions that would otherwise be fought, avoided, or rationalized. Common ground functions in this context as a means for facilitating decoding and for preventing receivers from rebalancing psychological elements in unintended ways. The second function for common ground is more direct. In this case, receivers need only be reminded that they are not entirely happy about discrepancies between their wishes and their expectations, the means they use and the ends they accomplish. By indicating that they share or have shared these problems with the receivers, persuaders not only increase their perceived importance, they also show themselves to be at one with the receivers in a search for balance-restoring solutions. Quite obviously, these are important advantages to the co-active strategy of persuasion that should be abandoned only with receivers who have proven themselves to be recalcitrant.

Getting
Attention

William McGuire (1969) has observed that in their rush to suggest techniques by which the motivational defenses of receivers can be penetrated, the experts on persuasion frequently overlook the fact that receivers must first decode the message. He points out that many failures at persuasion have their origin at this stage of the communication process, rather than at what he calls the *yielding* stage. Already we have seen how many factors in persuasion are important precisely because of their effects on decoding. Receiver variables like intelligence, level of education, interest, and need for cognitive complexity are among these factors. So are message variables like magnitude of discrepancy, revelation of intent, and explicit vs. implicit conclusion-drawing. Clever though it may be, for example, to imply conclusions rather than stating them, the implicit approach does little good if the receiver is unable to deduce the persuader's conclusion.

In this chapter and in the next one, we focus on methods of facilitating decoding in speeches and essays. Here we consider factors that provoke attention and interest. Then, in Chapter 10, we move to an exploration of means by which receivers may be clearly oriented toward what the persuader has to say. Particular attention is given to the introduction of the speech or essay.

Level of Attention

As with the woman in the song from *Porgy and Bess,* attention is a sometime thing. Like a radio, it can be turned on or off; but unlike the radio, when we turn ourselves off there is not even a click. Oftentimes, in fact, listeners who appear to be listening most are listening least. We can see them now, seated at the front of our classroom, their eyes riveted upon us, and their heads in dateland, dinnerland, or dreamland.

Attention to a stimulus may be *focal, peripheral,* or *subliminal.* At the moment that you are reading the word "passage" in this passage, you are probably attending in one degree or another to hundreds of stimuli, some of them sharply focused, others of them vaguely sensed. Even the focus of your attention is likely to wander about among a number of stimuli at a rate so rapid that you hardly notice the scanning process. At a peripheral level, you are probably aware of an itch here, a car noise there, but only barely. Strictly speaking, a consciously attended stimulus—whether at the focus or the periphery—is a combination of minute stimuli that have had sufficient duration and intensity to penetrate into awareness. Below the level of awareness, at the *subliminal* level, are stimuli that some theorists believe produce extrasensory perception. It has been maintained that receivers can be influenced dramatically as a result of being confronted with subliminal stimuli; for example, that they will buy more popcorn in theaters that flash pictures of popcorn across the movie screen at the subliminal level. Whether this is so is very much in doubt, but it is known that these stimuli may produce measurable affective reactions and modify perceptual judgments. (Hawkins, 1970; McConnell, Cutler, and McNeil, 1970).

Attention is a starting point for persuasion, but it does not begin or end with the first utterances of a communicator and it may be as much dependent on nonverbal cues as on what is said. Since so much research on persuasion utilizes "captive" audiences, there is a tendency to forget that in "real-life" situations receivers can generally choose whether or not to expose themselves to a message. As any campus leader will affirm, it takes careful planning and real ingenuity to initiate and sustain interest in most campus causes.

The job of getting attention may begin months before a speaking event through whatever steps are taken to publicize it. For an important revival meeting, such as those that used to be staged by Dwight Moody before the turn of the century (Huber, 1955), preparations would begin with the announcement that the renowned minister would be coming to town. Excitement might be generated by construction of a huge tabernacle in the city to be visited and by the news that special trains had been arranged to travel to the site across specially laid tracks. Local ministers would be asked to build expectations for the revival meetings in regular Sunday services. Tickets printed in different colors (to increase feelings of status—the colors had no significance in themselves) would be distributed. At the start of the meeting, Moody would remain in the background until prayers were said and hymns were sung by local ministers and choirs. Only then would he appear to deliver his sermon. As he well knew, his first moments on stage were important, not only for the words he uttered but also for the impression that nonverbal cues would be making: his appearance, his voice, his gestures, the attention given to him by the dignitaries on stage, and so on. Efforts to maintain attention were continued throughout the speech, and even afterwards, as additional hymns were sung and meetings arranged for those who "saw the light."

Our strong suspicion is that academics can learn a good deal about attention-getting from advertisers, pitchmen, con artists, and the like, although they might not always want to recommend the techniques that have been used. Long John Nebel (1961, p. 51), himself a supersalesman, has described the pitch used by one Dr. Johnny Friendly, a circuit-riding huckster of yore whom he characterizes as "a frock-coated, silver-haired, mello-voiced messiah of the open road." Friendly's product was Imported Far East Chinese Salve but one would never know it from his opening gambits. The pitchman would first produce a box which he would show to the small town folk who gathered around him. Intimating that it contained a two-headed baby that he might show them before he left, he would then sell several silver dollars for a quarter apiece. Next he would display some exotic "Jeriboam jewels," all the while claiming that he could give these magnificent Oriental gems away because he was not a salesmen but a "manufacturer's representative" whose job was only to promote interest in a product at the company's expense.

"Word by word, confidence by confidence, the master medicine man built his pitch. The doctor arranged the "jewels" across the front of the table to glitter in the flickering flares. He told humorous stories, but all eyes were on the golwing "gems." Finally he was ready to "turn the tip" (make the sale). This would be easy if there were a few "live ones" or "go-fers" in the crowd—people ready to go or spring for the merchandise. But in any event the turn must be made smoothly and with conviction.

"Now neighbors," Dr. Friendly would say, "the real reason for my being here. You older men who have felt rheumatic pain, listen closely. You ladies, not so young as you used to be, who know the hurt of arthritis, this is important to you. All you girls who don't feel so very good when the moon is high, and you young bucks who go stiff in the muscle after a day of heaving hay—you listen. This is for everyone who doesn't like pain or ache. Man, woman, or child—and to tell the truth, it's pretty great for horses, too. Mild as milk, strong as a tornado. What is it called? Imported Far East Chinese Salve! That's it. Imported Far East Chinese Salve. Expensive? You're darn right it's expensive. They don't give away stuff like this. No sir, they don't. This half-pound size is twelve-fifty. Hold it, friends, take it easy. I don't mean that it costs you twelve-fifty—I mean that it costs me twelve-fifty. I have to make a little to live on, don't I, friends? That is, it would cost me twelve-fifty—if I was selling it. But I am not selling it! I am making it available at cost. Not my cost, but the manufacturer's cost of seven dollars. You hear me, friends, seven dollars for a large half-pound of the world famous Imported Far East Chinese Salve. But I must extract from you one important promise. If I make available to several of you this valuable medicinal product, then you must in turn do me a favor. You must promise to be a walking, talking advertisement for Imported Far East Chinese Salve. You must tell one and all about its marvelous therapeutic powers.

"And finally, to show that I represent a company that thinks highly of its representatives—and that's what you must promise to be—to those who are the leading voices for Far East Chinese Salve in this territory I will give one genuine, more than thirty-carat Jeriboam Jewel! That is what I said and that is what I mean. To those who are the largest representatives of this product in this town, those who take the greatest number of jars, I will give away absolutely free and with no hidden costs, one thirty-carat, genuine, authentic Jeriboam Jewel! Five for you, sir. Right. And three for you, young lady . . . eight over there . . . and . . ." (pp. 51–54).

James Winans (1917), a pioneer in the field of persuasion, once said that "What holds attention governs action." So difficult is the task of getting attention in a world bombarded by competing messages that modern day advertisers often seem to take his overstated dictum quite literally. To locate the stimulus patterns that are the most eye-catching, they have undertaken ingenious studies of pupillary eye-movement in relation to page placement and layout in magazines. Before a shampoo bottle is put out on the market, the bottle's size, shape, color, and feel may be subjected to psychoanalytic study of its symbolic significance to the consumer. Oftentimes, too, the modern advertiser borrows a page from the behavioral scientist and conducts field experiments on competing message alternatives. Given a choice between a jangling radio jingle and a humorous commercial, most of us would no doubt prefer the latter. Yet through empirical tests in several comparable cities, the Terminex people found their "Termites? Try Terminex!" advertisement increased sales far more than a series of comic conversations between two termites that we judged to be hilarious. Sometimes we suspect that the jangling jingles used in advertisements for headache pills do little more than cause the very headaches they purport to relieve.

Social science notwithstanding, the attention-getting techniques of modern advertisers are not all that different from those of the travelling pitchmen, as Long John Nebel has himself observed (1961, p. 54):

> And what is the format today? The announcer presents the entertainers and you watch and enjoy. Then the medicine man appears and makes the pitch. He tells you about the acid in your stomach, your unhappy blood, or melancholy muscles—and then he offers you something that has special ingredients that work "almost like magic." He tells you this is a special offer ("I may not pass this way again") and he pushes the giant economy size. Basically this is the same medicine show that rolled around the country for many, many decades, in an exciting and colorful carriage, behind the great white horses, driven by "Dr. John Friendly" or "Professor Brown" or "Chief Granite Cloud."
>
> And neighbors, if you think the last few pages have been interesting, well then—just move in a little closer; just a little closer, please, and I'll reveal to you the wonders of . . .

External and Internal Factors of Attention

What sorts of things get our attention? Strictly speaking, all attended stimuli are internal, but we may make a loose distinction between "out-there" and "in-here" stimuli—between the sighting of an apple and the pangs of hunger, for example. Internal stimuli partially affect what external stimuli we attend to. If we are extremely hungry, for instance, we may pay little attention to a lecturer or may even misperceive some of his or her words as referring to food. External stimuli may also affect what internal stimuli we attend to. In one case the job of the persuader is to provide external stimuli that will call to mind favorable stimuli within the perceptual field of the receiver.

Some external stimuli have the power to "demand" or "compel" attention, whether we want them to or not. Let us briefly note some of the characteristics of these stimuli and then consider internal determinants of attention to "out-there" stimuli.

External factors.

1. *Intensity.* Generally speaking, a loud noise or bright color will be more arresting than a sound or sight that is less intense.

2. *Contrast.* The use of italics in this text is one method we use to set off important concepts from those we consider less important, but imagine if the entire book was written in italics.

3. *Novelty.* What is *nunsnɐ* (try looking at the word in italics upside down) may attract attention, and because we expect the the familiar, you may not have noticed that there is an extra "the" in this sentence. On this dimension, external and internal determinants are inextricably interrelated.

4. *Movement and change.* Other things being equal, we are likely to notice a moving car more readily than a stationary car. If we are travelling on the open road, we are more likely to be drawn to a change in scenery than to the same old stuff.

5. *Repetition.* A slight imperfection in a phonograph record may go unnoticed until it has been played half-way through, and we may then begin to ignore it once we become accustomed to it. This is a typical pattern for repeated stimuli of low intensity.

Internal factors. There was a music professor at Swarthmore College who, every April, took his students outside to teach them how to smell the Spring. Thereafter, his students were sensitized to stimuli that had simply gone unnoticed in the past. They had developed a *set* or *readiness* to respond. Each of us is likely to have somewhat different attention sets as a result of training, different interests, needs, wants, and so on. There are, however, certain internal determinants of attention to "out-there" stimuli that are fairly constant from individual to individual.

1. *The vital, the immediate, the tangible, the near at hand.* Some things become so salient or important to us at times that nothing else counts. When receivers are immediately and directly threatened with loss of security or safety, for example, no gimmicks are needed to get their attention. The problem itself will be of sufficient interest.

2. *Drama, conflict, suspense.* However repelled many campus administrators were by the confrontations of the late sixties, none could ignore them. Most exciting news events have an aspect of theater about them.

3. *Exploration, mastery, fulfillment of curiosity.* These are some of the *competence* motives that we discussed in Chapter 5. As White (1959) has suggested, we will endure a great deal simply to be able to explore, to learn, to grow. The persuader's job may be to vitalize and channel an already existing *need to know.*

4. *Resolution, completion, rebalancing.* Countering, but in some ways complementing, the need for competence is the desire to reduce imbalance. As we suggested in Chapter 5, when imbalance is intolerable we are likely to search for balance-increasing information. At a sort of primitive rebalancing level, we are even drawn to configurations of visual stimuli, such as geometric forms, that "fit together," offer "closure," form a "good gestalt" (Krech and Crutchfield, 1948). If they do not "fit" we tend to make them fit at a perceptual level.

5. *Release, escape, enjoyment.* The attention-getting value of humor is well known. It is also true that we are drawn to materials that offer escape from or vicarious support for fears, frustrations, and hostilities.

6. *Minimal effort.* Unless otherwise motivated, we are likely to give greater attention to front-page news than to news on page three, to keep the television set tuned to the same channel, and so on.

Attention to Nonverbal Cues in Communication Situations

The foregoing lists of external and internal factors of attention may be readily applied to communication situations. Here we will focus on the nonverbal cues that receivers are likely to attend to in face-to-face interactions.

Bodily cues. Public speakers were at one time advised to gesture and posture mechanically, as though they were actors in a highly stylized Restoration drama. Much more important than obedience to mechanical formulas is the communicator's capacity to transmit *warmth, enthusiasm, vitality, poise,* and *directness.* It turns out that these intangibles are often communicated through subtle, nonverbal cues, and that they are frequently picked up at a peripheral or even subliminal level by the receiver. Although "the whole body speaks," as Charles Woolbert has said (1916), one's eyes and mouth are especially revealing.

Nonverbal cues may supplement verbal cues but they may also belie them. Erving Goffman (1959) has commented on two observational techniques used by the Trobriand Islanders, a people who habitually tend to mask their own feelings while being highly curious about the feelings of others. If guests were visiting, the host would peek out at them through a window as they stood by the door, their faces not yet "arranged" for polite conversation. Once a conversation had begun between two persons, the wily Trobriand Islander would watch the unguarded expressions of the nonparticipants who formed an audience for the exchange rather than focus on the faces of the participants.

Many observers have commented on the way John F. Kennedy's hands could be eloquent even when they rested motionless upon a podium. In sharp contrast to the Kennedy style, we can recall a press conference at which Richard Nixon was giving a highly capable performance in a manner so relaxed that one could only marvel at his confidence. Suddenly the camera zoomed to a close-up of the hand that Nixon was not using for gesturing. It was clenched tightly, belying the "cool" image he had sought to promote.

In Chapter 3 we briefly referred to research which bore out the reliance receivers place on nonverbal messages when they are inconsistent with the verbal. Indeed, Mehrabian (1971, p. 43) has concluded from experimental research that when liking of a source is at issue, the relative impact of discrepant verbal, vocal, and facial cues is approximately as follows: Total liking = 7% verbal liking + 38% vocal liking + 55% facial liking.[1]

The importance of facial and gestural cues was borne home to us in an experiment conducted by a former student. Saul Fox (1974) has hitchhiked in 40 states and several countries, and has read widely in the research literature on nonverbal communication. In general, his readings helped reinforce his earlier impressions that there are more effective ways of hitchhiking than those traditionally employed. Accordingly, Fox asked friends to hitchhike back and forth along the same thoroughfare, and to

---

1. Mehrabian's *Silent Messages* (1971) provides a useful introduction to experimental research on nonverbal communication, and so does Argyle's (1969) *Social Interaction*. We are especially enamored with the work of Erving Goffman (1959, 1961, 1967) whose writings on impression management combine the theoretical rigor of the social sciences with the observational sensitivity of great novelists.

"... more important than obedience to mechanical formulas is the communicator's capacity to transmit warmth, enthusiasm, vitality, poise, and directness." *Top left:* Photo of journalist I. F. Stone. *Top right:* Photo of anthropologist Margaret Mead (by Walter Steinbacher). *Bottom:* Photo of Senator Edward Kennedy (by Art Braitman). (All photos courtesy of *Temple News*.)

alternate randomly between Method A, the traditional method, and Method B, the "scientific" approach. Here were the major characteristics of his Method B:

1. H (the hitchhiker) stands at 45° angle to road, rather than traditional 90° angle. H is now in psychological path of motorist and cannot as easily be dismissed as an irrelevant object.

2. Rather than the traditional rigidly extended arm, clenched fist, and protruding thumb, H extends arm loosely and presents raised hand and open palm (as when getting attention in a classroom) toward oncoming traffic. This relaxed, friendly posture begs recognition and bespeaks desire for familiarity. Moreover, it acts as larger "flag" than the closed fist and calls attention to his facial area, where the greatest amount of persuasion occurs.

3. H seeks eye contact with motorist and attempts to maintain its duration beyond the conventional "glance" period by emitting an eyebrow flash at the moment contact is made. If eyes lock onto each other for more than a brief instant, motorist becomes psychologically responsible for making some type of response to H. Raised eyebrows serve as an additional "asking" cue and may even put the question of a ride on a level beyond that of simply asking for one by communication of a presumption of assent to a previously asked question. In other words, it may signify, "Is it true that you are willing to give me a ride?".

Method B proved significantly more effective. Whereas the H had a 27 percent chance of getting a ride within ten minutes using the traditional method, he (or she) got a ride within ten minutes 52 percent of the time using the scientically based approach.

Vocal Cues. By comparison to message content, probably too much attention is paid by student speakers to characteristics of their own voice and diction. As with bodily cues, vocal cues should not *distract* from the message, and by well-placed pauses and vocal emphases, they may increase a listener's interest, but most of us are overly sensitive to them. The keys to good vocal delivery are variety adjusted to content and a willingness and capacity to express feelings. Pitch, rate, and volume should vary with what is said and the variety should be exaggerated if the speaker is not accustomed to emoting in front of others.

Contextual Cues. Some time ago, we conducted workshops for persons whose job it was to interview claimants for unemployment compensation. The official doctrine of the Bureau was that since unemployment insurance is something workers purchased like any other insurance (indirectly in this case), the claimant is entitled to respect, a patient and fair hearing, and full information about his rights. A visit to a branch office proved otherwise to us. Not that the interviewers were necessarily unfriendly; they did not have to be. Contextual cues were sufficient. The office was a huge room with metal cages separating the bulk of the office staff from the claimants. At each step in the filing process the claimant was obliged to stand in long lines. In some communication situations, interaction among members of the audience is of distinct benefit to the persuader. A multitude of voices shouting support for the speaker may help make neutral bystanders into enthusiasts, for example. Not so in this situation. Each face in line reinforced gloom in the others. The gray walls, the signs with their lists of prohibitions, the printed forms whose legal jargon even the interviewers could not translate into intelligible English—all of these bespoke indifference and even hostility to the claimant more effectively than any words spoken by the interviewers.

Applying Factors of Attention to the Verbal Message

There are a number of ways that attention to a verbal message can be sustained, all of them involving applications of the external and internal factors of attention that we listed earlier. The language of a speech or essay should be alive, vivid, exciting, robust. Main ideas can be made memorable by use of slogans, mottoes, aphorisms, alliterative and rhythmic statements, and by parallel phrasing. Better to say "Don't put a cold in your pocket," suggests Stuart Chase (1953), than to say "Handkerchiefs are unsanitary." Supporting materials may be made more interesting by rounding out statistics, paraphrasing long or dull quotations, using analogies, contrasts, and metaphorical language, and by judicious use of humor.

Persuaders can profit from examination of the attention-getting devices used by weekly news magazines such as Time and Newsweek. The difference between the same story in a newspaper and in a news weekly is often a difference between news made brief and news made interesting. The newspaper reader wants the essential facts first and the details later, if at all. Hence, the job of the reporter is to present the "four W's and the H" of an event in the lead paragraph: the Who, What, When, Where, How, and sometimes the Why. The readers of a news weekly ask for and get a writing style that captures attention from first page to last. In addition to the other devices we have named, the weeklies make heavy use of *factual illustrations*. A factual illustration contains the same "four W's and an H" that are found in the first paragraph of a news story, but it adds concrete and vivid *imagery*. A one paragraph statement about an assault by the Egyptians on a Kibbutz in Israel might become a story about two children and the horror they experienced, complete with names, family background, minute descriptions of their living quarters following the attack, a full paragraph of the sounds made by the mortars, and so on. Because it builds drama, conflict, concreteness, novelty, and many other attention factors into the story, the factual illustration is probably the most reliable attention-getter that persuaders may utilize. It is a picture painted with words.

The overall structure of a message can contribute to a listener's or a reader's interest. It is especially effective to *think with* the receiver: to identify a problem and then think with him about its causes; to identify a general tendency and then reason with him to a determination of its effects; perhaps to identify a series of proposals and then examine each systematically in light of generally acceptable criteria.

Most important of all are the opening statements made by the communicator. Even in a "captive" audience situation, and even when the social context is conducive to careful listening, the speaker must often fight his way past apathy and competing stimuli. Consider the job of a visiting speaker at a campus convocation. At first the listener makes a *physical* adjustment. Books are placed under the seat. A sweater is pulled off. The student leans on one buttock, then decides to try the other. Next comes the *social* adjustment, and this may go on for several minutes. "Hi Freddy. Hi Louise. Guess who I saw at the cafeteria this morning . . ." In the midst of all this is the guest lecturer, all but forgotten on the stage.

Because so many stimuli compete for attention at the beginning of a speech, some persuaders use startling statements or other shock techniques. Our favorite story concerns Robert G. Ingersoll, the notorious nineteenth century lecturer, who, as a confirmed agnostic, had a penchant for engaging crowds of Fundamentalists smack dab in the middle of the Bible Belt. Ingersoll was not much for common ground techniques. After an open-air crowd had been assembled he would turn to his audience and say, "If there is a God, let him strike me dead in forty seconds." And thereupon he would pull out a large stop-watch, gaze up at the sky, and begin a verbal countdown. Wary of the inevitable thunderbolt, the crowd would back away and Ingersoll, with a triumphant smile, would yell, "What's the matter? Don't you trust God's aim?"

In fairness to the faithful, let it be said that the religious leaders of Ingersoll's day were no slouches at the same shock techniques. A contemporary of Ingersoll's, Henry Ward Beecher, visited many of the same towns as the infidel. Among his favorite topics for a sermon was blasphemy. It was therefore quite a shock to one of his church audiences when he bellowed out: "Goddamnit, it's hot!" After sufficient disbelief was registered, Beecher leaned forward and said, "Yes, ladies and gentlemen, that's the phrase I heard from the mouths of many of you as I ambled through your town this afternoon."

A list of "openers" for a formal speech should probably include the startling statement, the humorous anecdote, the pithy reference to the audience or the occasion, the factual illustration, and the brief quotation.

Generally speaking, whatever is said should not only get attention but should also help to *orient* the receiver, a subject to which we turn next.

Summary

Utilizing attention-getting materials is important throughout a speech or essay but *vital* at the beginning. Among the external or environmental factors that compel attention are: (1) intensity, (2) contrast, (3) novelty, (4) movement and change, and (5) repetition. Attention is also determined in part by internal factors; we "set" ourselves to receive some stimuli and to ignore others. Internal determinants of attention include: (1) the immediately vital, (2) drama, conflict, suspense, (3) exploration, mastery, curiosity, (4) resolution, completion, rebalancing, (5) release, escape, enjoyment, and (6) that which requires minimal effort.

Because the receiver ordinarily gets but one opportunity to hear a speech (written materials can of course be reread), capturing audience attention becomes especially crucial. Fortunately, the speaker need not rely on words alone. The oral and physical delivery of the speech can build on the external and internal factors of attention named above. Most important in delivery are the attitudinal cues one transmits. The speaker should appear warm, enthusiastic, alive, direct, and confident.

Strongly recommended in this chapter was the use of the factual illustration, both as a form of support for the thesis of the presentation and as a means of creating attention and interest. Other standard "openers" include the startling statement, the humorous anecdote, the quotation, and the reference to the audience or occasion.

10
Orienting Receivers

"First I tell 'em what I'm gonna tell 'em. Then I tell 'em. Then I tell 'em what I told 'em."

Why follow the example of the minister quoted above? Why not simply "tell 'em?" Although persuaders may sometimes wish to conceal intent or mask illogic behind a veil of ambiguity, at least some understanding of a message is almost always prerequisite to acceptance of an advocated proposition. Orienting an audience by telling them what you are going to tell them is the starting point from which audience understanding may be achieved. It is especially important when speeches or essays are long and complex, when there is minimal opportunity for audience feedback, when readers cannot be expected to reread written messages carefully, and when they must have the "big picture" first if the bits and pieces of a message are to fit together for them later. An appropriate orientation makes the job of "telling them" that much easier. Once receivers have been "told" in detail, it is then generally expedient to *summarize* the message by placing it in a compact verbal package tied by an appealing verbal ribbon.

The task of orienting receivers belongs primarily to the *introduction* of a formal speech or essay. Although it is presented first, the final draft of the introduction should not be prepared until the communicator has a firm notion of what he or she will say in the body and conclusion of the message. Our experience has been that persuaders tend to make conclusions too long and introductions too short. They are anxious to delve into the meat of their presentations, and once into it, they have difficulty wrapping it up succinctly.

Orienting Functions of the Introduction in Speeches or Essays

Along with establishing common ground and getting attention, the introduction should ordinarily perform a number of orienting functions. Depending on the audience, persuaders may accomplish several of these functions by means of a single sentence, or they may omit some entirely, or they may be required to elaborate on each of them at great length.

Indicating subject and position. Receivers should generally have a clear notion of *what* it is the communicators will be discussing, and *why*. As we indicated in Chapter 7, communicators run a risk if they leave their position implied or conceal it until the very end of the message. Not knowing what communicators are driving at—where their logic is heading—receivers may misperceive intent or lose interest in the message. Generally speaking, positions should be stated *in terms of the reaction desired from the audience*. As precisely as possible, persuaders should indicate what they want receivers to believe, feel, desire, and do, even if the details of the proposal must await exposition in the body of the message. Rather than saying: "I think something should be done about auto-insurance costs," one might say: "I'm here to ask your support for a 'no-fault' insurance plan for our state that will cut your auto-insurance costs by at least 20 percent."

Indicating what will be excluded. The counterpart of revealing what will be talked about is indicating what will be excluded from your speech or essay. Statements of subject and position are often misleading until they are qualified. Continuing with the example just given, the speaker might say: "Now, I'm not here to advocate just any 'no-fault' plan—certainly not the kinds of plans that many have rightly called unconstitutional, those that deny citizens the right to sue a company for extra damages in cases of severe injury or death. What I'll be asking you to support is the 'Denenberg plan' put forth by former Insurance Commissioner Herbert Denenberg of the Commonwealth of Pennsylvania. . . ."

Offering definitions of key terms. What is "no-fault" insurance? On almost any controversial issue such as this one, there are bound to be key terms that need defining. The most familiar form of definition is the *dictionary definition*. It names something, puts it into a category, and then separates it from other members of that category. "No-fault" insurance might be defined as "a system of auto insurance that provides immediate and automatic payment, regardless of fault, to all persons who suffer injuries or property damage in auto accidents."

In and of themselves, dictionary definitions tend to be too abstract. Oftentimes it is helpful to supplement them with other definitional types such as *definitions by example and definitions by contrast*. Persuaders should recognize, however, that in adding color to a definition they may also be introducing bias. Definitions should ordinarily be unobjectionable. They should be regarded as "ground rules" that must be accepted by the "players" if the "game" of communication is to proceed. To supplement the dictionary definition, the communicator might proceed as follows:

> Let's suppose that you run into someone on a rain-slicked highway who failed to signal that he was turning. Who's at fault? Chances are that if anyone claimed injury the case would go to court under the present system. Lawyers for the victor would get one-third to one-half the settlement fee; the victor would get the rest. "No-fault" insurance largely eliminates the role of the lawyer. Injury and property settlements are based on formulas and they are awarded directly to both parties. The idea is to reduce insurance premiums by reducing legal fees, at the same time providing increased protection to drivers.

Offering background information. In a five-page essay or a ten-minute speech, a persuader might well want to introduce historical or other background material before entering upon the body of the message. How many states have "no-fault" insurance at present? How did the idea originate?

What other states are considering it? These are just some of the factual questions that might be discussed briefly in the introduction.

Offering acceptable first premises. In addition to the other benefits to be derived from emphasizing source-receiver commonalities on underlying assumptions, values, or other first premises, these attempts at establishing common ground serve to orient receivers to the types of arguments that will be presented later. Like the vacuum cleaner salesperson in an earlier example, the advocate of "no-fault" insurance might set the audience up by suggesting general criteria against which any system of auto insurance should be evaluated. Later in the speech or essay, he or she might re-introduce these criteria and show that the system compares favorably with others.

Offering analyses and explanations. Chances are that the body of a speech or essay on "no-fault" insurance will begin with an indictment of the present system: its manifest evils, and the reasons that it must be replaced rather than simply repaired. Such an indictment assumes that there is something wrong with the system in principle; that the alleged evils stem from the *very nature* of the system rather than from particular practices associated with it. But what is "the system"? What are its underlying principles? Oftentimes, the basic principles of the system are not at all obvious. An indictment of the present auto insurance system might well be preceded by analyses and explanations of its underlying principles—its inherent assumption, for example, that every accident is caused by a "guilty" party to the accident.

Let us consider another example. Suppose you favor a "right-to-work" law, a law on the books in several states that prohibits compulsory unionism. Suppose, further, that you believe many unions to be corrupt. What is inherently or intrinsically wrong with compulsory unionism? Is it the fact that unions are corrupt? Certainly not. Many unions that require membership as a condition for continued employment are not at all corrupt. Analysis of the system must proceed further lest a receiver decide that corruption needs to be eliminated, but not compulsory unionism. Part and parcel of compulsory unionism, however, is the principle that even if a union is corrupt, workers *must belong to it without choice*. An explanation of this subtle but important distinction in the introduction of a speech or essay would go a long way toward making later indictments believable. We shall comment further on the place of logic in persuasion in Chapter 11.

Previewing the structure of the speech or essay. A well-organized speech or essay is likely to increase source credibility and be easier to understand (McGuire, 1969). Although the research evidence on the relationship between organizational structure and comprehension is surprisingly incon-clusive (Thompson, 1967), until additional evidence is forthcoming it is undoubtedly safer to assume that a tightly structured message will be better understood than a poorly structured one. Minimally, a well-organized speech or essay subordinates minor ideas to major ideas, avoids overlapping, divides (and subdivides) material in terms of a single significant principle, and allows ideas to flow in a logical progression.

Whatever the structure of the body of a speech or essay, it is generally useful to preview it in the introduction. The communicator might indicate that he or she will first discuss evils in the present system, then their causes, and then their solutions. Or he or she might preview only the first section of the body of the message. The communicator might identify the three or four inherent evils that will constitute his or her indictment of the present auto-insurance system and the order in which they will be discussed. Previews provide attention sets; they key receivers in to main ideas and their logical relationships.

Orienting Material in the Conclusion of a Speech or Essay

By the end of the introduction the receiver's orientation should be well along but it should continue throughout the remainder of the message. Additional terms may need defining, other sections previewed, further explanations provided, and so on. Particularly helpful are *transition statements and internal summaries*, devices that help to remind receivers about what has been said and where the message is heading. Also quite helpful are striking *main headings* that serve to introduce new sections of the message.

Generally speaking, the body of the speech or essay should be organized for maximum psychological impact, rather than in terms of aesthetic symmetry or other aesthetic niceties. In this connection, Cohen (1957) has provided experimental support for the age-old principle that problems should be presented before solutions, rather than the other way around. Two messages were constructed on the subject of grading and presented to equivalent audiences. One message first discussed the evils of the present system of grading and then suggested that grading on a curve would be a welcome reform. To the other group, Cohen's proposed reform was presented first, followed by a discussion of the problems. The need-plan order was found to be more effective, both in the short run and in a measure of delayed effect, presumably because it appeared more interesting and was better understood.

Also affecting decoding in the body of a speech or essay is the order of presentation of strong versus weak arguments. Let us suppose that a persuader has five reasons for opposing gas rationing, and that two of them are especially strong. Should the persuader use an "anticlimax" order on the assumption that placing the strongest arguments first will stimulate interest and encourage comprehension? Or should a "climax" order be employed on the assumption that what is heard last is remembered best? This issue has engendered considerable controversy and stimulated a good deal of research. Unfortunately, there are no clearcut answers to the question other than that arguments presented in initial and final positions are more readily decoded than those in middle positions (Karlins and Abelson, 1970). On the basis of his research, McGuire (1969) gives a slight edge to the anticlimax order, and, from our own experience, we are inclined to go along with him.

Under any circumstances, the introduction and body of a speech or essay should avoid stilted language. Above all, the communicator should refrain from utilizing what some have called "tool" language. In this chapter, especially, we have introduced a number of "tools" for getting attention and orienting receivers. These devices are most effective when communicators do not call attention to them—when they do not say, for example: "Here is a preview of the body of my speech . . ." or "Let us pause for an internal summary. . . ."

Orienting Material in the Body of a Speech or Essay

Just after he had finished his now famous "Checkers" speech in 1952, Richard Nixon broke down and cried. Here he had delivered a masterful defense against charges of political corruption, providing evidence and arguments that could turn near certain political defeat into a moment of personal glory. Yet the speech called for telegrams of support and Nixon, poor fellow, had neglected, in the conclusion of his speech, to tell viewers where the telegrams should be sent.

Fortunately for Nixon, the telegrams went everywhere, and in sufficient abundance to insure his political future. Other persuaders are not as fortunate, however. A chief failing of many persuasive presentations—especially those that require overt action from receivers—is that they do not tell receivers in clear enough terms just *how* they should act. Oftentimes it is necessary to provide quite explicit instructions for action in the conclusion of a message—in the case of a radio advertisement, for example, to provide a telephone number or an address and to repeat it several times.

Even where overt action is not called for by the persuader, it is extremely useful to wrap things up for receivers, to remind them of the basic points made in the presentation and to restate the persuader's overall position.

Decoding and Forgetting

One of the best-established findings from research on persuasion is that the effects of messages tend to wane over time as their contents are forgotten. Partly for this reason, the persuasive campaign enjoys clearcut superiority over the "one-shot" effort at persuasion. The campaigner is able to reorient the audience on each subsequent occasion, making good use of the principle of *repetition with variation*. As long ago as 1933, Peterson and Thurstone (1933) found that several commercial films on a subject presented to the same audience were considerably more effective than any one of them alone. More recently, Zajonc (1968) and Tucker and Ware (1971) found that mere exposure to the name of an attitude object increases the likelihood of favorable attitudes toward that object. Zajonc was even able to induce more favorable reactions toward certain nonsense syllables merely by showing them on a screen more frequently than other nonsense syllables used in his study.

Surprisingly, some loss of memory by receivers may work to the advantage of persuaders, especially if they have low credibility. Hovland and Weiss (1951) and Kelman and Hovland (1953) have found that receivers tend to disassociate source and message over time. As a consequence, messages by high credibility sources exhibit the characteristic decline in effect, but messages by low credibility sources show what they call a *sleeper effect*. Recipients of these messages become more favorable to the advocated proposition as time passes. This is probably one of the reasons that commercial advertising—patently insincere though it may be—is often effective. The radio disk jockey who promoted Rizzo's Pizza may have had low credibility, but six months later the message lives on with an existence independent of its original source.

One Final Comment: The Issue of Selective Decoding

As we suggested in Chapter 3, decoding is selective. Incoming messages do not penetrate to awareness if they are of low intensity, and they are screened out or distorted if they are too complex or too disturbing. This does not mean that all nonsupportive information is screened out or distorted. As Festinger (1957) and others have theorized, our interest in learning and adapting is too great to prevent us from tolerating some dissonance-increasing information. For many years, it was accepted as a truism that receivers actively seek out supportive information and actively avoid nonsupportive materials. Recent research and careful reinterpretations of past research have cast doubt about the universality of this doctrine. In the first place, selectivity is far less pronounced than was formerly supposed (Sears and Freedman 1967). Second, while there is correlational evidence that people who agree with a particular position also tend to expose themselves to materials which support it, this evidence does not conclusively demonstrate that support for the position is the *cause* of exposure. In many cases reviewed by Sears and Freedman (1967), factors such as sex, religion, and social class were also correlated with exposure and provided equally good or better explanations of why supporters of a position were disproportionately represented in a given audience.

Although it may well be that people do selectively seek supportive information, the evidence is far less clear that they selectively avoid non-supportive material (McGuire, 1969). There is fairly convincing evidence that receivers are selective once they have made a choice or commitment in favor of something (Brehm, 1956; Insko, 1967), but far less evidence in situations where no decisions have yet been made.

One factor does consistently emerge from the research on selective decoding, and that is that people attend and strive to comprehend material that appears to them to serve a useful, practical purpose (Adams, 1961; Freedman, 1965). If persuaders want unpleasant material to be decoded, the evidence seems to indicate that they can achieve that goal if they show audiences that they have a vested interest in receiving it.

Summary

The task of orienting receivers belongs primarily to the introduction of a formal speech or essay. Ordinarily, the receiver should learn in the introduction what the communicator will be discussing and why. It is generally wise to indicate not only your subject but also your position; and not just what will be covered, but also what will be excluded. Definitions should be fair and reasonably complete. Other optional materials for the introduction include: (1) background information, (2) analyses and explanations of difficult concepts or systems, (3) statements of first premises, and (4) previews or partitions of the body of the speech or essay.

To increase comprehension, persuaders should use colorful main headings and transitions or internal summaries between main sections of the body of the message. Dry language, including "tool" language, should be avoided at all costs.

The body of the speech should be organized for maximum psychological impact. A need-plan order is generally preferable to a plan-need order; an anticlimax order slightly preferable to a climax order.

In speeches, especially, it is important to build on the principle of repetition with variation. The conclusion of the speech should, at a minimum, restate main points and, where action is called for, indicate specifically and repeatedly the steps to be taken.

Building
a Case:
Logic,
Psycho-Logic
and
Rhetorical
Proof

What does it mean to "prove" a case in persuasion? Does it make any sense to speak of politicians "proving" to their constituents that tax increases are necessary, or of sales representatives "proving" that their company's product should be purchased, or of ministers "proving" that there is life after death? If so, is case-building in these typically rhetorical situations the same as case-building on scientific issues—a matter of assembling evidence and arguments according to the logician's "laws" of logic? Or is logic pretty much irrelevant to persuasion?

Intuitively, we know that "proof" of sorts is provided in rhetorical situations. We say that a persuader has "proven" or established a case when we find it plausible, probable, or even compelling. No doubt all of us have had the experience of being unable to sustain a previously held conviction in the face of a persuader's withering arguments.

Yet, if "proof" is provided in typically rhetorical discourse, we also know that it is not quite the same as "proof" in scientific discourse. What, then, are the differences? How are the "laws" of logic, as prescribed by logicians, related to the principles of "psycho-logic," identified by balance theorists (see Chapter 5)? Most important, what are the implications of these similarities and differences for persuaders?

In this chapter we shall be discussing these questions in some depth as we present our own conception of proof in persuasion as *distinctively rhetorical*. Before developing our position, we shall want to consider further what criteria logicians use to determine logical adequacy. If nothing else, these criteria constitute departure points for identifying distinctive characteristics of rhetorical proof. But more significantly, they constitute standards which readers might well wish to apply when functioning as discriminating receivers of persuasive communications.

Having briefly presented our position, we shall then want to explore its practical implications. Here we shall offer advice on case-building dealing with such issues as the following:

1. Whether and when to reveal underlying premises;

2. How problem-solution arguments can be adapted to different types of audiences;

3. How claims of logical consistency or inconsistency can be used to establish value principles;

4. How to blend reason and emotion, logic and "psycho-logic" in deductive arguments;

5. How to select psychologically compelling evidence;

6. How to deal with potential objections or other potential sources of resistance by receivers.

Characteristics of Logical Conclusion Drawing

Whether in drawing analogies, making causal inferences, applying a general principle to a specific instance, or concluding that such and such is likely to happen, the hallmarks of logical-conclusion drawing are clarity and consistency. These criteria may be applied to the two basic types of logic, briefly discussed in Chapter Two, *deductive logic* and *inductive logic*.[1]

Deductive Logic

A conclusion may be said to be *deductively* valid when it follows from clearly stated premises. It is invalid (i.e., fallacious) when the conclusion does not follow. Let us look at a number of valid and invalid triads, known as *syllogisms* by logicians.

1. All men have four legs.
   You are a man.
   Therefore, you have four legs.

Every syllogism has a major premise (e.g., all men have four legs), a minor premise (e.g., you are a man), and a conclusion. Strictly speaking, the deductive validity of a conclusion has nothing whatever to do with the *material* truth of either the conclusion or its premises. Syllogism 1 is valid despite the fact that its major premise and conclusion are untrue. In fact, the syllogism would be just as valid if its key terms were reduced to letters having no meaning:

All A's have B.
X is a case of A.
Therefore, X has B.

Here, on the other hand, is an example of a syllogism that would be invalid, even if all three sentences were true:

2. Dogs have four legs.
   Fido has four legs.
   Therefore, Fido is a dog.

Or, to put the syllogism in more abstract terms:

All A's have B.
X has B.
Therefore, X is a case of A.

---

1. An excellent introduction to principles of logical consistency is found in Ehninger and Brockriede (1963), *Decision by Debate*. See, in particular, their discussion of the Toulmin model (beginning in Chapter 8) which is especially instructive in showing how deductive and inductive logic are related to each other.

Without getting into technicalities (a comprehensive discussion of formal logic is outside the province of this book), we ask the reader to consider the possibility that Fido—despite its name—*may be* a cat or a giraffe or even a table! This can be illustrated with circles:

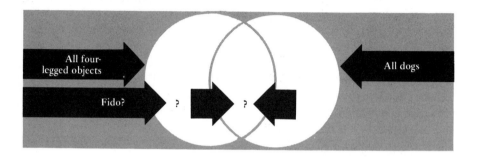

The foregoing are known as categorical syllogisms. They involve applications of categories to cases. There are three other forms of the syllogism, illustrated below, known as the *hypothetical* ("if-then") syllogism, the *disjunctive* syllogism, and the *conjunctive* syllogism, respectively.

3. If methadone treatments work in New York, they should work in Cleveland.
   Methadone treatments work in New York.
   Therefore, they should work in Cleveland.

4. Either Joan is guilty or she is innocent.
   Joan is guilty.
   Therefore, she is not innocent.

5. Joan could not have been in New York and Cleveland at the same time.
   She was in New York at time X.
   Therefore, she was not in Cleveland at time X.

Deductive arguments may be used in a number of *types of reasoning*. Example 3 happens to illustrate a type of reasoning known as *reasoning by analogy*. An analogy asserts or implies that the relevant similarities between two objects, events, or ideas outweigh their relevant dissimilarities. In this case, the analogy rests on the assumption of significant similarities between New York's addiction problems and Cleveland's.

The syllogism may also be used in *cause-to-effect* reasoning, and in *effect-to-cause* reasoning, both illustrated below:

6. Only if you eat spinach will you become strong.
   You will not eat spinach.
   Therefore, you will not become strong.

7. Eating spinach is all that you need to become strong.
   You have eaten spinach.
   Therefore, you have become strong.

Finally, syllogistic deductions may be used in arguments from sign:

8. Whenever there is smoke, there is probably fire.
   I see smoke.
   Therefore, there is probably a fire.

Examples 3 through 8 are valid syllogisms, but it is easy to imagine that with slight modifications they could be made into invalid syllogisms. In general, the rules of deductive reasoning are quite exacting. Here are some tests of valid categorical syllogisms:

- Is the syllogism confined to three basic terms (e.g., in syllogism 8, the basic terms are "smoke," "fire,' 'and "I")?
- If premises are qualified by such words as "some," "many," "few," is the conclusion similarly qualified? For example, it would be invalid to conclude that because Jones lives in a *mostly* Democratic state, he is *definitely* a Democrat.
- Is what logicians call the *middle term* ("men" in example 1) found in both premises, and absent from the conclusion? Note that in example 2, this principle is violated.
- If both premises are affirmative, is the conclusion affirmative? If one of the premises is negative, is the conclusion negative? (Both of the premises may not be negative.)

Thus far, we have treated each syllogism as though it existed in isolation. It is possible, however, to join syllogisms together into a structurally consistent whole, the conclusions from one syllogism serving as premises for others. Those familiar with geometry are aware that it constitutes a structurally consistent *system* of logic. The mathematician's deductions are tied together by a set of basic axioms and postulates. The same axioms and postulates are used in a number of syllogistic deductions, and, for this reason, no single conclusion is inconsistent with any other conclusion. A logically coherent system of logic has a Christmas tree shape; it is consistent along *vertical* and *horizontal* dimensions. In the following diagram, there is vertical consistency between levels 1 through 4 and horizontal consistency among propositions at any single level:

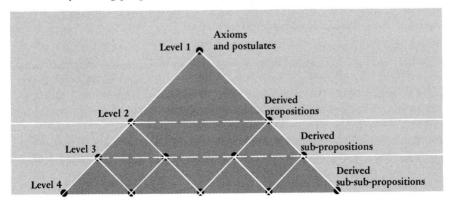

Good scientific theories *approximate* the structural consistency of purely mathematical systems. If they are structurally consistent, there is a vertical chain of syllogisms linking abstract and specific assertions: concrete hypotheses deriving from general hypotheses; general hypotheses deriving from theorems; theorems deriving, in turn, from higher-order premises and resting ultimately on what philosophers call *first principles.* Scientific theories are also dependent on *inductive proof,* as we shall see, but they have the triangular, Christmas tree shape of mathematical systems. It is for this reason that the basic principles of quantum theory could suggest hypotheses about a wide variety of phenomena—from atomic energy to electricity—or that the disparate behaviors of primates and lower-order animals may be explained by the single set of principles found in Darwin's theory of evolution.

Inductive Logic

Whereas deductive reasoning is concerned with establishing the validity of a conclusion, inductive reasoning is concerned with establishing the material truth of a claim—usually one that will serve as a premise in deductive arguments. Strictly speaking, induction is perfect only when all cases are available for study. Consider the generalization: "All students in this class are left-handed." If all students in the class were present, and if the observer had some way of establishing that all were left-handed, he or she could readily assert the truth of the claim.

Rarely, however, are all cases available for study—either in a physical sense or in a practical sense. When a pollster seeks to determine whom the citizenry will vote for in a national election, it is necessary to survey a sample of potential voters and to infer the characteristics of the population from knowledge of the sample. Such an inference is known as an *inductive leap.*

The rules of induction are imprecise. At best, induction establishes the probability of a generalization, not its certainty. Still, it can be said that one is following the rules of inductive logic if one's evidence is reliable and representative, and if one's generalizations are limited to the evidence presented. Evidence consists, essentially, of two kinds: *facts* and *opinions.* Here are some criteria for evaluating evidence:

1. *Factual Evidence*
Are the factual claims true? Are they verified or verifiable? Are they accurately stated? If they are second-hand reports—from reporters or witnesses, for example—is the source reliable, unprejudiced, competent? Did they observe the event? Were they physically and mentally capable of accurate reporting? Were they detached and unbiased?

Are the facts representative? Are they universal or isolated instances? Do they cover a sufficient period of time? Are they sufficient in number to establish the inference? Are there no significant negative instances?

2. *Opinions*

If the opinions of alleged authorities are cited, are they reliable authorities? Are they persons of wisdom and experience? Better still, have they engaged, competently, in research on the subject? Are they free from prejudice and exaggeration? Are they logically consistent?

If opinions are cited as reflections of popular sentiment, rather than as those of authorities, are they reliable, trustworthy, representative, etc.?

Some types of inductive claims are inherently more supportable than others. It is one thing to conclude from an election poll, for example, that a plurality of the voters favor candidate X; it is quite another thing to predict the outcome of the election on the basis of that poll. And if predictions about masses are unreliable, imagine how difficult it would be to predict the vote of each individual who comprises that mass.

The problems of induction are enormously increased when the inference called for is a causal generalization. It might be established with a high degree of probability that political power is highly correlated with wealth, but does this mean that political power caused wealth or that wealth caused political power? Perhaps some third factor, such as intelligence, caused both.

Inductive generalizations are even more problematic when, as is so often the case with major premises, it is not clear what the premise means in operational terms. Consider the assertion: "Most people are illogical." Unless the term "illogical" is defined in such a way that the category can be applied to cases (we hope we have done that in this section), there is no way of supporting or refuting the assertion. Assertions often appear to be clear, but upon careful examination they turn out to be circular statements or metaphysical statements which no amount of evidence can prove or disprove. In these cases, as we shall point out, intelligent argument can only proceed after there is agreement about definitional criteria. In a sense this is true of all inductive generalizations; they are true or false only in terms of agreed upon standards. Still, there is a vast difference in testability between saying "She is sitting in a chair" and "She is one of the most beautiful people in this city."

Problems of the kind we have been discussing have prompted scientists to give careful consideration to definitional problems, have led them to develop and test measuring instruments with extreme care, and have sparked the development of sophisticated survey and experimental methodologies. Even then, scientists deliberately understate their conclusions rather than overstating them. Although their inductive generalizations may be imprecise, they still provide a standard in terms of which the inference-drawing of others may be compared.

Induction and deduction work hand in hand. In logical reasoning, conclusions beget premises and premises applied to one case are shown to be applicable to others. Evidence is used to establish the material truth of premises, and deduction is used to derive conclusions from those premises. The general is tied to the specific and the specific is tied to the universal. As we shall see, these are not always easy standards to live by.

Logic and Psycho-Logic: The Concept of Rhetorical Proof

One school of philosophers has long maintained that the rules of logic are none other than the laws of human thought; hence, to persuade the receiver, one need only present arguments in a logically compelling manner.

Unfortunately, this extreme position has found little support from psychological research. At best, the evidence suggests that people seek psychological consistency (i.e., balance, dissonance-reduction, etc.), or, to use Abelson and Rosenberg's (1958) apt phrase, they obey the rules of their own *psycho-logic*. As we saw in Chapter 5, the means by which they achieve psychological consistency often reveal their illogic. Here, for example, is a classic illustration of prejudice, reported by Gordon Allport (1954, pp. 13–14):

> Mr. X: The trouble with Jews is that they only take care of their own group.
>
> Mr. Y: But the record of the Community Chest shows that they give more generously than non-Jews.
>
> Mr. X: That shows that they are always trying to buy favor and intrude in Christian affairs. They think of nothing but money; that is why there are so many Jewish bankers.
>
> Mr. Y: But a recent study shows that the percent of Jews in banking is proportionately much smaller than the percent of non-Jews.
>
> Mr. X: That's just it, they don't go in for respectable business. They would rather run night clubs.

If the rules of logic, as laid down by logicians, do not correspond to the laws of thought, then why bother discussing logic in a textbook on persuasion? There is, indeed, a temptation to succumb to one extreme in the process of rejecting another: to conclude, as some S-R learning theorists have done, that persuasion is a matter of simple conditioning, or to decide that people are governed solely by their emotions.

Precisely because it rejects both extremes, our own position is difficult to convey. In general, we believe that logic has an important place in persuasion, but that it must be adapted to the needs and capacities of receivers, and to the distinctive nature of the rhetorical situation. Specifically, our position is based on the following judgments and observations:

1. Whatever they may say to others, persuaders should satisfy themselves that the propositions they endorse are logically defensible. Moreover, on

ethical grounds, they may well decide to be *ineffective,* at least in the short run, if being effective means being grossly illogical.

2. Logic and emotion are not antithetical. It used to be thought that a persuasive appeal could either be logical or emotional, as if logic and emotion occupied separate boxes in a receiver's psyche. Now it is recognized that an effective argument may be 100 percent logical and 100 percent emotional. An argument for seat belts, for example, may appeal to the emotion of fear while being inductively and deductively sound. Although it is true that logical reasoning may be impaired under conditions of high emotional arousal, moderate degrees of arousal may actually facilitate thought. In any case, it is not necessarily "illogical" to be emotional.

3. The logician's rules of logic and people's own rules of "psycho-logic" are not entirely incompatible.

4. The need for psychological consistency includes the need to feel that what we believe at least *appears* logical. Were this not so, we would never invent rationalizations to account for seemingly illogical cognitions. What *appears* logical may also *be* logical by a logician's standards. If we value the jury system, it is usually because we also value justice and believe that the jury system is the best way of achieving justice. If we accept the advice of others, it is often because it is sound advice. If we buy a Ford instead of a Chevrolet, it is usually because we have evidence to support our preferences. These are examples of psychologically balanced cognitions, which, to some extent, at least, also meet the logician's tests of logical adequacy.

5. *Within limits,* as we indicated in Chapter 5, all of us may *tolerate* psychological consistency for the sake of logical consistency. A farmer desires rain but looks up at the sky and concedes that it will not rain. An old man longs for immortality but concedes that he will die. In most cases, sanity compels us to recognize that where there is a will, there is not always a way.

The foregoing principles underscore the importance of logic in persuasive discourse, but now let us introduce some additional principles which, while not inconsistent with the former, enormously complicate the picture.

6. The ethical obligation to be logical in persuasive discourse may have to be balanced against other considerations. If being illogical is the only way to accomplish highly desirable ends, the persuader may well be justified in departing from standards of logical adequacy.

7. As we argued in Chapter 2, even the philosopher and the scientist are not exemplars of pure logic. If this is true of philosophers and scientists,

certainly it is true of ordinary persuaders and their audiences. Consider some of the differences:

a) Typically, persuasion involves propositions requiring *judgments* rather than demonstrations; it deals with what seems plausible or wise rather than what seems certain or true.

b) Compared with most scientific and philosophical discourse, the issues argued by ordinary persuaders are *emotionally involving* rather than *emotionally neutral,* and they are often debated in *highly charged* settings.

c) The situation imposes *time* or *space* limitations on what can be communicated.

d) Persuaders and receivers must usually act on the basis of *fragmentary* information.

e) Compared to scientists and philosophers, most "ordinary" receivers have greater *intellectual limitations.*

f) The truth of an inductive generalization or the conclusion from a logical deduction may be too *unpleasant* or too *threatening* to be tolerated. In these cases, we may *rebalance* cognitions by various means of *psychological fight* or *flight,* many of them discussed in Chapter 5. Some of these may work to the advantage of the persuader but others may be counterproductive.

Given what we have said thus far, it follows that the persuader must neither ignore the rules of logic nor rely on them exclusively in persuading others. Needed, as Aristotle observed long ago, is a conception of *rhetorical proof,* one which, while not disdainful of logic, envisions its role *within the framework of the rhetorical situation and of the receiver's needs and capacities.* Such a conception must recognize the central role of psychological balancing and rebalancing in the persuasive process. At the same time, it must recognize that what is psychologically consistent may also be logically consistent in some ways; furthermore, that receivers may tolerate some degree of psychological inconsistency. Rhetorically proven arguments may be defined as those arguments by persuaders on questions of judgment which lay audiences accept as plausible.

Our intention in the remainder of this chapter is to offer guiding principles of rhetorical proof and to indicate in a general way how they may be adapted to different audiences. Drawing heavily on Aristotle, on the modern-day balance theorists, and on bits and pieces of other formulations, we hope to show how persuaders may utilize logic, but also depart from the strictures of logic, in changing or in reinforcing attitudes, in dealing with critical audiences or with sympathetic audiences.[2] Since what one receiver finds plausible another may find implausible, the principles that we offer must necessarily remain imprecise. Nevertheless, it should be possible for the persuader to glean applications from these principles for his or her own uses and, at the very least, to gain greater awareness of the factors that bear upon audience acceptance of advocated propositions.

Principles of Rhetorical Proof

Recall that a good scientific theory comes close to being a structurally consistent *system* of thought. It offers not one syllogism but an interconnected *chain* of syllogisms. Its propositions or theorems stand, not in isolation, but, rather, are tied together by explicitly stated higher-order premises and first principles. Any single proposition or theorem suggests logically deducible hypotheses. Since each hypothesis derives, ultimately, from the same set of premises, it, too, is logically consistent with other hypotheses. Finally, each hypothesis is tested against rigorous standards of evidence. When the hypothesis is confirmed, it constitutes an argument in support of the theory.

By strict standards of deductive and inductive logic, the propositions that persuaders customarily endorse would be as well defended as the propositions or theorems in good scientific theories. Figure 11.1 illustrates such a case diagrammatically. The arrows outlined in black are designed to indicate vertical consistency at all levels of discourse. Using the scientific model as a basis for comparison, let us see how rhetorical proof may incorporate, but also depart from, the scientist's standards of logical adequacy.

Rhetorical Proof and Underlying Premises

Just as scientific theorems are based on higher-order premises and first principles, the propositions of judgment (belief, value, or policy) which persuaders defend are also based on underlying premises. These consist of basic values, beliefs, and definitions.

Take, for example, the proposition of policy that physicians should not practice abortion. Theoretically, this proposition could be linked in a logically consistent vertical chain to higher-order beliefs and values. Lead-

---

2. The relationship between formal logic and the persuader's "practical" logic is addressed periodically in such journals as *Philosophy and Rhetoric* and the *Quarterly Journal of Speech*. We are especially indebted to Jesse Delia (1970) whose essay on foundations of rhetorical proof opened our eyes to relationships between traditional Aristotelian theory and modern-day balance theories.

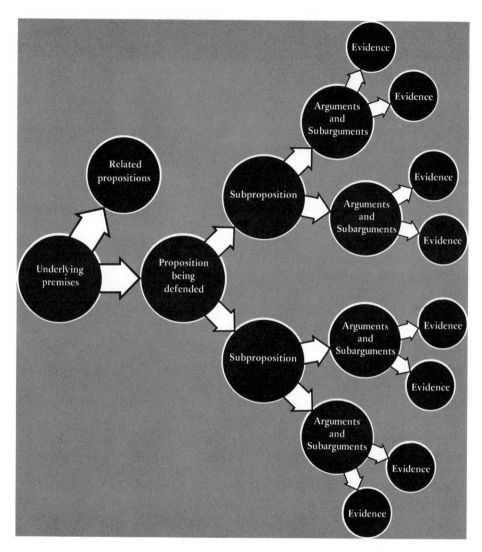

Fig. 11.1 Diagram of a logically consistent case

ing to the advocate's conclusion might be the following interconnected syllogisms:

If there is willful destruction of a fetus, there is willful destruction of life.
Abortion is willful destruction of a fetus.
Therefore, abortion is willful destruction of life.

Physicians should not willfully destroy life.
Abortion is willful destruction of life.
Therefore, physicians should not practice abortion.

These are but two syllogisms in the vertical chain, but we can easily imagine the possibility of other links. If asked why it is that physicians should not willfully destroy life, we might reply that no one has that right. And if asked why we hold this value, we might reply that all life is sacred. And if pushed further, we might say that the Bible tells us so. And if asked why we believe the Bible, we might say it is the word of God. And if pushed even further, we might say that our belief in God rests, finally, on a first principle—faith.

To what extent must persuaders justify the propositions they endorse by explicitly stating and defending each underlying premise? As a general answer, we can say that so elaborate a defense is seldom necessary and, when necessary, is rarely effective.

As is emphasized in our chapter on common ground, persuasion ordinarily begins from shared premises; i.e., from agreement on basic values, beliefs, and definitions. If, in opposing abortions, the persuader anticipates disagreement on the premise that physicians should not willfully destroy life, it might be advisable to search for a different justification, one with which the audience would be more likely to agree. Barring that possibility, the underlying premises might have to be defended, but it will generally be possible to find an earlier stopping point than the point at which, in the foregoing illustration, the persuader was obliged to defend the authenticity of the Bible. Chances are that if even this premise required justification, the persuader would be unsuccessful no matter how logical his case. This is the experience that persuaders generally have with extremely hostile audiences or with others whose world views diverge sharply from their own. With such audiences, it is imperative that persuaders not take anything for granted. Using the "yes-yes" or "yes-but" techniques described in Chapter 8, they may inch along from premise to premise, perhaps not even articulating the main proposition until the very end, or even waiting until a second or third meeting with the audience to confront them on highly controversial issues. In general, our most basic beliefs and values are well protected by *defense mechanisms*, some of them listed in our discussion of rebalancing alternatives. These include such relatively "mild" and commonplace devices as wishful thinking and rationalization and such severely handicapping mechanisms as regression and complete avoidance. We can better understand the difficult persuasive task of psychoanalysts when we recognize that they try to get patients to alter basic self-perceptions and expectations in the face of highly resistant defense mechanisms.

Audiences vary in terms of the degree to which they are aware of their own underlying premises, but in general it can be said that for all of us there exists a large storehouse of basic beliefs and values which remain unexamined unless called to our attention by persuaders (Bem, 1970). If asked whether objects continue to exist after we have stopped looking at them, most of us would reply that "Of course they do, it goes without saying." This is one of those "facts of life" that we take for granted. As Bem (1970) points out, there are many such unexamined premises comprising our most basic beliefs and values. Most of us are not consciously aware of the faith that we have in the validity of sensory experience. Nor, on the other hand, are we likely to decide that a mountain gets smaller as we move away from it, despite the fact that its image on our retina changes. We retain faith in perceptions such as these, even as they distort immediate sensory experience.

Other unexamined beliefs have to do with the trustworthiness of what Mead (1934) has called *significant others*. Much of what we know comes to us second-hand. Yet, in childhood, at least, we are not likely to question the authenticity of authority figures; their facts become our facts. Even as adults, most of us rely on some persons or reference groups whose judgments remain unquestioned. Moreover, we seldom question cultural truisms. Practically all of us have been sufficiently acculturated that we cannot imagine other ways of representing time than by our culture's calendar and our culture's clock. Nor are we likely to question the correctness of our grammar or other sociolinguistic conventions such as "This is my foot."

Still other unexamined premises take the form of stereotypes, categorical generalizations that we fuse together as "fact" from sensory impressions and accepted second-hand reports. We tend to associate stereotypes with racial or ethnic generalizations, but the belief that Iowa is flat is a stereotype to many, as is the notion that snakes are dangerous or that effeminate persons are homosexuals. One wag defined a "category" as "a set of differences which, for a particular purpose, don't seem to make a difference." Chances are that we are not always mindful of the differences, and that is when categories become stereotypes.

In general, persuaders may capitalize on unexamined premises without necessarily making them explicit. They may appeal to unquestioned authorities, rest their cases on cultural truisms, or imply stereotypes, yet not state them categorically. Instead, they may speak in what Aristotle called *enthymemes*. An enthymeme is a syllogism with one premise (usually a shared premise) left implicit. Since the deductive logic of a case rests on a series of syllogisms, we can appreciate how tedious it would be to state all of them formally. The informal style of the enthymeme permits us to take verbal shortcuts. Instead of stating the two syllogisms which might have comprised only a small part of the opposition to abortions, the persuader might have said, in enthymematic form:

Since abortions involve willful destruction of life, it's my position that physicians should not commit them.

Premises in syllogisms need not be stated when they are self-evident, when stating them would be linguistically awkward or artificial, or—and this creates fits for ethically minded rhetoricians—when stating them would give the ghost away. Especially since so many of the receiver's own premises are unexamined, it is often effective to conceal controversial premises or to leave them implicit.

Under what circumstances is it helpful to call attention to unexamined premises? Generally speaking, it pays to do so when one wants to arouse an already sympathetic audience or when one wishes to challenge an audience-held premise that is believed to be vulnerable. We shall discuss both of these points later in this chapter.

Besides unexamined premises, what other shared premises can persuaders appeal to? One function of premises is to *motivate* receivers: to activate their attention, interest, and emotions. With this function in mind, some rhetoricians have compiled lists of *motive appeals*, compilations of biological and acquired needs and wants that can be incorporated into premises and linked to propositions being defended. Here, in no special order, is one such list:

Cleanliness	Mothering	Ambition
Hunger	Power	Curiosity
Pleasure	Domesticity	Creating
Rest	Activity	Devotion
Health	Sex	Status
Protection	Reproduction	Independence
Belonging	Conformity	Dependence
Fear	Anger	Property
Cooperation	Acquisition	Gregariousness
Conflict	Exploration	Sympathy

The trouble with such lists is that they provide no index of which values might be most important at any one time to a particular audience. We value dependence, but also independence, cooperation, but also conflict. The list itself is insufficient.

An improvement upon merely listing motives or values is Maslow's (1943) *hierarchy* of motives. Maslow lists the following motives in rank order: (1) physiological needs (i.e., food, water, sleep, etc.); (2) safety needs (i.e., stability, order, freedom from violence or disease, etc.); (3) belongingness needs (i.e., giving and receiving love, affection, etc.); (4) esteem needs (i.e., recognition, respect from others, self-respect, etc.); (5) self-actualization needs (i.e., genuine fulfillment, realization of potential, etc.).

Maslow argues that although many human acts are multimotivated, we must often postpone some gratifications for others, and cannot even begin to think about satisfying some needs until we have satisfied others. His hypothesis helps to explain why American propaganda campaigns have often failed when directed at third world peoples. Frequently, they have defended the values of democracy and freedom to people preoccupied with safety and physiological needs. Conversely, his hierarchy may help to explain why so many young people cannot accept the premises of their parents. Reared as children in more affluent surroundings than were their parents, accustomed to having physiological and safety needs satisfied, they are not as preoccupied with these needs and care more about self-actualization.

In the final analysis, neither a list of generally accepted needs or wants nor a hierarchy of motives is a substitute for careful analysis of particular audiences and contexts. Here we believe that Merton (1946) was right in stressing the importance of *symbolic fitness.* The choice of appeal must "fit" well with the nature of the audience, the topic, the speaker or writer, and the setting. For example, although financial gain is ordinarily a compelling motive, it would not have been appropriate for Kate Smith (a "mother-figure") to appeal to financial gain in selling war bonds (a symbol of patriotism) to housewives during her radio marathons at the time of World War II. Better to play on appeals to sacrifice and patriotism, and this she did. An appeal to financial gain would be more appropriate coming from the Secretary of Commerce in an address to business executives, especially if the government bonds were being sold during peacetime.

Maslow's need hierarchy refers to ends or objectives. Still other generally held premises have to do with *optimization values,* standards which most of us apply in judging alternative ways of achieving our objectives. These are especially helpful to persuaders since they suggest the types of subpropositions they may use to defend any or all propositions of policy. Because of their special importance, we shall take them up separately in some detail.

Rhetorical Proof and Optimization Values

Whether in making decisions about our personal lives or in appraising social or political systems, most of us adhere to fairly rational standards of judgment. How we apply those standards is something else again, as we shall see.

Generally speaking, we *assume the desirability of existing policies or systems unless a need for a change has been demonstrated.* Car owners do not change their cars unless they perceive something wrong with the old car. Physicians do not operate unless the patient has a defective respiratory system, circulatory system, or other system. In the same way, most of us would not endorse basic changes in welfare laws unless we believed there was something seriously wrong with those laws. Existing policies and systems are presumed "innocent" until proven "guilty."

The second of our optimization values is that *the solution must fit the need*. Rather than buying a new car when the old one gets a flat tire, we are more likely to repair the flat tire. Rather than operating, physicians may prescribe medication to heal a minor respiratory problem. Rather than getting rid of welfare policies on grounds that they are inefficiently administered, we are likely to prefer keeping the policies but getting at the inefficiencies. On the other hand, a proposed policy should not, if possible, fall short of the need. If we need a car and if the old car is wrecked beyond repair, we feel compelled to get a new one. If medication will not suffice, the physician may decide to operate. If inefficient administration is inherent in the present welfare law, we may feel obliged to support a new law.

The third of our optimization values is that, *compared to other possible policies, the proposed policy must offer the most advantages and the fewest disadvantages*. A brand new Porsche might handily solve our driving needs, but its cost may be excessive by comparison to other alternatives which might also solve our driving needs. An operation might be successful, but it might lead the patient into bankruptcy. A new welfare law may be desirable, but it may not be as practical and workable as other possible counterplans.

The foregoing appear to be rational decision criteria and, indeed, they do suggest subpropositions in terms of which the persuader may rationally defend propositions of policy. In arguing for a change of systems or a major repair of systems, persuaders should show that problems exist which are caused by present policies, that their solutions will remove or reduce these problems, and that, compared to other solutions, theirs are superior. In arguing that present policies should be retained more or less as is, defenders of the status quo should take opposite positions on these issues. Their first obligation is to refute objections to the present system by showing how, in principle and in practice, it does the job. Second, they may defend the subproposition that proposed changes would not solve existing problems nearly as well. Finally, they may argue that proposals for change would introduce new and greater evils. Table 11.1 presents an illustration of the underlying premises and subpropositions that might be used to support a proposal for change.

We said earlier that although people's optimization values are rational, the way they apply these standards often reveals their irrationality. In the first place, the conditions that we label as problems or nonproblems are often branded as such on highly questionable grounds. As a result of the auto manufacturers' careful indoctrination campaigns, our old car can constitute "a problem" simply by being two years old. In the absence of substantive criteria for choosing among aspirins, mouthwashes, or premium beers, the advertiser may promote a product, and we may buy it, on the basis of snob appeal, color preference, or because it's "lighter." Nor are these tendencies confined to advertised products. In the face of glaring in-

Table 11.1   The Overall Structure of a Case: An Illustration

Underlying Premises (not necessarily stated explicitly)	
Definition	Foreign aid is a system of grants and technical assistance to other countries.
Basic Values	Well-being of others; efficiency; support from other nations.
Optimization Values	Systems should be changed if they create serious problems or fail to solve them; proposals for change should remove or reduce existing problems; compared to other possible policy alternatives, proposals for change should offer maximum gains at minimum costs.
Main Proposition	The United States should replace its system of bilateral foreign aid with a system of aid channeled through the United Nations.
Subproposition	I. The present system of bilateral aid is in need of change. A. The recipients of our aid are growing poorer. B. Bilateral aid is inefficient. C. Recipient nations have turned against us.
Subproposition	II. A system of aid channeled through the United Nations would remove or reduce these problems. A. Under such a system, recipient nations would grow richer. B. Such a system would be more efficient. C. Recipient nations would give us support.
Subproposition	III. Compared to other solutions, aid through the United Nations would offer maximum gains at minimum costs. A. Halting all aid would create even more poverty and bitterness. B. Aid through the World Bank would be less efficient. C. Aid through the United Nations would not be impractical. D. Aid through the United Nations would not prevent us from exercising control over our aid.

justices, the general public may label the injustices as "nonproblems" and the protestors who complain about them as "problems."

Second, most of us tend to prefer short-range solutions to long-range solutions. Oftentimes, we seek gratification of immediate needs at the expense of more basic, enduring needs. This is not simply a matter of whim or caprice, as in impulse buying. In his important study, Platt (1971) has shown that one riot commission after another since 1919 has called for a "two-pronged" approach to ghetto riots: getting at the miserable conditions of life that spawn them, and developing more effective techniques of riot control. Commensurate with its labeling of the rioters as "problems" and the injustices as "nonproblems," the public has generally pushed for and gotten better riot control while rejecting solutions which might get at basic causes.

Finally, the human being tends to be, at best, a "satisfier" rather than an optimizer (H. A. Simon, 1947). Rarely are we in a position to even consider all of the possible policy alternatives and when we are, we tend to choose not the best solution but the "least worst" solution nearest at hand. In part, this is due to defective inductive or deductive reasoning, problems that we shall take up later in this chapter. Even the best of us, however, appear unable to cope with the enormous complexities of contemporary life. Consider, for example, the problem of setting up a budget for a college or university. Ideally, such a procedure would involve the following steps: (1) agreement by responsible authorities on the organization's goals; (2) specification of goals and subgoals and translation into measurable criteria; (3) quantitative weighting of goals and subgoals; (4) determination of costs per unit of goal accomplishment by all alternative means; (5) allocations of available funds on the basis of demonstrated need and potential for goal accomplishment. What this means is that every school in a college and every department in a school would have to justify proposed budgets in relationship to need and potential for goal accomplishment, relative to other programs in other departments and schools. Weiss (1973) points out that this is rarely if ever done, and we can easily understand why. Imagine how difficult it would be to get "responsible authorities," each with vested interests, to agree on a rational system for weighting goals and subgoals. Imagine the problems involved in translating into dollar figures the benefits to be derived from teaching poetry. Imagine the frustrations involved in attempting to decide on a rational basis how much money chemistry should get in relation to poetry. And even assuming that these activities could be accomplished rationally, imagine the task of selling these decisions to schools and departments whose budgets might be cut drastically thereby. Instead, administrators in universities and other organizations "muddle through," a term used by Braybrooke and Lindbloom (1963) to refer to the way budgetary decisions are actually made. Goals remain deliberately vague as a way of justifying any or all decisions. The existence of a program becomes its own justification. Knowing this, administrators use the "leg in the door" technique to give programs an existence. Deals are made, preferences are determined by favoritism, and satisfaction of the organization's personnel becomes more important than achievement of the organization's goals.

Side by side, then, we have reason mixed with unreason: individuals opting for rational decision criteria but applying them in ways that make them the victims of artificially created wants; telling themselves that they want the most for the least but settling for solutions that postpone rather than solve problems; certainly not making decisions in a wholly rational manner on complex issues. There are, of course, individual differences on these matters. Some knowledgeable persons do apply intelligent performance standards in purchasing autos, rather than buying color or style or status. Some budgets have greater rational justification than others. To one degree or another, however, and especially on complex issues, the real is likely to fall short of the ideal.

Recall now that persuasion deals in appearances and takes place on the receiver's terms. Applied to policy propositions, this means that the persuader must *appear* to satisfy the receiver's optimization criteria. Rhetoricians have labeled the issues of need, workability, and relative superiority of proposals as *stock issues* because they apply to all propositions of policy. They provide a convenient framework for organizing the body of a persuasive speech or essay.

Within that framework, however, messages may vary considerably. With intelligent, well-informed, critical audiences, the case for a policy proposition is unlikely to succeed on most topics unless it approaches the rigor of scientific discourse. With unintelligent, less formal, uncritical listeners or readers, especially those who are initially sympathetic, the persuader may get by with a considerably less defensible case.

Generally speaking, persuaders need not deal systematically with all stock issues and subissues, and they need not mention policy alternatives which the receivers themselves have not considered. On most propositions of policy, there are likely to be some issues and subissues on which both are agreed. Even the most critical receiver would probably grant that there is an overpopulation problem in India, that the pollution problem is serious, or that the electoral college system is antiquated. Given the speaker's time limitations or the writer's space limitations, it would be inefficient to dwell at length on these issues. This does not mean that they should ignore them entirely. They should point out areas of agreement as a way of building rapport. They should work from areas of agreement as a way of preparing receivers for their treatment of controversial issues. And they may dramatize agreed-upon problems or other issues as a way of arousing emotion. Still, their emphasis should be on controversial issues. Granted, for example, that the pollution problem is serious, what do they intend to do about it?

With *sympathetic* audiences, there are obviously bound to be more areas of agreement. Receivers may even agree that a proposed solution is workable and practical, that it is superior to the existing system, and that it contains few disadvantages. The controversy may hinge, if at all, on whether the proposed solution is the best available solution. Once again, it would be inefficient to deal, systematically, with agreed upon issues. The persuader may, in fact, focus entirely on activating commitments.

The *hostile* audience presents problems of a different order. Here, the receiver is likely to find each stock issue controversial, but *for that very reason* the persuader should probably not deal with each of them systematically in a single speech or essay. In a first speech to a chapter of the National Rifle Association, for example, it would probably be inexpedient to advocate strict licensing and control of all firearms, even if this is the persuader's ultimate goal. Occasionally, skilled persuaders may dare a head-on clash, but their goals are usually more modest. They may, for example, devote the entire speech to the problem of accidental deaths and injuries from firearms and only hint at the need for tighter regulations.

Rhetorical Proof and Consistency Between Propositions

All of us endorse propositions about a number of varied issues. We may be opposed to abortion, for capital punishment, against socialized medicine, for aid to Chile, and so on. If, as persuaders, we were to emulate good scientific theorizing, any single proposition that we defended before an audience would not only be linked in a vertical chain to explicit underlying premises, it would also be tied, horizontally, to other propositions we endorse.

Let us suppose that we entertained all four of the above propositions and that our case against abortion was premised on the assumption that all life is sacred. Logically speaking, if we favored capital punishment we would be obliged to apply the premise to this proposition as well. Perhaps, if pressed, we might draw a distinction between taking the lives of innocent people and taking the lives of murderers. But, again, even after having limited the sacredness of life principle to innocent people, the question is whether we could apply it consistently to other cases. Mightn't socialized medicine save innocent lives by providing more comprehensive services to the poor? Might the Chilean government use our aid to kill innocent people? If so, do we really believe the higher premise?

Still another alternative would be to insist that although socialized medicine may save some lives, it represents a denial of freedom by government, and freedom is more important than life itself. In this case we would be attempting to resolve our self-imposed dilemma by assigning priorities to values. But again, it might be asked, does aid to the Chilean government contribute to the freedom of the Chilean people or does it help to enslave them? If a mother wants an abortion, shouldn't she be free to get one?

Stated generally, the tests for consistency between propositions are as follows:

1. Can the underlying premises that we call upon to defend one proposition also be applied consistently to other propositions that we accept?
2. As an alternative, can we show that two issues are sufficiently different as to warrant any apparent inconsistency?
3. If we have offered a distinction to justify an apparent inconsistency between two propositions, can the distinctions themselves be applied consistently to other propositions?

The issue of consistency between propositions arises often in rhetorical interactions. Quite commonly, it is raised by receivers, and under those circumstances, persuaders had better be prepared to defend themselves. At other times it is raised by persuaders themselves. Those who have a consistent record on a number of related propositions may wish to advertise that record as a way of bolstering their images. Those interacting with receivers who share their positions on these related propositions may emphasize that agreement as a way of establishing the premises underlying the proposition they are now defending. "Most of us," a persuader might say, "are horrified by child killings and we are appalled when we hear that even a puppy has been mistreated. Under the circumstances, all of us must reject the killing of unborn children by abortion."

Correspondingly, the persuader may call attention to inconsistencies in the receiver's positions on related propositions. Because they are not easily reconciled, the basic values that most of us hold exist in a precarious state of balance. We want freedom but also order, spontaneity but also control, property rights but also human rights, stability but also change, what is equitable but also what is profitable. Adding to our problems is the fact that our value priorities are seldom examined carefully (Bem, 1970). We may be consciously committed to the above named values, but we are unlikely to weigh them in relation to each other in any systematic way. Failing to examine them, we are apt to apply them inconsistently from case to case. Hence, we may be for law and order but also cheat on our income tax. We may believe that government officials should always follow orders but also believe that Nixon's political staff should not have followed orders in the Watergate affair. An awareness of our value priorities may not guarantee consistency; far from it. Chances are, however, that greater awareness would reduce inconsistencies of this sort or enable us to make distinctions by which apparent inconsistencies might be justified. Here is where the persuader comes in. By calling attention to inconsistent positions, the persuader stands a chance of unbalancing our cognitions in ways that could produce conversions.

Sad to say, persuaders may hold inconsistent positions on related propositions and nevertheless escape undetected. Politicians may cover over inconsistencies with ambiguous statements or vague generalities. Moreover, so long as a logical inconsistency accords with a receiver's biases, the receiver may be quite content. We turn now to a general discussion of deductive reasoning in persuasion.

Rhetorical Proof and Deductive Reasoning

As we have already seen, deductive reasoning (however invalid) plays a vitally important role in persuasion. The propositions and subpropositions we defend are shown to follow from shared underlying premises, including premises about optimization values. Positions on related propositions are shown to be deducible from these same premises. Underlying premises are justified to doubting audiences as deductions from still higher-order premises and first principles. We may add, finally, that every inductive argument from evidence presupposes an implicit or explicit definitional premise in terms of which the evidence is judged to be relevant to the argument. Thus, when it is argued that so and so is probably guilty because of a conviction in a jury trial, the underlying premise is that a jury's conviction constitutes a definition of probable guilt. As we indicated earlier, an inductive generalization is true or probably true only in terms of specified standards of truth or probability.

In general, the research evidence suggests that receivers can do fairly well at detecting deductive fallacies when provided with syllogisms containing emotionally neutral symbols, explicity stated premises, and explicitly stated qualifying terms such as "some," "most," or "all" (see McGuire, 1969; Miller, 1969). Moreover, they may arrive at highly imaginative deductions even when they violate the rules of deductive logic. So far as inexplicit, ego-involving arguments are concerned—the very kinds of arguments which persuaders are likely to put forth—the picture is quite different. On arguments such as these, our need for logical consistency appears to take a back seat to our need for psychological consistency. In what may be a too extreme interpretation of the evidence, Morgan and Morton (1944) have concluded, for example, that "a person is likely to accept a conclusion which expresses his convictions with little regard for the correctness or incorrectness of the inferences involved" (p. 39).

There is some countervailing evidence, and we should report a sampling of it if for no other reason than to underscore our overall thesis that the human being is neither a logical nor an illogical creature but something of both. In one dramatic study, Rosenberg (1960) hypnotized subjects into believing the contrary of premises in syllogisms they had previously endorsed. Under the influence of posthypnotic suggestion, these same subjects modified their conclusions so as to make them syllogistically consistent with their premises.

In another study, Rokeach (1968) was able to get students to change their value preferences or their attitudes toward civil rights demonstrations by showing them that their attitudes and value preferences were mutually inconsistent. Surprisingly, these changes were even more pronounced after a period of several months than they were three weeks after the experiment. As Bem (1970) notes, however, the subjects in this experiment may have been attempting to say what they thought was socially desirable rather than reflecting their true attitudes or values.

In other research, McGuire (1960a; 1960b) showed that the wish-fulfillment need could be tempered, somewhat, by the need for logical consistency. Subjects were asked to rate both the believability and the desirability of a number of statements that were interspersed with other statements so that their syllogistic relationship would not become immediately apparent. McGuire found that when subjects were confronted with a logical inconsistency in one triad (agreement with two of its three statements, for example), they had at least a partial tendency to eliminate the inconsistency, not only in that triad, but in other triads where inconsistencies had not been made manifest by the experimenter. Furthermore, if subjects were persuaded to change a premise that formed part of a valid syllogism, they tended in many cases to modify the conclusion that followed from the altered premise. Although this occurred more frequently when the conclusion was valued, it also occurred when the conclusion was considered undesirable.

These individual studies notwithstanding, the general run of evidence suggests that we are apt to accept invalid but self-confirming deductions and either to reject valid but undesired conclusions or change the premises so as to make the conclusions acceptable. With respect to the first of these categories, it was Aristotle who first recognized that certain syllogistic forms are inherently difficult for most persons. Consider, for example, the following syllogism:

> Communists are for removing trade barriers with Cuba.
> Senator Kennedy is for removing trade barriers with Cuba.
> Therefore Kennedy is a communist.

Probably only the most extreme rightwingers would buy the above argument today, but note that with slight changes of content we have the same "guilt by association" arguments that were so enthusiastically mouthed during the fifties by supporters of the late Senator Joseph McCarthy:

> Communists are for recognizing Red China.
> Adlai Stevenson is for recognizing Red China.
> Therefore Adlai Stevenson is a communist.

Or, even more glaringly:

> John Smith is a communist.
> Joe Smith is John Smith's brother.
> Therefore Joe Smith must be a communist sympathizer.

What makes these arguments effective, apart from the fact that they may accord with our own prejudices, is that we frequently do not have the time or the inclination to pursue issues exhaustively. Instead, we rely on signs that something is probable. The foregoing are all *arguments from sign*. As in the above cases, persuaders may utilize these forms to show that their enemies are in league with the devil, but they may also use them —sometimes quite plausibly—to establish the expertise of a source or to show that the ideas they favor are blessed by sources their audiences admire. For example:

> The people who have been in Vietnam know what's going on there.
> Joe Alsop spent many months in Vietnam.
> Therefore Joe Alsop must be an expert on Vietnam.

Or:

> Gerald Ford is for good things.
> Gerald Ford is for revenue sharing.
> Therefore revenue sharing is good.

Related to fallacious sign reasoning is specious causal reasoning, and here, once again, there is a tendency to accept invalid conclusions. Consider this slight deviation from a valid syllogism presented earlier:

> Eating spinach helps to make you strong.
> You will not eat spinach.
> Therefore you will not become strong.

This is a common fallacy in cause-to-effect reasoning. The example mistakes a *contributing* cause for a *necessary* cause, one required to produce an effect. Here, on the other hand, is an example of specious effect-to-cause reasoning:

> Most heroin addicts smoked marijuana before they took heroin.
> You smoke marijuana.
> Therefore unless you stop you will become a heroin addict.

Here it is fallaciously assumed that whatever preceded an occurrence must be its cause; furthermore, that what is true in most cases must be true in all cases. Marijuana smokers are fond of pointing out that heroin addicts drank milk before they took heroin. Should you stop drinking milk?

As for the rejection of valid syllogisms, it would appear that we are particularly prone to twist or distort when the conclusion from premises constitutes an assault on our favorable self-perceptions. For the smoker, for example, the following valid syllogism may be psychologically unbearable:

People who do not look out for their own interests are fools.
Smoking is detrimental to my own interests.
I am a fool.

To be sure, some of us are sufficiently detached to be able to acknowledge the validity of syllogisms such as these, although chances are we will still find the conclusions unpleasant and perhaps intolerable. To use other examples from Chapter 5, it may, on an intellectual level, be perfectly logical to us that we live in the city but prefer living in the country, or that our friends disliked a movie we liked. Still, it may be psychologically intolerable to us to discover that we do not always do what we prefer to do or that those whom we respect differ with us on matters of taste.

Given a logically derived conclusion that we find psychologically intolerable, we generally sacrifice at least one type of logical consistency but do not abandon logic entirely. Oftentimes, we change a premise so that it will yield a more tolerable conclusion. Thus, a paranoid schizophrenic may create a delusionary world of objects that are attacking him, but given his inductively improbable premise, his deductive reasoning may be impeccable. Or, to take more typical cases, smokers may be inductively accurate in surmising that they smoke and that smoking is harmful to health; yet they may make the invalid deduction that smoking isn't harmful to their personal health. Seeking to maintain the fiction that they always do what they want to do, persons who live in the city but prefer the country may try to justify their behavior on grounds that they like to be near galleries and art museums, even though they never visit them. Or they may conclude that the country is bad for their imagined allergies.

In view of the fact that individuals may sacrifice deductive consistency for psychological consistency, what choices are open to persuaders?

First, we should reemphasize that although illogic is sometimes effective, persuaders may *choose* at times to be ineffective over the short run, rather than violate syllogistic rules. Ethical questions are obviously raised by the foregoing, and we leave them for the reader to decide.

Second, persuaders may work to make noxious deductive arguments more psychologically acceptable to receivers. By approaching issues in a nonthreatening manner, they may make psychologically inconsistent cognitions at least tolerable to the receiver. Moreover, the basic self-perceptions and expectations that cause cognitions to be dissonant may themselves be altered, not only on an intellectual level ("I realize what you're saying is logical, but it still bothers me"), but on an emotional level as well. Smokers, for example, may be persuaded that it is quite normal for persons not to always maximize their own interests. As a result, they may not need to invent rationalizations or maintain the fiction that smoking does not affect their health. Some degree of psychological inconsistency in the face of smoking would of course be useful in getting smokers to stop, but if the receivers are too threatened, they are unlikely to face the issue realistically.

Assuming that persuaders wish to be effective at all costs, they should still avoid glaring fallacies. These will vary, of course, depending on how critical the audience is, but as a general rule, persuaders should not offer arguments to their peers which they themselves recognize are manifestly illogical. It would not do, for example, to recommend one policy while acknowledging that another offers greater benefits and fewer disadvantages. Arguments from sign, however, especially arguments from sign with implicit premises or qualifiers, may be quite plausible, and may not constitute an affront upon the receiver's sensibilities. Particularly with uncritical, sympathetic receivers, invalid deductions may be quite effective.

Rhetorical Proof and Inductive Logic

Ideally, every inductive argument that is used to support a proposition or subproposition should stand like a bridge, evenly supported across its span by evidence which is solidly grounded in the bedrock of reality. Evidence should be well documented and should be shown to be relevant to the argument.

Other things being equal, the persuader should use "good" evidence and should not overgeneralize from evidence (see our discussion of evidence earlier in this chapter). McCroskey (1969) has concluded from a summary of 21 experiments, many of them his own, that reliable, representative, and comprehensive evidence is more likely to produce attitude-change than no evidence or "poor" evidence.

This should not be interpreted to mean, however, that ordinary persuasive discourse can measure up to the standards set for inductive logic in the sciences. It is much easier to isolate variables in the scientific laboratory than in everyday life, and much easier, also, to interpret evidence with detachment. Even under the best of circumstances, the persuader is unlikely to have access to complete information and must normally rely on fragmentary, second-hand reports. Moreover, insofar as the receiver depends on the persuader for evidence, the receiver must *always* rely on second-hand reports.

In some circumstances, "good" evidence is unnecessary. McCroskey (1969) has found that where the evidence was "old hat," or where the primary source was highly credible, the inclusion of such evidence did not contribute to attitude-change. For evidence to change attitudes, it had to be shocking in some way or come from a source whose credibility was not so high that receivers would have accepted the conclusion in the absence of evidence.

Let us add, too, that other things are seldom equal. Although good evidence is generally more convincing than bad evidence, lay receivers

THERE ARE, IN ALL FROM 8,000 TO 10,000 TONS OF GASES, VAPORS AND SOLIDS BEING THROWN INTO THE AIR OF THE AVERAGE LARGE CITY EVERY DAY — TWO THIRDS OF IT FROM THE AUTOMOBILE

When referring to statistical data, the persuader should take pains to make the data come alive. (Photo courtesy of *Temple News*.)

often accept conclusions based on limited, unrepresentative evidence, even when they are inclined to be critical. One theorist (Abelson, 1968) has gone so far as to argue that most of our beliefs about the real world consist of isolated "opinion molecules" consisting of "a fact, a feeling and a following." For instance: "I've found many times that Vitamin C has prevented colds in my family (fact), and most of my buddies at work think there must be something in it too (following). So I don't think much of the scoffers (feeling).

It has long been recognized that giving just a few examples to support an argument can be quite effective, especially when they are presented dramatically and given additional support by trustworthy documentation. Because examples are vivid and concrete, they are often more psychologically compelling than the most carefully assembled statistical evidence. Generally speaking, persuaders should *combine* specific examples with testimony and statistics, and when they refer to statistical data they should take pains to make the data come alive.

As with deductive arguments, the conclusions from intolerably dissonant inductive arguments will be rebalanced by receivers, assuming that they have been open enough to expose themselves to them. Among the most commonly employed rebalancing mechanisms used under these circumstances are *wishful thinking* and *denial*. Wishful thinking occurs when, in the absence of evidence, or contrary to evidence, we believe something because it is desirable. We may want admission to a highly selective college so badly that we come to regard acceptance as a virtual certainty. Or we may believe so strongly in a utopian "ism" that we become convinced of the utopia's inevitability. Denial is the refusal to believe something because it is undesirable. We may find the idea of a nuclear war so menacing that we refuse to believe it can happen.

When an intolerable expectation or perceived actuality is more compelling than a wish and too convincing to be denied, we *rationalize* or retreat to other mechanisms such as compartmentalization, discussed in Chapter 5. A rationalization is a kind of "self-persuasion" in which we tell ourselves that what we know is true is also desirable. The "fattie" who decides that "One more piece of candy can't hurt" provides an instance of rationalization. So do persons who insist that if they had their lives to live over, they would not change a thing.

Quite obviously, these rebalancing mechanisms may work to the detriment of those seeking to *change* attitudes, but, by the same token, they may play into the hands of those seeking to reinforce existing attitudes. Consider the role of agitators addressing a sympathetic audience. Rather than labeling some of the audience's unexamined premises as "stereotypes," they may play on those stereotypes, intensifying perceived differences between in-groups and out-groups in the process. Rather than depicting the complexities of the system, its pros and cons, they may capitalize on the audience's desire to minimize or deny the bad and hear only the good. Similarly, in defending a program for change, they may offer what Smelser (1963) has called *"if-only beliefs"* about the benefits to be gained and rationalizations about possible ill effects.

Lest only the agitator for change be pictured in this way, readers need only think back to the ceremonial speeches they have heard on such subjects as "The American Way." Here, proponents of change become the stereotypical enemy, wish-fulfillment beliefs about the virtues of the system are offered in place of sober analysis, and rationalizations are offered to justify existing evils.

An even more extreme instance of rationalization was dramatically illustrated in a study conducted by Festinger, Riecken, and Schachter (1956). These authors managed to infiltrate a Doomsday sect that had "received word" of the exact date that all but the faithful would be destroyed. On the day before Doomsday, the group was split into those who could not spare time from their daily labors and a group of ten that had gathered at the leader's home to make preparations for the moment (12:00

A.M.) when they would be whisked off by friendly flying saucers and spared the Armageddon.

Midnight passed without incident, of course, and after several hours the followers were a sorry bunch. Suddenly, however, a radiant look appeared on the leader's face. In a style that aped the King James version of the Bible, she announced to those at her home that their faith had saved the world.

The conclusions that we offered about deductive reasoning in persuasion also apply in a general way to inductive reasoning. Granted that specious or inadequate inductive arguments may be effective, the persuader may refrain from using them on ethical grounds or in order to secure important secondary effects. With critical receivers, moreover, careful inductive reasoning or controversial issues is necessary. Even with highly defensive receivers, good evidence can be compelling when presented in a nonthreatening manner.

Rhetorical Proof and Counterarguments

In our discussion of rebalancing mechanisms in Chapter 5, we suggested that persuaders must not only unbalance cognitions to change attitudes, they must also *close off* undesired forms of rebalancing if they are to rebalance cognitions in intended directions. This is particularly true of the various forms of psychological *fight*: rationalization, differentiation, derogation of the source, search for social support or supportive information, and minimization of the importance of a dissonant relationship.

Let us note that each of these mechanisms may be conceptualized as ways of finding *counterarguments* to maintain or reestablish one's initial attitudes. In some cases, as with minimizing, differentiating, and rationalizing, receivers formulate their own counterarguments. In other cases, they set out to secure counterarguments from other sources of opinion or information.

Now let us suppose that the logic of your case has been compelling enough to cause doubts in the receivers' minds about the wisdom of their own positions. Chances are that unless you can anticipate and deal with their counterarguments or with those to which they will become exposed, significant attitude change will either not take place or it will not persist. This can be accomplished in part by associating your proposition with sources to whom the receiver normally turns for social support, by evidencing your own expertise and trustworthiness, and by underscoring the importance of the issues. Even more significantly, it requires the use of a "both sides" approach (Hovland, *et al.*, 1953). This can be illustrated by a "classic" study in persuasion consisting of two related experiments on the same subjects.

Early in 1945, the U.S. Army wished to persuade its troops that victory in the European theater did not mean that the war in the Pacific would soon be over. Using this as the topic for an experiment, army psychologists constructed two alternate radio broadcasts for presentation to randomly assigned groups of soldiers. One version offered a one-sided series of arguments; a more balanced but otherwise comparable version added arguments for a more optimistic position. Both messages urged the same pessimistic conclusion and were alike in all other relevant respects. So as to prevent the soldiers from becoming aware that they were participating in an experiment, the attitude questionnaires were disguised as part of a general survey. Once the data were collected the group receiving the one-sided approach was compared with the group receiving the two-sided approach so as to determine which approach was most effective. The researchers found that neither technique of persuasion enjoyed a clear superiority over the other although both were influential. What they *did* discover was a bit more complex. The one-sided approach was most persuasive with predisposed listeners and with those who lacked a high school diploma. The "both-sides" approach had greater success with listeners who were initially undecided or in opposition, those who were better educated, and those who were later exposed to counterarguments.

Anticipating and minimizing counterarguments is often essential with opposed, critical audiences, but for other reasons it may be important with uncritical, sympathetic audiences, especially in dealing with unchallenged cultural truisms. McGuire (1969) has likened such cultural truisms to being in a germ-free environment. In both cases, there is no apparent "danger" but paradoxically, for that reason, the organism is extremely vulnerable should germs (i.e., counterarguments) suddenly appear. Extending the analogy, receivers should be more resistant to counterarguments if they are "immunized" or "inoculated" against them. By getting a small "dose" of the "poisonous elements" they should become better motivated to stay on guard and they should develop the intellectual wherewithal to combat them when they occur.

McGuire has tested this important theory in a number of experiments involving several variations of experimental conditions. In general, it can be said that resistance to counterarguments is greatest when (1) the receivers not only hear arguments that support a truism but also refutations of counterarguments; (2) the receivers are not simply handed supportive arguments or refutations of counterarguments but must also construct their own refutations of novel counterarguments that they were not warned to anticipate.

Ordinarily, it is probably ineffective to mention counterarguments that the receivers themselves would not have anticipated and would not be likely to receive from others. Should such arguments be mentioned, they should also be refuted. But where persuaders seek to reinforce attitudes that enjoy a "monopoly propaganda" position in our culture, it is probably a good idea to unsettle the receivers and to help them cope with potential counterarguments.

Summary

By strict standards of logic, the persuader's arguments before a lay audience would approach the level of clarity and consistency which characterizes scientific arguments before learned audiences. Conclusions would follow deductively from premises. Generalizations would follow inductively from reliable, relevant, representative evidence. Propositions and subpropositions would be linked together by clearly articulated underlying premises.

In varying degrees, persuaders may make good use of deductive and inductive logic. At the very least, their arguments should *appear* reasonable. With highly critical and well-informed audiences, fallacious deductive logic and poor or inadequate evidence may cause boomerang effects.

Still, it must be recognized that people's preeminent need is not for logic but for adherence to the rules of their own "psycho-logic." Logically consistent arguments may not be incompatible with those rules, and within tolerable limits, dissonance-increasing arguments may be accepted, but beyond those limits, persuaders may anticipate resistance through various forms of psychological fight or flight.

Hence we see the need for "proof" in persuasive discourse, but "proof" defined in terms of what a given audience will accept as plausible. Consideration of the nature of rhetorical proof has been the focus of this chapter.

Rhetorical proof begins from shared premises. These include *optimization values*, generally held preferences for the old over the untried, for solutions which remove or reduce identifiable problems and for solutions which offer the most benefits for the fewest costs. Questions pertaining to these values constitute *stock issues* since they arise no matter what proposition of policy is being advocated.

Other shared premises include unexamined beliefs, basic values, and value priorities. Generally speaking, persuaders need not make all shared premises explicit. Instead, they may speak in the form of *enthymemes*, truncated syllogisms with one implied premise or conclusion (usually a shared major premise). The persuader may emphasize shared premises as a way of building rapport, or arousing emotion, or demonstrating that the advocated position is consistent with his or her positions on related propositions.

On the kinds of ego-involving issues about which persuaders are likely to argue, most audiences experience some difficulty in adhering to the rules of deductive logic, especially when the conclusions that logically follow are inconsistent with their values, expectations, and self-perceptions; hence the tendencies toward rationalization, denial, wishful thinking, and other forms of rebalancing. Some deductive forms are especially troublesome (e.g., arguments from sign) and thus enable the persuader to use logical fallacies effectively, at least in the short run. Whether this should or should not be done is an ethical question which we have left open. Rather than sacrificing logical consistency under these circumstances, the persuader may either attempt to increase the receiver's capacity to tolerate imbalance or choose to be ineffective. The same is true of inductive arguments.

Other things being equal, the persuader should use "good" evidence, but if the evidence is "old hat" or if the source is highly credible, such evidence may be ineffective. Particularly with sympathetic audiences, poor evidence that reinforces prejudices may be quite effective. Examples and illustrations are especially compelling.

To prove a case rhetorically, the persuader must close off undesired avenues for rebalancing. Several of the most common rebalancing mechanisms may be conceptualized as means of finding counterarguments to refute dissonance-producing arguments. Anticipating these mechanisms, the persuader may employ a "both-sides" approach. Where audiences are initially sympathetic, the persuader may "immunize" or "inoculate" them against the danger of counterarguments from others to which they might otherwise be vulnerable.

Of all the issues raised in this book, the relation between logic and "psycho-logic" is among the most important and also the least understood by rhetoricians. This much can be said for sure: that the human being is neither a purely logical animal nor a purely illogical animal, but a curious combination of both.

Leading
Persuasive
Campaigns

We have repeatedly emphasized in this book that significant changes in audiences are unlikely to come about through a single speech, essay, or other "one-shot" communication; hence the reason for persuasive campaigns—organized, sustained attempts at influencing groups or masses of people through a series of messages. Some campaigns are mammoth undertakings, involving a large variety of spokesmen, media, channels, messages, and audiences. As we shall see, such efforts are not without their special problems.

Most campaigns fit roughly into one of the following categories: (1) *Image-oriented* campaigns are typified by corporate public relations efforts and by contests for political office. (2) *Indoctrination* campaigns promote values that are noncontroversial within a given context. Examples include campaigns to make children into patriotic Americans and campaigns to sell a company to new employees. (3) *Charity* campaigns are designed to serve a disadvantaged group, either through monetary donations or volunteer service. (4) *Product-oriented* campaigns are the province of advertisers, merchandisers, salespeople, and the like. (5) *Self-help* campaigns are those conducted ostensibly for the benefit of the audience being addressed. Health and safety campaigns and religious campaigns are outstanding examples. (6) Finally, there are *institutional change* campaigns of the kind practiced by local citizen's groups, special interest lobbies, and reform-oriented protest movements. The aim here may be to change personnel (e.g., hire more black policemen, fire the police chief), practices (e.g., stricter enforcement of housing codes), policies (e.g., laws, executive edicts), or institutional values and priorities (e.g., publish or perish, job discrimination against women).

This chapter will focus on characteristics of campaigns that are not simply extensions of principles covered in earlier chapters. We will focus, in other words, on unique features of persuasive campaigns: both the greater potential for influence that comes from being able to approach audiences developmentally and the greater potential for problems that can arise from such efforts. Special attention will be directed to campaigns for institutional change.[1] We will also include a section on political campaigns

---

1. The term "institution" is sometimes used to refer to an established law, custom, or practice (e.g., constitutional law, the Miss America Pageant, Fourth of July orations). We shall use the term in its organizational sense to refer to a *relatively enduring, publicly sanctioned collectivity, empowered by law or custom to perform societal functions.* Examples include educational institutions, governments and government agencies, established political parties, business organizations, and mainstream religious denominations. *When uninstitutionalized groups act in concert to change institutions from without, we may speak of the collectivity as a protest movement.* Our discussion of institutional change campaigns in this chapter will include (but not be restricted to) *moderate* type protest

involving the electronic media. As the title of this chapter implies, we will be primarily concerned with campaigns in which readers of this volume may be likely to take leadership roles—relatively small-scale campaigns such as those which are limited to a local community or an institution such as a university.[2] Many of our examples will be drawn from actual cases of this kind.

Campaigns in Stages: A Developmental Model

Charles Larson (1973, p. 166) has observed that campaigns

> ... do not run on the same level or pitch throughout; they do not repeatedly pound away on the same pieces of information; they do not always have the same strategy at various times in their existence. Instead, successful campaigns grow and change and adapt to the change in audience response to them, and as new information and issues become apparent.

What Larson is saying, of course, is that campaigns proceed developmentally, through stages, each stage building on the last, yet exhibiting a "life" of its own. The following outline of stages and their respective components is intended to be quite general, so as to encompass a wide variety of campaign types. As indicated in Fig. 12.1, the stages in our model do not terminate as each "next" stage begins; planning, for example, is a continuous process throughout any campaign.

Planning

Although plans for a campaign must periodically be modified in light of new developments, there are certain steps which must be taken at the outset.

1. **Goal-setting.** To be considered here are intended primary effects (the basic purpose or purposes of the campaign) as well as secondary effects (for example, effects on the image of the campaign organization); immediate goals as well as long-range goals; goals for the campaign as a whole as

---

movements, those utilizing essentially co-active strategies of persuasion. It will largely *exclude*, however, the efforts of more militant collectivities. A discussion of their efforts at campaigning, if we can call them such, belongs more properly in the next chapter. We will, in fact, in the next chapter, provide a detailed comparison of moderate and militant approaches to institutional change.

2. An excellent introduction to campaigns of this kind is found in Bettinghaus (1968; rev. ed., 1973). We shall be drawing heavily on his book in this chapter. For those interested in running political campaigns, we recommend Napolitan (1972) and Shadegg (1964). Both books are written by experienced political consultants.

Some campaign perennials. *Top left:* Union group campaigning for increased wages and benefits. *Bottom left:* Political campaign rally. *Top right:* Street-preaching. (Photos, respectively, by Ken DeBlieu, Valentin I. Jablokov, and David Spease; courtesy of *Temple News*). *Bottom right:* "Fire the coach" (Photographed by Bill Watkins, courtesy of *Philadelphia Magazine*).

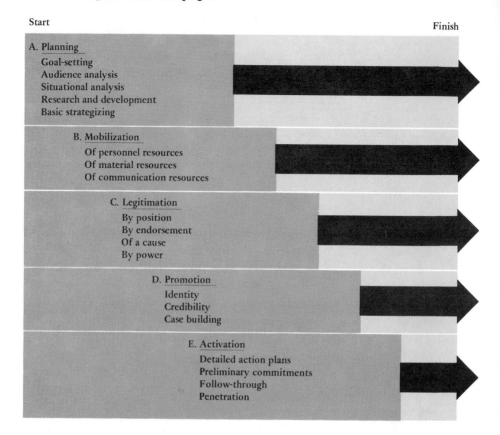

Fig. 12.1 Campaign stages and components

well as subgoals for each stage of the campaign. Generally speaking, it is well to formulate primary goals at several levels: (a) what you would ideally like to achieve; (b) what you expect to achieve; and (c) the bare minimum that would still make your campaign worthwhile. Oftentimes, the large-scale campaign is of questionable value when measured against the amount of time, effort, and money expended. According to one study, for example, (Etzioni, 1972), driver education campaigns have saved lives at the cost of $88,000 per life. Compare this with the introduction of mandatory seat belts and other safety accessories in new cars, estimated to cost only $87 per life saved!

Not long ago, a group called *The People's Fund* was set up as a radical alternative to *The United Fund*, Philadelphia's main fund-raising agency for established community service organizations. Its immediate primary purpose was to raise funds for out-of-favor groups such as the Black Panthers and the Gay Alliance but it hoped, secondarily, to promote co-operation among radical organizations. Ultimately, it sought a union of these groups around a socialist banner, but in the meantime its planners had to consider whether the funds it could expect to secure would be worth the time, effort, and money it would have to expend. Note the variety of goals that its planners had to keep in mind.

2. **Audience analysis.** Especially important in campaigns is analysis of the many audiences that are targeted for persuasion in terms of their varied reasons for potential support or opposition. One former student organized a campaign to block construction of an asphalt company in the small town where he lived. The student's motive in opposing the asphalt company was purely selfish; he lived downwind from it. He recognized, however, that not everyone in the community could be expected to oppose it for this reason, and, indeed, that many wanted the company for financial reasons. The student organized his campaign around the potential danger to children from large asphalt trucks speeding through the town's narrow, sidewalkless highways.

3. **Situational analysis.** More so even than for a single speech, careful attention must be paid to prior situational factors, to the climate prevailing at the onset of the campaign, and to events as they are likely to unfold. On April 30, 1973, Richard Nixon launched a campaign to restore some measure of public confidence in himself and his Administration. Nixon knew not only that he would have to account for recent incriminating disclosures but that the stage was set for a more thoroughgoing investigation by a special prosecutor and for the opening of hearings by the Senate Select Committee on Watergate on May 15. Some people wondered why Nixon did a turnabout in his speech by praising the news media. It may well be that he anticipated the need for a favorable—or at least not unfavorable—press in the months ahead.

4. **Research and development.** What management experts refer to as the R & D function of business organizations has its counterpart in persuasive campaigns. It involves the gathering of arguments and evidence to be used in building persuasive messages as well as the development of know-how for implementation. The failure to take these necessary steps is commonplace among amateur campaigners. We recall one well-intentioned student who attempted to launch a campaign to require bicycle safety education in the public schools. Intuitively, he decided that the best way to get action was to testify at a meeting of the Philadelphia School Board. Unfortunately, he had not yet come up with a plan for such a program or discovered how and where decisions of this kind are made in the school system or sought to determine whether there were any groups that might have been interested in aiding his campaign or even developed documented proof of the existence of a problem.

5. **Basic strategizing.** Although campaign strategies must frequently be revised in light of new developments, it is nevertheless possible at the outset to formulate global strategies. Should the politician run a high visibility campaign or maintain a "low profile"? Should the candidate engage in image-building or run a "negative" campaign of attack on the opponent? Is it more advantageous to remain mute or ambiguous on highly controversial issues or to attempt to enlarge one's constituency by seeking to convert the skeptical? George McGovern could not have anticipated the Eagleton fiasco in early 1972, but he might have recognized that his strong stands on amnesty, abortion, and marijuana during the early primaries would eventually catch up with him during the post-Convention campaign.

Basic strategies must of course be formulated with the other planning factors that we have identified clearly in mind. Advertisers from Eastman Kodak ran a camera-purchasing campaign aimed at families with expectant mothers; they did so on the basis of evidence that these families were least likely to own cameras and most likely to purchase them. A Midas Muffler campaign zeroed in on the inadequacies of ordinary service stations; it did so on the basis of evidence that these stations were their stiffest competition and were highly vulnerable to attack. In the same way, groups seeking institutional change must formulate strategies with an eye toward maximizing their resource capabilities. John Gardner's *Common Cause* and Ralph Nader's action groups provide excellent models of campaign organizations that consistently come up with innovative and appropriate strategy plans, geared to concrete, solvable problems.

Mobilization

Mobilization consists in locating, acquiring, developing, and exploiting the *resources* necessary to run the campaign.

1. **Personnel resources.** Unlike one-shot messages by individual communicators, persuasive campaigns require organization. The effectiveness of any campaign organization is dependent on adherence to its program, loyalty to its leadership (or active commitment to shared leadership), a collective capacity and willingness to work, energy mobilization, and member satisfaction. A hierarchy of authority and division of labor must be established in which campaign workers are persuaded to take orders, to perform menial or time-consuming tasks, and to forego social pleasures.

The problems of personnel mobilization are more acute for the leaders of voluntary organizations (e.g., charities, political parties, self-help groups) and especially for those who head protest movements seeking institutional change. Whereas commercial sales organizations, for example, may induce productivity through tangible rewards and punishments, protest movements, as voluntary collectivities, must rely on ideological and social commitments from their members. These commitments may endow a movement with great energy for a period of time, but as we have seen in recent years, commitments of this kind are difficult to sustain.

There is no simple way to mobilize volunteers for sustained efforts. A spirited, energized membership is the strength of many voluntary campaigns, yet morale cannot be secured through abdications of leadership or of leadership tasks. Members may feel the need to participate in decision-making, to undertake pet projects on their own initiatives, to put down leaders or other followers, to obstruct meetings by socializing, or to disobey directives. The leadership cannot ignore these needs, especially today, when members are likely to be well educated, independent, given to "doing their own thing."

Still, they cannot accede to all of them either. The problem of leadership was well illustrated at the central office of Vietnam Summer, a national coalition of antiwar organizations which had formed, on an *ad hoc* basis in 1967, to present a coordinated attack on the Johnson administration's participation in the war. According to Keniston (1968), the inexperienced, all female, secretarial staff demanded and received equal status and responsibilities with the seasoned, all male, political staff. As a result of this early experiment in women's liberation, experienced organizers were forced to perform menial chores during the organization's most hectic period while the former clerical workers advised major projects.

2. **Material resources.** A clever group can work toward fulfilling several campaign requirements simultaneously. At Temple University recently, several students sought to organize a campus chapter of PIRG, a consumer-action group in the Ralph Nader image. The leadership recognized that they would need money, lots of it, to build and maintain the organization and advance its goals. Conceivably, a foundation grant might have been forthcoming, but they sought another fund-raising approach, one that would help legitimize the group and promote its values at the same time. A "mini-campaign" was launched for a campus referendum on whether money should be raised for the group by means of a voluntary dues checkoff on student tuition bills. The vote was favorable, and the group went next to the administration with a strongly worded request that it execute the checkoff—or be in the embarrassing situation of opposing a Nader-like organization that had widespread student support. Not surprisingly, the administration proved anxious to please.

Watergate has shown dramatically that there are often hidden costs associated with acquiring material resources. A great many of the Nixon administration's difficulties were tied to an excessive zeal for the campaign dollar: the Rebozo slush fund, the alleged favors granted the dairy industry, I.T.T., swindler Robert Vesco, and others in exchange for money. Yet favoritism toward large donors is the rule, not the exception, in politics, and it extends to other voluntary organizations. The power of the purse often dictates or influences policies of colleges and universities, social welfare lobbies, and charity organizations. Campaign leaders must frequently ask themselves whether the courtship of "fat cat" contributors is worth the price of a loss of independence.

3. **Communication resources.** One need for money in large-scale campaigns is to purchase or control communication resources. They include access to channels of influence and to the mass media as well as basic information and know-how needed to communicate effectively. Commercial organizations have long purchased market analyses, mailing lists, media expertise, and media time—paying, in the case of television advertisements, as much as $50,000 for a one minute commercial. The modern political campaigner, of course, now purchases these same resources. As we shall see in the next chapter, organizations seeking institutional change are often denied access to media or to channels of influence—unless, ironically, they stage militant protests that compel attention.

Legitimation

To say that someone has legitimacy is to say that others have conferred upon that person the right to exercise authoritative influence in a given area or to issue binding directives. These others, meanwhile, tacitly acknowledge a corresponding obligation to take him or her seriously or to follow his or her directives. Scientists have enormous legitimacy, to the point where, in psychological experiments on legitimacy, even the psychologists have been astounded. Simply on the basis of such instructions as "The experiment requires that you continue," Milgram (1963) was able to persuade subjects to administer what they believed were dangerous electrical shocks to their peers. Pepitone (1955) encountered little resistance in getting subjects to sort out waste baskets filled with disgusting debris. Frank's (1944) subjects continued for a full hour in attempts at balancing a marble on a small steel ball. Orne (1962) has commented despairingly on his inability to find tasks so noxious that subjects would not perform them. Indeed, in one experiment (Orne and Evans, 1965), subjects picked up what they believed were poisonous snakes while others agreed to place their hands in nitric acid and to throw it in the face of a lab assistant. Seldom, of course, do campaigners have that degree of legitimacy.

Legitimations are the grounds upon which legitimacy is established. A campaign or campaign organization may be legitimated in any of several ways.

1. **Legitimacy by position.** A common type of legitimacy is that which inheres in a role or position within government, business, or some other established institution. Without knowing anything about the Surgeon

General of the United States, we may heed the advice offered in an anti-smoking campaign sponsored by that individual because the position confers a certain authority.

Groups seeking institutional change are often well advised to secure positional legitimacy by attaching themselves, if they can, to some established institution—a church, a university, perhaps even the very institution they seek to change. Community organizer Saul Alinsky (1971) spoke of the importance of being invited into the communities he sought to influence, and students seeking campus change have often found it useful to get appointed to university committees or commissions. During the height of the campus confrontations at Temple University in 1969, the Academic Vice President challenged the legitimacy of a militant student group, claiming it had no right to speak for the student body. On his own initiative, he devised a mechanism for student representation in which student delegates to an all day student-faculty-administration conference would be elected by departments, thus bypassing the militant group. Rather than challenging this procedure, the militant group simply organized the departments, making sure their supporters were well represented among the delegates.

2. **Legitimacy by endorsement.** The next best alternative to the power of positional legitimacy is endorsement by those who have it. Bettinghaus (1973, p. 257) speaks of "checking in with the power base," which for him includes not only those in official positions of power but also informal opinion leaders:

> The role of the legitimizer is a peculiar one. He is seldom active in the early stages of a social-action campaign. He does not make speeches in favor of the proposal. He does not write letters to the newspaper, and he frequently will ask that his name not be associated with the new idea. He may not want to give a formal approval to a new proposal. But he can effectively block the adoption of a new idea by saying, "No!" If he simply agrees that a proposal is a desirable one, he may well clear the way for future operations by the change agent and eventual adoption of the proposal.

3. **Legitimacy of a cause.** Those seeking minor reforms in an institution or the adoption of innovations in a community may well be granted positional legitimacy or at least the blessings of key legitimizers. But those seeking more widespread changes are likely to threaten and be threatened by the institution or community's sanctions and taboos: its laws, its maxims, its customs governing manners, decorum, and taste, its insignia of authority, and so on.

Still, the change-minded group may utilize co-active persuasion to establish its legitimacy by representing its cause as one that any virtuous individual must endorse. Programs may be defended in the name of God or the Founding Fathers or the Constitution or Natural Law. Here the promotion and legitimation stages are merged.

4. Legitimacy by power. The last resort for campaigners is to establish legitimacy by sheer power. Properly, a discussion of this alternative belongs in the next chapter. The point is that groups seeking change must often fight for the right to be heard or to negotiate in their own interests.

Promotion

Once a campaign group has taken effective steps to plan, mobilize resources, and secure legitimations, it is in a powerful position to promote its cause before a wider audience. Effective promotion, in turn, should open doors for the group that may have been closed before in terms of personnel, material, and communication resources as well as endorsements by key influentials.

In the ideal persuasive campaign, there is continuity from beginning to end of the promotion process. An advertising campaign may "go public," for example, with messages somewhat mysteriously alluding to a new product that is soon to appear on supermarket shelves. Mystery may continue as a theme once its identity is revealed, the product somewhat humorously being described as having magical qualities, its label and packaging reinforcing that concept. Rather than the usual endorsements by attractive celebrities or "just plain folks," subsequent ads may feature testimonials by actors associated with suspense theater. Should the product become an established competitor in its field, later ads may tone down the mystery theme, playing now, perhaps, on its reputation for dependability.

This example illustrates, once again, the importance of having an overall campaign strategy at the promotion stage. Larson (1973, p. 174) speaks here of providing audiences with an "invitation to the drama." He argues that it is the dramatic which compels major interest in any campaign; that the materials of the drama should be enacted through deeds, rather than pedantically stated; and, above all, that the "plot" of the drama should provide unity to the campaign. The "plot" may be the familiar underdog saga of the honest politician fighting the "pols" against overwhelming odds, as in the McGovern campaign of 1972. Or it may be Richard Nixon as the Good Sheriff in 1968, with plans for peace abroad and law and order at home. Or it may be the familiar "Camelot" theme, as in the Kennedy campaign of 1960. In campaigns for institutional change and in self-help campaigns, the drama often has a negative focus and is embodied in religious metaphors: a "crusade" against evil or evil men or a quest for "purification" or "purgation" from the evil in ourselves.

Various steps have been proposed by different campaign theorists as substages within the promotion stage. The following is intended to be quite general.

1. **Identity.** Political candidates are nowhere without name recognition. Commercial advertisements do better getting negative attention than no attention. Worthy charities must somehow stand out from others making a claim on the public's generosity. So it is that campaign managers work assiduously at formulating memorable slogans, devising labels and catchy jingles, and finding clever ways to build repetition of the same campaign themes.

Effective identification symbols are those which serve members of the campaign organization (giving them an identity) as well as the larger public. Many militant movements of the sixties chose identification symbols, it seemed, mostly to promote in-group solidarity. Black militants, for example, announced themselves with faded levis, "Honkie" epithets, in-group songs, handshakes, flags, ceremonies, hairstyles, and speech patterns. These symbols were more appropriate for a combative approach to persuasion than for a co-active approach. In recent years, the Black Panthers (the name still frightens) have toned down their divisive image as they have moved toward bridging distances between groups. Similarly, where once the Democrats and Republicans featured in-group images at their party conventions (e.g., party emblems and flags, pictures of party heroes), now, with the conventions televised, the emphasis is on identification symbols that link the party with the people and that even make a pitch for members of the opposition.

2. **Credibility.** Moving beyond the creation of a favorable and memorable identity, the campaign leadership must establish its own believability as well as the credibility of the group as a whole. The first step for leaders is to promote respect, trust, and attraction from their own followers. Here, especially, deeds are important, not just words. Occasionally, followers will be taken in by a charismatic firebrand, but for the most part they will want concrete evidence that this individual has their interests at heart, is capable of delivering, and possesses such qualities as intelligence and expertise, honesty and dependability, maturity and good judgment.

Establishing personal or group credibility to the satisfaction of suspicious outsiders may be considerably more difficult. On this score, Zimbardo (1972) has offered a number of suggestions to college students on how they might canvas door to door in behalf of highly controversial or hostility-arousing positions. His pointers on establishing credibility (paraphrased below) bear close resemblance to those we offered in earlier chapters. With some modification, they may be adapted to other campaigns.

a) Impress the target with your expertise, concern, and dedication, being forceful but not overbearing.
b) Make some points which are against your own best interest; indicate the sacrifices you have made and would be willing to make.
c) Have a respected person introduce you.
d) Begin by agreeing with what the audience wants to hear.
e) Minimize your manipulative intent until you ask for commitment.
f) Avoid group situations where the majority are known or expected to be against you.
g) Socially reinforce target persons by listening attentively to what they have to say, by maintaining eye contact and close but comfortable physical proximity, by individuating them (using proper names, for example) and helping them to individuate you (e.g., through appropriate personal anecdotes), by nodding or saying "good" or "that's interesting," on specific points and by smiling to reinforce more general classes of behavior, and, in general, by showing respect and appreciation for them.
h) Show genuine enthusiasm and concern on the issues.
i) To reduce the natural resentment accorded to college student types, differentiate yourself from audience stereotypes by a neat appearance, by showing respect, even awe, for how hard the target persons work, and by intimating, through off-hand examples, that you are not privileged and spoiled.
j) Work in pairs that differ in some obvious characteristic such as temperament, age, or sex, but that provide the bases for similarities by one or both with the target persons.

3. **Case building.** Any persuasive campaign must build a case within the framework of the stock issues discussed in Chapter 11. A need must be established and the candidate, product, charity, self-help program, or what have you, must be shown capable of filling that need. In campaigns, of course, persuaders have the advantage of being able to pound home the same message repeatedly (using the principle of repetition with variation) or to stretch out a suspicion-arousing case over a series of stages—focusing on problems and principles in the beginning, for example, and pushing their own favorite solution in subsequent messages.

The main case-building principle we wish to emphasize here is embodied in the saying: *"Different strokes for different folks."* Particularly when campaigning for institutional change, separate attention must be given to three different groups: campaign participants, members of the general public, and organizational decision-makers.

a) *Campaign participants.* It is a truism of voluntary campaign organizations that they fail as often from fragmentation from within as from resistance from without. Within these organizations, interfactional conflicts invariably develop over questions of value, strategy, tactics, or implementation. Purists and pragmatists clash over the merits of compromise. Academics and activists debate the necessity of long-range planning. Others enter the campaign with personal grievances or vested interests. Preexisting groups that are known to have divergent ideological positions are nevertheless invited to joint or affiliate with the campaign because of the power they can wield. These and other differences may be reflected at the leadership level as well. Rarely can one campaign leader handle all of the leadership roles and tasks of the campaign. Hence the need for a variety of leadership types: theoreticians and propagandists to launch the campaign, political or bureaucratic types to carry it forward. There may also be cleavages between those vested with positions of authority in the campaign, those charismatic figures who have personal followings, those who have special competencies, and those who have private sources of funds or influence outside the campaign.

The problems of building a case before the general public without offending one or another faction within the campaign organization were well illustrated by "Key '73," a religious crusade that was supposed to have combined the evangelical thrust of some 140 denominations, 250 thousand congregations, and 100 million Christians. (*Time*, Feb. 19, 1973). As might be expected, this amorphous group was compelled to deal in generalities and deliberate ambiguities, avoiding doctrinal issues or questions about the role of the church in respect to social injustices or political oppression. Quite obviously, this is an extreme case since the campaign membership allegedly included half the nation's population, but it can be a considerable problem for other campaign organizations as well.

Saul Alinsky (1971) has suggested several things that can be done to solidify community action organizations, not all of them applicable to other campaign types or less militant campaign styles. First is the familiar tactic of focusing on a common enemy. Second, he suggests that it is often expedient to lead your people in a "cinch fight," one that will demonstrate to them their success capabilities. If at all possible, he advises, the actions they take in advancing the group's cause should not drag on too long and should be enjoyable. Also important is the need to revitalize the membership by periodically introducing new issues and varying the tactics employed. Above all, he suggests, "Never go outside the experience of your people . . . [and] whenever possible, go outside the experience of the enemy" (p. 127).

Our own "rule" for the leaders of voluntary campaigns is more general: Whatever case you construct for persuading outsiders, build with an eye toward solidifying campaign participants.

b) *General public.* The case taken before the public must vary, of course, with the type of campaign, and with the nature of the audience being addressed. Here we will focus once again on campaigns for institutional change and we will highlight less militant tactics than those proposed by Alinsky.

Bettinghaus (1973) has suggested a series of steps in building a case before the general public: establishing a need for the social systems involved, identifying and defining goals for relevant individuals and groups, securing agreement on methods to accomplish change, and constructing a formal plan of work to be accomplished.

With respect to need, Bettinghaus identifies several techniques that can be used. First, there is basic education. Through face-to-face contacts and exploitation of the available mass media, the change-oriented group can lay out its facts and its arguments. Second, the group may conduct questionnaire surveys. In addition to aiding the group's efforts at audience analysis, questionnaires may in themselves be persuasive documents, compelling reflection by people who might not otherwise have perceived the existence of a problem, and generating survey data which, if favorable to the group's cause, may be used to convert fence-sitters. Third, Bettinghaus advises demonstrations or trials—pilot projects that may evidence both need and feasibility. Fourth, the group may call attention to precedents for the proposed action within the community or institution, as well as envy-arousing precedents in other communities. The need for a new high-school gymnasium may be argued, for example, on grounds that several high schools in nearby towns have added new gym facilities. Finally, the group may exploit crises that develop by building on the immediately felt need.

With respect to goals, methods, and work plans, Bettinghaus advocates an essentially participatory pattern of persuasion, one in which members of the general public share in the development of project proposals or at least are asked to play a policy confirmation role. Here the campaigner must be politically sensitive. The ideal solution may be unacceptable; the politically feasible solution may be one that provides a little something for everyone.

c) *Key decision-makers.* Locating those with real power or influence in organizations is not always easy. Groups seeking institutional change are often referred to persons whom Tom Wolfe (1970) has labeled "flak catchers," minor functionaries with fancy titles who are assigned to hear out complainants and, if possible, to soothe their ruffled feelings. Unless change-oriented groups understand how influence flows and where the buck stops in a given institution, they are liable to be given the runaround. Oftentimes, moreover, key decision-makers are not identifiable by their titles. One such person at Temple University, for example, held the modest title of Registrar. Another was secretary to a dean. Both exerted more influence than several university vice-presidents.

A general rule of institutional change—to be discussed more fully in the next chapter—is that key decision-makers are unlikely to take significant action on conflict-arousing issues unless direct or indirect pressure is applied. Proposals for innovations designed to improve the overall efficiency of the institution are likely to be greeted with open arms; proposals in support of group interests at the expense of other group interests are likely to be resisted unless accompanied by a show of strength. This is not to say that co-active appeals will have no effect. The campaign group may call attention to the endorsements it has received or its other sources of legitimacy. Moreover, if the decision-makers are personally impressed with a proposal, they may act within the *limits* of their freedom and perhaps even stretch those limits. Still, they are likely to be subject to a sea of cross-pressures that constrain them from taking major action. University presidents, for example, are not simply *power-holders;* they are also *power brokers* who must balance the conflicting demands of students, faculty, alumni, parents, community leaders, etc. Co-active persuasion used to incite the anger of the student body may constitute just the right sort of indirect pressure needed to influence the president. Secretly, a given president may welcome the pressure; without it, it might be virtually impossible to present a case to other key decision-makers such as trustees or state legislators.

Activation

Building a compelling case is not enough. Unless the campaigner seeks only to communicate information or to modify attitudes, it is necessary to make special provisions for the action stage.

1. **Detailed action plans.** Campaigns often fail because the campaign target lacks specific information on how to act. Voters must be told where to vote and how to vote. People with problems must learn how to get help. In the case of campaigns for institutional change, there are bound to be misinterpretations unless plans for action are concretized. Bettinghaus (1973, p. 268) has enumerated the types of detail needed in a proposal for a community innovation such as a new recreation center:

> The formal plan of work will include decisions about financing, operational steps to be taken in implementation, the time sequence that has to be followed, and most important, the specific tasks which each individual associated with the implementation will have to perform. Making these decisions will result in an organizational structure charged with actually carrying out the operations. This structure will provide for appropriate lines of authority, a detailed task description for each individual, and the relation of the operational group to other community groups and institutions.

2. **Preliminary commitments.** Professional campaigners have learned that it is wise to secure partial, preliminary commitments from people before the final action is taken. Short of obtaining cash donations, the charity solicitor may work toward obtaining campaign pledges. Short of securing

even verbal agreements to purchase new cars, the automotive sales organization may provide all sorts of inducements just to get people to the showrooms. If at all possible, the preliminary commitment should be of a public nature and should entail some effort on the part of the individual. For reasons to be discussed in the next chapter, the attitude of the individual should be strengthened by the act of overt commitment. Zimbardo (1972, p. 90) also suggests that the campaigner "provide several levels of possible behavioral alternatives for the person." The campaign pledge card, for example, may list several monetary alternatives: $1, $5, $10, $100. Says Zimbardo, "pushing the most extreme is likely to get a greater level of compliance even if the extreme is rejected."

3. **Follow-through.** On Election Day, each major party mobilizes a large campaign organization for poll-watching, telephoning, chauffering, baby-sitting, etc. Advertisers seek to make buying a habit among those who have made initial commitments. Revivalist campaigns work at translating instant "conversions" into weekly attendance at church.

Campaign organizations seeking institutional change may be granted authority and resources to put programs into operation themselves (at least on a trial basis), or they may get promises of action from the institution itself. In the case of the latter, we have seen more than one externally initiated program fail for lack of administrative follow-through. The campaign organizations have been at least partially to blame for not maintaining the pressure. A good rule of institutions is that institutional policies are what their administrators do about them. Often, it is precious little.

In the case of programs administered initially by the campaign organization itself, there is a similar danger that once the innovation has been effectively sold, campaign activists will become lazy or indifferent or begin caring more about their reputations than about the persons they claim to be serving. At some point, the new innovation must be institutionalized, and this is another juncture fraught with potential problems. In the mid-sixties, several students at Temple University helped form a voluntary organization named *Conscience* that successfully ran a day camp for disadvantaged children. For three summers, the organization endured, even thrived on, its poverty, its dearth of trained leaders, and its lack of formal ties to the university. Then, with the members' consent, the university began providing large amounts of money, facilities, and technical assistance. The support was now there but the spirit was gone. The appropriate socioemotional adjustments for institutionalization had not been made.

4. **Penetration.** In the ideal campaign those reached directly become persuaders themselves. Advertisers dance for joy when radio listeners begin humming aloud the jingle they have heard in the commercial. New converts to a religious group are often asked to proselytize in its behalf. And

political campaigners often rely on opinion leaders to carry their television messages to others. In each case there is *penetration* beyond the initial receivers to their own interpersonal networks.

The effective conclusion to a campaign for institutional change occurs, not simply when the change is put into practice, but when others begin hearing about it, speaking favorably about it, and even attempting to emulate it. Serving as a model for others is often a small campaign group's most important accomplishment.

Political Campaigns and the Electronic Media

Looking back on recent contests, we can easily see that the model of stages and components (Fig. 12.1) which was applied primarily to institutional change campaigns in the foregoing section of this chapter applies equally well to political campaigns. In the 1972 presidential contest, for example, McGovern was clearly no match for Nixon on just about every count imaginable. The Nixon effort was planned to perfection: a dramatic scenario calculated to win over disaffected Democrats by picturing the incumbent as being "above politics," and the contender as immoderate, inconsistent, and clumsy. The McGovern organization, it seemed, did everything it could to reinforce the negative image. Among its more notable failures at the planning stage were the Eagleton fiasco, its scheduling of speeches (a magnificent nominating speech by Edward Kennedy was presented in the wee hours of the morning; a half-hour McGovern speech on network television was scheduled to compete with *Love Story*, which drew 80 percent of the television audience), and its failure to analyze the needs and aspirations of the swing vote.

McGovern did exceedingly well at mobilizing resources during the primaries: soliciting millions in small donations through a direct-mail campaign, building a large army of volunteers, and capturing media attention by his early successes in the primaries (when McGovern walked into New Hampshire a month before the first primary, he had a three percent popularity rating in the polls and could not even muster up an essential accoutrement of any major political campaign, a press bus). Still, he was no match for the Nixon organization, and with each evidence of failure at the promotion stage there came a corresponding diminution in the generosity of his financial backers and in the ardor of his campaign staff.

A basic problem was legitimacy, and this was to hurt him grievously when he attempted to promote his candidacy. The convention left deep wounds among key decision-makers within the Democratic Party, many of whom either bolted the party or sat out the election. McGovern had legitimacy by power and position but he seemed unrepresentative of the party's mainstream and thus lacked legitimacy by endorsement.

Some of McGovern's promotional problems were stylistic; his voice reminded one scribe of Liberace. More serious, according to James Reston (*New York Times*, October 4, 1972), was his basic misreading of the American people—pushing them too far and too fast on gut issues. It is a truism of American politics that the successful campaigner is one who can capture the ideological center. Gary Wills (*New York Times Magazine*, November 5, 1972) has taken this principle one step further, arguing that political candidates must "not only 'out-middle' each other, but also engage in compensatory blandishments toward those who have least reason to trust them" (p. 37). McGovern appeared to have learned this lesson to late ("By the end of this year's campaign, McGovern could rhetorically out-policeman Nixon at home and out-Rabbi him abroad"—Wills), and his shifts on basic issues only served to undermine his initial base of support.

By the conclusion of the Eagleton affair in early September, the die was cast. Over 60 percent of the American public had made preliminary commitments (often public commitments to friends and relatives; here the interpersonal network is important) for Nixon—or against McGovern. Hence, when the Watergate break-in was revealed in the press, the public could not assimilate it or connect it with Nixon; they had already been too well activated to alter their behavioral intentions.[3]

The Image-Building Function of the Electronic Media

Our retrospective on the Nixon-McGovern contest should serve to illustrate how large-scale political campaigns may be incorporated within our model. Still, so far as these campaigns are concerned, the model makes insufficient provision for the role of the mass media, and particularly television.

At the very least, television makes it possible for a national candidate to appear "live" before many more millions of people than is possible by face-to-face communications. More than the other media, it can augment or diminish the effects of a candidate's messages by its reportage and its analyses and interpretations of the news. Newscasters like Walter Cronkite and news commentators like Eric Sevareid have become highly trusted figures on the political landscape, and they enjoy considerably greater exposure than newspaper reporters and columnists. Impressive, too, is the ability of television to shape events; the demonstrators outside the 1968 Democratic Convention in Chicago undoubtedly would have behaved differently, for example, had the television cameras not been trained

---

3. For a comprehensive and highly readable history of the 1972 presidential contest, see White's (1973), *The Making of the President; 1972*. White has, in fact, chronicled each of the presidential campaigns since 1960.

upon them. But even more impressive is telvision's capacity to build composite political images out of the bits and pieces of personality that a candidate's media and public relations experts may choose to expose to the voting public:

> *Voice:*   Mr. President, what about the high cost of living?
>
> *Eisenhower:*   My wife, Mamie, worries about the same thing, I tell her it's our job to change that on November 4.

In this, the first of the campaign-by-television spectaculars, Eisenhower turned to Madison Avenue for help on selling his grandfatherly image. Before that—even as late as the forties—although politicians had made widespread use of radio, the *forms* of their presentations over the electronic media constituted mere extensions of the platform speech styles that they had habitually employed in the past. After that, politicians were almost invariably sold like pantyhose and popcorn:

> *Camera:*   Little girl picking daisies while babbling a countdown.
> Camera fades to a countdown at an atomic testing site.
> Scene dissolves into a mushroom-shaped cloud.
>
> *Johnson:*   These are the stakes: to make a world in which all God's children can live, or go into the dark. We must love each other or we must die.

The potential of television to create image facades that bear little or no relation to realities is perhaps best illustrated by a commercial in behalf of Clair Engle, an incumbent seeking reelection to the Senate in California in 1964. Engle had undergone brain surgery, had a paralyzed arm, and could barely walk or talk, but a repeatedly filmed and carefully edited television commercial created an image of health. Fortunately for the voter, Engle died before the primary (Nimmo, 1970, pp. 141–2).

The "minimal effects" hypothesis. Despite the apparent potential of commercials like these, there is precious little evidence that they are effective. About the only documented evidence of their power to influence is contained in a recent study by Patterson and McLure (1974) who found that certain advertisements for Nixon in 1972 produced shifts among voters with low involvement.

In fact, the most popularly voiced generalization by hard-nosed empiricists about political campaigns is that the media have *minimal effects* on voter attitudes or behaviors. Political campaigns in general, and mass media communications in particular, may well *reinforce* existing attitudes or help *mould* attitudes among the indifferent or the conflicted, but they have "minimal effects" in the sense that rarely do they *convert* people from one political preference to another (Klapper, 1960; Berelson and

Steiner, 1964). Supporters of the hypothesis argue that mediated campaign messages aren't trusted; that potentially discrepant information is listened to, perceived, remembered, or utilized selectively; and that in any case, most political campaigns neutralize each other. So the net effect is that most people vote in terms of prior predispositions (Klapper, 1960) and/or in terms of past habits of party identification (Campbell, *et al.*, 1960).

The "minimal effects" hypothesis needs to be tempered in several ways. First, moulding and reinforcement effects are hardly inconsequential: they create new partisans and help mobilize and activate old ones. Nor are relatively small conversion effects insignificant in political terms since they may swing close elections. Second, the data on which the minimal effects hypothesis is based come primarily from studies of voter reactions to presidential campaigns during the post-convention periods (Labor Day to Election Day) of 1948, 1952, and 1956. The conclusions from these studies do not necessarily apply to Congressional or gubernatorial contests. Nowadays, moreover, some presidential contenders actively campaign as early as two years before the election. Their messages, and mass media treatments of their messages, may have significantly greater conversion effects during the preconvention period and especially in the state primaries. Finally, the conclusions do not necessarily apply to more recent contests where there has been considerably greater split-ticket voting. There is evidence that voters of today are somewhat better informed (Neumann, 1974) and more intellectually consistent (Anderson and Petrocik, 1974) than they were in the fifties, a period that encouraged political indifference and voting in terms of party identification. At any rate, Miller, *et al.* (1973) have found that in the 1972 presidential contest, issues and images, as much or more than party identification, accounted for the Nixon landslide.

Campaigns by television as entertainment and drama. If today's voters are more informed or more consistent, they are still not paragons of intellectual enlightenment, and their reasons for selecting a candidate on the basis of images or issues may have little relationship to the facts (Sears, 1969). This has led some pundits to speculate that the majority of citizens—those with low political involvement—get gratification from political campaigns chiefly because of the drama and entertainment they provide (Blumler and McQuail, 1969; Edelman, 1967; Nimmo, 1970). For most people, the electronic media are about the only sources of political exposure. Television, especially, is said to fill a social void in people's lives. Campaigns by television provide objects on which they can project their wishes and illusions, fears and hostility. They become fans of political parties and candidates in much the same way they identify with football teams or baseball heroes. And rather than demanding hard information from the newscasters, they insist upon "human interest" materials that will provide escape from duty and routine and items for small talk among friends (Stephenson, 1967). Says Edelman (1967, p. 9):

> If political acts are to promote social adjustment and are to mean what our inner problems require that they mean, these acts have to be dramatic in outline and empty of realistic detail. In this sense publishers and broadcast licensees are telling the exact truth when they excuse their poor performance with the plea that they give the public what it wants. It wants symbols and not news.

If this hypothesis is valid (Nimmo, 1970, pp. 179–199, makes an excellent case for it), then the implications for political campaigners are clear. Rather than competing with *Love Story*, as McGovern did in 1972, the politician must romance the voter—courting the uninvolved voter especially with dramatic acts off camera and visual/verbal messages on camera that portray him as being like a favorite character in a television series or a celebrated movie star.

In this connection, Larson (1973, pp. 184–185) quotes a letter from Ross Cummings, a political consultant in Oklahoma, who conducted a rather unique poll to determine which of several candidates—each of whom roughly resembled a television or movie personality—had the best chance of winning the gubernatorial race. Rather than naming the actual contenders, the poll asked only about political preferences for their entertainment counterparts:

> We used James Bond, Perry Mason, Ben Cartwright, Andy Griffith and Gomer Pyle. . . . Our known political contenders fit these characters loosely. . . . Well, Ben Cartwright won handily, garnering some 60% of the votes, and pointing to a tendency on the part of the voters to favor an older candidate. Andy Griffith did poorly even in "Little Dixie," indicating a pull-back from an unrelieved rural image. James Bond ran last, indicating dissatisfaction with handsome young playboy types. Perry Mason was second, but far enough behind Ben Cartwright to indicate that rugged, patriarchal directness was a more desirable characteristic than urbane, articulate competence.

A footnote: Ben Cartwright won the primary but lost the election. This should serve to remind us that prognoses about political persuasion, as with other rhetorical predictions, are fallible.

Summary

Utilizing a model of campaign stages and components, this chapter has focused on the unique characteristics of persuasive campaigns: both the greater potential for influence that comes from being able to approach audiences developmentally, and the greater potential for problems that can arise from such efforts. Given special attention in this chapter were relatively small-scale campaigns for institutional change, of the kind likely to be engaged in by readers of this book. A separate section of the chapter was devoted to political campaigns via the electronic media.

Typical treatments of persuasive campaigns focus on the promotion stage. We have argued that *planning, mobilization* of resources, and efforts at *legitimation* must precede *promotion* of the product, candidate, etc., before the general public, and must continue through to the final campaign stage: *activation.* Voluntary campaigns, especially, tend to falter at the mobilization stage for lack of inducements to discipline and cohesion. And voluntary campaigns for institutional change tend to fail also from insufficient pressure on key decision-makers or from lack of follow-through at the activation stage.

A persistent theme in this chapter has been the importance of the dramatic. Few campaigns succeed solely on the basis of the information they provide or the didactic arguments that they offer. Information is important, but it must be embedded in symbols and actions that spark the imagination and invite participation from a public that seeks excitement and psychological gratification as much as it does hard evidence and material satisfactions. Political campaigns must be good theater, and through television, in particular, the candidate can create "mini-dramas" that project a favorable image with which voters can identify.

13

Persuasion in Social Conflicts: Alternatives to the Co-active Approach

From time to time we have argued that however applicable the traditionally prescribed co-active approach to persuasion may be for most rhetorical situations, it is only of limited value in social conflicts. Recall from Chapter 6 the defining elements of the co-active approach. First and foremost, it is a rhetoric of *identification*, building as it does on *common ground* between source and receiver. Second, we suggested, it is persuasion *free of threats or punishments*—a rhetoric of appeals and arguments, rather than a rhetoric of power. Third, it is *rational* persuasion, at least in the sense that the co-active persuader attempts to *appear* reasonable and rational. Fourth, it proceeds by modifying attitudes or attitude components as a *precondition* for changes in behavior. Finally, it is, ideally speaking, a *democratic* approach in the sense that the co-active persuader seeks *no special advantage* over those with whom he disagrees other than that which accrues from the persuasiveness of his arguments and appeals. We shall argue in this chapter that for each of these characteristics of the co-active approach there are combative alternatives—rhetorical in at least a peripheral sense —which might well be more appropriate for conflict situations. As a general proposition, we shall argue that rather than being an alternative to money, punitive force, or other forms of power, persuasion in conflict situations is either *an instrument of power, an accompaniment to power, or a consequence of power. In conflict situations, rhetoric serves power and power serves rhetoric.*

What are social conflicts? Who seeks to influence whom, how, and for what purposes? What are the relative advantages and disadvantages of combative approaches to persuasion? After discussing these questions, we move to a comparison of co-active and combative strategies as applied to protest movements for institutional change. Finally, we look at expressive strategies as still another alternative to the co-active approach.

Nature of Social Conflicts

In Chapter 1, we defined a social conflict as a *clash over incompatible interests in which one party's relative gain is another's relative loss.* An explication of that definition should help readers to see why the traditionally prescribed approach may be of limited value.

First, a social conflict is not simply a misunderstanding or semantic confusion or communication breakdown; it goes deeper than that. Situation comedies are rife with apparent crises between husband and wife or boss and employee in which the source of tension is an error of fact or interpretation that is easily correctable with a bit of dialogue. These might more accurately be labeled as *pseudoconflicts.*

Second, the notion of a clash of interests presupposes something more than a disagreement, difference of opinion, or academic controversy. This point deserves considerable emphasis since there is a widespread tendency to minimize or wish away conflicts by treating them as though they were mere disagreements. To underscore the point, picture the difference between a newspaper columnist arguing that the auto workers deserve higher wages and the same argument coming from the head of the United Auto Workers in the midst of a collective-bargaining session. The columnist would have been arguing a controversial position, it is true, but it is questionable whether he or she would have had anything more than an academic and passing interest in the matter. The union leader, by contrast, is quite clearly involved in a social conflict, evidenced by a clash over incompatible interests. Similarly, two people—even two intimates—may subscribe to divergent religious principles without necessarily being in conflict. Their interests might well become incompatible, however, if one felt morally compelled to convert the other, or if, as in a marriage, both had to decide how to rear their offspring. (Note that conflicts over principles arise whenever one party makes unacceptable claims upon the other, or when, in the face of divergent goals, their activities must be coordinated.)

To have an interest in something, then, is to covet or value it personally, whether it be an item of scarcity such as money or a principle such as equal pay for equal work. For two people (or groups) to have *incompatible interests*, each must stand as an obstacle to maximum realization of the other's interests. Two people may disagree on the market value of a house that is up for sale without necessarily being in conflict. But should the disputants be seller and potential buyer, they would indeed be in conflict. (Note that they might well reach an amicable compromise and still have been in conflict; as in any such bargaining situation, each party's relative gain over what he or she could have paid or received is the other party's relative loss.)

Third, the same persons may be embroiled in a conflict on one level and in a controversy or disagreement on another level. Consider the case of two undergraduates engaged in a classroom debate over Israel's annexation of Arab territories. To the extent that either party may receive a poor grade or suffer loss of reputation from doing badly in the debate, they are, indeed, engaged in a conflict. But the conflict is not over Israel's relationship with her Arab neighbors! *That* remains a disagreement or difference of opinion. A conflict may involve value differences or personal animosities or competition for scarce resources, but, once again, *the personal interests of one party must be threatened by the other party.*

Already it should be clear that appeals to reason or common ground may not be sufficient to resolve social conflicts; indeed, in such conflicts as between labor and management, buyer and seller, husband and wife, Israel and Egypt, the combatants might well have reason to remain antagonistic. Let us now turn to our fourth point, which is that, to a greater degree than in classroom discussions or bull sessions between friends, attitudes in conflict situations are linked to beliefs about relative power capacities.

In a college debate, one has the luxury to decide that such and such is what two conflicting parties *ought* to do, irrespective of the nature of the context and of each side's willingness and capacity to reward or punish the other. The realities of conflict situations generally militate against agreement on "ideal" solutions. Trust levels tend to be low, ego-involvement high, channels of communication closed or restricted, and neither side able to enforce its conception of an "ideal" outcome. Hence, "peace with honor" may be a truce agreement following a military stalemate. What is considered "honorable" or "desirable" is necessarily what one can hope to get *under the circumstances.* Correspondingly, as we shall see, conflicting parties each may struggle to alter the other's circumstances as a way of modifying the other's beliefs and attitudes. What emerges most often is an implicit or explicit *compromise.*

Influence in Social Conflicts

The foregoing example might lead some readers to search for some term other than "persuasion" to describe the means by which decisions are influenced in conflict situations. Would it not be more appropriate to say that the foreign ministers of Israel and her Arab neighbors are "constrained" by their adversaries or "coerced" into agreement? Is there not a difference between *voluntary compliance,* arrived at through freedom of choice, and *grudging compliance,* coerced through restrictions on choice? And even where agreements are reached through promises of reward rather than threats of punishment, mightn't some term other than "persuasion" be found to describe the means of influence that has been employed?

These are troublesome questions, not easily resolved. Indeed, many theorists (e.g., Fotheringham, 1966; Bettinghaus, 1973) would label all acts of force "coercive" and they would maintain that persuasion and coercion are not only separable but antithetical. Still others (e.g., Gamson, 1968; Parsons, 1963) would distinguish persuasion from *constraints* and *inducements.* According to Gamson, persuasion changes "minds" (beliefs, values, or attitudes) without altering the target's situation, while inducements and constraints alter situations without changing minds:

> Constraints are the addition of new disadvantages to the situation, or the threat to do so, regardless of the particular resources used. A student group threatening to hold a sit-in unless the university administration takes a desired course of action is using constraints. So is the U.S. government when it drops "antipersonnel" bombs on North Vietnam in an effort to make that government's participation in the war in South Vietnam more "punishing" (p. 75). . . . Inducements are the addition of new advantages to the situation

or the promise to do so, regardless of the particular resources used. The [target] acts as the partisan group desires in exchange for some resource which they have received or will receive. There is a specific good or service involved as a *quid pro quo* in such an exchange (p. 77). . . . Persuasion involves some change in the minds of the [targets] without adding anything new to their situation. It involves making them prefer the same outcomes that the influencer prefers (p. 79).

Admittedly, there are important differences reflected in these conceptual distinctions. It *is* one thing to purchase agreement, another to win agreement through sound arguments: one thing, again, to coerce involuntary acceptance of a proposition, another to secure voluntary acceptance through what might be called "pure" persuasion. In practical terms, combatants who secure grudging compliance must constantly maintain a surveillance and enforcement capability since their adversaries might cease to comply or might even retaliate once their backs are turned. This is not so in the case of "pure" persuasion.

Still, for a variety of reasons to be elaborated upon later in this chapter, we would reject the notion that persuasion and coercion or persuasion, inducements, and constraints can so easily be dichotomized or trichotomized. Our quarrel is not so much with classification systems of the kind proposed by Gamson, but rather with the mistaken assumption that is so readily drawn from them—namely, that actions in conflict situations may be labeled as fitting within one *or* another category. Consistent with the overall thesis stated earlier—that, in conflict situations, rhetoric serves power and power serves rhetoric—we would argue that elements of persuasion and inducement or persuasion and constraint are generally manifested in the same act. Seldom is persuasion truly "pure" but then again neither do inducements or constraints take place without rhetorical elements.[1] Here we will only list some of the many ways in which these means of influence are interlinked:

- Promises and threats do not automatically induce or constrain. In order for them to be effective, the influence-agent must persuasively establish the credibility of his promises or threats.

- Apart from whatever direct impact they may have, the actual use of rewards or punishments (as opposed to the mere promise or threat of

---

1. Kriesberg (1973, p. 109) makes this same point. He pictures a triangle in which "pure" persuasion, rewards (i.e., inducements), and coercion (i.e., constraints) are at the corners of the triangle. Any given act of influence in social conflicts falls somewhere within the triangle. Most acts of influence, he observes, involve healthy doses of persuasion.

We recommend the Kriesberg book as an introduction to conflict theory. The first three chapters are nontechnical and provide an excellent summary of major conflict variables.

same) may have communicative value. As we saw in Chapter 2, even acts of force or violence may contain implicit appeals and arguments.

- Knowledge that a boss, parent, or other power figure has the capacity to reward or punish us may cause us to pay greater attention to this person's words of advice than we would to those of a power equal.

- Inducements and constraints may restrict choice but they seldom eliminate it entirely. So long as there is some freedom of choice there is also room for argument—hence, opportunity and need for persuasion.

- Under some circumstances, to be discussed below, changes in behavior produced by "adding advantages" or "adding disadvantages" to the adversary's situation may lead to genuine changes in the adversary's attitudes. Contrary to Gamson, inducements and constraints *can* change "minds" in a very fundamental sense.

- Acts that seem on the surface to be instances of "pure" persuasion may be made compelling by dint of the influence-agent's capacity to purchase or control the *instrumentalities of persuasion:* media access, information, channels of influence, and the like.

These briefly mentioned ways in which rhetoric and power may go hand in hand should suggest the flavor of conflict interactions and provide an advance indication of what we mean by "combative alternatives" to the co-active approach to persuasion. This is not to say that the co-active approach has no place in social conflicts, for, as we shall now see, most conflicts require some combination of cooperativeness and combativeness.

Cooperation and Competition in Mixed-Motive Conflicts

One of the paradoxical features of practically all social conflicts is that the adversaries are motivated, simultaneously, to cooperate and compete with each other. Seldom is either party served by annihilating the enemy, or taking all his money, or totally incapacitating him. Real-life conflicts, in this sense, are not like foot races or games of chess or poker. Instead, they are of the *mixed motive* variety. To understand this fact of social conflicts is to understand why purely combative strategies of influence seldom make sense.

Consider, once again, the case of a labor-management conflict over wages. Admittedly, it is in the interests of labor to *get* as *much* as possible, and it is likewise in the interests of management to *give* as *little* as possible. Each, moreover, has combative weapons available (prolonged strikes, layoffs, etc.) by which to severely punish or cripple the enemy. Why don't they use them more often?

The obvious answer is that they have much to lose by acting combatively and much to gain through cooperation. Morality aside, let us

Moves and Countermoves in the Prisoner's Dilemma Game

Many of the essential features of mixed motive conflicts are illustrated in what has come to be known as the prisoner's dilemma game (PD). The table presented below is known as a *payoff matrix*. Player Y has two pos-

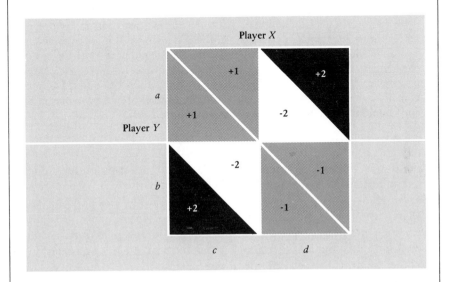

sible moves, *a* and *b*. If Y plays *a*, he receives either +1 or −2 units of reward, depending on X's move. If Y chooses *b*, he gets +2 or −1 units of reward, depending on X's move. X's payoffs are similarly determined by a combination of both players' moves. The two players must choose simultaneously.

As can be seen, each player has a possible cooperative choice (*a* or *c*) and a possible competitive choice (*b* or *d*). Each knows that the competitive choice is best for him personally, for it offers the possibility of the greatest gain. But—and this underscores the interdependent nature of mixed motive conflicts—if both players make the competitive choice, both lose. What constitutes "winning" and "losing" in this type of conflict? What is the most rational strategy for achieving "victory"?

One of the advantages of games such as this one is that they help us to understand a great variety of conflicts, from marital squabbles to labor-management contests. In both types of conflict, for example, goals often remain ambiguous over the life of the relationship, each party alternating betwen mutual accommodation (the *ac* combination) and victory at the expense of the other. (In some bad marriages that we know of, each side willingly suffers −1 outcomes solely for the perverse joy of seeing the other experience −1 outcomes.) At the same time, of course, the game necessarily oversimplifies life's situations. In real life, for example, each side may have more than two options; moves may alternate, rather than occurring simultaneously; payoffs are not known in any quantitative sense; and the distribution of rewards and punishments may vary from that presented in the above table. Nevertheless, the game captures the ambiguities and paradoxes of conflict interactions, and that is no small accomplishment.

We urge that you play this game with someone in three stages: 1. For 50 trials (each trial involves one simultaneous move by each player), all talk between you should be prohibited. After the 50 trials are over, compute total scores for each of you. The scores will themselves be a form of communication about how each of you plays the game. 2. For the next 50 trials, verbal communication should again be prohibited. This time, however, each side's move should be revealed after each trial. 3. For the next 25 trials, you may verbally communicate before each trial. Pay careful attention to the ploys and counterploys used in making threats and promises.

---

examine the interests of labor and management in terms of the potential costs and benefits exchanged by acting combatively or cooperatively (Gergen, 1969).

First, we should remember that purely coercive influence entails relatively high *delivery costs*. To punish another, or even to threaten effectively, one must mount an offensive capability. Co-active persuasion, on the other hand, may cost little or nothing.

Second, because conflicts involve reciprocal influence, each side must calculate the repercussions of its actions in terms of possible *retaliation costs*. The use of force may carry the day, but only at the price of incurring the wrath of the adversary who may strike back with even greater fury.

Third, the use of purely combative strategies over an issue such as wages may block the resolution of other, subsidiary, issues. The ensuing buildup of antagonisms may so impede communication and reduce trust as to make what once were considered trivial questions into significant and unresolvable matters of principle.

Fourth, strategies of a purely combative nature often enrage non-adversaries who then bring their own influence to bear on the situation. Some combative acts are punished by law, others are vilified by the press, and still others cause backlash reactions from the mass public.

Thus far, we have stressed the costs involved in employing purely combative strategies, but we should add, finally, the benefits possible from employing cooperative, co-active means of influence. Conflict theorists like to speak of costs and benefits in terms of a hypothetical conflict *pie*, and they are fond of pointing out that the size of the pie is by no means finite. Should a labor-management conflict escalate beyond control, the size of the pie is reduced. On the other hand, should the two sides find a way to increase productivity and profits, the size of the pie is increased. Cooperation on one issue can breed a spirit of harmony on other issues and reduce the need for offensive capabilities.

So what is the "optimal" influence strategy for mixed motive conflicts? Is it any strategy that so pleases the adversary as to yield speedy agreement? No again! Speedy agreements are often inequitable agreements, and when one side does all the giving and none of the getting, its strategy of cooperation constitutes a sellout.[2]

Summarizing this discussion, we can say that the test of a method of influence in conflict situations is *neither* whether it produces speedy consensus nor whether it yields the largest share of a finite conflict pie. Choices between strategies must be framed in more complex ways. For example: Compared to alternative methods of influence, does the strategy in question offer the greatest possibility for benefits at the smallest possible cost? Is the strategy in the common interest as well as the competitive interest? In addition to producing overt compliance, will it produce interpersonal liking and trust and perhaps even favorable attitudes toward the actions being recommended? One generalization seems reliable for sure: that the optimal method of influence will involve some combination of cooperativeness and combativeness.

The Audiences for Social Conflicts

Even if it assumed (however erroneously) that purely combative strategies are required for dealing with the adversary, it should be remembered that the leadership of conflict groups such as labor and management must address a variety of audiences besides the opposition; indeed, that co-active

---

2. A preference for speedy conflict resolutions is often held by persons who identify more with the need for order and stability in social or political systems than they do with the interests of any one party to an interfactional conflict within the system. We may say that they are *system-oriented* rather than *actor-oriented*. From a system-oriented perspective, conflicts are "bad" because they are disruptive of the system's interests. A nationwide strike may cripple the economy, for example. Hence, the emphasis is on how conflicts may be prevented, minimized, or quickly terminated in the system's interests. Of course, conflicts may also take place between actors and systems, as when protestors take on officials of the government. In these cases, especially, system-oriented persons are likely to take a dim view of combative stratagems. For a general discussion of actor-oriented versus system-oriented perspectives, see Simons (1972) and Gamson (1968, Chapter 1). Attitudes toward disruptive protests often hinge on whether one is actor-oriented or system-oriented. See, for example, the fascinating debate between Fortas (1968) and Zinn (1968).

persuasion with some of these audiences is necessary in order to constrain or coerce the adversary. Co-active persuasion has a place even in the most embittered clashes between adversaries.

Figure 13.1 presents a simplified model of actors, reactors, and communication patterns in a mixed-motive conflict characterized by two competing groups. In the figure we show five pairs of messages (each leadership component sends comparable types of messages) directed to five different audiences.

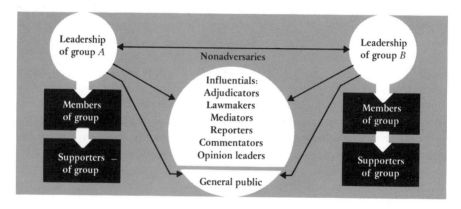

Fig. 13.1 Leader-generated messages and their audiences in a mixed-motive conflict between two groups

(1) *Leader to supporters.* In industrial conflicts, international conflicts, conflicts between political parties, etc., there are generally people who sympathize with one side or the other without functioning as active members. Co-active persuasion is used primarily to recruit and indoctrinate these supporters. The larger and more committed the following, the larger the power base. Hence, leaders seek to foment a sense of grievance, a feeling of collective identity among the following, a belief in the legitimacy of the group and its leaders, hostility toward the opposition, and confidence in the in-group's power to succeed.

(2) *Leader to hard-core members.* The same co-active rhetoric used to recruit and indoctrinate supporters is also used to intensify the commitments of hard-core members, but in addition they must be mobilized to do the hard work of the adversary group.

(3) *Leader to general public.* If significantly awakened, the general public can tip the balance in social conflicts, either by constraining one or the other side or by bringing indirect pressure on the adversaries via lawmakers, the courts, and so on. Hence, the leaders of adversary groups

engage in public relations campaigns aimed at justifying their means and ends and delegitimizing the opposition. In some cases, the leadership may use combative methods of influence on the general public as a way of exerting indirect pressure on adversaries or influentials.

(4) *Leader to influentials.* Each side regularly courts these persons, and in regulated conflicts, may be bound by the decisions of adjudicators or reciprocally influenced by mediators. Combative influence may also be employed here as a way of bringing indirect pressure on adversaries.

(5) *Leader to leader.* In rough-and-tumble conflicts between adversaries, direct co-active persuasion between leaders may be highly restricted but it may still take place via messages to nonadversaries. As conflict escalates, messages ostensibly directed at other leaders may actually be meant for the ears of nonadversaries or followers, as a way of confirming the rigidity or stupidity or immorality of the opposition. It may also be used, of course, to get the opposition's attention and their willingness to negotiate and compromise.

These, then, are the basic types of leader-generated messages in social conflicts. As we move now to a discussion of combative alternatives to the co-active approach we should be mindful that the same act of influence may serve different rhetorical functions for different audiences.

Combative Alternatives to the Co-Active Approach

Earlier it was suggested that for each of the components of the co-active approach, there are combative counterparts, rhetorical in at least a peripheral sense in that they all involve human communications designed to influence behavior by modifying beliefs, values, or attitudes in intended directions. Table 13.1 lists these strategies alongside their co-active equivalents. Strictly speaking, these should not necessarily be viewed as alternatives since, as was indicated earlier, those in conflict may employ combinations of co-active and combative approaches.

No attempt will be made in this section to decide between strategems in any absolute sense although we will describe advantages and disadvantages as well as the conditions in which each approach is likely to be most effective.

I. Rhetoric of Division

Whereas the rhetoric of identification aims at bridging distances between adversaries, the rhetoric of division is distance-increasing. Divisive rhetoric accuses, belittles, vilifies. The speaker is right, the listener wrong; the speaker is superior, the listener inferior. Differences are underscored, and they tend to be exaggerated through invective and ridicule.

Table 13.1 Co-Active Versus Combative Strategies of Persuasion

Co-Active	Combative
Rhetoric of identification: appeals to common ground; affirmation of shared values by means of symbolic acts.	Rhetoric of division: emphasis on differences between antagonists; use of invective, ridicule, symbolic acts of force.
Motivational appeals, including fear appeals, compliments, appeals to duty, etc. Avoidance of monetary inducements or coercive constraints.	Rhetoric of inducements and constraints; promises and rewards; threats and punishments for noncompliance —used to alter beliefs, values, and attitudes, not just behavior.
Rational persuasion; appearance of being rational and reasonable.	Appearance of being irrational or unreasonable; loss of control.
Changes in beliefs, values, or attitudes as a precondition for changes in behavior.	"Forced compliance" techniques: changes in behavior as a precondition for changes in beliefs, attitudes, and values.
No special effort to purchase or control media, channels, or other instrumentalities of "pure" persuasion.	Use of money or other sources of power to gain selective control over instrumentalities of "pure" persuasion.

In addition to verbal polemics, persuaders may engage in symbolic acts of division, including acts of force or violence of the kind described in Chapter 2. They may pour blood on draft board files or desecrate the flag or interrupt highway traffic or sit-in at segregated lunch counters, each such move designed as an act of protest and an implicit appeal for justice.

What are we to make of the rhetoric of division? From what we have said in Chapter 8, it would appear that under most circumstances, a rhetoric of identification is infinitely superior. Recall that common ground facilitates decoding, increases attraction, and in the case of relevant dispositional similarities, is likely to increase respect and trust. Appeals to common ground are also more likely to engender a spirit of cooperation in conflict situations. In one experiment (Sherif, 1958), intergroup rivalries between campers were considerably reduced when supraordinate goals were introduced which could not be obtained by the efforts of either group alone. The environment was arranged in such a way as to make the campers more conscious of their commonalities than of their differences. The campers, for example, were confronted with common dangers, such as a water shortage, and they were required to mobilize their resources in order to secure a much desired film. Sherif found that intergroup friendships increased, name-calling and derogation of out-groups decreased, and blatant glorification and bragging about the in-group diminished.

Of course, liking, trust, and even cooperativeness are not the only criteria for evaluation, as we have seen. From an actor-orientation, a rhetoric of division may still be preferable, especially in intense conflicts against recalcitrant opponents. One advantage of ridicule, obscenities, vilification, and so on, is that it may call attention to strongly held feelings in ways that polite and conciliatory language does not. In hurling abuse at one's adversaries, one often aims at gaining increased support from sympathizers or potential sympathizers. A rhetoric of division against the persuader's opponents is simultaneously a rhetoric of identification for those already in sympathy with the persuader's views. Symbolic acts of force and violence may be especially moving, both because of their dramatic qualities, and because, in risking punishment from a more powerful adversary, persuaders evidence the credibility of their commitment to the cause they consider just.

Divisive rhetoric may also, in some cases, moderate the opposition of conflict antagonists. The rhetoric of identification is predicated on the assumption that receivers will entertain reasonably high estimates of themselves and of the groups with which they are affiliated. This is not always a valid assumption, as we saw in Chapter 8. Many receivers are likely to be self-rejecting, either as a general predisposition or as applied to specific topics or to relative differences between themselves and other groups. The phenomenon of self-rejection appears to be the psychological dynamic behind appeals to guilt, envy, or embarrassment and is by no means confined to groups that have been accorded second-class status. The potential for evoking guilt has been a powerful weapon in the hands of protest groups, especially when directed at persons who consider themselves fair-minded. (We will return to this point in the discussion of threats.) When issued by persons in positions of authority, scoldings for behavior considered inept or improper may cause considerable embarrassment. In his discussion on "making Machiavelli work for peace," Zimbardo (1972, p. 97) has observed that a combination of guilt and embarrassment may be registered by receivers toward persons or groups who have been traditionally stigmatized by society, with a consequent tendency to try to get rid of the offensive-appearing sources by buying them off.

II. Rhetoric of Inducements and Constraints

Recall that inducements involve rewards or promises of reward for compliance and that constraints involve punishments or threats of punishment for noncompliance. We will be concerned in this section not with the direct impact on overt behavior that inducements and constraints may have but

on their rhetorical value as means for modifying beliefs, values, and attitudes.[3] Already we have noted that the capacity of power figures to reward
or punish is likely to cause those dependent upon them to give greater attention to their suggestions. Knowledge that the boss can promote us or
fire us, for example, should predispose us to take his or her ideas more
seriously. This constitutes a rhetorical advantage for the power figure even
though it does not guarantee ungrudging compliance.

Apart from serving as adjuncts to argumentative discourse, as in the
previous example, inducements and constraints may constitute messages in
their own right. In this connection, Schelling (1960, p. 117) has drawn a
distinction between "speech" and "moves," the latter including inducements and constraints:

> Talk is not a substitute for moves. Moves can in some way alter the game,
> by incurring manifest costs, risks, or a reduced range of subsequent choice;
> they have an information content, or *evidence* content, of a different char-
> acter from that of speech. Talk can be cheap when moves are not. . . . While
> one's maneuvers are not unambiguous in their revelation of one's value sys-
> tems and may even be deliberately deceptive, they nevertheless have an
> evidential quality that mere speech has not.

Despite the communicative potential of "moves," it is not always advisable to employ them. This is particularly true of threats, the use of
which, according to Raven and Kruglanski (1970) often produces such undesired rhetorical effects as the following: (1) perception of hostile intentions; (2) curtailment of dialogue; (3) increased intransigence; and (4)
mobilization of counteractive resources.

With respect to inducements, Raven and Kruglanski distinguish between small and large rewards. Relatively small rewards or promises of
small reward are likely to have the opposite effects of threats: (1) suspicion

---

3. Experimental research on inducements and constraints is most often conducted by involving subjects in conflict games. In a typical game, each side has
a choice of cooperating with the adversary or competing with him, and both must
move simultaneously. Potential "payoffs" from combinations of the players'
choices are stipulated in advance.

For an example of a widely used conflict game, see the Prisoner's Dilemma,
described in the box on page 255. An excellent introduction to game theory and
bargaining is found in Schelling (1960), *The Strategy of Conflict*. A rather comprehensive review of game theoretic research on inducements and constraints is
presented by Tedeschi, Schlenker and Bonoma (1973). Steinfatt and Miller (1974)
have presented the best review we have seen on the use of communication in
conflict games. Game theorists and researchers, unfortunately, do not always distinguish between the effects of inducements and constraints on overt behavior
and their effects on attitudes, beliefs, and values. One source that does is Raven
and Kruglanski (1970).

of benign intent; (2) desire for dialogue; (3) an impulse to respond in kind; and (4) a search for mutually acceptable solutions. As for large rewards, Raven and Kruglanski have this to say (p. 92):

> For one thing, it may seem inappropriate to dispense considerable rewards to the other side in the absence of the assurance of reciprocation. Thus, the interacting parties may hesitate a long while before communicating their intention to bestow "massive" favors on one another. Also, communicated promises of rewards are less likely to appear credible to the recipient to the extent that the rewards appear excessively large. Furthermore, sudden reception of considerable benefits might arouse suspicion and resentment, as when the rewards are interpreted as "bribes" or attempts at trickery. On the assumption that one is never given something for nothing, the individual's perceived salience of the outcomes at stake (i.e., one determinant of subjective conflict) is likely to increase. In addition, the feeling that the other side is being untruthful may instigate a strong feeling of resentment and lead to a resolution to resist the influencer on *interpersonal* grounds.

For these reasons, those seeking to constrain others often seek to disguise selfish intent or, in other ways, to depersonalize noxious demands. They may justify their insistence on compliance (and threat of punishment for noncompliance) on grounds that the situation dictates their directives or that they are merely doing their job. So as to escape the onus of constraints they may get others ("hatchet men") to do their dirty work. Finally, as with divisive rhetoric, they may justify threats or threatening acts on grounds that the target is morally culpable. Raven and Kruglanski (1970, p. 93) acknowledge that this may be a particularly persuasive use of threats but they add an interesting qualifying comment:

> Threats may also facilitate conflict resolution when issued under the aegis of a cause accepted as legitimate by the opposite side. The usefulness of threats (vs. other modes of influence) in these circumstances is due to their dramatic value. . . . For example, a majority may uphold values strongly opposed to suppression of, or discrimination against, minorities, yet continue such practices while remaining unaware of the inconsistency. This state of affairs is particularly likely to prevail when the majority (as often happens) finds the situation convenient and/or profitable. Under these conditions mild protests by the minority are likely to go unnoticed and only strong dramatic effects (such as may be achieved by the use of coercive, violent means) are likely to jolt the majority out of its apathy and force it into making the choice between actively defending the status quo, thereby taking a counter valuative stand, and supporting the moral values involved, which implies change in the direction demanded by the threatening group. . . . The effects of combining legitimacy and threats becomes complicated further by the fact that, in our own culture, coercion has an almost inherent aura of illegitimacy. Thus, it is likely that when faced with incongruency involved

in a "legitimate threat," the individual's reaction to threats will become polarized. Some persons may react to the legitimacy of the demands and comply with the requests advanced by the threatening group, while others may respond to the illegitimacy of coercion and counter it in kind.

Still another disadvantage of large rewards, of course, is that they entail greater delivery costs—a larger transfer or resources. For this reason, persons in positions of power often dispense symbolic or psychological benefits in place of tangible benefits such as money. Thus, for example, the Johnson administration's "War on Poverty" includes a high-sounding "Rent Supplement" bill that appropriates less than one dollar per person per year to needy families; the Nixon administration follows with a "Work Incentive Program" that offers little promise of employment following training; and the Ford administration announces a "Tax Rebate" program with great fanfare but quietly retrieves that money, and more, with an indirect tax on petroleum consumption. According to Murray Edelman (1967), it is the first rule of politics that those elites having political clout get concrete rewards such as tax loopholes and corporate subsidies while the masses get symbolic substitutes that cost little.

The rhetoric of conflict is concerned to a considerable degree with verbal messages about the meaning of inducements and constraints. In bargaining, for example, each side interprets its own offers and counteroffers in a favorable light and impugns the adversary's promises of reward. So as to conserve delivery costs, use is made of such rhetorical ploys as bluffing, issuing vague rather than explicit promises, and packaging meager inducements attractively so that they will have the appearance of great worth ("selling the sizzle but not the steak").

As was noted earlier, persuasion functions at least peripherally in social conflicts in establishing the *credibility* of threats and promises—the willingness and capacity of the influence-seeker to actually punish in the event of noncompliance or reward in the event of compliance. Here the nonverbal is of extreme importance since verbal claims are so often ambiguous, deceptive, or untrue. Nonverbal behaviors may reinforce verbal claims or belie them. For example, the credibility of a verbal threat may be enhanced by actual displays of power. On the other hand, recall the scene from the movie, *Take the Money and Run*, where Woody Allen attempts to hold up a bank. In the typical old-fashioned gangster movie, the bank robber looked like a bank robber, and by disposing unceremoniously of those who got in his way, he left no doubt about his willingness and capacity to inflict punishments. The scene from the Woody Allen movie parodied the classic bank holdup. By contrast to truly credible bank robbers, Woody is bespectacled, emaciated, and nervous. Moreover, the toy pistol that he brandishes has been carved out of soap and inadvertently exposed to the rain. Woody does not have a chance.

Later in this chapter we will discuss still another aspect of the rhetoric of inducements and constraints—their use as a strategy for securing belief or attitude-change *following* behavior-change. Let us now turn to an examination of how the appearance of "irrationality" may be used to advantage in conflict situations.

III. Appearing Unreasonable or Irrational

From time to time we have argued in this book that, particularly with the kinds of untrusting and potentially hostile audiences one is likely to encounter in conflict situations, it is more effective to understate rather than overstate, present arguments in balanced fashion rather than one-sidedly, offer "good" evidence rather than "poor" evidence or no evidence, and appear competent and trustworthy rather than incompetent and untrustworthy.

These generalizations still stand, but they need to be tempered somewhat as applied to the making of threats and to attempts at deterring constraints by adversaries. For these purposes, conflict situations appear to invite a logic of their own; one which, by the standards of co-active persuasion makes those pursuing their own interests appear highly irrational and unreasonable. Rather surprisingly, it is often effective to seem undependable or entirely out of control.

Schelling (1960) emphasizes this point repeatedly. How, for example, does A convince B of a willingness and capacity to seize a traffic lane that they both want? Not by "rational persuasion" in the usual sense, although that cannot be ruled out entirely, but by opening the car window and screaming that the brakes have failed, or by advancing the car while looking away from the other driver, or by acting insane, inebriated, or retarded, or as though seizure of the lane is a matter of principle.

Looking back at this example, we can see several ways in which apparent *loss of self-control* may help make threats persuasive or, correspondingly, help make resistance to threats effective.

1. *Appearance of external constraints.* Being constrained by a brake failure provides license for A to forge ahead. In this case the apparent constraint stemmed from mechanical causes; in other situations constraints are imposed by individuals. Thus, for example, a union may vote to constrain its negotiators from being able to postpone a strike deadline. This apparent loss of power actually may increase the negotiator's bargaining power since the rule binds the adversary as well.

In general, external constraints, or any other sources of reduced control, make us less vulnerable to the pressures which might be exerted upon us by our adversaries. This writer learned to his chagrin recently that the

Philadelphia police are forbidden from retracting parking tickets once they have written them, even if they have made a mistake. Similarly, professors at some schools are not allowed to change a grade once it has been written into the official record. The rule makes them less vulnerable to student pressures.

2. *Madness, ignorance, retardation, physical symptoms.* By acting insane, or by refusing to look at a competitor for the contested traffic lane, our driver gains a kind of power that is not too different in a functional sense from that which is provided by external constraints. Examples like these can be found in social situations as well. A bored party-goer may announce that she has developed a severe headache which compels her to leave early. A seducer may claim that his advances are motivated by uncontrollable passions.

Perhaps the most convincing way to show that you mean business is to actually lose control. Thus, the seducer may actually get carried away, and the party-goer may actually get a headache. Watzlawick, *et al.* (1967) have convincingly argued that the schizophrenic's symptoms are an unconscious way of warding off perceived threats from the outside world. Taking the traffic lane example to its extreme, the driver bent on victory might place a brick on the accelerator and climb on to the back seat. That would indeed be convincing.

3. *Standing on principle.* By acting as though seizure of the traffic lane is a moral right, the driver acts not very differently from heads of state. Seldom does one nation initiate or escalate belligerent actions against another without having first invented moral justifications for its assaults. Acts and threats of force are almost always accompanied, too, by expressions of anger, indignation, and the like. Justificatory discourse of this sort is meant partly for third parties and partly to demoralize the adversary, but it is also another way of saying that the nation has reached the limits of its control. When President Nixon renewed the bombing of Hanoi and Haiphong in December of 1972, he let it be known that he was furious at the North for its alleged violations of the spirit of a tentative truce agreement that had been hammered out by Henry Kissinger in October and November of that same year. Whether Nixon was actually furious probably only Mr. Nixon knows, but the impression left in press briefings was that he would now stop at nothing to achieve "peace with honor." By acting indignant in defense of a principle, the President was able to couple a moral plea with strong evidence that he did indeed have the willingness to coerce.

Just as it is between nations, so it is between persons or between groups. The parent's menacing stare is accompanied with the reminder that rules are to be obeyed; the child's temper tantrum is coupled with a plea for justice. Labor and management blame each other for impending strikes, and the threat of an affair or a divorce is frequently justified in terms of what the other spouse has done.

We are not saying, of course, that people *ought* to threaten each other using the means we have described; that raises ethical questions which need to be considered separately. Nor are we saying that these means are always effective; only that they *may* be effective. Attempting to persuade through apparent loss of control is clearly *risk-taking*. Suppose the other driver is also a lunatic. Suppose the labor negotiator who is constrained from postponing a strike deadline is dealing with a company that would welcome a strike. Quite obviously, this principle is not meant for all contingencies. At the very least, any threatener who attempts to succeed by acting "irrationally" should be very certain that the opposition will react rationally.

IV. The "Forced Compliance" Paradigm: Changing Attitudes or Attitude Components by First Changing Behaviors

The strategies to be examined in this section involve a reversal of the "normal" sequence of persuasion. Under "normal" circumstances, a message is communicated, the receivers reevaluate their own thinking, modify their beliefs, values, or attitudes, and then change their behavior. If, as so often happens, the receivers remain intransigent or modify their attitudes or attitude components but not their behaviors, the co-active persuader simply tries again.

But now consider the not atypical case of workers who, having been promoted to supervisory positions, gradually begin to look down on their former mates where before they were antimanagement. A number of explanations have been offered to account for phenomena of this kind, the most prominent of which is Festinger's (1957) "forced compliance" hypothesis. Actually, the term "forced compliance" is somewhat of a misnomer since, in most of the research experiments conducted by Festinger and his colleagues, subjects were induced to comply and they were given some degree of choice in the matter. Still, the important point for our purposes is that changes in behavior produced by inducements and constraints can *lead to*—rather than follow from—genuine changes in attitudes or attitude components.

Festinger accounts for this phenomenon in terms of his theory of cognitive dissonance (1957), which we introduced in Chapter 5. In the example given above, the newly promoted supervisors discovered a discrepancy between their attitudes and the behavior required of them in their new role. Recall that discrepancies of this kind are said to be psychologically uncomfortable or "dissonant," and one way the supervisors can reduce that dissonance is by modifying their attitudes.[4]

Although contentions about the conditions under which people may be most readily persuaded following "forced compliance" remain a matter of lively debate, the many studies in this area—several of them to be reviewed in the next chapter—leave little doubt but that, contrary to the old saw, "a man persuaded against his will" . . . "is not necessarily" . . . "of the same opinion still." As McGuire (1969, p. 180) has concluded, the question is no longer whether overt compliance tends to become internalized but "under what conditions it occurs in the greatest amount."

Festinger's hypothesis is of special interest to us because it concerns situations in which the persuader actually *creates* attitude-behavior discrepancies for receivers by pressuring them to engage in various counter-attitudinal activities. According to Festinger, two things must happen before attitudes will be modified following forced compliance. First, receivers must be *pressured enough so that they will comply, but not so much that they will feel as though they have had no choice.* The pressure, then, must be subtle, mild, or indirect. If it is too forceful it may produce grudging compliance, but it will probably intensify negative attitudes. Second, receivers must be *prevented from reducing the "dissonance" they experience in other ways.* If receivers can claim that they acted because they had to, or if they can find other rationalizations for performance of their discrepant acts, then they need not modify their attitudes. The general proposition advanced by Festinger is that the *less justification provided to receivers for complying with counter attitudinal requests, the greater the likelihood that they will modify their attitudes.*[5] Let us consider a number of offshoots of this general proposition.

---

4. Once attitudes have changed as a consequence of behavior change, they should, in turn, influence future behavior; otherwise, by definition, they are not truly attitudes. Kelman (1974) makes this frequently overlooked point in his excellent article.

5. Probably the most popular competitor to Festinger's theory is Bem's (1965, 1970) self-perception theory, which was briefly summarized in Chapter 5. Bem does not disagree with Festinger's interesting predictions but he seeks to place a different interpretation on the findings from forced compliance research. Specifically, he maintains that one need not assume a painful drive such as dissonance to be operating when one modifies his attitudes or beliefs following changes in behavior. In the normal course of events, people simply learn about themselves from looking retrospectively at their behavior, in much the way they learn from other external cues. The notion of dissonance, he maintains, is vague and inelegant.

1. *Role-playing and degrees of choice, effort, and justification.* The example given earlier of workers who modified their attitudes in ways consistent with their new role requirements involved what some theorists have labeled "self-persuasion." That self-persuasion of this sort may occur in a relatively permanent role is not surprising, but experimenters have been able to produce attitude shifts in more transient role-playing situations. In several experiments involving pressure to role-play, subjects have been asked to defend positions that they did not privately support: for example, to write essays favoring higher tuition. Among the variables investigated in these studies have been the amount of choice afforded the subject (e.g., Cohen and Latané, 1962), the degree of effort involved in role-playing (e.g., Zimbardo, 1965), or the number or quality of reasons given for compliance (e.g., Brock and Blackwood, 1962). In general, the results of these studies have supported Festinger's predictions. Those subjects who acceded to the experimenter's pressure to comply were more likely to modify their attitudes under conditions where they felt they had choice in the matter, or where they could not rationalize away their discrepant behavior on grounds that compliance was effortless or justified by the circumstances.

2. *Boring tasks and severity of threat.* Several forced compliance experiments have involved getting subjects to perform extremely boring tasks. In one well-known study (Brehm, 1962) fraternity pledges were "asked" by a fraternity brother to copy random numbers for three hours. They were threatened either with paddling (low threat) or a tribunal with possible expulsion (high threat) if they did not comply. Although the threat of paddling was regarded as less likely to be carried out than the tribunal, Brehm's findings still provide general support for Festinger's theory. As reported to a supposed third party (an Interfraternity Council), compliant pledges threatened with paddling experienced less dissatisfaction with the boring task than pledges in the high-threat condition of the experiment. Presumably, those in the high-threat condition did not need to modify their attitudes toward the task. They could hate doing it and still do it on grounds that they had little choice.

As might be expected, the very opposite of the generalization about severity of threat applies to situations in which the activity in question is something we initially regard as pleasant or valuable. The evidence suggests that, other things being equal, paying a high price for something that was valued in the first place increases our attraction for that object. In one experiment, Aronson and Mills (1959) applied varying degrees of punishment as conditions for entrance into an ongoing discussion forum. Unbeknownst to the subjects, the actual discussion to which they were later exposed was prearranged to be extremely boring. Still, the subjects given severe initiations rated it highly; more highly, at least, than those given mild initiations. Presumably, the experience of a severe initiation was dissonant with the experience of unanticipated boredom. Rather than admit to themselves that they had been bored, the subjects modified their attitudes toward the discussion and persisted in their desire to join the group. There are other possible interpretations of these findings. Still, the "dissonance" explanation cannot be ruled out. Further confirmation has been provided by Gerard and Mathewson (1966).

3. *Forced compliance and disliked communicators.* One of the real "surprises" predicted and evidenced by dissonance theorists is that *disliked communicators are more apt to secure attitude-change following forced compliance than highly attractive communicators.* Ordinarily, of course, we are swayed more by attractive sources than by unattractive sources. But what happens in the special case where we are pressured into doing something that we would not otherwise be inclined to do? Dissonance theory argues that when the source of pressure is attractive we can rationalize away the discrepancy between our attitudes and behaviors by saying to ourselves that we performed the noxious task as a favor to the source. But when the source is unattractive, that potential rebalancing alternative is foreclosed. Hence, we have little choice but to modify our attitudes.

This inobvious principle has been consistently supported by research (Smith, 1961; Zimbardo, *et al.*, 1965; Powell, 1965). In the Zimbardo study, for example (as in the Smith study before it), pressure was placed on subjects to perform the noxious task of sampling fried Japanese grasshoppers. As in many other "forced compliance" studies, the "force" exerted upon subjects to comply stemmed not from explicit threats by the communicators but, rather, from their role or position as authority figures conducting scientific research. Although the subjects were "strongly urged" to eat the unusual food, it was also made quite clear that they could refuse, and many, in fact, did just that.

One sample used in the study consisted of ROTC students who were told by either an attractive or an unattractive ROTC officer that the experiment was concerned with physiological and intellectual reactions to food deprivation. The attractiveness variable was manipulated quite cleverly by the experimenters. Here is Zimbardo's description (Zimbardo and Ebbeson, 1969, p. 74):

> *Positive Role.* The communicator (playing the role of an experimenter) interacted with his "assistant" according to a prearranged script in which, for the positive condition, he gave politely phrased requests to the assistant, called him by his first name, responded to a "mistake" by the assistant with equanimity, and in general was considerate and pleasant. But at all times it was clear that he was in charge of the experiment and in control.
>
> *Negative Role.* However, the negative condition demanded that the communicator be perceived as unpleasant, a person one would not want to know,

work with, or work for. This perception of the negative communicator was largely induced by his quite formal interaction with the assistant. When the assistant mistakenly brought in the "wrong" experimental food (a tray of eels in aspic instead of grasshoppers), the communicator, who was in the process of talking to the subjects in his most pleasant manner, suddenly blew up and said, "Oh dammit, can't you remember the schedule? That food is for the next group. . . . Let's get with it and hurry up about it!" As the assistant left, obviously embarrassed, the communicator shrugged his shoulders disgustedly, *then reversed his role behavior in front of the subjects* and proceeded again in the same tone as previously.

The results of the Zimbardo, *et al.* study are quite revealing. About half the subjects in both experimental groups refused to participate, and *their* attitudes toward fried Japanese grasshoppers became less favorable. Of those who did participate, the attractiveness of the communicator made a considerable difference. By a wide margin (as much as 50 percent), subjects who ate the grasshoppers for the negatively valued communicator increased their ratings of the food more than those who complied for the positively valued communicator.

There are, it seems to us, at least three important lessons for persuaders which are illustrated by the Zimbardo study. First, the study attests to the *extraordinary power of legitimate authority* as a vehicle for getting people to perform noxious tasks. In Chapter 12 we saw that getting people to eat fried grasshoppers is a mild accomplishment compared to some of the things which "legitimate authorities" have been able to get others to do, but let us simply note here that both the liked and disliked communicators achieved a considerable degree of compliance simply by dint of their positions as authority figures acting in the name of science. Second, the study illustrates how pressure to comply is *apt to produce* "backlash" effects among those who refuse to bend. This research finding, it would seem, should help us to understand some of the "backlash" effects which have occurred on the political level in recent years. Finally, the study's main finding—that disliked communicators created more attitude-change following compliance—*underscores the importance of closing off other possible dissonance-reducing alternatives* for the receiver once attitude-behavior discrepancies have been created.

Taken together, the literature on Festinger's mini-theory of "forced compliance" provides us with a handle on some of the more inobvious ways in which attitudes may be modified in social conflicts. The basic principle, once again, is that under certain conditions, described above, it is possible to change attitudes by first bringing pressure on people to change their behaviors. That principle has a number of applications. Contrary to the notion, for example, that attitudes cannot be legislated, we can see that new laws or executive decrees may indeed lead to attitude-modifications by creating attitude-behavior discrepancies. We can see, too, why those in authority frequently take potentially unpopular action first and then seek confirmation of their policies afterwards. Once policies are put into practice, the easier dissonance-reducing alternative for those affected is to modify their attitudes. Another potentially powerful weapon, as we have seen, is counterattitudinal role-playing. In conflict situations, this device is often employed by those in positions of institutional authority. One way to blunt opposition, for example, is to give potential partisans important positions of responsibility within the system. Partisans are not simply "bought off"; they are also placed in a role in which the need to publicly defend official positions may lead them to modify their own attitudes.

The finding that we value attitude objects all the more if we have had to pay dearly for them also has direct application to conflict situations. Machiavelli observed long ago that those in power could reduce domestic discontent by going to war. We should not be surprised to learn that wounded veterans of the Vietnam War identified more with the war effort than soldiers who escaped unscathed. Antiwar sentiments are dissonant with the price they have paid while prowar sentiments provide justification for their wounds. Seizing on this same principle, protest leaders and other movement strategists have deliberately placed their followers in situations where they would be subjected to repressive actions by "the enemy." Many a protestor has been radicalized by tear-gasings, macings, and arrests.

Festinger's hypothesis may also help to account for changes in the attitudes of targets of militant confrontations. At Temple University (and, we suspect, at many other places as well), it was common practice during the sixties for militants to make demands, to be rebuffed by faculty members and administrators who lacked sympathy for their means or ends, to reassert their demands, in the context, this time, of a show of force, and to find that many of their targets now regarded the demands as reasonable and even desirable. At least two ingredients were present in these confrontations that dissonance theorists name as factors contributing to attitude-change following forced compliance: sources low in attractiveness and just enough coercion to produce compliance (not so much that the targets felt they had no choice). As the targets of confrontation found themselves unable to resist the demands made upon them, the resulting discrepancies between their attitudes and actions might well have led them to modify their attitudes. Still another factor that has been discussed was probably operative for at least some of the targets: the phenomenon of "self-persuasion" following counterattitudinal role-playing. The president of the university, for example, was obliged to defend new policies before legislators, alumni, trustees, and so on. If he was not initially in sympathy with the demands of the protestors, we suspect that his own speeches in defense of the proposals helped to convince him.

V. Purchase or Control of the Instrumentalities of Persuasion

Democratic theory holds that truth will most likely emerge from a competition of ideas when all parties to a controversy have equal access to communication resources, the instrumentalities of "pure" persuasion. As indicated in the previous chapter, these include media, media time, information, channels, spokesmen, etc.

Truth is not inconsequential, of course, in mixed-motive conflicts. To the extent that two conflicting parties also have interests in common, they might wish to insure equal opportunity for persuasion, at least on some issues, in order that rational solutions to their common problems might emerge. There is considerable evidence from research on group problem-solving (McGrath and Altman, 1966) that problem-solving is facilitated when the leader does not attempt to impose solutions, when he or she encourages give and take, and when there is, in fact, active participation from persons with divergent viewpoints.

Still, however appealing the norm of free and equal participation may appear from the perspective of democratic theory, it hardly needs saying that the capacity to gain control over the instrumentalities of "pure" persuasion can be a decided advantage in conflict situations. In recognition of this truism, democratic governments take pains to prevent antagonists from having undue advantage in courtroom disputes, labor-management relations, electoral contests, and many other conflict situations. This has not stopped rich, or in other ways powerful, antagonists from obtaining a selective advantage. Oftentimes, it is the leaders of governmental institutions who are the chief culprits. Here are some illustrations of how the instrumentalities of persuasion may be controlled for political purposes.

Control of information. As David Wise (1973) makes clear in his book, *The Politics of Lying*, governments routinely control opinion by controlling information. A particularly effective technique of control is to deny information to antagonists, and then, when they attempt to persuade others, to accuse them of being uninformed. With equal impunity, three presidents used this technique against antiwar protestors—first by classifying politically embarrassing information, then by asserting that few would protest if they, too, had access to the secret documents. As Wise makes clear, secrecy is also a favorite weapon in conflicts between governmental agencies.

Purchase or control of communication expertise. It has become a political axiom that in order to get elected to major office, one must either be wealthy or have rich friends. Campaign funds are used, not only to purchase media time, but also to hire skilled ghost writers, public relations experts, make-up men, and so on. On the other hand, money or other forms of power may be employed to defuse the communicative potential of the opposition. Effective advocates may be jailed or bought off. As in Nixon's "negative campaign" of 1972, money may also be used to hire hecklers, to disrupt the opposition's fund-raising efforts, or to set opposition party contenders against each other.

Control of terms and definitions. Crucial to the perpetuation of modern-day political power is control over the meanings of terms which help to justify the actions of a given regime and simultaneously serve to demean those who would challenge that regime. As we saw in Chapter 2, terms in the influence "family"—persuasion, coercion, rhetoric, education, rational argument, violence—are not exempt from political efforts at definitional control. Here is what the Skolnick Report (1969, pp. 4–5) has to say about the concept of "violence."

> The kinds of acts that become classified as "violent," and, equally important, those which do not become so classified, vary according to who provides the definition and who has superior resources for disseminating and enforcing his definitions. The most obvious example of this is the way, in a war, each side typically labels the other side as the aggressor and calls many of the latter's violent acts atrocities. The definition of the winner usually prevails. Within a given society, political regimes often exaggerate the violence of those challenging established institutions. The term "violence" is frequently employed to discredit forms of behavior considered improper, reprehensible, or threatening by specific groups which, in turn, may mask their own violent response with the rhetoric of order or progress. In the eyes of those accustomed to immediate deference, back talk, profanity, insult, or disobedience may appear violent. In the South, for example, at least until recently, the lynching of an "uppity" black man was often considered less shocking than the violation of caste etiquette which provoked it.

Control of media. Totalitarian governments are notorious for controlling educational, entertainment, and news media, but the phenomenon reaches to basically democratic systems as well. Richard Nixon is quoted in the House Judiciary Committee version of the White House tapes as threatening to use every means available to deny renewal of a license to a station owned by the publisher of the Washington Post, the newspaper that broke the Watergate story. Efforts at intimidating the news media began with a speech by former Vice-President Agnew in 1969 and were escalated in subsequent years.

The political constraints on educational media become most apparent when educators dare to strike out for new ways of teaching and learning. Thus, for example, the "New History" program, currently in vogue in about one quarter of the nation's high schools, has come under severe attack for stimulating critical analysis, rather than unquestioning praise, of the way Americans have behaved in the past. Among the critics has been Pat Buchanan (June 8, 1975), former speechwriter for Richard Nixon. He writes (p. 17):

> It is ludicrous that we should sit still for this. Americans have the right to have their tax-supported schools teach their children not only to revere the great men of America's past, but to understand, respect, appreciate and defend the society and systems in which Americans have chosen to live.
>
> The mythology, the shared beliefs, the heroes of American history are part of the cement that binds together this diverse society. They are part of the common heritage of all Americans, which every citizen should know. And if the purveyors of the "New History" feel their academic freedom is traduced by having to portray Lincoln and Jefferson as great and good men, then let them practice their academic freedom in an unemployment line.

Control of access to key channels of influence. As indicated in the previous chapter, certain channels within institutions are dead ends for those seeking influence; they function essentially as "flak-catching" receptacles. Others, reserved for the powerful, open doors to goal accomplishment. During the Arab oil embargo in early 1974, those with direct access to the office of the former energy czar, William Simon, were often able to get quick relief. Others who simply wrote to the energy office received pre-printed postcards. According to reporter Jack Anderson (*Philadelphia Evening Bulletin*, February 24, 1974), "each gets a routine 'thank you' and a promise that 'every consideration will be given to the consumer.'"

Seldom, of course, is the flak-catching function of a channel made public; thus, for readers of the *Philadelphia Evening Bulletin* (July 3, 1973), the following squib might have been revealing:

> Under pressure, The Prison Board of Trustees decided some time ago to hold public hearings. But it needed a format. So the Board of Education was asked how it ran its open sessions, and one member provided a format which included this reference to citizen speakers: "At the conclusion, written statements are submitted to the board. If not, minutes are used. Speakers are told that consideration will be given. Generally, these (the speakers) are forgotten."

Control of Agendas. An agenda may not tell people what to think but it will tell them what to think and talk *about*. Recent evidence suggests that agenda-setting may be a prime function of the news media in electoral contests (McCombs and Shaw, 1972). Bachrach and Baratz (1970) have provided evidence that political elites perform a similar function within legislative bodies. Especially pervasive, they argue, is their control over "nondecision-making"; they decide what political issues will not be discussed. In diplomatic and labor management negotiations, the substance and sequence of an agenda may be fought over vigorously since it provides a framework for what will be decided.

Looking back on these examples we can see a pattern whereby the well entrenched can appear ostensibly as "pure" persuaders while obtaining a rhetorical edge by their control of communication resources. Given public preferences for "pure" persuasion over coercion or bribes, behind-the-scenes control of communication resources can be a decisive advantage in conflict situations. Utilizing co-active appeals in public while negotiating from power in private, political elites can even create the impression that no rational grounds exist for conflict between themselves and the poor and powerless—all the while enjoying their special privileges. Even should denial of equal opportunity for persuasion be publicly exposed, it will be tolerated within limits. Control of the instrumentalities of "pure" persuasion is the ultimate weapon in political conflicts—far more dependable than threats or punishments.

Co-Active versus Combative Persuasion as Institutional Change Alternatives

In the previous chapter, we focused on co-active campaigns for institutional change and in this chapter we have provided several examples of how militant protest groups have used the combative approach to secure institutional change. Here we will provide a detailed comparison of the two approaches, showing, too, how they may be combined in what might be called an *intermediate* strategy of persuasion. Our purpose in this section is partly to illustrate principles already covered in the chapter, but also to provide change-oriented readers with a sense of the options they have available. In the final section of the chapter, we will consider another alternative, the *expressive* approach.[6]

Distinguishing Features

Little needs to be said at this point about the strategies of co-active persuaders. As applied to protests against institutional policies or practices, they are the quintessential *moderates*, the embodiments of reason, civility, and decorum in human interaction. Moderates collect petitions, send tele-

---

6. The sixties generated a rash of books on contemporary methods of protest. See, for example, Alinsky (1971), Fanon (1966), Gregg (1966), Lipset and Schaflander (1971), Roszak and Roszak (1969), and Skolnick (1969). Interested students will also profit from reading theoretical works on social movements and collective behavior. See, for example, Gamson (1968), Kriesberg (1973), Oberschall (1973), Smelser (1962), and Toch (1965).

grams to their Congressional representatives, write books, picket and march peacefully, organize voting blocs, file lawsuits, and so on. Exuding earnestness, charm, and an aura of competence, they get angry but do not shout, issue pamphlets but never manifestos, inveigh against social mores but always in the value language of the social order. Their "devil" is a condition or a set of behaviors or an outcast group, never the persons they are seeking to influence. Those persons are, rather, part of the moderates' "we" group, united, if only by lip-service, to their beliefs. To the extent that moderates are successful at garnering mass support for their positions, their actions might well threaten those in power and might thus constitute a kind of combative persuasion, but their threats are generally muted or implied, and they always operate within limits prescribed by "The System." For the most part, moderates seek to reduce the psychological distance between the movement and those outside it by speaking the listeners' language, adjusting to their frame of reference, adapting to their needs, wants, and values. The approach was well-articulated by Roy Wilkins (1964) of the NAACP when he suggested that the "prime, continuing racial policy looking toward eradication of inequalities must be one of winning friends and influencing people among the white majority" (p. 11).

If co-active persuaders assume or pretend to assume an ultimate identity of interests between the movement and its antagonists, militant combative persuaders act on the assumption of a fundamental clash of interests. In mixed-motive conflicts, each can lay claim to a part of the truth and each can boast support from proud philosophical traditions. The moderate's commitment to co-active persuasion is rooted in the Greco-Roman democratic tradition, in Judeo-Christian conceptions of the brotherhood of man, in Emerson's faith in human educability, in John Stuart Mill's conviction that truth will survive any open competition of ideas, and in the writings of countless others. Militants, by contrast, are inclined to be mistrustful of ordinary citizens or to assume that the systems they oppose are likely to be intractable. With Marx, they are apt to believe that the masses have lost sight of their "real" interests or that those in power are unlikely to surrender it willingly. Although Machiavelli wrote for princes and not for protestors, the militant is inclined to accept that scribe's view of persuasion as an adjunct to force rather than its alternative. Likewise, the militant would probably go along with Henry James when he wrote that "Life is, in fact, a battle. Evil is insolent and strong; beauty enchanting but rare; goodness very apt to be weak, folly very apt to be defiant; wickedness to carry the day; imbeciles to be in great places, people of sense in small, and mankind generally unhappy."

The nonverbal language of protestors tends to provide a remarkably reliable measure of degrees of militancy. Whereas the moderate tends to be dressed and groomed in accordance with prevailing conventions, the

The persuasive power of these protest symbols comes from the way they are linked together to express identifications and divisions. *On this page:* "Doves" linking Nixon and death, murders at Kent State and murder in Vietnam. *Opposite page:* Two symbols inadvertently joined together—pro-war marchers against backdrop of SELLOUT. (Courtesy of *Temple News*)

militant tends to flaunt those conventions. In quasi-expressive groups such as the Yippies, "doing it" became more important than "saying it," and followers expressed their rejection accordingly. Paper money was dropped from the balcony of the stock market; marijuana was smoked in public; the flag was sewn on to the seat of a protestor's levis. Hostility was expressed in gestures, dialect, manners, musical rhythms, and ceremonies.

So too with verbal symbols. While one militant group shouts four-letter words at authorities, another insists that it is the Establishment which uses obscenities when it speaks of "body counts," "kill ratios," "protective reaction strikes," "free-fire zones," and "saturation bombing." Meanwhile, the society's "devil" terms are fashioned into "god" terms. A light-skinned Negro declares himself "black," an alienated youth declares herself to be a "freak," a militant feminist group calls itself "WITCH."

This is not to say that militants offer no appeals to shared values. They do, indeed, but in ways that call into question other widely held values. In general, the militant tends to express greater degrees of dissatisfaction. Whereas the moderate tends to ask "how" questions, the militant asks "whether" questions. Whereas the moderate sees "inefficiencies" in existing practices, the militant sees "inequities." Whereas the moderate might regard authority figures as "misguided" though "legitimate," the militant would tend to regard these same figures as "willfully self-serving" and "illegitimate." Whereas both might pay homage to law, the militant is more apt to derogate man-made laws in the name of "higher" laws. For many moderates, American participation in the Vietnam war became inadvisable because "we could not win." For many militants, the basic question was whether we *ought* to win. Moderates began to ask whether Vietnam was vital to our national security. Militants asked whether national security was as important as our obligations to international law.

Moreover, as we have said, militants may extend the scope of their "devil" to ordinary citizens, whereas the moderate tends to soft-pedal any differences with the citizenry. Partly so as to satisfy their own militant following, the leaders may charge the masses with moral culpability or, at best, with being fools or puppets.

The actions of militants are not all of a piece by any means. The practice of "classic" civil disobedience, for example, borders on being "intermediate" between militancy and moderacy. So as to test the constitutionality of a law, that law is violated. However, the law in question is violated openly and nonviolently, no other laws are breached in the process, the rights of innocent persons are not interfered with, and, if found guilty, the law violator willingly accepts his punishment (Fortas, 1968). Contrast this strategy with acts that can more clearly be labeled as combative in nature: confrontational acts, strikes, boycotts, riots, political bombings and kidnappings—all the way to organized guerrilla warfare. By means of verbal polemics and direct action techniques, protestors who practice combative persuasion threaten, harass, cajole, disrupt, provoke, intimidate, coerce. Although the aim of pressure tactics may be to punish directly (e.g., strikes, boycotts), more frequently they are forms of "body rhetoric," designed to dramatize issues, enlist additional sympathizers, delegitimize the established order, and—except in truly revolutionary situations—force reconsideration of existing laws and practices, or pave the way for negotiated settlements.[7]

The campus confrontations of the late sixties provided clearcut illustrations of the use of combative strategies by militants. Some were fairly

---

7. Case studies of militant protest include Avorn (1968), Fogelson (1971), Lipset and Wolin (1965), Tompkins and Anderson (1971), and Walker (1968). We recommend that you pick up one such case study and see if the protest group can be characterized by the language and actions we have ascribed to militant protestors.

A Typical Manifesto by a Militant Group of the Sixties
The Seattle Liberation Front Program for Action

A. We shall create our revolutionary culture everywhere.

B. We will fight American imperialism.

C. We will struggle for the full liberation of women as a necessary part of the revolutionary struggle.

D. We shall resist the destruction of our physical environment.

E. We support the struggle of black and other Third World people for self-determination.

F. We must turn the schools into training grounds for liberation.

G. We will destroy the university unless it serves the people.

H. We relate to the liberating potential of drugs in our culture for both mind and body.

I. We must show working people that the international struggle for socialism is their struggle as well.

J. We will take communal responsibility for basic human needs.

K. We must break the power of the landlords and provide beautiful housing for all, *not cardboard tracts*.

L. We will tax the corporations, not the working people.

M. We will defend ourselves against law and order.

N. We must transform ourselves into more loving and committed human beings.

mild while others were quite disruptive, but all of them sought to perform attention-getting, radicalizing, and delegitimizing functions through actions which combined verbal exhortations with pressure tactics.

The confronter joined in a deliberate violation of the institution's written and unwritten code of conduct, fastening on those taboos which symbolized its false ideals and inequitable practices. Representatives of liberal institutions were thus presented with a king-sized dilemma. Suppression of the confrontation would belie the institution's appearance of liberalism and feed the flames of protest. Yet permitting violations of the code would, in effect, sanction other violations and undermine the offices of authority in the institution. And so, after promising a fair hearing and pleading in vain for a return to more moderate tactics, the institution acted to check or suppress the violations and punish the violators, frequently breaking its own rules in the process. In this way its representatives were able, temporarily, to contain the confrontation, but, in doing so, they "completed" the rhetorical act by revealing their own "ugliness." As Scott and Smith (1969) have described it:

> The use of force to get students out of halls consecrated to university administration, or out of holes dedicated to construction projects, seems to confirm the radical analysis that the establishment serves itself rather than justice. In this sense, the confronter who prompts violence in the language or behavior of another has found his collaborator (p. 8).

It should not be surprising that the public and quasi-public institutions of so-called liberal democracies are most susceptible to confrontation. Or that the Democratic Party is more vulnerable than the Republican Party, the "socially responsible" corporation more vulnerable than the self-serving corporation, the "progressive" university more vulnerable than the "conservative" one. Institutions which are unabashedly tyrannical may suppress unsanctioned forms of dissent. Institutions which come near to achieving their publicly stated objectives provide little reason for such dissent. But institutions whose façades are more impressive than their interiors provide the grounds for confrontation and are ill-equipped to counter it.

The problem for most "liberal" institutions is not simply that they profess liberal ideals. It is that these ideals are incompatible with other organizational objectives which, although less publicly affirmed, are nevertheless just as pressing. However Christian its Christian Ethic, the church must answer to the less noble demands of its parishioners. However, responsible its doctrine of social responsibility, the business corporation must make money. However democratic the Democratic Party's ideals, its officials must pay homage to the bosses and large contributors who constitute its power elite. Norman Mailer (1968) has written of a "schizophrenia on which America is built . . . a land of opportunity where a white culture sits upon a black; a horizontal community of Christian love and a vertical hierarchy of churches—the cross was well designed; a politics of principle and a politics of property, a land of family, a land of illicit heat . . ." and so on (p. 96).

Let us emphasize once again that even the most militant acts of protestors are likely to have rhetorical elements. At the very least, militants must establish the credibility of their threats and alter their target's perceptions of what is expedient under the circumstances. Beyond that, their symbolic acts of force may well engender support from those outside the movement, and even if they are not initially inclined to support the movement's programs, changes in their behavior produced by "forced compliance" might well lead them to modify their attitudes. Consider in this context the ghetto riots of the sixties. Many theories have been offered to account for these riots, some of them alleging that they were simply a form of entertainment, or that the rioters were only interested in what they could steal. Yet the evidence suggests that the rioters were fairly representative of the communities in which they lived; that they enjoyed widespread support from other residents; that riot targets were selective; and, most significantly, that the majority of riots occurred immediately following the assassination of Martin Luther King (Fogelson, 1971; Skolnick, 1969). On this basis, those more in sympathy with the rioters characterized their acts as rhetorical. Whatever their intent, it is clear that the riots called attention to grievances, fostered community solidarity, and provided ammunition for lawmakers who had been pushing for anti-poverty legislation. Coser (1967) has described the Watts uprising as a kind of "collective bargaining by riot." [8]

Advantages and Disadvantages of Moderate and Militant Approaches

So different are the rhetorical conceptions of moderate and militant strategists that it strains the imagination to believe that both approaches may work. Yet the decisive changes wrought by militant rhetorics in recent years give credence to the view that co-active persuasion is not the only viable alternative. Let us compare, in general terms, the strengths and limitations of moderate and militant approaches.

1. Militant tactics confer visibility on a movement; moderate tactics gain entry into decision centers.

Because of their ethos of respectability, moderates are invited to participate in public deliberations (hearings, conferences, negotiating sessions, etc.), even after militants have occasioned those deliberations by prolonged and self-debilitating acts of protest. On the other hand, the militant has readier access to the masses. Robert C. Weaver (1966) spoke for many moderates of the mid-sixties when he lamented that "Today, a publicized spokesman may be the individual who can devise the most militant cry and the leader one who can articulate the most far-out position" (p. 3).

2. For different reasons, militants and moderates must both be ambivalent about "successes" and "failures."

Militants thrive on injustice and ineptitude displayed by their targets. Should "the enemy" fail to implement the movement's demands, militants find themselves vindicated ideologically, yet frustrated programmatically. Should some of the demands be met, they are in the paradoxical position of

---

8. Gamson (1975) has accumulated considerable evidence from a study of a representative sample of "challenging" groups that groups seeking political influence tend to be successful at gaining acceptance and preferred outcomes if, and *only* if, they are willing and able to use violence, strikes, boycotts, or other combative stratagems. His is one of the very few studies in the area that scientifically examines the effects of alternative modes of protest.

having to condemn them as palliatives. Moderates, by contrast, require tangible evidence that the larger structure is tractable in order to hold followers in line; yet "too much" success belies the movement's reason for being (Turner and Killian, 1957). Not uncommonly, militants and moderates escalate their demands when faced with the prospect of success, but this makes them vulnerable to charges of bad faith. Self-proclaimed militants can avoid this problem by demanding at the outset considerably more than the system is willing to provide, but should self-proclaimed moderates do likewise, they invite charges of being "too militant."

3. Militant supporters are easily energized; moderate supporters are more easily controlled.

When George Wallace vowed, after losing a local election, that he would never again be "out-niggered," he was referring to a phenomenon that has its counterpart on the left as well. Turner and Killian (1957) have suggested that strong identification by members with the goals of a movement—however necessary to achieve *esprit de corps*—may foster the conviction that any means are justified and breed impatience with time-consuming tactics. The use of violence and other questionable means may be prompted further by restrictions on legitimate avenues of expression, imposed by the larger structure. Countering these pressures may require that the leaders mask the movement's true objectives, publicly disclaim the use of tactics they privately advocate, promise what they cannot deliver, exaggerate the strength of the movement, etc. A vicious cycle develops in which militant tactics invite further suppression, which spurs the movement on to more extreme methods. Having aroused their following, however, the leaders of a militant movement may become victims of their own creation, unable to contain energies within prescribed limits or to guarantee their own tenure.

On the other hand, leaders of moderate groups frequently complain that their supporters are apathetic. As Turner and Killian (1957, p. 337) have pointed out: "To the degree to which a movement incorporates only major sacred values its power will be diffused by a larger body of conspicuous lip-service adherents who cannot be depended upon for the work of the movement."

4. Militants are effective with "power-vulnerables"; moderates are effective with "power-invulnerables"; neither is effective with both.

Targets of protest may be labeled as "power-vulnerables" to the degree to which (a) they hold possessions of value and therefore have something to lose (for example, property, status, high office); (b) they cannot escape from a source's pressure (unlike suburbanites, for example, who could escape, physically or psychologically, from the ghetto riots of the sixties); (c) they cannot retaliate against a source (either because of normative or physical constraints). As we indicated earlier, such targets as university presidents, church leaders, and elected government officials are highly vulnerable—especially if they profess to be "high-minded" or "liberal"—, as compared to the mass of citizens who may lack substantial possessions, be able to escape, or feel no constraints about retaliating. We indicated in the previous chapter that as leaders of institutions allocate priorities in the face of conflicting pressures from other groups, they are unlikely to act on the programmatic suggestions of protest groups—even when they are sympathetic—unless pressured to do so. Hence, co-active strategies alone are likely to be ineffectual with them, whereas combative strategies should stand a better chance of modifying their attitudes. On the other hand, combative strategies are likely to be less effective with "power-invulnerables" than co-active strategies, and they might well invite back-lash effects. Where the movement and the larger structure are already polarized, the dilemma is magnified. However much they may wish to plead reasonably, wresting changes from those in public positions requires that leaders build a sizeable power base. And to secure massive internal support, leaders must at least *seem* militant.

"Intermediate" Strategies

It should be clear that in choosing between co-active and combative strategies of persuasion, the protest leader faces a series of dilemmas: neither approach is likely to meet every rhetorical requirement nor resolve every rhetorical problem, and, indeed, the introduction of either approach may create new problems.

So it is that the leadership of a protest movement may attempt to resolve or avoid the aforementioned dilemmas by employing "intermediate" strategies, admittedly a catchall term for those efforts that combine militant and moderate patterns of influence. They may alternate between appeals to common ground and threats of punishment, or speak softly in private and stridently at mass gatherings. They may form broadly based coalitions that submerge ideological differences or utilize speakers with similar values but contrasting styles. Truly the exemplars of oxymoronic postures, they may stand as "conservative radicals" or "radical conservatives," espousing extreme demands in the value language of the social order or militant slogans in behalf of moderate proposals. In defense of militancy, they may portray themselves as brakemen holding back more militant followers. In defense of moderate tactics, they may hold back their followers without loss of reputation, as Jerry Rubin and Abbie Hoffman did in urging non-violence on their "Yippie" following during the 1968 Democratic Convention in Chicago: "We are a revolutionary new community and we must protect our community. . . . We, not they, will decide when the battle begins. . . . We are not going into jails and we aren't going to shed our blood. We're too important for that. We've got too much work to do" (Walker, 1968, pp. 136–137).

Intermediacy can be a dangerous game. Calculated to energize supporters, win over neutrals, pressure power-vulnerables, and mollify the opposition, it may end up antagonizing everyone. The turned phrase may easily appear as a devilish trick, the rationale as a rationalization, the tactful comment as an artless dodge. To the extent that strategies of intermediacy require studied ambiguity, insincerity, and even distortion, perhaps the leaders' greatest danger is that others will find out what they *really* think.

Still, some strategists manage to reconcile differences between militant and moderate approaches and not simply to maneuver around them. They seem able to convince the established order that bad-tasting medicine is good for it and seem capable, too, of mobilizing a diverse collectivity within the movement.

The key, it would appear, is the leader's capacity to embody a higher wisdom, a more profound sense of justice: to stand above inconsistencies by articulating overarching principles. Few will contest the claim that Martin Luther King, Jr., epitomized the approach. Attracting both militants and moderates to his movement, King could win respect, even from his enemies, by reconciling the seemingly irreconcilable. The heart of the case for intermediacy was succinctly stated by King himself in a speech which Robert Scott has analyzed (quoted by Scott, 1968, p. 84): "What is needed is a realization that power without love is reckless and abusive and love without power is sentimental and anemic. Power at its best is love implementing the demands of justice, and justice at its best is power correcting everything that stands against love."

The major protest movements of the sixties all seemed to require combinations of militant and moderate approaches. Militants were counted upon to dramatize the Vietnam issue, moderates to plead forcefully within inner circles. Threats of confrontation prompted city and state governments to finance the building of new schools in ghetto areas, but it took reasonableness and civility to get experienced teachers to volunteer for work in those facilities. Demands by revolutionary student groups for total transformations of university structures helped impel administrators to heed quasi-militant demands for a redistribution of university power. Support for the cause by moderate groups helped confer respectability on the movement. Thus, however much they might have warred among themselves, militants and moderates each performed important functions.

A Brief Look at the "Expressive" Alternative

As we indicated earlier, many young persons today believe that neither militant nor moderate (nor "intermediate") approaches to protest are "where it's at." Yet if asked whether they sought significant changes in society's institutions, they would respond affirmatively and might even label themselves "revolutionaries." Proponents of this position include many women's liberationists, gay liberationists, back-to-nature advocates, and others concerned, fundamentally, with matters of life style. An important component of the viewpoint is the doctrine of Expressivism, which we characterized somewhat critically in Chapter 2 as a kind of "anti-rhetorical rhetoric." Although we are by no means convinced that the approach can be applied to all arenas of protest, we recognize it as a viable approach to some issues, and believe that its proponents offer a significant critique of conventional approaches to protest. Here is a brief summary of the position as we have heard it argued.

In their preoccupation with strategies of persuasion, militants and moderates are really barking up the wrong tree. Institutions do not change until people change, and people do not change as a result of the machinations of movement strategists. They change when an idea is ripe for the times, and when they have come to that idea as a result of direct personal experiences. Amitai Etzioni (1972) speaks of an "iron law of sociology that states that the fate of all popular movements is determined by forces they do not control" (p. 35). He is probably not too far from the truth.

In point of fact, moderates and militants are really cut from the same cloth, and, most ironically, they are not very different from the social order that they seek to change. Scratch at the source of our society's ills and you will find a set of dehumanizing values that are also reflected in conventional protest groups. Like the society at large, moderate and militant leaders scheme, manipulate, exploit—even their own followers. And when they get caught up in their own manipulations their only solution is to manipulate some more. The underlying mentality is that of the bureaucrat or the technocrat. In all probability it is an extension of the male's culturally sanctioned wish to dominate, as epitomized by Stokeley Carmichael's statement that the position of women in the Black Power movement should be—"prone." Ultimately it is a self-defeating mentality because, in addition to dominating other people and the surrounding physical environment, protest leaders get out of touch with their own feelings and begin to think of their cause as a set of cold abstractions.

That is why movements such as Women's Liberation are truly revolutionary. Their target is not so much particular laws or practices but the values giving rise to society's institutions—its public philosophy. Only when these values are changed can the institutions of our society be changed.

The alternative to conventional strategies, then, is an honest, unstructured, leaderless, nonmanipulative exchange of ideas and feelings among people, as exemplified by consciousness-raising sessions among women.[9]

---

9. A "how-to-do-it" guide to consciousness-raising in women's groups is found in *Ms. Magazine*, July, 1972, pp. 18, 22, 23.

It is not simply a compromise between the way of the moderate and the way of the militant but a genuine alternative. In Karlyn Kohrs Campbell's (1973, p. 79) terms, there is an "affirmation of the affective, of the validity of personal experience, of the necessity for self-exposure, and self-criticism, of the value of dialogue, and of the goal of autonomous, individual decision-making." The goal, however, is to make the "personal political" (Campbell, 1973, p. 79), and it is in this sense that movements such as Women's Liberation are not simply self-help movements but protest movements seeking institutional change.

This is not the place for a full-scale debate over the merits of the "alternative" approach. Nor would we wish to debunk it entirely in any case since we believe it has considerable value. Allow us, however, to make brief note of some counterarguments, if only so that readers will be in a better position to judge for themselves.

1. It is not necessarily true that institutions do not change until the masses of people change. We have seen in this chapter, in fact, that the reverse may occur: changes in behavior compelled by new laws or edicts may lead to changes in the public's attitudes.

2. While it is true that claims of success by the leaders of conventional movements are frequently overstated, it is also true that movements of this kind have exerted considerable influence in recent years. Witness, for example, the substantial triggering and catalytic effects of the antiwar movement. If anything, we suspect that these movements could have profited from greater attention to matters of rhetorical strategy.

3. It is true that the leaders of moderate and militant movements tend to be manipulative, and in this sense no different from "exploiters" in the larger society. There is great danger in this, we agree, especially if power considerations come to outweigh all other considerations. But just as one movement may lose sight of its values, another may become so preoccupied with value questions that it becomes impotent. The question is one of balance, and here proponents of the "alternative" approach are faced with the same conflicts among rhetorical requirements as conventional movements.

4. Consciousness-raising sessions have undoubtedly helped to politicize women, and, indirectly, they have also helped to "liberate" men. Still, one suspects that they are only a first step. Traditional methods of protest are needed to get laws enacted, business practices changed, and so on. These fights have thus far been led by relatively conventional women's protest groups.

5. Even if movements such as Women's Liberation enjoy spectacular success in the years to come (we suspect they will), the expressive approach should not necessarily be adopted by other protest groups. Women,

It would be a pity if women's liberation meant "liberation" from conventional politics. We are encouraged that women like Bella Abzug, Shirley Chisolm, and Angela Davis now occupy prominent positions in political life. (*Top left:* photo of Davis, copyrighted by Ken DeBlieu; *top right:* photo of Abzug, by Anne Casey; all photos courtesy of *Temple News*.)

after all, are a majority in this country, and many of them already hold considerable power in one institution, the family. Poor blacks, by comparison, face a more entrenched and intractable "enemy."

Summary

A social conflict is a clash over incompatible interests in which one party's relative gain is another's relative loss. Conflicts are not simply misunderstandings, semantic confusions, or communication breakdowns; nor are they disagreements, differences of opinion, or controversies—they are always something *more than that*. Divergent interests are at stake, interests so important to one or both parties that they lead actors to combine rhetoric with power and reactors to modify beliefs, values, or attitudes partly with an eye to the other's relative power capacities.

Although the co-active approach to persuasion (as discussed in the previous six chapters) is appropriate for most rhetorical situations, it is often highly inappropriate for social conflicts, especially when relied upon exclusively. Unfortunately, theorists have often attempted to wish away conflicts or to recommend the same rhetorical strategies for them as they would for nonconflict situations. Adding to our misunderstanding has been the assumption that acts of influence must be either dichotomized as persuasion or coercion, or trichotomized as persuasion, inducement, or constraints. Rather than being an alternative to these forms of power, persuasion in conflict situations is generally either an instrument, accompaniment, or consequence of power.

The combative approach was introduced as the major alternative to co-active persuasion for conflict situations. For each of the characteristics of the co-active approach, we identified contrasting strategies which, together, constitute the combative approach. They include: (1) divisive techniques, such as ridicule, obscenities, and symbolic acts of force; (2) inducements and constraints that function to modify beliefs, values, or attitudes; (3) the appearance of irrationality or loss of control; (4) "forced compliance" techniques designed to modify behaviors as a precondition for modifying beliefs, values, or attitudes; and (5) purchase or control of the instrumentalities of pure persuasion: information, communication expertise, terms and definitions, media, access to channels, and agendas. In general it can be said that whereas combative strategies offer the greatest assurance of attainment of primary objectives, they also incur the largest costs and frequently produce unwanted residual effects. The advantages and disadvantages of combative strategies were compared in this chapter with special attention given to "forced compliance" techniques.

We moved then to a detailed comparison of co-active and combative persuasion as means by which protest movements may secure institutional change. As applied to protest movements, these terms actually refer to a range of choice on a continuum from ultramoderate to ultramilitant. Moderates and militants differ in terms of the degree to which they are willing to work within "the system," the scope and intensity of the "devils" they attack, and the extent to which they rely on appeals to common ground or, on the other hand, find it necessary to bolster appeals and arguments with displays of power or delegitimizing techniques such as confrontation. Perhaps the most fundamental difference between the two is in terms of orientation. Whereas co-active persuaders assume or pretend to assume an ultimate identity of interests between the movement and its antagonists, militants act on the assumption of a fundamental clash of interests. Since most conflicts are of the "mixed motive" variety, involving combinations of common and conflicting interests, each can lay claim to a part of the truth.

Choosing between moderate and militant approaches is far from easy. Militant tactics confer visibility on the movement and open the doors for negotiation, but it is the moderate who frequently gains entry into the actual negotiations. Militant supporters are easily energized; moderate supporters are more easily controlled. Militants are effective with "power-vulnerables"; moderates are effective with "power-invulnerables"; neither is effective with both. Some movements attempt to combine the attractive features of moderate and militant approaches by use of "intermediate" strategies. Other movements, such as Women's Liberation, have looked askance at both moderate and militant approaches to strategizing and have sought to develop alternative strategies that are essentially *expressive* in nature. In general, we would not recommend the use of combative strategies *unless* more moderate methods have been found wanting, the situation requires immediate and drastic action, and there is strong likelihood that these strategies will be at least partially successful.

Part

3

Analysing
Persuasion

We may think of the critic in a sense as a prism: filtering, defining and analyzing the light shed by a rhetorical event. Not only the light but the prism itself is an object of rhetorical interest. As the prism turns, different colors and shades are brought to our attention, each having a single source but each so fused in the single source that only the prism may articulate it. On the other hand, the critic is not an inanimate object, like a prism, with only the capacity for passive reflection. The critic's humanity is necessarily inherent in his work. His critical act is constituted of and by his choices and judgments.

From the Report of the Committee on the
Advancement and Refinement of Rhetorical Criticism
(Bitzer and Black, 1971, p. 224)

Doing
Rhetorical
Criticism

Why is it that Lincoln's Gettysburg Address is so memorable? If I were to give that speech all over again, how would I do it differently? Would Ibsen's *A Doll's House* be any better if it were less rhetorical? Did Gerald Ford's speeches on Watergate in 1974 help or hurt his chances of being nominated and elected in 1976? What do first-grade primers tell us about sex-role stereotypes in our culture, and what do these readers do to our children? Is there a predictable pattern in concession speeches by candidates who lose elections? Is there really a consistent relationship between the number of footnotes in a scientific article and its chances of being published? Why is it that so many people fall for Bayer Aspirin advertisements? Since stylistic simplicity is so highly valued in our culture, how is it that Martin Luther King, Jr., was able to get away with a highly ornate style?

Each of these questions and thousands more like them constitute legitimate starting points for critical analyses of rhetorical happenings. Critics or analysts (we use the terms interchangeably) may be motivated by outrage at an apparent misuse of language or logic or a pretension to objectivity that is belied by the facts. Their critical impulse may spring from a pragmatic interest in persuading others or in determining how others attempt to persuade them. They may have an irreverent streak and thus be inclined to demythify claims or claimants to universal truth. They may appreciate a rhetorical effort and want to know why it was so admirable. Or they may simply be puzzle-solvers by temperament who enjoy unravelling some of the mysteries of persuasion. In each case, they will attempt to make sense of the rhetorical act or event, either as an object of interest in its own right or because it helps illuminate some larger issue, problem, or theoretical question. Criticism serves *consummatory* functions when it stops at evaluation or explanation of a rhetorical effort. It performs *instrumental* functions when it focuses on persuasive discourse as case-study material in service of a larger end such as theory-building or theory-testing. Recall that we stressed the importance of theory-oriented criticism in Chapter 1.

It should be apparent that we have no choice but to be rhetorical critics if we are to function intelligently as consumers of persuasive communications; furthermore, that post-mortems on our own rhetorical efforts and on the efforts of others can help sharpen our skills as practitioners of persuasion. The motive for criticism need not be selfish, of course, and, in fact, the best criticism speaks to a wide audience. Focusing on a significant rhetorical object or issue, it corroborates commonplace observations or makes the inobvious apparent or provides justification for an evaluation or theoretical perspective. In all cases, it does more than describe a work or the critic's gut reaction to it. Like the objects of their analyses, critics are themselves persuaders with cases to present and defend. We may not entirely agree with the analysis, but we must respect it if the case has been well argued.

We strongly urge that you try your hand at writing rhetorical critiques or analyses, if for no other reason than that the act of applying principles covered in this book will help you to better assimilate them. In this chapter, we offer suggestions on how to proceed.[1] The final chapter of the book provides sample materials for analysis.

Choosing a Topic or Question

The critic has wide latitude in terms of topic selection. The object of analysis may be written or oral, verbal, or nonverbal. It may be an historical remnant that has enduring significance or a contemporary event of ephemeral interest. The critical analysis may be confined to a speaker or speech or even to a segment of a speech. On the other hand, it may extend to a comparison of speakers or speeches, or to an entire campaign or movement, or to an identification of rhetorical patterns in a form or genre of persuasion such as public-service advertising or debate in Congress.

Depending on the scope of the project, critics may fasten on minute details or paint the rhetorical canvas with broad brush strokes. In the case of the former, they may help us to discover meanings in commonplace objects that had previously gone unnoticed. Here, for example, is Lloyd Brown's (1974, p. 34) analysis of a simple billboard advertisement:

> The scene is Main Street, Any City, U.S.A. The likeness of Colonel Sanders beams benevolently down on snarled traffic from a large, well-lit billboard which he shares with the inevitable bucket of Kentucky Fried Chicken and with an eye-catching phrase in bold lettering, "Woman's Liberation." Once again, the motivation seems straightforward enough—a very popular talking-point becomes the huckster's attention-getter. But note, too, how subtly significant shifts and distortions in images and language have simultaneously effected a selling pitch on the ideological level. "Women's Liberation"—the collectivist associations of the original phrase have been replaced by an individual emphasis that evokes "freedom." And, equally important, the exhortatory and prophetic connotations of the original rallying cry have been shoved to the background of our consciousness by the concrete, three-dimensional presence of that imposing bucket: liberation is now, it is of the present,

---

1. Because a great variety of goals and methods are encompassed by the term "rhetorical criticism," this chapter can do little more than introduce the subject. In Chapter 1 we referred the reader to various textbooks on goals and methods (Black, 1965; Brandt, 1970; Campbell, 1972; Scott and Brock, 1972), and from time to time in this chapter we shall be recommending more specialized works as well as examples of types of criticism.

it is already here. The almost tangible physicality of the Colonel and his bucket is a reassurance of incontrovertible facts: the fact of Kentucky Fried Chicken restaurants, the fact of "secret recipes," "herbs," "spices," warm succulence, and not least, the established fact that the little woman has been "liberated" from the stove this evening—just as she has been freed from drudgery by all the gadgetry of a marvellous technological paradise. The gastronomic image confronts and transforms the feminist's rhetoric— no need for exhortatory threats and prophecies about liberation for "women"; "woman" is already a "liberated" individual, emancipated, enfranchised, and packaged like so many Kentucky fried breasts and legs for our (male) consumption. As for those who agitate for humanistic rather than merely physical liberation, the patriarchical features of the benign Colonel are a sufficient rejoinder—it is a man's world.

Where the unit of analysis is much larger—a campaign or movement, for example—the critic cannot possibly comment on every feature of the rhetorical landscape or examine it from every angle. Needed is a thesis, model, or theoretical framework by which to structure the analysis. Edwin Black (1970), for example, chose a metaphor as a guiding framework. He argued that the themes of victimage, guilt, corruption, and counterviolence that characterize the rhetoric of the Radical Right are corollaries of its unique and unifying preoccupation with the metaphor of "communism-as-cancer." Griffin (1964) analyzed the rhetoric of the New Left movement in terms of Burke's (1945) dramatistic model. He traced its emergence and development in the past two decades and argued that its socialistic "god" words and "devil" words were still too unacceptable in this country for it to be able to "speak in its own name" (p. 135). We (1969) analyzed the effectiveness of campus confrontations during the late sixties in terms of the theory of "power-vulnerability" briefly discussed in Chapter 13. Recall that our argument was that the heads of professedly liberal-minded universities were sitting ducks for the confronter's delegitimizing rhetoric, and that authoritarian methods of retaliation only exacerbated their image problems.

Readers should find ample materials here and in the next chapter for the development of guiding frameworks presented earlier in the book: the balance theories introduced in Chapter 5, the "super-representative" thesis presented in Chapter 8, the developmental model of campaign stages and components presented in Chapter 12, the classification system for comparing co-active and combative strategies presented in Chapter 13, and so on. The choice of framework must obviously be fitted to the object being studied. Moreover, the critic should indicate what the model excludes. We have found it quite useful, for example, to analyze protest movements (e.g., Black Power, the anti-war movement) in terms of the rhetorical requirements incumbent on the movement's leadership, the rhetorical problems created by conflicting requirements, and the strategies and tactics developed by the leadership in an effort to ameliorate those problems and fulfill those requirements (Simons, 1970). By focusing on the rhetoric of movement leaders, however, our framework neglects the admittedly important role of spontaneous mass behavior in protest movements and we have had to make this clear.

By no means must rhetorical criticism be confined to paradigm cases of persuasion, such as those which have occupied most of our attention in this book. We have found, to the contrary, that analyses of peripheral cases (i.e., those identified in Chapter 2) are often more rewarding. Here the critic can teach us something merely by showing *that* a given item or pattern of discourse is rhetorical. He can advance the thesis, for example, that ostensibly objective high-school history textbooks tend to be rhetorical in the sense that they manifest a consistent ideological bias. Or that a poem which we would ordinarily not regard as rhetorically inspired actually constitutes a plea for recognition by the author (see Chapter 15).[2]

Where a given work is obviously rhetorical, the critic of peripheral cases can still perform a service by showing us *how* it persuades—how the illusion of scientific rigor is created in a dietary manual; or how forms and colors are used to make a rhetorical statement in Picasso's *Guernica;* or how theatrical devices are used to propagandize in Odets's *Waiting for Lefty;* or how the *New York Post* manifested a pro-Israeli bias in its reporting of the Yom Kippur "war" of 1973.

Virtually no human act or artifact need escape rhetorical attention, although it should be acknowledged that other perspectives on the object of analysis may be equally valid. A poem, for example, might be examined syntactically, or as an historical curiosity, or as an exemplar of literary form. None of these analyses would be rhetorical, however. *The rhetorician's distinctive task would be to examine the poem in terms of the implicit or explicit appeals and arguments it offers and its potential or actual effects on particular audiences.* A report of a Speech Communication Task Force on rhetorical criticism (in Bitzer and Black, 1971) made this same point when it argued that rhetorical criticism was definable, not in terms of any special object of study, but in terms of the special set of lenses worn by the rhetorician (p. 220). In this way, too, it is distinguishable from syntactical analysis, historical analysis, literary criticism, or what any of a number of other disciplines might do by way of analyzing a human act or artifact.[3]

---

2. For excellent examples of rhetorical analyses of literary works, see Tompkins on James Joyce (1968) and Sloan on John Donne (1962, 1965). For an interesting theoretical treatment of the rhetoric of musical form, see Irvine and Kirkpatrick (1972).

3. The writer was a member of that task force and owes thanks to his colleagues on the committee for many of the viewpoints expressed here.

Because rhetorical criticism has a way of growing like topsy, inexperienced critics are well advised to bite off *less* than they think they can chew. Rather than appraising a speech in terms of every standard conceivable, critics might restrict their evaluations to its probable short-run effectiveness or to the logical adequacy of its arguments. Rather than examining every speech made by George Wallace in the 1968 Presidential contest, they might focus on a typical speech, or perhaps restrict themselves further to consideration of Wallace's handling of hecklers on that occasion.

We believe that critics can place effective limitations on the scope of their projects and still make especially valuable contributions by focusing on a work solely in terms of some larger problem, issue, or theoretical question that it helps to illumine. The item of discourse need not be as intrinsically significant as a Presidential oration or a Papal decree (in and of itself, it may be quite trivial), but it must have implicative value. Such theory-oriented criticism may simply be tacked on to an otherwise object-oriented critique, but it also can constitute the exclusive purpose of analysis. We will be discussing it at length in the next section.

Goals and Methods

We have already seen that the same object of analysis can be treated in a variety of ways. Although the precise choice of goals and methods cannot be prescribed, it is possible to identify major types of critical tasks and means of accomplishment appropriate to each. That, at least, is our intent in this section.

I. Message-Centered Analysis

Whether the object of critical scrutiny is as large as the discourse of a mass-media campaign or as small as a thirty-second commercial, the critic can often perform a valuable service simply by telling us *what* it says, *how* it says it, and/or what it *reveals* about its creator(s). Message-centered analysis is a search for meanings, methods, and motives—either as an end itself or as an important adjunct to one of several other critical functions to be discussed later in this section. At times, the critic attempts to impose order on a body of discourse by identifying substantive patterns or documenting the use of various rhetorical devices. At other times, the task involves more than classifying and documenting; it might better be described as explicating, interpreting, or demystifying. The critic as demystifier goes beneath the surface to reveal hidden motives and ideological commitments, unrevealed strategies and tactics, unstated assumptions, implicit appeals and arguments, and subtle nuances of style. Depending on the particular task, the critic may function quite scientifically, or, like an artist, may deliberately place his or her own imprimatur on the analysis. We begin by describing a procedure at the scientific end of the continuum, quantitative content analysis.

Classifying and documenting: quantitative content analysis. Perhaps you have noticed that television advertising no longer excludes blacks; that, in fact, many advertisements reflect black culture realistically, rather than depicting blacks as middle-class whites who happen to be colored black or brown. Or perhaps you have observed that the villains in Kerry Drake episodes frequently meet violent endings and rarely go to trial. Or that a given newspaper consistently gave less space to political candidates whom it opposed editorially. Or that Richard Nixon used personal self-references when he wished to boast of an accomplishment, but positional references ("Your President," "As commander-in-chief," etc.) when he was acting defensively.

Each of these observations constitutes the basis for an hypothesis, and each hypothesis can be tested by means of quantitative content analysis. (cf., Berelson, 1952; Kerlinger, 1964). The method is by no means a panacea for message-centered critics, but it can be used advantageously to document informal observations that are operationally translatable into a reliable counting procedure.[4]

For purposes of illustration, let us look at Lyle Shannon's (1954) analysis of the comic strip, *Little Orphan Annie.* Shannon's thesis was that the strip "presents a picture of the world ... in which the hard-working captains of industry struggle against a vicious and uncompromising underground in order to protect capitalism, earn large profits, and thus assume their social responsibilities, i.e., be charitable to the needy."

As in all content analysis, the critic needed first a representative sample of the discourse. He chose all appearances of the strip on Sundays from April 18, 1948 to July 2, 1950, a total of 110 items. Next, he needed mutually exclusive categories of analysis and reliable indicators of those categories. To establish the strip's values, for example, Shannon used approved and disapproved "god" words and "devil" words as indicators. As a check on observer bias, he had two assistants scrutinize the strips in addition to himself, and he provided specific directions. For example: "The character may appear in the section one or more times but we shall count an appearance on this date as *one* appearance regardless of the number of times that the artist shows the character." Finally, the observers counted indicators as instances of categories. Here is a sampling of findings:

> Thirty-nine weeks were spent in conflict with foreign agents whose identities were thinly disguised and presumably Russian. ... Foreign spies and their

---

4. For some excellent examples of content analysis of mass media messages, see Gerbner, *et al.* (1969).

radical American counterparts are far and away the wiliest opponents; their numbers are overwhelming as contrasted to other opponents, such as hoodlums, young and old. . . . On six occasions Annie vigorously condemns lazy, mean people who are unwilling to work. . . . Orphans are approved five times and work is approved six times. . . .

The great advantage of quantitative analysis is that it is relatively objective. Rather than providing informal illustrations of bias in newspaper coverage of political candidates, analysts might count column inches of space devoted to the contestants. Rather than offering anecdotal proof of shifts in the way television advertising portrays black Americans, they can randomly select a sampling of ads from each of several time periods and get independent observers to help in classifying the models depicted in them. Where meanings or persuasive techniques are inobvious, however, critics must generally fall back on qualitative methods of analysis.

Probing beneath the surface: qualitative content analysis. Rosenfield (1968a) has likened the critic to a spectator at an athletic contest who knows first and foremost how to look at the game. No textbook chapter can tell critics how to look, but we can provide some pointers on what to *look for* in a search for the inobvious:[5]

1. Look first at the overall form of the message to determine what it is *like*. Classify the message in conventional ways (e.g., a lawyer's brief as forensic rhetoric; a legislative debate as deliberative oratory), but also leap across familiar boundaries so as to gain other perspectives on its meanings, methods, and motives. Giving free rein to your imagination, allow yourself to see a keynote address as a religious ritual and a papal decree as a political maneuver; a car advertisement as an attempted seduction and a pastoral poem as an advertisement for self; a treatise on naturalistic phenomena as a defense of class privileges and a pornographic novel as an expression of puritanical outrage. Using what Burke (1969) calls "perspective by incongruity," deliberately place the persuader in bed with strange sleeping partners. One stuffy churchwarden is like another stuffy churchwarden, to be sure, but their adherence to proprieties also makes them analogous in a way to the corner gang member who dresses and behaves in strict conformity to another set of proprieties.

2. Look for examples in the message that reflect its overall tone. On the matter of tone, Karlyn Kohrs Campbell (1972, p. 15) has this to say:

Statements about tone are inferences drawn from stylistic qualities. The critic may describe tone in an infinite number of ways: as personal, direct,

---

5. An excellent example of strictly textual analysis is found in Leff and Mohrmann's (1974) critique of Lincoln's speech at Cooper Union. Most message-centered analyses also examine extrinsic factors, as we shall see shortly.

ironic, satirical, sympathetic, angry, bitter, intense, scholarly, dogmatic, distant, condescending, "tough" or realistic, "sweet" or euphemistic, incisive, elegant, and so on. Each such label should reflect, as accurately as possible, whether the language is abstract or concrete, socially acceptable or unacceptable, technical or colloquial; it should reflect sentence length and complexity.

3. Look for *metacommunications*; i.e., communications about how the communicator perceives his (or her) audience, how he perceives himself, how he perceives the audience seeing him, how he wishes they would perceive him, and how he wishes they would interpret the content of his message. Recall from Chapter 3 that clues to interpersonal attitudes are often most reliably revealed through nonverbal communications. Through gestures and inflections, action language and body language, the communicator may unwittingly provide messages about the message.

4. The *structure* of the message provides another clue to the way communicators see their subject matter, or, more importantly, how they want others to see it. Here, once again, we turn to Campbell (1972, p. 16):

> A historical-chronological form emphasizes development over time. A narrative-dramatic form reflects an organic view of reality and assumes that vicarious sharing of integrally related experiences is essential to the understanding of a concept or situation. A problem-solution form emphasizes the need to discover a concrete policy in order to resolve a troublesome situation. A cause-effect form stresses the prediction of consequences. A topical form selects certain facts of the subject and suggests that others are relatively unimportant. A taxonomical form focuses on the interrelationships between the parts of a process or between the parts and the whole. Each structural form represents a choice of perspective that emphasizes certain elements of the material over others.

5. Look closely at *supporting materials*. Reconstruct arguments for the purpose of discovering patterns of consistency and inconsistency. Look especially at what gets *unsaid* or treated *ambiguously*. Identify enthymematic major premises as well as unstated but implied conclusions. Compare the arguments, appeals, and evidence in the message with those that could have been used. Behind each such choice there lurks a strategy or tactic.

6. Identify terms that express alignments and divisions. Look first at what Chesebro and Hamsher (1973, p. 285) call *entitlement* terms, words that organize and define issues and positions on issues. Is a dispute between labor and management labeled a conflict or a controversy? Is a meeting between the two a confrontation or a discussion? Look next at "god" words and "devil" words. See what symbolic oppositions are created and which terms are treated synonymously. See also what divisions are implied by common ground identifications. When the President praises "Mr. Aver-

age American," for example, who gets damned by implication? See, especially, how terms of approval and disapproval cluster together to reflect ideologies (i.e., integrated systems of belief). It is a reasonable conjecture, says Rokeach (1968), that Leftists will champion equality, conservatives will champion freedom, liberals will champion both, and extreme Rightists will champion neither. See, finally, if you can discover an overarching metaphor that captures the discourse, as Black (1970) did in an example provided earlier.

7. Look for *exceptional* or *unusual* elements. See how the persuader violates rhetorical principles or acts differently from other persuaders in similar roles. Stylistic oddities often reveal attitudes and motives. At the Senate Watergate Hearings, for example, why did Administration bigwigs so rarely say "As I remember" and so frequently say "To the best of my recollection at this time"? Why did John Dean "communicate telephonically" rather than "talk on the phone"?

8. Having moved from a macroscopic examination of forms and tones to a microscopic examination of terms and stylistic oddities, move back again to the general, seeing if each manifested choice, perhaps inexplicable by itself, contributes in some way to the overall thesis and purpose of the persuader.

Combining quantitative and qualitative analysis. In most cases, the critic of discourse functions partly as scientist and partly as artist. Some characteristics of a message or group of messages can be classified and enumerated with great objectivity; others cannot. Where a work of criticism cannot rely on a codified system of quantification to support its claims, the persuasiveness of the critique rests heavily on the skill of the writer. We shall discuss the writing of the critical analysis later in this chapter.

II. Causal Analysis

Beyond asking what a message says, how it says it, and what it reveals about the persuader's motives, the critic often asks *whether* it was effective and *why*. Here the purpose of the analysis is generally pragmatic. Campaign managers want to know whether their candidates are getting through to the public. Ordinary citizens want to erect defenses against con artists. Burke (1967) had a consumer protection function in mind when, through an analysis of Hitler's *Mein Kampf*, he sought to discover how this "medicine-man" sold his "snakeoil." At other times, the goal is a contribution to history. Marie Nichols (1954) examined Lincoln's speaking, for example, to determine how the rhetorical choices of a publicly significant figure shaped the destinies of the nation. Causal analysis involves examination of the discourse, but the message is no longer a self-contained symbolic environment.

To determine whether a rhetorical effort was effective, it is sometimes possible to secure published opinion poll data or to conduct surveys on one's own. Atkins and Reeves (1974), for example, surveyed a sample of voters just prior to Spiro Agnew's resignation speech and a comparable sample just after the speech. The before-after comparison enabled them to glean immediate effects on such issues as perceived credibility, judgments of guilt or innocence, and degrees of sympathy for Agnew's plight. A classic effects-oriented survey was conducted by Robert Merton (1946) on reactions to a radio marathon in which singer Kate Smith was promoting the sale of war bonds. Listeners were extremely moved by the day-long affair and Merton had a methodology appropriate to the occasion. In addition to a cross-sectional poll of almost 1000 respondents, his staff conducted 75 in-depth interviews to determine gut reactions. Although readers are unlikely to have the resources available for studies of that magnitude, it is often possible, and frequently eye-opening, to conduct small-scale surveys —for example, of student reactions to a series of television advertisements or to a campus event.

Rarely, however, do critics have direct evidence of effects, let alone proof of why the message was persuasive or unpersuasive. Here they must rely on their own judgment and on bits and pieces of indirect evidence.

Suppose, for example, that the object of analysis is Edward Kennedy's Chappaquiddick speech of July 25, 1969, the text of which is presented in Chapter 15. At the very least, the critic can appraise the speech *artistically;* that is, in terms of whether the speech *ought* to have been effective, and why, given what we know about the situation confronting the speaker, and given what we know in general about the *art* of persuasive speech-making.

The artistic approach usually begins with an analysis of factors extrinsic to the speech text itself: the historical context, the audience, the immediate occasion, and the speaker's goals and aspirations. How had the news media reported and characterized the sequence of events leading up to the speech? What did people know (or think they knew) about these events, and how much interest had the events aroused? In particular, what competing "theories" or collective impressions had been built up in the public's mind about Kennedy's role in the Kopechne drowning? What did the general public think of Kennedy, both before and after Chappaquiddick? Was he trusted? respected? liked? envied? feared? What was his standing among state and national politicians? What prompted the speech at that time? Was his own explanation of the sequence of events coming under increasing scrutiny? And what of the future? To what extent, for example, did Kennedy's long-range political ambitions influence his speech purposes and strategies?

The second step is message-centered and raises the very same types of questions that were illustrated earlier in the chapter. In addition to making commonplace observations about the message, the Kennedy critic might dare to speculate a bit. Billed as a "Statement to the People of Massachusetts," the speech was aired on national television—does this suggest additional motives for its delivery? By constituting his audience as the people of Massachusetts, was Kennedy attempting to get the entire nation to accept *their* verdict as its own—knowing full well that a "jury" of his own direct constituents would be most sympathetic? Was his self-portrayal particularly well suited to the largely Roman Catholic "jury" that resides in Massachusetts—a Job-like character seeking absolution from bad acts (venial sins) but adamantly insisting on what the theology values most: good intentions? The brevity of the speech befitted a man who was too traumatized by an event to discuss it at length, but was it too concise—suggesting a possible coverup?

The third step involves a fusion of the first two steps, the extrinsic and the intrinsic. Here, in making inferences about effects and causes, the critic may attempt to answer one or both of the following sets of questions: (1) In light of his speech purposes, did Kennedy respond with reasonable effectiveness to the exigencies of the rhetorical situation confronting him? Which rhetorical choices were most appropriate and which were least appropriate? (2) Independent of his goals and of contextual constraints, what were the probable short-term and/or long-term consequences of the speech on those who heard it or heard about it? How did it *function* for receivers and why? To answer either of these sets of questions, critics using the artistic method would apply accepted principles of persuasion to the case at hand in forming their verdicts.

Readers might well object that there is something too conjectural and perhaps even circular about the artistic approach. Too conjectural, because there is inevitably a gap between principles and practice. Generalizations about the art of persuasion, however sound, cannot always be applied reliably to the particular case. And circular, perhaps, because strict adherents to the artistic method have no independent means of establishing the validity of their principles. The principles are presumed to be valid because they were applied by persuaders presumed to be effective because they applied the principles. . . ! (This is a major reason why behaviorally oriented theorists perform controlled experiments to establish the validity of rhetorical principles. Artistically oriented critics are free to borrow and apply them, but frequently they don't.)

Rather than relying entirely on the artistic method, the critic might well search for tangible evidence of effects and causes, however indirect the evidence may be, and however many new questions might be raised about the critic's use of *post hoc* reasoning. An examination of newspapers and magazines from the period might reveal, for example, that thousands of letters of support flowed in from Kennedy's constituents; that Kennedy held his own among newspaper columnists; that the general public reacted sympathetically, especially to Kennedy's references to his long-suffering family; that Kennedy continued to stand well among Democratic politicians and retained a high popularity rating in the Gallup polls; but, on the other hand, that years after the event, most people still believed his chances of becoming President had been hurt by Chappaquiddick and a number of investigative reporters were raising serious questions about it. Was the speech effective in the short run but ineffective in the long run because it did not stand up to sound standards of reasoning and evidence? We shall see that this question borders on evaluative criticism, a subject we take up next.

III. Evaluative Criticism

Many critics insist that it is not enough to explicate a message or to infer rhetorical effects and causes. " 'Good' criticism," says Campbell (1972, pp. 21–22), "is evaluative. It makes clear and unmistakable judgments about the quality, worth, and consequences of the discourse." Oftentimes, an evaluation is implied in causal analyses or message-centered analyses, but there are dangers in not making judgments explicit. Says Campbell, the critic has an obligation to identify and defend the criteria used to evaluate a rhetorical effort, and to show how the criteria apply in the particular case. We shall focus here on ethical standards of evaluation.[6]

Standards of sound argumentation. Whether a rhetorical effort was effective or ineffective, it may still be damned because it was untruthful and illogical, or praised because the audience was too stupid or biased or unhinged to appreciate it. Rationalists frequently assume that unsound argumentation also dooms a rhetorical effort to be ineffective, at least in the long run. Note that this assumption is manifest in William Buckley's (1973, pp. 30ff.) analysis of Richard Nixon's first major Watergate speech, delivered April 30, 1973 (the text of the speech appears in Chapter 15):

> The rhetoric apart, I thought the speech mortally flawed by low analytic cunning. Mr. Nixon sought to construct an august scaffolding for himself,

---

6. One can learn a good deal about rhetorical criticism by comparing different critiques of the same persuasive discourse. Two excellent, but quite different, analyses of Richard Nixon's speech of November 3, 1969 were provided by Hill (1972) and Campbell (1972). Hill focused solely on assessing whether and how it worked on Nixon's target audience; Campbell insisted on pronouncing moral judgments. Was the speech a "good" speech? In addition to reading their critiques (a copy of the speech itself is presented in Campbell), also read the exchange between Hill and Campbell (pp. 451–460) on how the speech "should" have been evaluated, appearing in the same issue of the *Quarterly Journal of Speech* in which Hill's article is found.

whence to preside over the restoration of the public rectitude. He produced a spindle, on which he impaled himself. The structure of the speech compressed into a single sentence: *"Although it is clearly unreasonable that I as President—laboring full-time to bring peace to our generation and to combat inflation and to make it safe to walk the streets at night—should be held responsible for the excesses and minor illegalities of the entire executive and political staffs, nevertheless, because I am that kind of man, I do accept responsibility, and I commence my discharge of it here tonight by firing two innocent men."*

To appraise the logic of a speech or other message form, readers may apply standards suggested in Chapter 11. Was it clear? Were its key terms defined fairly? Did conclusions arrived at deductively follow from their premises? Did inductive generalizations follow from the evidence presented? In reasoning by analogy or from signs or from cause to effect or effect to cause, did the persuader avoid potential fallacies? Were correlations treated as proof of causation? Were *post hoc* fallacies exhibited? Was the overall structure of reasoning vertically and horizontally consistent? Did the plans proposed meet the needs presented, or, for example, did the persuader produce a plan that would only get at effects after he or she insisted that any solution must get at causes of the problem?

The truthfulness of evidence can also be appraised internally by applying other standards suggested in Chapter 11, but the critic should generally locate external sources to confirm or disconfirm the evidentiary claims presented. A reading of the Watergate tape transcripts, for example, should reveal, contrary to claims presented in his April 30th speech, that Nixon exercised considerable control over the 1972 campaign; that he was aware of illegal actions taken by Erlichman, Haldeman, and Kleindeinst (persons whom he praised in the speech), that rather than urge a full investigation and full disclosure in March, he urged his top people to "stonewall it," etc.

Appraisals in terms of truth and logic are often revealing, but one wonders whether they are always fair to the persuader. We argued in Chapter 11, you will recall, that the requirements for "rhetorical proof" cannot possibly be as stringent as those proposed by the logician—else practically all speaking on matters of judgment before ordinary mortals would fail the test. What the rhetorician calls effective the logician labels fallacious; few techniques of persuasion escape the logician's censure.

Not wishing to dispense with truth and logic, yet aware that these standards can be too exacting, some critics have sought a kind of compromise standard for evaluating the soundness of rhetorical argumentation, rooted in judgments about what "reasonable" persons would accept. Recall that John Stuart Mill proposed an external standard—whether the arguments advanced could survive in a "free marketplace" of ideas. Somewhat similarly, Perelman and Olbrechts-Tyteca (1969) have suggested that the test of an argument is whether those best equipped to hear it (an imagined "universal audience") could buy it. We may once again detect circular reasoning here: A reasonable argument is one reasonable people would accept because the arguments are reasonable because they are reasonable people. . . . Clearly, the debate over standards of sound argumentation in rhetorical discourse has not ended.

Standards of "purity." Oftentimes, the critic seeks not simply to demystify or to debunk. As we saw in Chapter 2, this critical stance is particularly suited to evaluations of peripheral cases of persuasion. The critic's thesis is that a given work or body of discourse (or creator of the discourse) not only *can* be viewed rhetorically (as one among many valid perspectives), but that it *is* rhetorical in the most pejorative sense of the term.

The structure of "purity" critiques is fairly straightforward. To make a case, the debunker begins by citing the rhetor's publicly stated claims to purity. This rhetor claims that her discourse is purely objective. That rhetor claims his administration has only the students' interests at heart. That rhetor purports to be interested only in the aesthetics of her art, and not in how others see it.

Next, the critic sets forth criteria for accepting or rejecting the rhetor's claims. If the rhetor is purely objective, for example, presumably there should be no distortion, concealment, or misrepresentation of factual data.

Applying these criteria, the critic now uses the rhetor's own words to debunk her. Evidence is presented to show that she is not what she purports to be; that she has not only dealt in appearances, as any rhetor does, but in illusions, deceptions and hypocrisies. Frequently, the critic introduces a dramatistic metaphor: Having looked at the public performance of the rhetor, let us see what she is really like by going "backstage." There we will discover that the exterior is only a façade.

The critic may stop at this point or he may add a fourth point—that the rhetor's discourse has adverse social consequences. He may argue, for example, that the administrator's rhetoric gives students a false sense of complaceny, or that the media's bias on an issue inhibits intelligent discussion of that issue.

Debunking is fairly easy to do and should be familiar to readers from examples provided in Chapter 2. Recall that Weigert (1970) debunked the "Immoral Rhetoric of Scientific Sociology." His argument went as follows:

1. The behavioral sociologist claims that the social sciences are potentially as objective as the physical sciences.
2. To be objective by the physical scientist's standards, the scientific sociologist would have to be able to replicate findings, isolate and control variables, discriminate between valid and invalid measures, predict with precision, etc.

3. Because it deals with complex aggregates of people, rather than isolatable physical entities, sociology is inherently different in kind, and not just degree, from the physical sciences. The rhetoric of scientific sociology is thus deceptive. Its rhetoric is a status-preserving mechanism that masks careerist interests behind a cloak of pure objectivity.

4. An important consequence of this deception is that sociology is in danger of becoming an ideology. If it does, this will inhibit its search for truth.

The great advantage of debunking is that it hoists the rhetor by his own petard, thus making him look silly, if nothing else—a prostitute pretending to be a virgin. The great danger, however, is that the critic's "mere rhetoric" epithet may be a substitute for careful argumentation. In debunking the rhetoric of another, critics often make dubious and inexplicit assumptions of their own about what the world is "really" like. Needless to say, they are duty-bound to be able to defend them. Otherwise, they had better retreat to the less aggressive stance of those critics who maintain that theirs is only one among many perspectives on a work.

Standards of effect. In the process of undermining a persuader's pretensions to "purity," the debunker impugns the persuader's *motives*. Judgments of truth and logic are two among many standards for evaluating the *means* of persuasion. Not altogether separable from judgments about motives and means are judgments about the *moral consequences* of a persuasive effort. Recall that in Chapter 7 we illustrated this approach as applied to intragovernmental discourse about Vietnam policy-making. There we argued that the planners had become caught up in their "god" words and "devil" words, the end result being that dissent was punished, reasonable public discussion was foreclosed, values inimical to the long-run interests of the society were promoted, and, most important, the planners could not extricate the nation from the Vietnam quagmire.

Effects evaluations might begin with the persuaders themselves. It might be argued, for example, that in the process of creating discourse for others, we also create ourselves and, furthermore, that we have a moral obligation to strive for self-actualization. What, then, do our habits of speaking do to our personalities? Another argument might weigh short-term gains against long-term costs. Even if we can succeed in the short run by underhanded tactics, what will this do in the long run to our reputations?

Judgments about consequences are more commonly cast in terms of effects on audiences or on the society at large. Did the rhetorical effort have the primary effect of promoting justice or injustice, equality or inequality, the public interest or the private interest? And what of its secondary effects, the consequences of the means employed to secure primary objectives? However noble the persuaders' ends and however worthy their efforts in terms of their primary consequences, does the use of such techniques as pandering, question-begging, obfuscation, etc., encourage others to do the same?

Moralistic arguments clothed in pragmatic terms have an aura of practicality about them and thus are attractive to many readers. Critics of moral pragmatism point out, however, that behind every utilitarian argument, there is ultimately the assumption of some moral absolute which the moral pragmatist asks us to accept on faith. It is often difficult, moreover, to establish the causal links in arguments about consequences—to demonstrate, for example, that the use of lies by one speaker reinforces the value of lying in the society as a whole.

We would suggest to readers that they combine judgments about means, motives, and consequences into a situational ethic that weighs each in light of circumstances (see our discussion in Chapter 2). We would caution readers, however, that no critical evaluation in terms of ethics is likely to be entirely compelling. Ours may be a minority viewpoint, but we would urge critics to focus nonevaluatively on message-centered analyses, on causal analyses, and on a type of criticism to be discussed next, theory-oriented analysis.

IV. Theory-Oriented Analysis

Recall that theory-oriented analysis differs from the other types of criticism discussed thus far in that it focuses on a rhetorical object primarily as case study material. The goal of the critic may be to undermine a popularly held theory or conceptual distinction or yardstick for evaluation. Or the critic may use the case to affirm a distinction or support a theory or suggest a hypothesis requiring further testing or derive lessons from the case for future persuaders in similar situations.

Perhaps the smallest type of theory-oriented analysis involves tests of the adequacy of concepts or conceptual distinctions. Recall, for example, our dissatisfaction with the persuasion-coercion dichotomy. We are happy to report that several case studies have helped to undermine that dichotomy. In one of them, Andrews (1970) attempted to illustrate how persuasion and coercion could work hand in hand:

> To deny coercion any place in the process of social change is perhaps to hope for the attainment of an ideal and not to describe realistically the rhetorical process. There is undoubtedly an intimate and compelling relationship between persuasion and coercion. The persuader, in his examination of alternatives, may find his position greatly strengthened when one alternative offered is the surrender to coercive methods. . . . In short, while persuasion may be viewed by some as the antithesis of coercion, persuasion may often depend on its opposite to achieve its goal (p. 187).

To support his thesis, Andrews focuses on the interplay of coercion and persuasion that led to the passage of the 1832 Reform Bill in England. Throughout the land there was riot and destruction by the lower classes. Parliamentary opponents of reform were greeted with less than adulation in their own boroughs. With great accuracy, one Liverpoolian managed to toss a dead cat on to the top of Lord Sandon's head. In Bristol, the rioting that took place during Sir Charles Wetherell's visit was so intense that he was forced to flee for safety by scurrying over several rooftops. Meanwhile, in Parliament, Whig MPs were sharply rebuked by Tories for submitting to the "universal bellow" of the violent masses. With good reason, the Duke of Wellington went so far as to accuse the ministry of having "coalesced with the mob," and even to have "encouraged" violent agitation for change (p. 193). The response by the Whigs was predictable; a variation on what we have called elsewhere (Simons, 1970) the "brakeman" theme. Far be it from them to approve mob coercion; they were merely responding to it pragmatically. Macaulay claimed to support the reform measure because "unless the plan proposed, or some similar plan, be speedily adopted, great and terrible calamities will befall us" (quoted by Andrews, p. 192).

Our second example involves a type of theory-oriented analysis that is becoming increasingly popular nowadays, the search for common characteristics in *genres* of rhetorical discourse. A rhetorical genre may be defined as a class of unique and distinguishable patterns of response to common situational exigencies. An assumption behind genre theories is that similar situations evoke similar strategic responses to them. One obvious advantage of genre theories is that, if valid, they help make rhetorical choices somewhat more predictable. A second advantage is that they provide a benchmark for evaluating the artistry of a persuader. We may ask, for example, whether the concession speech of a defeated political candidate simply conformed to the characteristics of the concession genre or whether it deviated in artistic ways. The search for distinctive genres generally begins with comparisons of two or more cases thought to be similar.

In one such study, Rosenfield (1968b) posited the existence of a genre which he called the *mass-media apologia*. It might be defined as a type of response over the broadcast media by a publicly significant figure to charges of moral transgression. The cases compared by Rosenfield were the "Checkers" speech of 1952, in which Richard Nixon, running for the vice-presidency, sought to dispel charges that he had improperly used a campaign fund, and an address in 1953 by ex-president Harry S Truman in response to charges that he had allowed a communist agent to hold high government office. Rosenfield found that both speakers: (1) were quite brief (23 and 30 minutes); (2) employed similar forensic strategies (motives were defended and factual accusations were either denied or justified in terms of higher values); (3) presented counteraccusations in the form of invective and innuendo about the moral qualities of their accusers; (4) offered documented support for claims in only the middle sections of their speeches; (5) disclosed new items of information, (6) but introduced no new arguments beyond those offered in public statements during the previous weeks.

Two cases obviously do not validate a genre theory or any other theory, but Rosenfield's probe was obviously a beginning, and an impressive one at that. (From an examination of the texts reproduced in Chapter 15, readers may note strikingly similar characteristics in the Nixon-Watergate speech and in the Kennedy-Chappaquiddick speech.) Since Rosenfield's pioneering essay, other scholars (e.g., Ware and Linkugel, 1973) have attempted to improve upon Rosenfield's conception. Each new case study of public figures in similar situations adds grist for the theoretical mill.[7]

The foregoing examples of theory-oriented analysis involved acts or events that were worth studying in their own right, but others may be quite trivial or commonplace. In the hands of a clever critic, several news clippings about recent bank robberies may be used to develop or affirm a theory about the nonverbal rhetoric of threats (Ellsberg, 1959); a school board debate on next year's budget may illustrate a theory about the relationship between rhetoric and rationality (Weiss, 1973); and an essay on clothing may serve as the springboard for a theory about "mystification" as a rhetorical device (Burke, 1969, pp. 118–123).

How does one "see" a theory illustrated or embodied in a case? As a starting point, critics needs to be well informed about existing rhetorical concepts, principles, and full-scale theories, as well as theoretical conceptions outside rhetoric's domain. Knowing about them is not enough, however; they also need to be able to "play" with them—to imagine their implications and applications to cases. Thereafter, they may choose one of two paths. Either they may select a theoretical conception and search for a case or cases that will in some way bear upon it, or, more commonly, they will begin with one or more cases and ask what is theoretically most interesting about it. Wayne Brockriede (1974, pp. 172-3) provided a typical example of the latter approach:

> . . . when criticizing the structure of the Truman Doctrine speech of 1947, Robert L. Scott and I observed that the speech did not follow the traditional model of a logical brief. . . . We wondered whether a model derived from the concept of musical counterpoint might more appropriately explain, in part, how Truman's auditors might have responded positively to the speech

---

7. For examples of other attempts at identifying and characterizing rhetorical genres, see Windt (1972), Wooten (1973), and Ivie (1974).

structured as it is. . . . After tracing the motifs, we engaged in some speculation about the extent to which speeches structured along the contrapuntal
model could have good effects on understanding, attitude change, and behavioral influence. In short, our study hypothesized a new approach to an
understanding of rhetorical discourse and invited others to confront and
pursue the possibilities.

Theory-oriented case studies are not a substitute for laboratory or field
experimentation on persuasion, but they can nevertheless illuminate uni-
versals in the process of focusing on particulars. If they do nothing else,
these studies can suggest hypotheses for testing by more rigorous means.

Earlier we suggested that, as one way of narrowing their critical tasks,
readers might well select and examine rhetorical objects solely in terms of
some single theoretical question raised or illustrated by the work. Usually,
a work will exhibit several dimensions of theoretical interest, and the critic
will be free to choose among them, at least as a point of focus. A colon in
the title of the paper can be used to highlight the theory-oriented nature
of the analysis. Here are some examples:

1. Sylvia Plath As Feminist Poet: The Paradox of Expressive Rhetoric
2. Berkeley Ten Years Later: A Case Study of the Effects of Campus Confrontations
3. Uses of Deliberate Ambiguity: A Study of Christ's Parables
4. The Anti-Ploy Ploy: Campaigning in the Wake of Watergate
5. Scientific Discourse as "Mere Rhetoric": The ESP Debate

Writing the Critical Analysis

"Whatever else it may be," insists Wayne Brockriede (1974, p. 165), "useful rhetorical criticism . . . must function as an argument." Where scientific
methods such as content analysis are employed, the weight of the argument is carried substantially, though not entirely, by the hard data presented. But what of the critic who subjectively interprets or evaluates a
given work or derives implications for theory from a single case? Here the
eye of the critic is not simply a camera lens that reflects the light cast by
the rhetorical object but a complex prism that refracts it in idiosyncratic
ways. How does the artistic critic get us to see what he or she sees, and
more than that, to accept his or her vision of the symbolic reality as valid
or correct?

The answer, it seems apparent, has something to do with linguistic
sensitivity. Like any other persuader, the critic has functions to perform
of a rather mundane nature. The introduction must identify a topic or
thesis and justify it as significant. Orienting materials must be provided in
the form of background information, previews or partitions, definitions

and explanations. Attention and interest must be captured and sustained throughout. The body of the essay must be structured strategically and clearly. Arguments must be offered and evidence adduced in support of them. And in the conclusion the critic must tie things together, summarizing major generalizations offered within the body of the critique and suggesting possible implications and applications.

But these bare bones of the critical essay in no way hint at the communication skills required of the artistic critic. We get a better glimpse of the art of criticism when we see good critics at work at the task of recreating the rhetorical event for their readers. Here critics offer more than a scorecard of players and acts; they order, yes, but in ways that lead inexorably to the inferences and judgments they will be making. In Mailer's (1968) essay on the tumultous 1968 Democratic National Convention, the scene opens with a long description of the Chicago stockyards. Page after page describes pigs taken to be slaughtered and dragged howling through the assembly line. There we meet Mailer's archtypical Chicagoan, a wide-nostriled, blood-stained ethnic who resembles nothing so much as the animals he is butchering. Yet we learn soon that Mailer respects these human carnivores: their wide nostrils were fashioned, after all, to do the hard work of our society. Then the scene shifts to O'Hare Airport where delegates and demonstrators in support of Eugene McCarthy are filing down the gangplank. Suddenly we see the inevitability of the violence that was to erupt on the streets of Chicago that August. For McCarthy's supporters are the paper-wielding, intellectual, narrow-nostriled denizens of our society. Chicago, 1968, hints Mailer, is symbolized by the nostrils of its antagonists. It is a tragic encounter because neither side can appreciate the virtues of the other.

As in Mailer's essay, good artistic criticism uses metaphors as linguistic economies. Global images are wrought from snatches of dialogue or from nuances of gesture. Here, for example, is Garry Wills' (1974, p. 17) description of John Erlichman, a powerful figure in the Nixon administration who was now defiantly standing trial in connection with the attempted theft of papers belonging to Daniel Ellsberg's psychiatrist:

> While St. Clair implied at the Court that Presidents are above the law, John Ehrlichman was arguing at his own trial that the President's men are above it too. He came into the courtroom cocky with an assurance that had grown from the trial's first stage, when David Young proved to be an unimpressive witness for the prosecution. On the stand, Ehrlichman suffered a momentary catch of nervousness in his throat—and put that rebellious member in its place. Ostentatiously, he poured water and drank, ran it around his mouth, swallowed, drew his top lip up, ran tongue across teeth, adjusted his jaw line back and forth to the proper firmness, then raised his eyebrows at the jurors—a whole toilette in ten seconds. Here, clearly, was a man in charge.

Even as evidence of the effects of a message is presented, the skilled artistic critic manages to avoid tedious accountings. Note, for example, how Marie Nichols (in Scott and Brock, 1972, pp. 78–9) interweaves historical materials to create a composite picture of immediate reactions by witnesses to Lincoln's first inaugural address:

> As Lincoln read on, the audience listened respectfully, with "intense interest, amid a stillness almost oppressive." In the crowd behind the speaker sat Horace Greeley, momentarily expecting the crack of the fire. At one point he thought it had come. The speaker stopped. But it was only a spectator crashing down through a tree. Otherwise, the crowd in the grounds "behaved very well." Buchanan sat listening, and "looking as straight as he could at the toe of his right boot." Douglas, close by on Lincoln's right, listened "attentively," showing that he was "apparently satisfied" as he "exclaimed, *sotto voce,* 'Good,' 'That's so,' 'No coercion,' and 'Good again.' " Chief Justice Taney did not remove his eyes from Mr. Lincoln during the entire delivery. Mr. Cameron stood with his back to the President, on the opposite side of Mr. Douglas, "peering off into the crowd." Senator Seward and the other Cabinet officers-elect "kept themselves in the background." Senator Wigfall of Texas, with folded arms, "leaned conspicuously in a Capitol doorway," listening to the inaugural, plainly wearing "contempt, defiance, derision, on his face, his pantomimic posture saying what he had said in the Senate, that the old Union was a corpse and the question was how to embalm it and conduct the funeral decently." Thurlow Weed moved away from the crowd, reporting to General Scott at the top of the slope, "The Inaugural is a success," as the old general exclaimed, "God be praised! God in his goodness be praised."

These fragments suggest that communication skills are an indispensable part of the artistic critic's methodological equipment. Like poets, artistic rhetorical critics capture the elusiveness of human experience. Simultaneously, they present arguments, erecting a logical structure that will support their contentions. And that, of course, is a fair description of what any persuader must do.

Summary

A colleague of ours, Trevor Melia, likens the various academic disciplines to observers, each on a different mountain top, looking down on the same valley of subject matter. From their vantage point atop "Rhetoric Mountain," rhetorical critics or analysts are inclined to see as rhetorical not only paradigm cases of persuasion, but also borderline or peripheral cases such as news reports, scientific discourse, plays and poetry, expressive acts, and ostensibly coercive acts. The scope covered by an analysis may range from a series of persuasive campaigns all the way down to a small excerpt from a ten-minute speech. In all cases, however, the rhetorical critic looks at discourse in terms of the implicit or explicit arguments and appeals it offers, and in terms of its potential or actual effects on the beliefs, values, or attitudes of particular audiences. More specifically, we have identified several critical functions.

Message-centered analysis is concerned with identifying and explicating meanings, methods, and motives. Where these are fairly apparent, the analyst may operate rather scientifically, utilizing a method known as quantitative content analysis. More often than not, however, the critic needs to probe beneath the surface to reveal hidden meanings, inexplicit strategies, and inobvious motives. Here we offered no formulas but did suggest some things to look for: (1) likenesses with ostensibly quite different rhetorical efforts which, upon closer examination, reveal similarities in form; (2) tonal qualities of the work; (3) metacommunicative cues (messages about the message); (4) structural characteristics of the message; (5) types of support materials included and, more important, excluded; (6) terms that express identifications and divisions; (7) exceptional elements, including stylistic anomalies, and (8) patterns of relationship among 1–7 above.

Other forms of rhetorical criticism build on message analyses but go beyond them. *Causal* analyses ask not only what a message says, how, and why, but whether a message was effective or ineffective and for what reasons. Effectiveness may be assessed from the perspective of the persuader, or it may be viewed functionally, in terms of intended and unintended consequences. In either case, analysts examine situational elements extrinsic to the rhetorical effort, as well as the message itself. In most cases, causes and effects must be inferred from indirect evidence and/or from judgments about how the message *ought* to have worked, given what the critic knows about the art of persuasion in general.

Evaluative criticism not only describes or explains a work, it pronounces judgment upon it, based on criteria the critic identifies and defends. The work may be described as illogical or untruthful, for example, or as having promoted good ends for bad reasons. Debunking is a popular form of evaluative criticism in which the critic cites a rhetor's claims to "purity" of motive and then undermines those pretensions.

The foregoing types of criticism are object-oriented and thus perform consummatory functions. The last type we discussed, *theory-oriented* criticism, utilizes rhetorical objects instrumentally, as case-study materials in service of a larger end such as theory-building or theory-testing. By looking at a rhetorical object solely in terms of its implications for theory, the critic can effectively narrow his topic and still perform a valuable function.

We strongly recommend that readers try their hands at writing rhetorical analyses. We cautioned, however, that good rhetorical criticism requires two skills that none of us come by easily: the ability to see well and the ability to communicate well. These are skills, ultimately, that any persuader must have.

15

Materials
for
Analysis

As should be quite clear by now, there are myriad ways of analyzing persuasion, a range of critical perspectives, and an infinite number of topics from which to choose. Full-scale analysis, as in term papers and theses, is certainly recommended, but the reader should not think of rhetorical analysis as necessarily requiring such extended efforts. Reasoned judgments about rhetorical efforts (not excluding your own efforts) should become a habit of mind, and they should be applied on a continuing basis both to the seemingly trivial events of your personal life and to the speeches, movements, and campaigns that make headlines in the newspapers.

Presented in this chapter is a wide assortment of ideas for analysis, sample discourses begging to be analyzed by you, and brief analyses by others. In addition to drawing inspiration from these materials for your own rhetorical analyses, we suggest that you use them to test your understanding of concepts and principles discussed in Parts 1 and 2 of the book. You should find, by the way, that any single item of discourse is illustrative of concepts and principles covered in more than one chapter. For example, the introduction to the Palmer Hoyt speech, transcribed on pages 344 to 345, should illustrate research generalizations about explicit versus implicit conclusion-drawing (from Chapter 7), principles of common ground (from Chapter 8), techniques of attention-getting (from Chapter 9), orienting functions of the introduction (from Chapter 10), and principles of psycho-logic (from Chapter 11).

Advertising

Advertising is a favorite subject for rhetorical analysis but few of us get beneath the surface of things. This book should help you in a general way to identify advertising strategies (they are basically no different from those used by other persuaders), and it may be supplemented by textbooks on specialized tactics (e.g., Barmash, 1974; Bogart, 1967; Dichter, 1960).

Suggestions for Analysis

1. Create a series of thirty-second commercials for radio or TV, and then justify your verbal and nonverbal choices in light of the psychological literature on persuasion. For example, you might wish to create an anti-smoking commercial. Should you use strong or weak fear appeals? A story about an ordinary person or one about a celebrity? A commercial conceding the benefits of smoking or one naming only its harms? To support your choices, use not only the literature of psychology books and journals but also the applied research presented in such periodicals as the *Journal of Marketing*.

2. Collect and then compare a series of magazine advertisements on similar products that differ primarily in terms of the psychological strategies they employ. For example, compare testimonials in whiskey ads by prestige figures, "plain folks," and "super-representatives." In addition to surmising how effective each ad *ought* to be in light of the psychological research literature on common ground and source credibility, try surveying a sample of drinkers to compare their reactions to the ads.

3. Try advertising yourself. For example, prepare a "mate wanted" advertisement for the Personals section of an underground newspaper and analyze the bases for your inclusions and exclusions. Or actually place two different "job wanted" ads for the same type job and compare the responses you get.

4. The volume of advertising in our society provides an opportunity to put the *analogue* method of criticism to work (see Chapter 14). Collect a large number of ads on the same subject to determine what qualities they have in common. How do they achieve common ground? get attention? orient receivers? provide the appearance of reasonableness? overcome problems or potential objections?

5. A useful starting point for analyses of advertising's *secondary effects* is Jules Henry's *Culture Against Man* (1963). He attributes many of our woes to advertising's "pecuniary philosophy,' a view of truth and logic as that which sells, and a view of men and women as inert trigger-action mechanisms. Try writing an essay paper on the secondary consequences of ads in a particular area such as processed foods or prescription tranquilizers. "If you give someone strawberry ice cream made with fresh strawberries," says Kurt Konigbacher of Booz, Allen and Hamilton, Inc., "you'd have a totally unacceptable product. People would say, 'I wouldn't eat that artificial stuff.' " Is commercial advertising of processed foods helping to make us into artificial human beings?

Sample Analysis: Erica Jong on Ads for Women

Erica Jong's best selling novel, *Fear of Flying* (1973), is interspersed with rhetorical analyses of everything from cocktail party chatter to psychotherapy sessions. Here is her colorful analysis of the secondary effects of advertisements addressed to women (p. 9):

> "Be kind to your behind." "Blush like you mean it." "Love your hair." "Want a better body? We'll arrange the one you've got." "That shine on your face should come from him, not from your skin." "You've come a long way, baby." "How to score with every female in the universe." "The stars and sensual you." "To a man they say Cutty Sark." "A diamond is forever." "If you're concerned about douching . . ." "Length and coolness come together." "How I solved my intimate odor problem." "Lady be cool." "Every

woman alive loves Chanel No. 5." "What makes a shy girl get intimate?" "Femme, we named it after you."

What all the ads and all the whorescopes seemed to imply was that if only you were narcissistic *enough,* if only you took proper care of your smells, your hair, your boobs, your eyelashes, your armpits, your crotch, your stars, your scars, and your choice of scotch in bars—you would meet a beautiful, powerful, potent and rich man who would satisfy every longing, fill every hole, make your heart skip a beat (or stand still), make you misty and fly you to the moon (preferably on gossamer wings), where you would live totally satisfied forever."

Interpersonal Relations

The study of persuasion in ordinary, day-to-day relationships invites special attention to nonverbal forms and symbolic acts, and provides an opportunity to see how social conflicts are played out rhetorically. Be especially alive to the way seemingly expressive acts function, consciously or unconsciously, to serve the interests of the communicator.

Suggestions for Analysis

1. Read Mehrabian's *Silent Messages* (1971) and the chapters on face work and on deference and demeanor in Goffman's *Interaction Ritual* (1967). Utilizing concepts and principles found in those books, analyze one or more of the following:

   a) Ingratiation techniques used by job applicants and status maintenance techniques used by employers;

   b) Impression management techniques used at cocktail parties or in dating situations;

   c) Techniques used by job supervisors to handle employee complaints or rule infractions;

   d) Methods used by toddlers to wrest privileges or avoid punishments from parents.

2. When cultural norms governing interpersonal relations change radically, as they have in recent years, the advice columns in magazines, marriage manuals, and etiquette books of yesteryear appear ludicrous. Compare prescriptive materials of the same type from fifty years ago and today.

3. Keep a careful record of your behavior in conflicts that arise between you and intimate friends or relatives over a period of a week. Then analyze your behavior in terms of its costs and benefits. How often do you:

   a) Directly communicate your feelings on a matter;

b) Carp, blame, or ascribe motives of badness or madness;

c) Use such "loss of control" techniques as developing a physical symptom or claiming ignorance, innocence, or incompetence;

d) Pout or sulk when frustrated or charged with wrong-doing;

e) Seek common ground for possible compromises or reconciliations;

f) Compliment or humor as a way of defusing hostility;

g) Blame yourself and beg forgiveness;

h) Threaten punishments for noncompliance;

i) Promise rewards for compliance;

j) Objectify or intellectualize the conflict, as though feelings were irrelevant to the matter?

4. Identify several acquaintances whose behavior seems to epitomize the "expressivist" life style (see Chapter 2). Are they genuinely spontaneous or is the appearance of spontaneity controlled and contrived? In what kinds of situations are their behaviors rhetorically adaptive and in what situations do they appear to be maladaptive?

Item for Analysis: Allen Ginsburg at a Senate Hearing

This selection is intended to typify what we have called, in Chapters 2 and 13, the "anti-rhetorical rhetoric" of the Expressivist position. Here is Ginsburg, poet of the Beat Generation, and later of the Hippie movement, before a Senate Judiciary Committee on Drug Use in 1966. Ginsburg's seemingly direct style subtly mocks the formal style expected at Congressional hearings. Is it an effective style for him, and for leaders of social movements in general?

> I hope that whatever prejudgments you may have of me and my bearded image you can suspend so that we can talk together as fellow beings in the same room of Now, trying to come to some harmony and peacefulness between us. I am a little frightened to present myself—the fear of your rejection of me, the fear of not being tranquil enough to reassure you that we can talk together, make sense, and perhaps even *like* each other enough to want not to offend, or to speak in a way which is abrupt or hard to understand.

Sample Analysis: Lois Gould on Lumpily Made Beds

Recall our argument (from Chapters 2 and 3), that many seemingly expressive acts are symbolic in nature, and are thus fair game for rhetorical analysis. We proposed that acts ranging from ghetto riots to fainting spells could be labeled as symbolic when other explanations for the act such as whim, incompetence, or biological need could be ruled out, or where there was direct evidence of rhetorical intent. Oftentimes, we argued in Chapter 13, denial of rhetorical intent is a "loss of control" strategy, designed to maintain power or deter an adversary in a conflict situation.

Among the best rhetorical critics around these days are women's liberationists. They have frequently described the seemingly innocuous acts of their companions as devices designed to maintain male domination. Targets of analysis have included such acts as automatically assuming the driver's role, both in the car and the bed, and, in this selection (Gould 1973), Gould's husband's not uncharacteristic habit of making lumpy beds. Rather than reproducing Ms. Gould's article in full, we have chosen to summarize the two main parts of her analysis in outline form:

I. My husband's habitual act is symbolic in nature.
   A. He is competent to make the bed unlumpily.
      1. He made his own bed in the army.
      2. He made his own bed in camp.
      3. He taught the children to make their beds neatly.
      4. Skills like these do not rust from disuse.
   B. He has as much time to make unlumpy beds as I do.
   C. He, as much as I, cares that the house is kept neat.
   D. Only with great reluctance did he begin making the bed at all.

II. The act symbolizes an interest in perpetuating power and privilege.
   A. Before acceding (with great fanfare) to my request that he make the bed at all, he offered the following arguments:
      1. Who makes the bed is unimportant.
      2. Making the bed would make me late for work.
      3. You do it faster and more efficiently.
      4. Why don't *you* hire a maid? . . . .
   B. Once he gave in, he said "There, I made the bed for you."
   C. If confronted over the bed's lumpiness, he would probably say:
      1. "What, for that matter, is a decent bed?"
      2. Why are you getting hung up on household sociology?
      3. Surely, you have better things to do than carp at me, now that you don't have to make the bed.
   D. These arguments give contextual meaning to the lumpy bed. Viewed in context, the lumpy bed is a way of saying:
      1. I'm a very important person.
      2. You're not a very important person.
      3. I therefore have a right to dominate in this relationship.

Is Ms. Gould reading too much rhetoric into the lumpy bed? We suspect not, and we suspect that readers can find similar examples from their own experience in which they have done, or been done in by, other seemingly expressive acts. Try analyzing some situations in a similar way from your own relationships with others.

Art and Entertainment

Painters, poets, dramatists, composers, humorists, etc., may not consciously seek to adapt arguments and appeals to particular audiences, and in many cases the persuasive techniques they employ and the effects they achieve are not readily discernible. In other cases, as in protest music, rhetorical intent and methods are quite obvious. Each type is fair game for rhetorical analysis.

Suggestions for Analysis

1. Select a work of art that is obviously rhetorical and analyze it the same way you would a political speech (see Chapter 14). Among plays, for example, take Ibsen's *Enemy of the People* or Clifford Odet's *Waiting for Lefty*. What was the nature of the audience and the situation? What was the author's apparent purpose? Did the arguments and appeals in the play seem well suited to fulfilling its purpose in light of the audience and situation? What were its probable effects?

2. To survey reactions to controversial situation comedies such as "Maude" or "Mash," telephone a random sample of persons just after a given episode has been played on television. First assess viewers' ideological positions on a variety of political and social issues. Then ask for interpretations of, and judgments about, the episode they have watched. See if ideologies, interpretations, and judgments are correlated.

3. Students of the visual arts will recognize that a number of movements in art since the turn of the century have been ushered in by explicitly rhetorical statements about what they were intended to accomplish. As Tom Wolfe (1975) has observed, the founders of movements such as surrealism and abstract expressionism have put pen to paper before they put paint on canvas. For any such movement, compare the founder's manifesto with the movement's products and accomplishments. Do they bear much relationship to each other? Has the movement's rhetoric gotten in the way of its art?

4. Before trying your hand at unravelling meanings, methods, and motives in inobviously rhetorical art, read biographical and historical materials that may shed light on the work. Learn, for example, that John Donne's poetry issued from both his religious concerns and his interest in the opposite sex, or that Bach had been a careful student of Aristotle's *Rhetoric*. Then examine the work of art in that context.

Item for Analysis: A Little Orphan Annie Strip

Maurice Horn (1971) has observed that "Compared to other mass media, the comics are not a highly effective instrument for either suasion or enlightenment. They are not as impressive as the movies, nor as authoritative as the written word, nor as pervasive as television."

Fair enough, Mr. Horn, as applied to one-shot exposures, yet the average readers of newspaper comics read their favorites over a period of years, get to know their leading characters almost as well as their personal friends, and often identify with them and imitate them in their daily lives.

We have deliberately selected this *Little Orphan Annie* strip because it so vividly illustrates Shannon's (1954) thesis about *Little Orphan Annie* which we discussed at length in Chapter 14. To detect less obvious rhetorical patterns in comic strips, it is generally necessary to sample randomly from a large number of episodes, and, even then, to be wary of taking the messages too literally.

Sample Analysis: Burke on Gray's Elegy

Before reading the interpretation provided below, train your own rhetorical lenses on these four lines from Gray's "Elegy":

> Full many a gem of purest ray serene
> The dark, unfathomed caves of ocean bear;
> Full many a flower is born to blush unseen
> And waste its sweetness on the desert air.

Kenneth Burke (1969, p. 125) has provided a rhetorical interpretation. First, he draws on Empson's *English Pastoral Poetry* for an explication of political meanings in the four lines. In summary:

1. The lines allude to society's neglect of such scholarly talents as this poet's.
2. Such neglected talents are presented in terms of virginal modesty (as of the blushing but unplucked flower).
3. The note of melancholy suggests that, while understanding "the conditions opposed to aristocracy," the poet will not protest, but will resign himself.
4. The churchyard setting, the universality and impersonality of the reflections, "claim as if by comparison that we ought to accept the injustice of society as we do the inevitability of death."

Then Burke suggests a possible fifth step, aimed at discovering not just political meaning but rhetorical strategy in the four lines:

> For have we the feeling that the poem is not wholly resigned. Isn't there a possibility that the virginal flower might be plucked after all? Can't the bowed posture of ingredients 3 and 4 be an unassuming appeal (of a nature that befits ingredient 2) for someone to correct the conditions of ingredient

Fri. Aug. 31, 1945   **O R P H A N   A N N I E—H I S   C R E E D**

From *Arf! The Life and Hard Times of Little Orphan Annie, 1935–1945*, by Harold Gray. New Rochelle: Arlington House. (Reprinted by permission of The News Syndicate Co., Inc.)

1? For here is a kind of resignation that might also, in "mystifying" terms, serve as a bid for preferment. The sentiments expressed are thus a character reference, describing a person doubly reliable, since he doesn't protest even when neglected. In an imaginary way the poem answers such questions as a personnel director would record on his files, if interviews and questionnaires were capable of such disclosures, rather than supplying merely such entries as would fit a punch card.

Political Cartoons

Political cartoons and other such visual forms provide rich subject matter for the study of the language of persuasion (introduced in Chapter 3). Although the techniques used to make the cartoon's point can be extremely sophisticated, the point itself is frequently rather simple. Cartoonists attempt to capture essences and they do so by drawing exaggerated caricatures and employing familiar symbols like the cross and the club which evoke strong emotional connotations. Oftentimes they use visual symbols as metaphors to characterize complex relationships. Cartoon drawing is highly enthymematic; it builds on large numbers of unstated premises shared by its audiences.

Suggestions for Analysis

1. To appreciate how much is said visually in political cartoons, try writing out their thesis statements and supporting claims in the form of editorials.

2. Compare political cartoons by different cartoonists on the same news event.

◀ Rizzo/Patronage artwork by Ralph Schlegel, *Philadelphia Magazine*, December 1974, pp. 136–137. Reproduced by permission of the publisher.

◀ Untitled political cartoon, courtesy of *Temple News*.

Poster by Ben Shahn: *This is Nazi Brutality*, 1942. (Courtesy Library of Congress)

3. Compare caricatures in political cartoons of leading political figures with photographs of these same figures.

4. Collect a large number of cartoons that use animals as dominant symbols. How frequently do they appear? How do they function rhetorically as metaphors?

Sample Item: Patronage at City Hall

Whenever you examine visual creations like those reproduced on pages 328 to 329, ask yourself whether the same point could have been made in another, and perhaps better, way. The article in *Philadelphia Magazine* which accompanies this art work by Ralph Schlegel (strictly speaking, it is not a political cartoon) was intended to alarm people about the growing power of Mayor Frank Rizzo and his widespread use of patronage as a political weapon. Does the art work make the point effectively? Is the octopus an appropriate symbol or might the artist have been better off using a different symbol such as a fishing net?

Sample Item: The Cross and the Club

Cartoons may be used to highlight an issue or to express a position on an issue. In this cartoon, reproduced on page 328, the issue of a clash between two types of authority is capsulized, but are the sympathies of the cartoonist revealed? Assuming he wished to land hard on police brutality, how might he have redrawn the same figures and cast them against a more communicative background?

Sample Item: Nazi Brutality

Like the political cartoon, the poster must present stark images in an arresting way. And, as in all persuasion, the images must be appropriate. Why, in this poster, did artist Ben Shahn choose to cover the face of the handcuffed prisoner, rather than evoke pathos by showing a tortured facial expression? Is the covered head consistent with the point being made?

Teachings and Preachings

In Chapter 2 we urged that you be especially wary of messages that claim to be objective, impartial, the authoritative word from on high, etc. These "teachings and preachings" often constitute a rhetoric of social control, designed to legitimize power, status, authority, or special privilege. Oftentimes, these discourses make a reasonable, if overstated case, but they should nevertheless be approached skeptically, as ideological statements that mask special interests and serve to maintain acceptance of existing hierarchical arrangements.

Suggestions for Analysis

1. Read Chapters 9, 19, 20, and 21 in Duncan's *Communication and Social Order* (1968). In light of his conceptual framework, analyze one or more of the following:

- a) Ideological bias in American history books;
- b) Religious indoctrination in Sunday School classes;
- c) Quarterly reports to stockholders by corporations;
- d) Supreme Court opinions on politically sensitive issues;
- e) Investigative reports by regulatory agencies;
- f) Orientation manuals for army recruits or new employees.

2. Read Weigert's (1970) article on the rhetoric of scientific sociology. See if his same arguments can be applied to introductory textbooks on other subjects, including this textbook on persuasion.

3. If we can generalize from Szasz's (1970) *Ideology and Insanity* or Weigert's article on scientific sociology, each of the professions in our society should have similar self-justifying rhetorics that mask ideologies with the pretense of objectivity. For many of the professions (e.g., law, social work, medicine, political science, etc.), see if you can identify the following genres:

- a) A rhetoric of special expertise (claims to valid theories and methodologies; insistence on specialized jargon);
- b) A rhetoric of social passage (justifications for professional training programs, licensing, etc.);
- c) A rhetoric of public service (boasts about how the profession serves the public interest);
- d) A rhetoric of self-regulation (insistence that the profession is regulating itself and corresponding denials that anyone else could possibly have the expertise to regulate it);
- e) A rhetoric of affiliation (characterizations of the profession as akin to higher status professions and different from lower status professions);
- f) A rhetoric of the rhetoric of "outsiders" (ridicule of heretics, traitors, debunkers, simplifiers, and other "cranks" as "pseudoprofessionals").

Item for Analysis: Gardner on "Pseudoscientists" [1]

Martin Gardner (1957) has devoted a good part of his professional career to debunking claimants to scientific status. Among the targets of his pointed thrusts have been ESP, the flying saucer theory, Alfred Korzybski's general semantics, Velikovsky's "big bang" theory, astrology, and various dietary schemes. Gardner is saying, in a way, that these theories and theorists are rhetorical in a pejorative sense, but note well that at least one of his criteria for distinguishing science from pseudoscience is also rhetorical! Can one help but test scientific claims by rhetorical standards? In what sense might these excerpts from Gardner's introductory chapter (pp. 3, 7–8, 11–12) be viewed rhetorically? What rhetorical techniques does Gardner employ?

One curious consequence of the current boom in science is the rise of the promoter of new and strange "scientific" theories. He is riding into prominence, so to speak, on the coat-tails of reputable investigators. The scientists themselves, of course, pay very little attention to him. They are too busy with more important matters. But the less informed general public, hungry for sensational discoveries and quick panaceas, often provides him with a noisy and enthusiastic following.

In the last analysis, the best means of combating the spread of pseudoscience is an enlightened public, able to distinguish the work of a reputable investigator from the work of the incompetent and self-deluded. This is not as hard to do as one might think. Of course, there always will be borderline cases hard to classify, but the fact that black shades into white through many shades of gray does not mean that the distinction between black and white is difficult.

Actually, two different "continuums" are involved. One is a scale of the degree to which a scientific theory is confirmed by evidence. At one end of this scale are theories almost certainly false, such as the dianetic view that a one-day-old embryo can make sound recordings of its mother's conversation. Toward the middle of the scale are theories advanced as working hypotheses, but highly debatable because of the lack of sufficient data—for example, the theory that the universe is expanding. Finally, at the other extreme of the scale, are theories almost certainly true, such as the belief that the earth is round or that men and beasts are distant cousins. The problem of determining the degree to which a theory is confirmed is extremely difficult and technical, and, as a matter of fact, there are no known methods for giving precise "probability values" to hypotheses. This problem, however, need not trouble us. We shall be concerned, except for a few cases, only

---

1. Martin Gardner, *Fads and Fallacies*, Dover Publications, Inc., New York, 1957. Reprinted through the permission of the publisher.

with theories so close to "almost certainly false" that there is no reasonable doubt about their worthlessness.

The second continuum is the scale of scientific competence. It also has its extremes—ranging from obviously admirable scientists, to men of equally obvious incompetence. That there are individuals of debatable status—men whose theories are on the borderline of sanity, men competent in one field and not in others, men competent at one period of life and not at others, and so on—all this ought not to blind us to the obvious fact that there is a type of self-styled scientist who can legitimately be called a crank. It is not the novelty of his views or the neurotic motivations behind his work that provide the grounds to call him this. The grounds are the technical criteria by which theories are evaluated. If a man persists in advancing views that are contradicted by all available evidence, and which offer no reasonable grounds for serious consideration, he will rightfully be dubbed a crank by his colleagues.

Cranks vary widely in both knowledge and intelligence. Some are stupid, ignorant, almost illiterate men who confine their activities to sending "crank letters" to prominent scientists. Some produce crudely written pamphlets, usually published by the author himself, with long titles, and pictures of the author on the cover. Still others are brilliant and well-educated, often with an excellent understanding of the branch of science in which they are speculating. Their books can be highly deceptive imitations of the genuine article—well-written and impressively learned. In spite of these wide variations, however, most pseudo-scientists have a number of characteristics in common.

The first and most important of these traits is that cranks work in almost total isolation from their colleagues. Not isolation in the geographical sense, but in the sense of having no fruitful contacts with fellow researchers. . . .

He does not send his findings to the recognized journals, or if he does, they are rejected for reasons which in the vast majority of cases are excellent. In most cases the crank is not well-enough informed to write a paper with even a surface resemblance to a significant study. As a consequence, he finds himself excluded from the journals and societies, and almost universally ignored by the competent workers in his field. In fact, the reputable scientist does not even know of the crank's existence unless his work is given widespread publicity through nonacademic channels, or unless the scientist makes a hobby of collecting crank literature. The eccentric is forced, therefore, to tread a lonely way. He speaks before organizations he himself has founded, contributes to journals he himself may edit, and—until recently—publishes books only when he or his followers can raise sufficient funds to have them printed privately.

A second characteristic of the pseudo-scientist, which greatly strengthens his isolation, is a tendency toward paranoia. This is a mental condition (to quote a recent textbook) "marked by chronic, systematized, gradually developing delusions, without hallucinations, and with little tendency toward deterioration, remission, or recovery."

News Reporting

The next time you pick up a newspaper or news weekly, read it as a rhetorical document. Look not only at pages labeled "Editorial" or "Commentary," but also at what is billed as straight news. Then see how "straight" it is.

Suggestions for Analysis

1. Examine several news media accounts of a major event that you have witnessed personally. Test the hypothesis that the news media tend to distort events by feeding the public's desire for drama, simplicity, and entertainment.

2. Along similar lines, test Edelman's (1967) claim that the news tends to be "dramatic in outline, empty of detail." Content analyze a random sample of five-minute news reports on radio. Compute the average length of each news item. Then determine the proportion of time devoted to news of murders, robberies, etc., versus more substantive events.

3. Compare two newspapers with diametrically opposed editorial stands on an issue in terms of their reportorial coverage of the issue over a period of weeks. See if there is a relationship between editorial position and news treatment. Along with such extrinsic variables as page placement, headline size, and proportion of space devoted to the issue, look for indications of bias in the way each story is written.

4. Recall the "agenda setting" hypothesis (briefly discussed in Chapter 12) that the news media do not tell us what to think but what to think about. With respect to Gerald Ford's plan for "slumpflation," for example (discussed below), they may provide a framework for evaluation of the proposal without explicitly supporting or rejecting it. Try applying the "agenda setting" hypothesis to a Presidential contest. Using a random sample of reports from a given news medium over a limited campaign period, tabulate instances of the following:

   a) Direct assessment of the candidate as a potential President (news judgments about his personal qualities, beliefs and attitudes, and skills);

   b) Assessments of the candidate's chances (judgments about whether a candidate is a "serious" contender, interpretations of "victory" and "defeat" from primaries; assessments of the impact of events on the candidate's chances);

   c) Characterizations of the campaign as a whole (images of "politics" and "politicians" as a whole; descriptions of the "climate" of expectations surrounding the campaign; identification of the "over-riding" issue);

d) Implied judgments about what standards of evidence and argument should be used in evaluating candidates, as revealed by standards the reporters themselves use (e.g., unsupported assertions of preference, reliance on candidate's statements of intentions, assertions supported by reports of observations, assertions supported by parallel evidence or historical evidence showing consistencies or inconsistencies).

Item for Analysis: Time on Ford's Plan for "Slumpflation"

The excerpt we have chosen is from the cover story of *Time*, January 27, 1975. As you read it, look first for obvious rhetorical statements and stratagems. See, for example, what blatant judgments it makes about problems, causes, and solutions. See what common ground techniques are used and how the credibility of leading actors in the conflict is established or impugned.

Then look beneath the surface. By implication and omission, *Time* is promoting some political values and rejecting or dismissing others. In *Time*'s view, what qualities in a politician are most admirable? How should differences between politicians be resolved? What is the range of possible solutions worth considering and what alternatives are to be ignored? Having answered these questions, then consider what vision *Time* offers of how politics is actually practiced in the United States. In *Time*'s view, what scale of values actually guides political decisions? Is the influence on politicians of lobbies and interest-groups conspicuous in this story? How, in contrast to *Time*, might a Marxist weekly describe political realities? Recalling Edelman's (1967) characterization of political news as functioning to lull us into political quiescence, ask yourself how he might analyze this piece. Recall, finally, our suggestion that you look for similarities in *form* between an object of rhetorical criticism and ostensibly quite different rhetorical objects. Might this rendering of political news be compared to a medical soap opera like Marcus Welby, M.D., in which Welby and other doctors are at odds about how to cure a rare ailment? Are there similarities here to a pregame warm-up show before a televised football game?

Ford's Risky Plan Against Slumpflation

It was anything but the standard State of the Union speech. Instead of congratulating himself on the achievements of his young and troubled Administration, Gerald Ford adopted the somber tone of a war-time leader calling for an all-out effort to repel the enemy. Instead of skipping lightly over a broad spectrum of national and foreign policies, the President concentrated almost exclusively on specific means to counter the worst economic slump since the Great Depression, the nation's almost 14% rate of inflation and the U.S.'s dangerous dependence on cartel-controlled foreign oil. Displaying the blunt candor that is his most politically attractive quality, the President proclaimed himself the bearer of "bad news," declared flatly that "the State of the Union is not good," and announced that he did not expect "much if any applause." Then he unfurled an economic and energy program of considerable scope, great complexity and huge risk.

If the policy works as Ford hopes, sales would revive, unemployment would moderate and the nation would be much better able to withstand another cutoff of foreign oil, since Americans would be compelled by higher prices to reduce their prodigious waste of energy. But if the program fails, the consequences could be dire indeed. The $16 billion in rebates and tax credits might be too weak to jolt the economy out of its alarming slumpflation; in that case, the nation could suffer a prolonged agony of unemployment rates higher than any since before World War II. In addition, the higher prices for oil and natural gas that Ford plans could restore the raging inflation that is only now beginning to relax its debilitating grip on the U.S.

Critical Crew. And Ford must sell his ideas to a highly critical crew of consulting physicians: the Democrats, who held overwhelming control of Congress. The Democrats slapped together their own program for doctoring the economy, but it was an imprecise series of compromises that even party leaders concede will be tough to enact. Still, in announcing the program, House Speaker Carl Albert of Oklahoma said: "We mean business. We intend to act."

The Democrats enthusiastically agreed on the need for a big and fast tax cut. Indeed, within a couple of months they may well enact a deeper slash than Ford has asked. But they fear that the President's energy proposals would push prices so high as to destroy the purchasing power that the tax reductions would create. Democratic Senator Adlai Stevenson III of Illinois estimates the chances of Ford's energy program getting through Congress as "zero."

When Ford was being escorted from the House by congressional leaders after his speech, his sometimes golfing partner, Democratic Floor Leader Thomas P. ("Tip") O'Neill, said: "Your conclusions were great, Mr. President, but we can't go down the same street together."

"Be charitable," said Ford, grinning. "See if you can give us a chance."

Responded O'Neill: "I don't see how these programs can work."

Later, Ford confidently—and probably overoptimistically—told an aide: "I think I can get 85% of this program." Indeed, he plans a series of speaking trips around the nation in late January or early February to explain—and sell—the program to the public.

Whatever the economic outcome, Ford clearly has seized the political initiative as only a President can. His State of the Union speech and a televised fireside chat from the White House two nights earlier, in which he previewed his programs, marked a welcome change from the drift and indecision, the platitudes and homilies of his first five months in office. The President sounded grim and forceful. Though he still used many cliches, the very flatness of some of his phrases ("Millions . . . are out of work. Prices are too high and sales are too slow

. . . the economic distress is global") had a kind of eloquence appropriate to a crisis.

Congressional Democrats will, and *indeed should,* quarrel with the program. But they cannot object to its two essential goals: fighting recession by cutting taxes, and reducing oil imports in order to break the stranglehold that the cartel of the Organization of Petroleum Exporting Countries is acquiring over Western economies. Those goals are exactly what the Democrats themselves have called for in innumerable speeches. Now that Ford has proposed specific programs to accomplish those ends, the burden is on the Democrats to come up with something better. Ford made the challenge as pointed as possible by calling on Congress to enact his tax cuts by April 1 and by announcing that he will impose new tariffs on imported oil on his own authority starting Feb. 1. Senate Democratic Leader Mike Mansfield conceded: "He stepped forward, showed some initiative." A high White House aide added, startlingly: "We know he is not home free, but we think he has taken a long step away from Bozo the Clown."

Conflict and Protest

The conflicts of the sixties and seventies have been played out by a variety of actors, some stridently proclaiming the need for institutional change, others resisting change with equal fervor, still others seeking to defuse hostilities with the voice of reason. All are worthy of rhetorical analysis.

Suggestions for Analysis

1. Recall that any movement must fulfill programmatic, value, organizational, and power requirements; that these requirements are often incompatible, thus leading to rhetorical problems; that strategies must be devised in light of these requirements and problems; and that the chosen strategy often begets additional problems. Try using the "requirements, problems, strategies" framework in an analysis of the rhetoric of a protest movement.

2. Combining the model of campaign stages presented in Chapter 12 with the discussion in Chapter 13 of alternatives available to movements seeking to secure institutional change, try launching a miniature movement of your own. For example, join with neighbors in an effort to get a traffic light erected at a busy intersection. Or organize nonsmokers in a campaign to prohibit cigarette vending machines on campus. Then do a post-mortem analysis of your efforts.

3. Applying Zimbardo's (1972) suggestions on canvassing, discussed in Chapter 12, try using coactive persuasion on a one to one basis with persons believed to be hostile to your position on a highly controversial issue. Write an audience analysis before and after each encounter (see Chapter 4).

Item for Analysis: Sally Gearhart on "The Lesbian and God-the-Father" [2]

Although the rhetoric of militant protest leaders frequently fails tests of sound argumentation, it may nevertheless serve to solidify the movement and to constrain power vulnerables. Subtitled "All the Church Needs is a Good Lay—On Its Side," this essay was deleted by an agency of the United Presbyterian Church in the U.S.A. from an issue of *Trends* in which it was scheduled to appear. Can you see why? Note first how Ms. Gearhart uses deductive logic to equate lesbians with "woman-identified women." Then note the way she characterizes enemies, evils, causes of problems, and solutions. Observe that it generally fits our description in Chapter 13 of militant rhetoric.

Of the host of things I'd like to share with you, a few at least bear mention:

I could speak with you about the twelve specific references to "homosexuality" in the Bible, about the misinterpretations that have been put upon them, about the fact that only one of these references includes any suggestion of female homosexuality.

Or, I might use a feature-article approach on "Lesbians I Have Known in the Church (and Still Know)." I doubt that many of you would be shocked at personal or experiential estimates of the number of lesbians in your congregations. I would, though, assure you that you don't find lesbians just among the single women in the church; nor, of course, are all single women lesbians. What may come as a bit of a surprise is that lesbians are to be found in significant numbers among heterosexually married women, women trapped by their commitment to families and to husbands, women who know deep in themselves that their most authentic love relationships have been and perhaps even now are with women.

Perhaps more important might be a recounting of the hundreds of lesbians I have met in the past year who have left the church. I could relate hair-raising stories of how the church attempted to dehumanize them, of how much pain they have suffered at its hands. I could tell you of the rage that erupts in some of them at the suggestion of anything Christian and of the tolerant laughter that springs from others at the mention of such devitalized concepts as "sin" or "salvation."

Or, I could fall into the old trap of trying to define a lesbian by male standards, by the same philosophy that says "All the lesbian needs is a good lay with a real man to make her normal." The male notion of the lesbian is the sexual one: she is a lesbian simply because she "has sex" with women. Nothing could be farther from the truth. But *if* we were talking in man-language about lesbianism, I'd want to point out that what lesbians and gay men do in bed is *technically* no different from what many of you do in bed with your wives or husbands (assuming you have a healthy and vivid sexual relationship). The pain

---

2. First presented as a speech at a pastor's conference in Berkeley, California, February, 1972.

is that although heterosexual couples do "it" and marriage manuals even recommend "it" to buck up an otherwise tired and dull sexual life, still you give lip service to the notion that the "missionary position" is the only proper mode of sexual expression. You support a hypocritical morality that sanctions only the sex act that is potentially progenerative. By your silence on any other mode of sexual expression you continue to oppress gay people every minute of every day.

But the main thing I want to share with you is twofold.

First, I cannot separate the lesbian from the woman. This is not only because my oppression has been more as a woman than as a lesbian (though that of course is true), but also because to me being a lesbian is what really being a woman means. I like to think that the way politically conscious lesbians "are" in the world today is the way all women were before the tyranny of the patriarchy. To be a lesbian is to be identified not by men or by a society made by men, but by me, by a woman. And the more I am identified by/for me, by/for my own experience, by/for my own values, the more a full woman I feel I become.

More and more woman-identified women are emerging every day. More and more lesbians. It's not that more and more women are leaping into bed with each other. That may be your fantasy—certainly it is a common male fantasy—as to what lesbianism is all about. And indeed, my understanding is that astounding numbers of women are extending their love relationships with other women into sexual dimensions. But that's not the distinguishing characteristic of a lesbian. Lesbianism is a life-style, a mind-set, a body of experiences. I would like to call any woman-identified woman a lesbian, and if she's really woman-identified, she'll feel good about being called a lesbian, whether or not she's had any sexual relationship with another woman.

The woman-identified women who are being reborn every day are those who are shaking off the chains forged by thousands of years of ecclesiastical propaganda—Shaking off their definition as male property, as male's helpmate, as the pure and empedestaled virtue-vessels that need chivalrous male protection. They are the unladylike women, the angry women, the ones who make you feel a little uneasy with their freedom of body, with the way they cross their legs or open their own car doors, or the way they look as though they'll give you a karate chop if you hassle them. They are the ones who apparently reach a deep and threatening place inside every man's gut, the ones who can make your stomach turn over because they represent a truth that your own stomach has always secretly known. Particularly if you are a man, you both hate and admire their independence, their strength.

The women being reborn today (that's the real meaning of resurrection) are the ones marching for the rights to their own bodies at abortion demonstrations. Often they are women of witch-like appearance, women in jeans and boots who have laid away the girdles and garters that bound them into the profiteering system. They are women whose faces are honest, whose hair flies free, whose minds and bodies are growing supple and steady and sure in their self-possession, whose love is growing deep and wide in the realities of newly discovered relationships with other women.

They don't need the church. The last thing they think about now is the church. They have within themselves what the church has claimed as its own and distorted so ironically for its own economic and psychological purposes these thousands of years.

Second, being a lesbian involves for me some growing political consciousness. That means I am committed to assessing institutions like the church, which, as far as women are concerned, takes the prize as the most influential and in itself the most insidiously oppressive institution in western society. The matter of its influence needs no elaborating. Its insidiousness lies most obviously in the fact that it has made women (particularly white women) not only victims but murderers in a complex and exploitative economic system. One of the greatest marks of women's oppression is our conviction that we are not oppressed.

I look forward with great anticipation to the death of the church. The sooner it dies, the sooner we can be about the business of living the gospel. That living cannot take place in the church as it is now, and I suspect that most of us here have known that for a long time. But if we count on "renewal" or "reform," then we understand neither the depth of the church's crime nor the nature of the women's movement. If we count on "renewal" or "reform," then clearly we have not heard the voices of Third World peoples here and abroad.

Renewal and reform are not enough. Renewal and reform are more often sops, liberal cop-outs and tokenism in the face of real and harder tasks. For example, with gritted teeth some denominations offer to ordain women. Then they expect me to rejoice in this, light bonfires on the hillside, and dance around the sacred flame. Far from rejoicing, I really feel sick, sick that woman energy shall now officially be made captive to the institutions, sick that in the very act of ordination a woman has separated herself from me and from others. She has played the church's game for good reason—in order to secure her survival. But in doing so, she hasn't challenged the church. She has only mounted another pedestal.

I am weary of the timid reassurances that "things are changing," or that "our congregation/pastor/district/seminary is different," or that you have to play the system's game to get into a power position so you can do some good. I mistrust with all my woman-heart the motive that keeps women committed to church renewal, i.e., "The church *needs* me." I am tired of hearing liberal church-people (both women and men) lay out transforming radical ideas in private and then collapse into meek submission in public when the chips are down. But I do understand why it happens: I know how important in this society it is to get a pay check.

I long to hear voices *in public church gatherings* insisting not only upon the death of the institutional church but upon specific ways of carrying out that goal. In other words, I want to hear voices (so bold in private) insisting *in public* upon programs that affirm plural relationship, collective and communal living, same-sex love relationships, childhood sexuality, masturbating, and self-love. I want loud voices protesting sex-role socialization: that is, our practice of brainwashing people with outside plumbing to assume the role of strong-dominant-active-in-telligent-conquering-HE-MAN and those with inside plumbing to assume that of weak-submissive-receptive-dumb-conquered-GIRL. Of course if such voices are heard, they are not likely to be heard again very often under the rafters of the institutional church. Such speakers have to be prepared to be ousted—and that, after all, may be the real point.

What is devastating and dehumanizing about the church is not its foundation of love, but the superstructure of patriarchial, theological claptrap that has been hoisted on that foundation. The superstructure shivers and quakes whenever the sanctity of the nuclear family or the traditional concepts of sexuality are called into question—and well it might shake, for it is these two concepts that are the bricks and mortar of the church.

The structure of the church (God over man, man over woman, father over family, clergy over laity, power over powerlessness) is vertical, hierarchical. The church's very identity depends on that hierarchy. This identity is dependent upon standards of success and failure, on authority, on competition. It is dependent upon who has power over whom. The idea is that God is at the top with power over all, and I as woman am at the bottom of the heap. Together with children my passivity is sanctified.

It will do no good to "renew" this monster. If the gospel is to live, then the vertical structure will have to be laid on its side—horizontalized—and that, to me, means the death of the institutional church.

Women who are being reborn these days do not want a man to step down from the pulpit so that a woman can step into it. They would do away with the pulpit altogether—do away with the physical setting apart of any person for purposes of "preaching" or "teaching."

Women of high consciousness do not want an equalization of the number of women and men on church councils. They would do away with councils themselves, with any body of people that is anything but voluntary and open to anyone concerned.

Women who are really getting it together don't want to be national presidents or bishops or pope. They don't want presidents, bishops, popes, and the like to exist at all, for the very definition of their office puts them above and below others.

Woman-identified women don't want the Bible rewritten to talk about God-the-Mother or Jesus the Savioress. The women I have in mind believe that each person creates herself out of her own experience and that we must all work out in community our salvation from the repressive system we've grown up with.

Women who think of a revolution don't want just to have "ladies' Sunday" in the local congregation, where women run the show. They want to do away with the show altogether, because as it presently exists, it is just that: a performance and not a participation. They do not want traditional worship, because that calls for craning their necks to look up or for bowing their heads in subjugation. They are only now learning what it means to look with love eyeball-to-eyeball with equals.

What can it mean to individuals in the church that they must begin to conduct the church's funeral, that they must themselves be agents of the church's death? It must mean at least risks never taken before. It might mean, on an action level, throwing out the phallic pulpit that sets one person higher than and apart from another. Or it might mean tearing out puritanical pews and putting in comfortable chairs and pillows for being-with rather than being-under. Then the otherwise unused building can become a crash-pad or a refuge for transients —surely the church should be in use every hour of every week in the shelter and care of human beings.

It might be a good thing to use a generic "she" and "woman" or "woman-kind" in all our conversations for a decade or two instead of the masculine generic so men can begin to understand what it feels like to be made invisible.

You pastors can refuse to preach anymore, refuse to be the "enlightened" shepherds of a blind flock. You can also suggest some primitive Christianity in the form of pooled salaries and resources in your congregation—which would be divided according to need. All of this, of course, is with full knowledge that if you try any of it you're likely to be spewed out of the mouth of the church (ironically, because you are *not* lukewarm). Then perhaps you can come into the streets and ghettos of the secular world where the gospel is being discovered and lived.

But to make such changes—if you should succeed—is still to treat only the symptoms. We don't really get anywhere toward toppling the church structure until we articulate loud and clear some fundamental assumptions.

1. That traditional Christian teaching is anti-life; it is antithetical to any liberation ideology; its enfleshment, Christian practice, is not enfleshment at all but one of the western world's most eloquent expressions of the fascist mind-set.

2. That traditional Christian concepts are the constructs of male thinking and depend for their perpetuation upon the myth of male superiority.

3. That because the submission of women is absolutely essential to the church's functioning, the church has a vested interest (economic and psychological) in perpetuating the institutions that most oppress women: the nuclear family and the sex-role socialization of children.

When we admit these things, then we can commit ourselves to one of only two paths: either toppling the hierarchy completely (which action would be the destruction of the church), or packing up whatever shred of personal worth we've got left and leaving the church entirely—hopefully in a hell-raising burst of glory that in itself may educate other Christians.

So, as a woman, as a lesbian, I invite you not to attempt reform of the church. I invite you to destroy it or to desert it. Personal integrity allows no other alternatives.

Item for Analysis: Baptist Conference on Rights for Gays

This selection is from a newspaper report of a press conference at which representatives of the Baptist Ministers Conference of Philadelphia and Vicinity voiced strong disapproval of a bill before the Philadelphia City Council which would bar discrimination against homosexuals in jobs, housing, and public accommodations. Once again, examine its argumentation. Do the belief and value assertions presented logically support the attitude of opposition to legalization of Gay rights?

The following are excerpts of arguments offered in a unanimously approved resolution by the group, as reported by William J. Nazzaro.[3]

> We object to the Gay Liberation Front suggesting that homosexual rights stand equal with civil rights for the black community—the two issues can in no way be compared.
>
> We feel that uninhibited, unrestrained, gay activity will serve as a detriment to the Philadelphia community, rather than to enhance or strengthen the moral fiber of its citizens.
>
> It is our opinion that the community has the right to demand the ouster of individuals engaging in homosexual activity, and, if passed, Bill 1257 will deny the citizens of Philadelphia that right."

Individual speakers at the press conference then went on to offer these, more extreme, statements:

> God himself frowns on homosexuality in the Scriptures. The bill would open a Pandora's box, like pornography. We'll have homosexuals all around us. I must take a stand for my children.
>
> If the bill passes, maybe child molesters, rapists, will demand their civil rights. . . . Sin brought down a President and the nation is slowly sinking down into the muck. We are close to the bottom of the barrel. God will judge us.

Finally, one clergyman added that because the Philadelphia school system has no dress code for its teachers, homosexual transvestites could conceivably report to their classrooms wearing articles of clothing of the opposite sex.

Item for Analysis: Palmer Hoyt at Little Rock, January 10, 1958

During the Fall of 1957, Little Rock, Arkansas, became the symbol of the South's resistance to court-ordered desegregation of public schools. In compliance with the Supreme Court's landmark decision three years earlier, the School Board of Little Rock set in motion a plan for gradual integration. This was resisted, however, by the townspeople, most of the state's newspapers and politicians, and especially the governor, Orval Faubus, who called in the National Guard in the name of States' Rights. In response, President Eisenhower brought in federal troops to enforce the desegregation ruling.

Given the climate of events, it should not be surprising that advocacy of school integration was a not-too-popular position in Little Rock on

---

3. William J. Nazzaro, "Baptist Conference Opposes Bill Granting Gay Rights," *The [Philadelphia] Evening Bulletin*, January 23, 1975, p. 17.

January 10, 1958, the day that Palmer Hoyt, Editor and Publisher of the Denver Post, addressed the Arkansas Press Association, with Orval Faubus sitting conspicuously in the audience.

As we noted earlier, the speech to a hostile audience poses the greatest challenge to co-active persuaders, requiring, particularly in the introduction, that they build good will and common ground in preparation for the inevitable clash over issues. Reproduced here is the introduction to Hoyt's speech. Hoyt skillfully emphasizes membership group similarities, refers to sources his audience can accept, wisely refrains from an explicit statement of his position, employs the "yes-yes" method of establishing major premises, and orients the audience to view the conflict from a broad pragmatic perspective. See if you can identify the techniques he employs.

Mr. President, Governor Faubus, members of the Arkansas Press Association, ladies and gentlemen, I am glad to be here tonight to talk to such a distinguished group of fellow newspapermen. And I am happy to have, at long last, the opportunity to meet one of America's most controversial figures—your own governor, the Honorable Orval Faubus.

My father was a Baptist preacher, and I was brought up on the Bible.

One of my favorite Bible stories was that of a gentleman, name of Daniel, who with a little urging, sauntered into a lion's den one day.

As a child, I used to wonder how old Daniel felt when the gate clanged shut and he found himself alone with those lions. Now I know. Because here I am. I'll have to agree that you are a nice-looking bunch of lions. Furthermore, I doubt if Daniel had the pleasure of being introduced by the head lion. But even so, it occurs to me that, lest I be devoured, I had best make my position clear.

You know, first, that I am a newspaperman. As such, over a period of almost four decades, I have worked for better human relations but I have learned that good human relations cannot be legislated. They are the product of time, education, and effort.

Some of you may look upon me as a "damnyankee." May I say, parenthetically, that I was 25 years old before I knew "damnyankee" was only one word.

A few of you, and I hope it is only a few, may regard me as a carpetbagger.

I would be less than realistic if I didn't concede that newspapermen, damnyankees and carpetbaggers, all three, seem at the moment to be fairly unpopular in this great commonwealth.

Before embarking on my main thesis tonight, may I say—this I do believe: No man can reflect upon the incident known as "Little Rock" without feelings of compassion for the people intimately and personally involved. A community within a Nation that is troubled by internal dissension, harassed by external critics and humiliated by internal civil disorder is no less a sorry spectacle than a nation itself in the grip of civil war.

Let the millions of Americans outside of Arkansas ask themselves if they, under similar provocation from within or without, could comport themselves with greater poise or restraint.

I shall not presume to levy judgment upon your gracious governor, Orval Faubus. What transpired here, after your school board set in motion a gradual program of integrating your public schools, has been exhaustively discussed by Arkansas' own press.

The facts have been widely and painfully appraised.

And, it seems to me that Little Rock's Arkansas Gazette, under the guidance of my friends, J. N. Heiskell and Harry Ashmore, reported accurately on the news of conditions within this city when the Arkansas National Guard was called into action. It is my personal view that the Gazette's editorial position has reflected great journalistic statesmanship. I have noted that the same is true of some other Arkansas papers.

It is not for me, as a newspaperman, damnyankee, carpetbagger, or whatnot, to evaluate the motives of any party to this case. I am, as you will see, less interested in motivation than in effect.

I have accepted your president's invitation to speak to you as a fellow American, and as such to point out what seem to me to be certain inescapable facts and conclusions.

The first is, that you and I and all of us in the free world are in a mess. If we don't do something about it soon, there will be no laws to squabble about and no way of life to preserve.

The second point is that we have all—our leaders and ourselves—had a hand in making this mess. We have been complacent about our ability to defend ourselves; selfishly materialistic and appallingly unconcerned with the consequences of our behavior upon the rest of the world—particularly the effects on the minds of men.

Suddenly we are awakened by the beeping of satellites, the flash of rockets not our own, and the unpleasant sound of angry words of men who do not love us.

And this is the background against which we may be on stage and performing an American tragedy in three acts.

As I have said, all three acts concern all of us, but one of them concerns you especially.

What are the acts of this unfolding, this implied tragedy?

The first is the effect and the impact of such episodes as the Little Rock case on our own respect for law and on our leadership of the free world.

The second act involves the economic challenges raised against the American people by the evil, if dedicated, geniuses in the Soviet Union.

The third act, and perhaps the climax of our tragedy, is built around the fundamental question of survival. Survival against internal economic collapse; survival against the threat of thermonuclear war or international blackmail in the age of the rocket, the missile and the platform in outer space.

Politics and Politicians

Since so much of this book has been oriented toward political communications, we hesitate adding here to suggestions already given. Our suggestions, then, will deal only with the items for analysis included in this section.

Suggestions for Analysis

1. Ghost write the speech you think Edward Kennedy should have given on Chappaquiddick, or the speech Richard Nixon should have given on Watergate. Justify the changes you have made from the original.

2. Compare the Kennedy and Nixon speeches in light of Rosenfield's hypothesis about characteristics of the "mass media apologia," as discussed in Chapter 14.

3. Examine analyses of the two speeches in newspapers and magazines immediately following each speech. In light of subsequent events and the perspective provided by time, do these analyses hold up?

Item for Analysis: Edward Kennedy on Chappaquiddick, July 25, 1969[4]

One week after the drowning of Miss Mary Jo Kopechne at Chappaquiddick, Senator Kennedy delivered this *apologia* on all three television networks.

My fellow citizens:

I have requested this opportunity to talk to the people of Massachusetts about the tragedy that happened last Friday evening.

This morning I entered a plea of guilty to the charge of leaving the scene of an accident. Prior to my appearance in court it would have been improper for me to comment on these matters.

But tonight I am free to tell you what happened and to say what it means to me.

On the weekend of July 18, I was on Martha's Vineyard Island participating with my nephew, Joe Kennedy—as for thirty years my family has participated—in the annual Edgartown Sailing Regatta.

Only reasons of health prevented my wife from accompanying me.

On Chappaquiddick Island, off Martha's Vineyard, I attended on Friday evening, July 18, a cook-out I had encouraged and helped sponsor for a devoted group of Kennedy campaign secretaries.

When I left the party, around 11:15 P.M., I was accompanied by one of these girls, Miss Mary Jo Kopechne. Mary Jo was one of the most devoted members of the staff of Senator Robert Kennedy. She worked for him for four years and was broken up over his death. For this reason, and because she was such a gentle,

---

4. Reproduced from Edward M. Kennedy, "Statement to the People of Massachusetts," *New York Times*, July 26, 1969, p. 10.

kind, and idealistic person, all of us tried to help her feel that she still had a home with the Kennedy family.

There is no truth, no truth whatever, to the widening circulated suspicion of immoral conduct that has been leveled at my behavior and hers regarding that evening. There has never been a private relationship between us of any kind.

I know of nothing in Mary Jo's conduct on that or any other occasion—the same is true of the other girls at that party—that would lend any substance to such ugly speculation about their character.

Nor was I driving under the influence of liquor.

Little over one mile away, the car that I was driving on an unlit road went off a narrow bridge which had no guard rails and was built on a left angle to the road.

The car overturned in a deep pond and immediately filled with water. I remember thinking as the cold water rushed in around my head that I was for certain drowning.

Then water entered my lungs and I actually felt the sensation of drowning. But somehow I struggled to the surface alive. I made immediate and repeated efforts to save Mary Jo by diving into the strong and murky current but succeeded only in increasing my state of utter exhaustion and alarm.

My conduct and conversations during the next several hours to the extent that I can remember them make no sense to me at all.

Although my doctors informed me that I had suffered a cerebral concussion as well as shock, I do not seek to escape responsibility for my actions by placing the blame either on the physical, emotional trauma brought on by the accident, or on anyone else.

I regard as indefensible the fact that I did not report the accident to the police immediately.

Instead of looking directly for a telephone after lying exhausted in the grass for an undetermined time, I walked back to the cottage where the party was being held and requested the help of two friends, my cousin, Joseph Gargan, and Phil Markham, and directed them to return immediately to the scene with me—this was some time after midnight—in order to undertake a new effort to dive down and locate Miss Kopechne.

Their strenuous efforts, undertaken at some risk to their own lives, also proved futile.

All kinds of scrambled thoughts—all of them confused, some of them irrational, many of them which I cannot recall, and some of which I would not have seriously entertained under normal circumstances—went through my mind during this period.

They were reflected in the various inexplicable, inconsistent, and inconclusive things I said and did, including such questions as whether the girl might still be alive somewhere out of that immediate area, whether some awful curse did actually hang over all the Kennedys, whether there was some justifiable reason for me to doubt what had happened and to delay my report, whether somehow the awful weight of this incredible incident might in some way pass from my shoulders.

I was overcome, I am frank to say, by a jumble of emotions, grief, fear, doubt, exhaustion, confusion, and shock.

Instructing Gargan and Markham not to alarm Mary Jo's friends that night, I had them take me to the ferry crossing. The ferry having shut down for the night, I suddenly jumped into the water and swam across, nearly drowning once again in the effort, and returned to my hotel about 2:00 A.M. and collapsed in my room.

I remember going out at one point and saying something to the room clerk.

In the morning, with my mind somewhat more lucid, I made an effort to call a family legal adviser, Burke Marshall, from a public telephone on the Chappaquiddick side of the ferry and belatedly reported the accident to the Martha's Vineyard Police.

Today, as I mentioned, I felt morally obligated to plead guilty to the charge of leaving the scene of an accident. No words on my part can possibly express the terrible pain and suffering I feel over this tragic incident.

This last week has been an agonizing one for me and the members of my family, and the grief we feel over the loss of a wonderful friend will remain with us the rest of our lives.

These events, the publicity, innuendo, and whispers which have surrounded them and my admission of guilt this morning—raise the question in my mind of whether my standing among the people of my state has been so impaired that I should resign my seat in the United States Senate.

If at any time the citizens of Massachusets should lack confidence in their Senator's character or his ability, with or without justification, he could not in my opinion adequately perform his duty and should not continue in office.

The people of this state, the state which sent John Quincy Adams and Daniel Webster and Charles Sumner and Henry Cabot Lodge and John Kennedy to the United States Senate, are entitled to representation in that body by men who inspire their utmost confidence.

For this reason, I would understand full well why some might think it right for me to resign. For me this will be a difficult decision to make.

It has been seven years since my first election to the Senate. You and I share many memories—some of them have been glorious, some have been very sad. The opportunity to work with you and serve Massachusetts has made my life worthwhile.

And so I ask you tonight, People of Massachusetts, to think this through with me. In facing this decision, I seek your advice and opinion. In making it, I seek your prayers. For this is a decision that I will have finally to make on my own.

It has been written a man does what he must in spite of personal consequences, in spite of obstacles and dangers and pressures, and that is the basis of all human morality.

Whatever may be the sacrifices he faces, if he follows his conscience—the loss of his friends, his fortune, his contentment, even the esteem of his fellow man—each man must decide for himself the course he will follow.

The stories of past courage cannot supply courage itself. For this, each man must look into his own soul.

I pray that I can have the courage to make the right decision. Whatever is decided and whatever the future holds for me, I hope that I shall be able to put this most recent tragedy behind me and make some further contribution to our state and mankind, whether it be in public or in private life.

Thank you and good night.

Item for Analysis: Richard Nixon on Watergate, April 30, 1973[5]

This was the first major speech by the President on Watergate. It was delivered soon after news of the coverup had broken in full fury in the newspapers and two weeks before the scheduled opening of the Senate Select Committee Hearings.

Good evening.

I want to talk to you tonight from my heart on a subject of deep concern to every American.

In recent months members of my Administration and officials of the Committee for the Re-election of The President, including some of my closest friends and most trusted aides, have been charged with involvement in what has become to be known as the Watergate Affair.

These include charges of illegal activity during and preceding the 1972 Presidential election and charges that responsible officials participated in an effort to cover up that illegal activity.

The inevitable result of these charges has been to raise serious questions about the integrity of the White House itself. Tonight I wish to address those questions.

Last June 17 while I was in Florida trying to get a few days rest after my visit to Moscow, I first learned from news reports of the Watergate break-in. I was appalled at this senseless illegal action and I was shocked to learn that employes of the re-election committee were apparently among those guilty. I immediately ordered an investigation by appropriate government authorities.

On Sept. 15, as you'll recall, indictments were brought against seven defendants in the case. As the investigation went forward, I repeatedly asked those that conducted the investigation whether there was any reason to believe that members of my Administration were in any way involved. I received repeated assurances there were not. Because of these continuing reassurances, because I believed the reports I was getting, because I had faith in the persons from whom I was getting them, I discounted the stories in the press that appeared to implicate members of my Administration or other officials of the campaign committee.

---

5. Reproduced from Richard M. Nixon, "Address to the Nation, April 30, 1973," *The Philadelphia Inquirer*, May 1, 1973, p. 4-A.

Until March of this year, I remained convinced that the denials were true and that the charges of involvement by members of the White House staff were false.

The comments I made during this period, the comments made by my press secretary in my behalf, were based on the information provided to us at the time we made those comments. However, new information then came to me, which persuaded me that there was a real possibility that some of these charges were true and suggesting further there had been an effort to conceal the facts, both from the public—from you—and from me. As a result, on March 21st, I personally assumed the responsibility for coordinating intensive new inquiries into the matter, and I personally ordered those conducting the investigations to get all the facts and to report them directly to me, right here in this office.

I again ordered that all persons in the government, or at the re-election committee, should cooperate fully with the FBI, the prosecutors and the grand jury.

I also ordered that anyone who refused to cooperate in telling the truth would be asked to resign from government service. And with ground rules adopted that would preserve the basic Constitutional separation of powers between the Congress and the Presidency, I directed that members of the White House staff should appear and testify voluntarily under oath before the Senate committee which was investigating Watergate. I was determined that we should get to the bottom of the matter, and that the truth should be fully brought out no matter who was involved. At the same time, I was determined not to take precipitative action and to avoid if at all possible any action that would appear to reflect on innocent people. I wanted to be fair. But I knew that in the final analysis, the integrity of this office, public faith in the integrity, would have to take priority over all personal considerations.

Today, in one of the most difficult decisions of my Presidency, I accepted the resignation of two of my closest associates in the White House—Bob Haldeman, John Ehrlichman—two of the finest public servants it has been my privilege to know. I want to stress that in accepting these resignations, I mean to leave no implication whatever of personal wrongdoing on their part. And I leave no implication tonight of implication on the part of others who have been charged in this matter. But in matters as sensitive as guarding the integrity of our democratic process, it is essential not only that rigorous legal and technical standards be observed, but also that the public—you—have total confidence that they are both being observed and enforced by those in authority, and particularly by the President of the United States.

They agreed with me that this move was necessary in order to restore that confidence, because Attorney General Kleindienst, though a distinguished public servant, my personal friend for 20 years, with no personal involvement whatever in this matter, has been a close personal and professional associate of some of those who are involved in this case, he and I both felt it was also necessary to name a new attorney general. The counsel to the President, John Dean, has also resigned.

As new attorney general, I have today named Elliott Richardson, a man of unimpeachable integrity and rigorously high principles. I have directed him to do everything necessary to insure that the Department of Justice has the confidence and the trust of every law-abiding person in this country. I have given him absolute authority to make all decisions bearing upon prosecution of the Watergate case, and related matters. I have instructed him that if he should consider it appropriate, he has the authority to name a special supervising prosecutor for matters arising out of the case.

Whatever may have appeared to have been the case before, whatever improper activities may yet be discovered in connection with this whole sordid affair, I want the American people, I want you, to know, to know beyond the shadow of a doubt that during my term as President, justice will be pursued fairly, fully and impartially no matter who is involved. This office is a sacred trust, and I am determined to be worthy of that trust.

Looking back at the history of this case, two questions arise: How could it have happened? Who is to blame? Political commentators have correctly observed that during my 27 years in politics, I have always previously insisted on running my own campaigns for office. But 1972 presented a very different situation. In both domestic and foreign policy, 1972 was a year of crucially important decisions, of intense negotiations, of vital new directions, particularly in working toward the goal which has been my overriding concern throughout my political career—the goal of bringing peace to America, peace to the world.

That is why I decided as the 1972 campaign approached that the Presidency should come first and politics second. To the maximum extent possible, therefore, I sought to delegate campaign operations, to remove the day-to-day campaign decision from the President's office and from the White House. . . .

Who then is to blame for what happened in this case? For specific criminal actions by specific individuals, those who committed those actions must, of course, bear the liability and pay the penalty. For the fact that alleged improper actions took place in the White House or within my campaign organization the easiest course would be for me to blame those to whom I delegated the responsibility to run the campaign.

But that would be a cowardly thing to do. I will not place the blame on subordinates, on people whose zeal exceed their judgment, and who may have done wrong in a cause they deeply believed to be right. In any organization, the man at the top must bear the responsibility. That responsibility therefore belongs here, in this office. I accept it. And I pledge to you tonight from this office that I will do everything in my power to insure that the guilty are brought to justice, and that such abuses are purged from our political processes in the years to come, long after I have left this office.

Some people, quite properly appalled at the abuses that occurred, will say Watergate demonstrates the bankruptcy of the American political system. I believe precisely the opposite is true. Watergate represented a series of illegal acts and bad judgments by a number of individuals. It was the system that has brought the facts to light and that will bring those guilty to justice. A system that in this case has included a determined grand jury, honest prosecutors, a courageous judge, John Sirica, and a vigorous free press.

It is essential that we let the judicial process go forward, respecting those safeguards that are established to protect the innocent as well as to convict the guilty. It is essential that in reacting to the excesses of others, we not fall into excesses ourselves. It is also essential that we not be so distracted by events such as this that we neglect the vital work before us, before this nation, before America at a time of critical importance to America and the world.

Since March, when I first learned that the Watergate affair might in fact be far more serious than I had been led to believe, it has claimed far too much of my time and my attention. Whatever may now transpire in the case, whatever the actions of the grand jury, whatever the outcome of any eventual trials, I must now turn my full attention—and I shall do so once again—to the larger duties of this office. I owe it to this great office that I hold. And I owe it to you, my country.

I know that as Attorney General, Elliott Richardson will be both fair and he will be fearless in pursuing this case wherever it leads. I am confident that with him in charge, justice will be done.

There is vital work to be done toward our goal of a lasting structure of peace in the world, work that cannot wait, work that I must do. Tomorrow, for example, Chancellor Brandt of West Germany will visit the White House for talks that are a vital element of "The year of Europe," as 1973 has been called. We are already preparing for the next Soviet-American summit meeting later this year.

This is also a year in which we are seeking to negotiate a mutual and balanced reduction of armed forces in Europe which will reduce our defense budget and allow us to have funds for other purposes at home, so desperately needed. It is the year when the United States and Soviet negotiators will seek to work out the second and even more important round of our talks on limiting nuclear arms, and of reducing the danger of a nuclear war that would destroy civilization as we know it. It is a year in which we confront the difficult task of maintaining peace in Southeast Asia and in the potentially explosive Middle East.

There is also vital work to be done right here in America—to insure prosperity, and that means a good job for everyone who wants to work, to control inflation—that I know worries every housewife—everyone who tries to balance a family budget in America, to set in motion new and better ways of insuring progress toward better life for all Americans.

On Christmas Eve, during my terrible personal ordeal of the renewed bombing of North Vietnam, which after 12 years of war, finally helped bring America peace with honor, I sat down just before midnight. I wrote out some of my goals for my second term as President.

Let me read them to you.

"To make it possible for our children, and for our children's children, to live in a world of peace.

"To make this country be more than ever a land of opportunity—of equal opportunity, full opportunity for every American.

"To provide jobs for all who can work, and generous help for all who cannot.

"To establish a climate of decency, and civility, in which each person respects the feelings and the dignity and the God-given rights of his neighbor.

"To make this a land in which each person can dare to dream, can live in his dream—not in fear, but in hope—proud of his community, proud of his country, proud of what America has meant to himself and to the world."

These are great goals. I believe we can, we must, work for them. We can achieve them. But we cannot achieve these goals unless we dedicate ourselves to another goal.

We must maintain the integrity of the White House, and that integrity must be real, not transparent. There can be no whitewash at the White House.

We must reform our political process—ridding it not only of the violations of the law, but also of the ugly mob violence, and other inexcusable campaign tactics that have been too often practiced and too readily accepted in the past —including those that may have been a response by one side to the excesses or expected excesses of the other side. Two wrongs do not make a right.

I have been in public life for more than a quarter of a century. Like any other calling, politics has good people and bad people. And let me tell you, the great majority in politics in the Congress, in the Federal government, in the state government, are good people. I know that it can be very easy, under the intensive pressures of a campaign, for even well-intentioned people to fall into shady tactics—to rationalize this on the grounds that what is at stake is of such importance to the nation that the end justifies the means. And both of our great parties have been guilty of such tactics in the past.

In recent years, however, the campaign excesses that have occurred on all sides have provided a sobering demonstration of how far this false doctrine can take us. The lesson is clear: America, in its political campaigns, must not again fall into the trap of letting the end, however great that end is, justify the means.

I urge the leaders of both political parties, I urge citizens, all of you, everywhere, to join in working toward a new set of standards, new rules and procedures—to ensure that future elections will be as nearly free of such abuses as they possibly can be made. This is my goal. I ask you to join in making it America's goal.

When I was inaugurated for a second term this past Jan. 20, I gave each member of my senior White House staff a special four-year calendar, with each day marked to show the number of days remaining to the Administration.

In the inscription on each calendar, I wrote these words: "The Presidential term which begins today consists of 1,461 days—no more, no less. Each can be a day of strengthening and renewal for America; each can add depth and dimension to the American experience. If we strive together, if we make the most of the challenge and the opportunity that these days offer us, they can stand out as great days for America, and great moments in the history of the world."

I looked at my own calendar this morning up at Camp David as I was working on this speech. It showed exactly 1,361 days remaining in my term. I want these to be the best days in America. I deeply believe that America is the hope of the world, and I know that in the quality and wisdom of the leadership America gives lies the only hope for millions of people all over the world, that they can live their lives in peace and freedom. We must be worthy of that hope, in every sense of the word.

Tonight, I ask for your prayers to help me in everything that I do throughout the days of my Presidency to be worthy of their hopes and of yours.

God bless America and God bless each and every one of you.

References

Abelson, R. P. (1968). Computers, polls, and public opinion—some puzzles and paradoxes. *Transaction* 5:20–27.

Abelson, R. P., and M. J. Rosenberg (1958). Symbolic psycho-logic: a model of attitudinal cognition. *Behavioral Science* 3:1–13.

Adams, J. S. (1961). Reduction of cognitive dissonance by seeking consonant information. *Journal of Abnormal and Social Psychology* 62:74–78.

Adelson, D. J. (January 18, 1970). What generation gap? *The New York Times Magazine* p. 10.

Alinsky, S. (1971). *Rules for Radicals*. New York: Random House.

Allport, G. W. (1954). *The Nature of Prejudice*. Cambridge, Mass.: Addison-Wesley.

Allport, G. W. (1935). Attitudes. In C. Murchison (ed.), *Handbook of Social Psychology*. Worcester, Mass.: Clark University Press, 798–884.

Anderson, B. F. (1971). *The Psychology Experiment*. Belmont, Cal.: Wadsworth.

Anderson, K., and J. Petrocik (May 31, 1974). Belief systems, party identification, and voting. Paper presented at American Association of Public Opinion Research Convention.

Anderson, N. H., and C. I. Hovland (1957). The representation of order effects in communication research (Appendix A). In C. I. Hovland (ed.), *The Order of Presentation in Persuasion*. New Haven: Yale University Press.

Andrews, J. R. (1969). Confrontation at Columbia: a case study in coercive rhetoric. *Quarterly Journal of Speech* 55:9–16.

———. (1970). The rhetoric of coercion and persuasion: the reform bill of 1832. *Quarterly Journal of Speech* 56:187–195.

Anisfeld, M., N. Bogo, and W. E. Lambert (1962). Evaluational reactions to accented English speech. *Journal of Abnormal and Social Psychology*, 65:223–231.

Apsler, R., and D. O. Sears (1968). Warning, personal involvement, and attitude change. *Journal of Personality and Social Psychology* 9:162–166.

Argyle, M. (1969). *Social Interaction.* New York: Atherton.

Aristotle. (1932). *Rhetoric.* Trans. by Lane Cooper. New York: D. Appleton Century.

Arnheim, R. (1944). The world of the daytime serial. In P. F. Lazarsfeld and F. N. Stanton (eds.), *Radio Research 1942–1943.* New York: Duell, Sloan and Pearce.

Aronson, E., and J. Mills (1959). The effect of severity of initiation on liking for a group. *Journal of Abnormal and Social Psychology* 59:177–181.

Aronson, E., J. Turner, and M. Carlsmith (1963). Communicator credibility and communicator discrepancy as determinants of opinion change. *Journal of Abnormal and Social Psychology,* 67:31–36.

Asch, S. E. (1946). Forming impressions of personality. *Journal of Abnormal and Social Psychology* 41:258–290.

————. (1952). *Social Psychology.* Englewood Cliffs, New Jersey: Prentice-Hall.

Atkins, C., and B. Reeves (June 1, 1974). Determinants and effects of exposure to mass media messages about the Agnew affair. Paper presented at the American Association for Public Opinion Research Convention.

Auer, J. J., ed. (1963). *Antislavery and Disunion, 1858–1861: Studies in the Rhetoric of Compromise and Conflict.* New York: Harper and Row.

Avorn, J. (1968). *Up Against the Ivy Wall.* New York: Atheneum Press.

Bachrach, P., and M. S. Baratz (1970). *Power and Poverty: Theory and Practice.* Oxford: Oxford University Press.

Baldwin, C. S. (1924). *Ancient Rhetoric and Poetic.* New York: MacMillan.

Barker, L. L., and R. J. Kibler, ed. (1971). *Speech Communication Behavior.* Englewood Cliffs, New Jersey: Prentice-Hall.

Barmash, I. (1974). *The World is Full of It.* New York: Delacarte Press.

Barnlund, D. C. (1968). *Interpersonal Communication: Survey and Studies.* Boston: Houghton Mifflin.

Becker, S. L. (1971). Rhetorical studies for the contemporary world. In L. Bitzer and E. Black, (eds). *The Prospect of Rhetoric,* pp. 21–43. Englewood Cliffs, New Jersey: Prentice-Hall.

Beisecker, T. D., and D. W. Parson, eds. (1972). *The Process of Social Influence: Readings in Persuasion.* Englewood Cliffs, N.J.: Prentice-Hall.

Bem, D. J. (1965). An experimental analysis of self-persuasion. *Journal of Experimental Social Psychology* 1:199–218.

————. (1970). *Beliefs, Attitudes and Human Affairs.* Belmont, Calif.: Brooks/Cole Publishing Company.

Berelson, B. (1952). *Content Analysis in Communication Research.* New York: Free Press.

Berelson, B., and G. A. Steiner (1964). *Human Behavior: An Inventory of Scientific Findings.* New York: Harcourt, Brace and World.

Berenda, R. W. (1950). *The Influence of the Group on the Judgments of Children.* New York: King's Crown Press.

Berger, P. L. (1963). *Invitation to Sociology—A Humanistic Perspective.* Garden City, New York: Anchor Books.

Bergin, A. E. (1962). The effect of dissonant persuasive communications on changes in a self-referring attitude. *Journal of Personality* 30:423–438.

Berlo, D. K. (1960). *The Process of Communication: An Introduction to Theory and Practice.* New York: Rinehart and Winston.

Berscheid, E. (1966). Opinion change and communicator–communicatee similarity and dissimilarity. *Journal of Personality and Social Psychology* 4:670–680.

Bettinghaus, E. P. (1968). *Persuasive Communication.* (Rev. ed., 1973). New York: Holt, Rinehart and Winston.

Bettleheim, B. (1943). Individual and mass behavior in extreme situations. *Journal of Abnormal and Social Psychology* 38:417–452.

Bickman, L., and T. Henchy, eds. (1970). Beyond the Laboratory: *Field Research in Social Psychology.* New York: Appleton-Century-Crofts.

Birdwhistell, R. (1970). *Kinesics and Context.* Philadelphia: University of Pennsylvania Press.

Bitzer, L. F. (1968). The rhetorical situation. *Philosophy and Rhetoric* 1:1–14.

Bitzer, L. F. and E. Black, eds. (1971). *The Prospect of Rhetoric.* Englewood Cliffs, New Jersey: Prentice-Hall.

Black, E. (1965). *Rhetorical Criticism: A Study in Method.* New York: MacMillan.

———. (1970). The second persona. *Quarterly Journal of Speech* 56:109–119.

Blumler, J. G., and D. McQuail (1969). *Television in Politics.* Chicago: University of Chicago Press.

Bochner, S., and C. A. Insko (1966). Communication discrepancy, source credibility and opinion change. *Journal of Personality and Social Psychology* 4:614–621.

Bogart, L. (1955). Adults talk about newspaper comics. *American Journal of Sociology* 41:26–30.

———. (1967). *Strategy in Advertising.* New York: Harcourt, Brace and World.

Bonchek, V. (1967). Commitment, communicator credibility and attitude change. *Dissertation Abstracts* 27:3929A–3930A.

Boorstin, D. J. (1962). *The Image.* New York: Atheneum.

Booth, W. C. (1971). The scope of rhetoric today: a polemical excursion. In L. B Bitzer and E. Black, (eds). *The Prospect of Rhetoric.* pp. 93–114. Englewood Cliffs, New Jersey: Prentice-Hall.

Brandt, W. J. (1970). *The Rhetoric of Argumentation.* Indianapolis: Bobbs-Merrill.

Braybrooke, D., and C. Lindbloom (1963). *A Strategy of Decision.* New York: Free Press.

Brehm, J. W. (1956). Post-decision changes in the desirability of alternatives. *Journal of Abnormal and Social Psychology* 52: 384–9.

Brehm, J. W. (1962). An experiment on coercion and attitude change. In J. W. Brehm and A. R. Cohen, (eds.), *Explorations in Cognitive Dissonance*, pp. 137–143. Englewood Cliffs, New Jersey: Prentice-Hall.

Brehm, J. W., and A. R. Cohen (1962). *Explorations in Cognitive Dissonance*. New York: John Wiley and Sons.

Brembeck, W. L., and W. S. Howell (1952). *Persuasion: A Means Of Social Control*. Englewood Cliffs, New Jersey: Prentice-Hall.

Bridgeman, P. W. (1959). *The Way Things Are*. Cambridge, Mass.: Harvard University Press.

Brigance, W. N., ed. (1943). *A History of American Public Address*. 2 vols. New York: McGraw-Hill.

Brock, T. C. (1965). Communicator-recipient similarity and decision change. *Journal of Personality and Social Psychology* 1:650–654.

Brock, T. C., and L. A. Becker (1965). Ineffectiveness of "overheard" counter-propaganda. *Journal of Personality and Social Psychology* 2:654–660.

Brock, T. C., and J. E. Blackwood (1962). Dissonance reduction, social comparison, and modification of others' opinions. *Journal of Abnormal and Social Psychology* 65:319–324.

Brockriede, W. (1974). Rhetorical criticism as argument. *Quarterly Journal of Speech* 60:165–174.

Brown, L. W. (1974). The image-makers: black rhetoric and white media. In J. L. Daniel (ed.), *Black Communication: Dimensions of Research and Instruction*, pp. 28–41. New York. Speech Communication Association.

Bryant, D. C. (1953). Rhetoric: its functions and its scope. *Quarterly Journal of Speech* 39:15–37.

Buber, M. (1958). *The I and Thou*, 2d ed. Translated by R. G. Smith. New York: Scribner.

Buchanan, P. J. (June 8, 1975) 'New History' makes mockery of America's great heroes. The [Philadelphia] Sunday Bulletin, p. 17.

Buckley, W. (May 20, 1973). Impeach the speech, not the President. *The New York Times Magazine*, p. 30.

Burhans, D. T., Jr. (1971). The attitude-behavior discrepancy problem: revisited. *Quarterly Journal of Speech* 57:418–428.

Burke, K. (1945). *A Grammar of Motives*. Englewood Cliffs, New Jersey: Prentice-Hall.

———. (1967). The Rhetoric of Hitler's "Battle." In Burke, *The Philosophy of Literary Form*. 2d. ed. Baton Rouge: Louisiana State University Press.

———. (1969). *A Rhetoric of Motives*, Reprint. Berkeley: University of California Press. Orig. published by Prentice-Hall, 1950. All references are to University of California edition.

Byrne, D. (1971). *The Attraction Paradigm*. New York: Academic Press.

Campbell, A., P. Converse, W. Miller, and D. Stokes (1960). *The American Voter.* New York: John Wiley and Sons.

Campbell, D. T., and J. Stanley (1963). Experimental and quasi-experimental designs for research on teaching. In N. L. Gage (ed.), *Handbook of Research on Teaching,* pp. 171–246. Chicago: Rand McNally.

Campbell, K. K. (1972). *Critique of Contemporary Rhetoric.* Belmont, California: Wadsworth.

————. (1973). The rhetoric of women's liberation: an oxymoron. *Quarterly Journal of Speech* 59:74–86.

Capaldi, N. *The Art of Deception* (2d. ed.) Buffalo, N. Y.: Prometheus Books.

Cartwright, D., and F. Harary (1956). Structural balance: a generalization of Heider's theory. *Psychological Review* 63:277–293.

Chapanis, N. P., and A. Chapanis (1964). Cognitive dissonance: five years later. *Psychological Bulletin* 61:1–22.

Chase, S. (1949). *Roads to Agreement.* New York: Harper and Bros.

————. (1953). Roads to agreement. *Vital Speeches* 19:279–282.

Chesebro, J., and C. Hamsher (1973). Rhetorical criticism: a message-centered procedure. *Speech Teacher* 22:62–70.

Chiaromonte, N. (July, 1968). Letter from Rome. *Encounter* 31:25–27.

Cohen, A. R. (1957). Need for cognition and order of communication as a determinant of opinion change. In C. I. Hovland (ed.), *Order of Presentation in Persuasion,* pp. 79–97. New Haven: Yale University Press.

————. (1964). *Attitude Change and Social Influence.* New York: Basic Books.

Cohen, A. R., and B. Latané (1962). An experiment on choice in commitment to counterattitudinal behavior. In J. W. Brehm, and A. R. Cohen (eds.), *Explorations in Cognitive Dissonance,* pp. 88–91. New York: John Wiley and Sons.

Corbett, E. P. J. (1971). Rhetoric in search of a past, present and future. In L. B. Bitzer and E. Black (eds.), *The Prospect of Rhetoric,* pp. 166–178. Englewood Cliffs, New Jersey: Prentice-Hall.

Coser, L. (1967). *Continuities in the Study of Social Conflict.* New York: Free Press.

Cousins, N. (July 10, 1971). The Pentagon Papers Continued. *Saturday Review* 54:18.

Cronbach, L. J. (1975). Five decades of public controversy over mental testing. *American Psychologist* 30:1–14.

Cronkhite, G. (1969). *Persuasion: Speech and Behavioral Change.* Indianapolis: Bobbs-Merrill.

Dahle, T. L. (1954). An objective and comparative study of five methods of transmitting information to business and industrial employees. *Speech Monographs* 21:21–28.

Davis, K. (1962). *Human Relations at Work,* 2d. ed. New York: McGraw-Hill.

Dean, R. B., J. A. Austin, and W. A. Watts (1971). Forewarning effects in persuasion: field and classroom experiments. *Journal of Personality and Social Psychology* 18:210–221.

Delia, J. G. (1970). The logic fallacy, cognitive theory, and the enthymeme: a search for the foundations of reasoned discourse. *Quarterly Journal of Speech* 56:140–148.

De Vito, J. A., ed. (1973). *Language: Concepts and Processes*. Englewood Cliffs, New Jersey: Prentice-Hall.

Dichter, E. (1960). *The Strategy of Desire*. Garden City, New York: Doubleday.

Duncan, H. D. (1968). *Communication and Social Order*. New York: Oxford University Press.

Duncker, K. (1938). Experimental modification of children's food preference through social suggestion. *Journal of Abnormal and Social Psychology* 33: 489–507.

Edelman, M. (1967). *The Symbolic Uses of Politics*. Chicago: University of Illinois Press.

Ehninger, D. (1972). *Contemporary Rhetoric: A Reader's Coursebook*. Glenview, Ill.: Scott Foresman.

Ehninger, D., and W. Brockriede (1963). *Decision by Debate*. New York: Dodd, Mead & Co.

Elkin, F. (1950). The psychological appeal of the Hollywood western. *Journal of Educational Sociology* 24:72–86.

Ellsberg, D. (1959). The theory and practice of blackmail. Presented as a Lowell lecture and reprinted in *Rand Papers*, 3883:1–38.

Ellul, J. (1973). *Propaganda: The Formation of Men's Attitudes*. Reprint. New York: Vintage. Originally published in English by Knopf, 1965.

Etzioni, A. (June 3, 1972). Human beings are not so easy to change, after all. *Saturday Review*, pp. 45–47.

Fanon, F. (1966). *The Wretched of the Earth*. New York: Grove Press.

Festinger, L. (1950). Informal social communication. *Psychological Review* 57: 271–292.

———. (1957). *A Theory of Cognitive Dissonance*. Stanford: Stanford University Press.

———. (Winter 1964). Behavioral support for opinion change. *Public Opinion Quarterly* 28:404–417.

Festinger, L., ed. (1964). *Commitment, Decision and Dissonance*. Stanford: Stanford University Press.

Festinger, L., H. Riecken, and S. Schachter (1956). *When Prophecy Fails*. Minneapolis: University of Minnesota Press.

Fine, B. J. (1957). Conclusion-drawing, communicator credibility and anxiety as factors in opinion change. *Journal of Abnormal and Social Psychology* 54: 369–374.

Fishbein, M. (1963). An investigation of relationships between beliefs about an object and the attitude toward that object. *Human Relations* 16:233–239.

——. (1967). Attitude and the prediction of behavior. In M. Fishbein (ed.), *Readings in Attitude Theory and Measurement,* pp. 477–492. New York: Wiley.

Fletcher, J. (1966). *Situational Ethics: The New Morality.* Philadelphia: Westminster Press.

Fogelson, R. (1971). *Violence As Protest.* Garden City, New York: Doubleday Anchor.

Fortas, A. (1968). *Concerning Dissent and Civil Disobedience.* New York: Signet.

Fotheringham, W. C. (1966). *Perspectives on Persuasion.* Boston: Allyn and Bacon.

Fox, S. (1974). The Rhetoric of Hitch-hiking. Unpublished paper.

Frank, J. D. (1944). Experimental studies of personal pressure and resistance. *Journal of General Psychology,* 30:23–64.

Freedman, J. L. (1964). Involvement, discrepancy and change. *Journal of Abnormal and Social Psychology* 69:290–295.

——. (1965). Preference for dissonant information. *Journal of Personality and Social Psychology* 2:287–289.

Freedman, J. L., and D. O. Sears (1965). Selective exposure. In L. Berkowitz, (ed.), *Advances in Experimental Social Psychology,* 2, pp. 57–97. New York: Academic Press.

Friendly, F. (1971). Television. *Harper's Magazine* 242:30–33.

Gamson, W. A. (1968). *Power and Discontent.* Homewood, Ill.: Dorsey Press.

——. (1975). *The Strategy of Social Protest.* Homewood, Ill.: Dorsey Press.

Gardner, M. (1957). *Fads and Fallacies in the Name of Science.* rev. ed. New York: Dover.

Gelb, L. (June 27, 1971). Why we did what we did in Vietnam. *The Sunday Bulletin.* Section 2, 1.

Gerard, H. B., and G. Mathewson (1966). The effect of severity of initiation on liking for a group: a replication. *Journal of Experimental Social Psychology* 2:278–287.

Gerbner, G., O. R. Holsti, W. P. Paisley, and P. J. Stone, eds. (1969). *The Analysis of Communication Content.* New York: John Wiley & Sons.

Gergen, K. J. (1969). *The Psychology of Behavior Exchange.* Reading, Mass.: Addison-Wesley.

Goffman, E. (1959). *The Presentation of Self in Everyday Life.* New York: Anchor.

——. (1961). *Encounters: Two Studies in the Sociology of Interaction.* Indianapolis: Bobbs-Merrill.

——. (1967). *Interaction Ritual.* Garden City, New York: Anchor.

Goldstein, M. J. (1959). The relationship between coping and avoiding behavior and response to fear-arousing propaganda. *Journal of Abnormal and Social Psychology* 58:247–252.

Gould, L. (1973). If your husband makes the bed, must you lie in it? *Ms.* 1:92–95.

Graham, J., ed. (1970). *Great American Speeches of the Twentieth Century, Texts and Studies*. New York: Appleton-Century-Crofts.

Gray, G. W. (1946). The precepts of Kagemni and Ptah-Hotep. *Quarterly Journal of Speech* 32:446–454.

Greenwald, A. G. (1965). Behavior change following a persuasive communication. *Journal of Personality* 33:370–391.

———. (1966). Effects of prior commitment on behavior change after a persuasive communication. *Public Opinion Quarterly* 29:595–601.

Greenwald, H. (1964). The involvement-discrepancy controversy in persuasion research. Doctoral dissertation, Columbia University.

Gregg, R. B. (1966). *The Power of Nonviolence*. New York: Schocken Books.

Griffin, L. (1964). The rhetorical structure of the "New Left" movement: Part I. *Quarterly Journal of Speech* 50:113–135.

Grover, D. H., ed. (1968). *Landmarks in Western Oratory*. Laramie: University of Wyoming Press.

Haiman, F. S. (1949). An experimental study of the effects of ethos in public speaking. *Speech Monographs* 16:190–202.

Hall, E. T. (1959). *The Silent Language*. Greenwich, Conn.: Fawcett Publications.

Hart, R. P., and D. M. Burks (1972). Rhetorical sensitivity and social interaction. *Speech Monographs* 39:75–91.

Hawkins, D. (1970). The effects of subliminal stimulation on drive level and brand preference. *Journal of Marketing Research* 7:322–326.

Heider, F. (1958). *The Psychology of Interpersonal Relations*. New York: John Wiley and Sons.

Henry, J. (1965). *Culture Against Man*. New York: Vintage.

Herzog, H. (1944). What do we really know about daytime serial listeners. In P. R. Lazarsfeld and F. N. Stanton (eds.), *Radio Research, 1942–43*. New York: Duell, Sloan and Pearce.

Higbee, K. L. (1969). Fifteen years of fear arousal: research on threat appeals. Psychological Bulletin 72:426–444.

Hill, F. I. (1972). Conventional wisdom—traditional form: the president's message of November 3, 1969. *Quarterly Journal of Speech* 58:373–386.

Hollingworth, H. L. (1935). *Psychology of the Audience*. New York: American Book Company.

Horn, M., ed. (1971). *75 Years of the Comics*. Boston: Boston Book & Art.

Hovland, C. I. (1959). Reconciling conflicting results derived from experimental and survey studies of attitude change. *American Psychologist* 14:8–17.

Hovland, C. I., I. L. Janis, and H. H. Kelley (1953). *Communication and Persuasion*. New Haven: Yale University Press.

Hovland, C. I., and W. Mandell (1952). An experimental comparison of conclusion drawing by the communicator and the audience. *Journal of Abnormal and Social Psychology* 47:581–588.

Hovland, C. I., and M. J. Rosenberg, eds. (1960) *Attitude Organization and Change*. New Haven: Yale University Press.

Hovland, C. I., and W. Weiss (1951). The influence of source credibility on communication effectiveness. *Public Opinion Quarterly* 15:635–650.

Howell, W. S. (1956). *Logic and Rhetoric in England, 1500–1700*. Princeton, New Jersey: Princeton University Press.

Hoyt, P. (1958). Civil Rights. The eyes of the world are upon us. *Vital Speeches of the Day*. Southold, N.Y.: City News Publishing Co.

Huber, R. (1955). Dwight Moody. In M. Hochmuth (ed.), *History and Criticism of American Public Address*. New York: Longmans Green 3:222–261.

Insko, C. A. (1967). *Theories of Attitude Change*. New York: Meredith Publishing Company.

Irvine, J. R., and W. G. Kirkpatrick (1972). The musical form in rhetorical exchange: theoretical considerations. *Quarterly Journal of Speech* 58:272–284.

Irwin, J. V., and H. H. Brockhaus (1963). The 'teletalk' project: a study of the effectiveness of two public relations speeches. *Speech Monographs* 30:359–368.

Ivie, R. L. (1974). Presidential motives for war. *Quarterly Journal of Speech* 60:337–345.

Janis, I. L., and P. B. Field (1959). Sex differences and personality factors related to persuasibility. In I. L. Janis and C. I. Hovland (eds.), *Personality and Persuasibility*, pp. 207–221. New Haven, Conn.: Yale University Press.

Janis, I. L., and C. I. Hovland, eds. (1959). *Personality and Persuasibility*. New Haven: Yale University Press.

Johannesen, R. L. (1971). The emerging concept of communication as dialogue. *Quarterly Journal of Speech* 57:373–382.

Jones, E. E. (1954). *Ingratiation: A Social Psychological Analysis*. New York: Appleton-Century-Crofts.

Jones, E. E., K. E. Davis, and K. J. Gergen (1961). Role playing variations and their informational value for person perception. *Journal of Abnormal and Social Psychology* 63:302–310.

Jones, E. E., and H. B. Gerard (1967). *Foundations of Social Psychology*. New York: Wiley.

Jones, E. E., K. J. Gergen, and R. G. Jones (1963). Tactics of ingratiation among leaders and subordinates in a status hierarchy. *Psychological Monographs* 77:566.

Jones, E. E., D. E. Kanouse, H. H. Kelley, R. E. Nisbett, S. Valins, and B. Weiner

(1971). *Attribution: Perceiving the Causes of Behavior.* Morristown, N.J.: General Learning Press.

Jong, E. M. (1973). *Fear of Flying: A Novel.* New York: Holt, Rinehart and Winston.

Kaplan, A. (1964). *The Conduct of Inquiry.* San Francisco: Chandler Publishing Company.

Karlins, M., and H. Abelson (1970). *Persuasion: How Opinions and Attitudes are Changed.* 2d. ed. New York: Springer Publishing Company.

Katz, D. (1960). The functional approach to the study of attitudes. *Public Opinion Quarterly* 24:163–204.

Katz, E. (1957). The two step flow of communication: an up-to-date report on an hypothesis. *Public Opinion Quarterly* 21:61–78.

———. (1963). The diffusion of new ideas and practices. In W. Schramm (ed.), *The Science of Human Communication.* New York: Basic Books.

Katz, E., and R. Lazarsfeld (1955). *Personal Influence: The Part Played by People in the Flow of Mass Communications.* Glencoe, Illinois: The Free Press.

Kelley, H. H. (1971). *Attribution in Social Interaction.* Morristown, N.J.: General Learning Press (also appears as first chapter of Jones, et al., 1971).

Kelman, H. C. (1961). Processes of opinion change. *Public Opinion Quarterly* 25:57–78.

———. (1974). Attitudes are alive and well and gainfully employed in the sphere of action. *American Psychologist* 29:310–324.

Kelman, H. C., and C. I. Hovland (1953). Reinstatement of the communicator in delayed measurement of opinion change. *Journal of Abnormal and Social Psychology* 48:327–335.

Keniston, K. (1968). *Young Radicals.* New York: Harcourt, Brace and World.

Kennedy, G. (1963). *The Art of Persuasion in Greece.* Princeton, N.J.: Princeton University Press.

Kerlinger, F. N. (1964). *Foundations of Behavioral Research.* New York: Holt, Rinehart, and Winston.

Kiesler, C. A., B. E. Collins, and N. Miller (1969). *Attitude Change: A Critical Analysis of Theoretical Approaches.* New York: John Wiley and Sons.

Kiesler, C. A., and S. B. Kiesler, (1964). Role of forewarning in persuasive communications. *Journal of Abnormal and Social Psychology* 68:547–549.

Klapper, J. T. (1960). *The Effects of Mass Communication.* Glencoe, Illinois: The Free Press.

Koch, S. (1964). Psychology and emerging conceptions of knowledge as unitary. In T. W. Wann (ed.), *Behaviorism and Phenomenology*, pp. 1–41. Chicago: Phoenix Books.

Kochman, T. (1969). Rapping in the ghetto. *Transaction* 6:26–34.

Krech, D., and R. S. Crutchfield, (1948). *Theory and Problems in Social Psychology.* New York: McGraw-Hill.

Kriesberg, L. (1973). *The Sociology of Social Conflicts.* Englewood Cliffs, N.J.: Prentice-Hall.

Kuhn, T. S. (1970). The structure of scientific revolutions. Vol. II, No. 2. *International Encyclopedia of Unified Science.* 2d ed. Chicago: University of Chicago Press.

Kutner, B., C. Wilkins, and R. R. Yarrow (1952). Verbal attitudes and overt behavior involving prejudice. *Journal of Abnormal and Social Psychology* 47: 649–652.

Lambert, W. E., S. Fillenbaum, R. C. Gardner, and R. C. Hodgson (1960). Evaluational reactions to spoken languages. *Journal of Abnormal and Social Psychology* 60:44–51.

Lapiere, R. (1934). Attitudes vs. Actions. *Social Forces* 13:230–237.

Larson, C. U. (1973). *Persuasion: Reception and Responsibility.* Belmont, California: Wadsworth Publishing Company.

Lazarsfeld, P. F., and H. Menzel (1963). Mass media and personal influence. In W. Schramm (ed.), *The Science of Human Communication.* New York: Basic Books.

Leff, M. C., and G. P. Mohrmann (1974). Lincoln at Cooper Union: a rhetorical analysis of the text. *Quarterly Journal of Speech* 60:346–358.

Linn, L. S. (1965). Verbal attitudes and overt behavior: a study of racial discrimination. *Social Forces* 43:353–364.

Lipset, S. M., and G. M. Schaflander (1971). *Passion and Politics: Student Activism in America.* Boston: Little, Brown.

Lipset, S. M., and S. S. Wolin (1965). *The Berkeley Student Revolt: Facts and Interpretations.* Garden City, N.Y.: Anchor Books.

Louch, A. R. (1969). *Explanation and Human Action.* Berkeley: University of California Press.

Maccoby, E., and C. Jacklin (1974). *The Psychology of Sex Differences.* Palo Alto: Stanford University Press.

Mailer, N. (1968). Miami Beach and the siege of Chicago. *Harper's Magazine* 237:41–130.

Maslow, A. H. (1943). A dynamic theory of personality. *Psychological Review* 50:370–396.

McCombs, M., and D. Shaw (1972). The agenda-setting function of mass media. *Public Opinion Quarterly* 36:176–187.

McConnell, J., R. Cutler, and E. McNeil (1970). Subliminal stimulation: an overview. *American Psychologist* 12:61–69.

McCroskey, J. C. (1969). A summary of experimental research on the effects of evidence in persuasive communication. *Quarterly Journal of Speech* 55:169–176.

McGinniss, J. (1969). *The Selling of the President, 1968.* New York: Trident.

McGrath, J. E., and I. Altman (1966). *Small Group Research.* New York: Holt, Rinehart, and Winston.

McGuire, W. J. (1957). Order of presentation as a factor in conditioning persuasiveness. In C. I. Hovland (ed.), *Order of Presentation in Persuasion*, pp. 98–114. New Haven: Yale University Press.

———. (1960a). A syllogistic analysis of cognitive relationships. In C. I. Hovland, and M. J. Rosenberg (eds.), *Attitude Organization and Change*, pp. 65–111. New Haven: Yale University Press.

———. (1960b). Direct and indirect effects of dissonance-producing messages. *Journal of Abnormal and Social Psychology* 60:354–358.

———. (1964). Inducing resistance to persuasion: some contemporary approaches. In L. Berkowitz (ed.), *Advances in Experimental Social Psychology*, I., pp. 191–229. New York: Academic Press.

———. (1969). The nature of attitudes and attitude change. In G. E. Lindzey and E. Aronson (eds.), *The Handbook of Social Psychology.* Vol. 3. 2d ed., pp. 136–314. Reading, Mass.: Addison-Wesley.

McLuhan, M. (1964). *Understanding Media: The Extensions of Man.* New York: Signet Books.

Mead, G. H. (1934). *Mind, Self and Society.* Chicago: University of Chicago Press.

Mehrabian, A. (1971). *Silent Messages.* Belmont, Cal: Wadsworth Publishing Co.

Mendelsohn, H., and I. Crespi (1970). *Polls, Television and The New Politics.* Scranton, Penna.: Chandler Publishing Company.

Merton, R. (1946). *Mass Persuasion.* New York: Harper.

Milgram, S. (1963). Behavioral study of obedience. *Journal of Abnormal and Social Psychology* 67:371–378.

Mill, J. S. (1859). *On Liberty.* Reprinted as a Crofts Classic. A. Castell (ed.) New York: Meredith Corporation, 1947.

Miller, A., W. Miller, A. Raine, and T. Brown (1973). *A Majority Party in Disarray: Policy Polarization in the 1972 Election.* Ann Arbor: University of Michigan Center for Political Studies.

Miller, G. R. (1964). An Experimental Study of The Relationships of Fear Appeals, Source Credibility, and Attitude Change. Mimeographed. Michigan State University.

———. (1969). Some factors influencing judgments of the logical validity of arguments: a research review. *Quarterly Journal of Speech* 55:276–286.

Miller, G. R., and H. W. Simons (1974). *Perspectives on Communication in Social Conflicts.* Englewood Cliffs, N.J.: Prentice-Hall.

Mills, J. (1966). Opinion change as a function of the communicator's desire to influence and liking for the audience. *Journal of Experimental Social Psychology* 2:152–159.

Mills, J., and E. Aronson (1965). Opinion change as a function of the communicator's attractiveness and desire to influence. *Journal of Personality and Social Psychology* 1:173–177.

Miner, H. (1956). Body ritual among the Nacirema. *American Anthropologist* 58:503–507.

Minnick, C. (1957). *The Art of Persuasion*. Boston: Houghton Mifflin.

———. (1968). *The Art of Persuasion*. 2d. ed. Boston: Houghton Mifflin.

Monroe, A. H. (1949). *Principles and Types of Speech*. 3d ed. New York: Scott, Foresman.

Moore, H. T. (1921). The comparative influence of majority and expert opinion. *American Journal of Psychology* 32:16–20.

Morgan, J. J. B., and J. T. Morton (1944). The distortion of syllogistic reasoning produced by personal convictions. *Journal of Social Psychology* 20:39–59.

Mortenson, C. D. (1972). *Communication: The Study of Human Interaction*. New York: McGraw-Hill.

Nader, R. (1965). *Unsafe At Any Speed*. New York: Grossman.

Napolitan, J. (1972). *The Election Game: And How to Win It*. Garden City, N.Y.: Doubleday & Co.

Nebel, L. J. (May 1, 1961). The Pitchman. *Harper's Magazine* 222:50–54.

Neumann, W. R. (June 1, 1974). *Political Knowledge: A Comparison of the Impact of Print and Broadcast Media*. Paper presented at the American Association of Public Opinion Research Convention.

Nichols, M. H. (1954). Lincoln's first inaugural. In W. M. Parrish and M. H. Nichols (eds.), *American Speeches*. New York: David McKay.

———. (1955). *A History and Criticism of American Public Address*. Vol. III. London: Longmans, Green.

Nimmo, D. (1970). *The Political Persuaders: Techniques of Modern Election Campaigns*. Englewood Cliffs, New Jersey: Prentice-Hall.

Novak, M. (1974). *Choosing our King*. New York: MacMillan.

Oberschall, A. (1973). *Social Conflict and Social Movements*. Englewood Cliffs, N.J.: Prentice-Hall.

Orne, M. T. (1962). On the social psychology of the psychological experiment: with particular reference to demand characteristics and their implications. *American Psychologist* 17:776–783.

Orne, M. T., and F. J. Evans (1965). Social control in the psychological experiment. *Journal of Personality and Social Psychology* 1:189–200.

Osgood, C., G. J. Suci, and P. H. Tannenbaum (1957). *The Measurement of Meaning*. Urbana: University of Illinois Press.

Osgood, C., and P. Tannenbaum (1955). The principle of congruity in the prediction of attitude change. *Psychological Review* 62:42–55.

Packard, V. (1958). *The Hidden Persuaders.* New York: Pocket Books.

Papageorgis, D. (1968). Warning and persuasion. *Psychological Bulletin* 70:271–282.

Parsons, T. (1963). On the concept of influence. *Public Opinion Quarterly* 27:37–62.

Patterson, T., and R. McClure (1974). *Political Advertising: Voter Reaction to Televised Political Commercials.* Princeton, N.J.: Citizens Research Foundation.

Paulson, S. (1954). The effects of the prestige of the speaker and acknowledgment of opposing arguments on audience retention and shift of opinion. *Speech Monographs* 21:267–271.

Pepitone, A., and W. Wallace (1955). *Experimental Studies on the Dynamics of Hostility.* Paper read at Pennsylvania Psychological Association Meeting. Described in A. Pepitone, Attributions of causality, social attitudes, and cognitive matching processes, by R. Tagiuri, and T. Petrullo (eds.), in *Person Perception and Interpersonal Behavior*, pp. 258–76. Stanford, Calif.: Stanford University Press, 1958.

Perelman, C. (1971). The new rhetoric. In L. Bitzer and E. Black (eds.), *The Prospect of Rhetoric*, pp. 115–122. Englewood Cliffs, N.J.: Prentice-Hall.

Perelman, C., and L. Olbrechts-Tyteca (1969). *The New Rhetoric: A Treatise on Argumentation.* Notre Dame: University of Notre Dame Press.

Perloff, M. (May 10, 1975). Soap opera bubbles. *The New Republic* 172:27–30.

Peterson, R. C., and L. L. Thurstone (1933). *The Effect of Motion Pictures on the Social Attitudes of High School Children.* Chicago: University of Chicago Press.

Pigors, P. (1949). *Effective Communication in Industry.* New York: National Association of Manufacturers.

Platt, A. M. (1971). *The Politics of Riot Commissions.* New York: Collier Books.

Poincaré, H. (1929). *The Foundation of Science.* New York: The Science Press.

Polanyi, M. (1958). *Personal Knowledge.* Chicago: University of Chicago Press.

Pool, I. D., and W. Schramm, eds. (1973). *Handbook of Communication.* Chicago: Rand McNally.

Powell, F. A. (1965). Source credibility and behavioral compliance as determinants of attitude change. *Journal of Personality and Social Psychology* 2:669–676.

Raven, B. H., and A. W. Kruglanski (1970). Conflict and power. In P. Swingle (ed.), *The Structure of Conflict*, pp. 69–109. New York: Academic Press.

Redding, W., and C. Sanborn (1964). *Business and Industrial Communication: A Sourcebook.* New York: Harper and Row.

Reston, J. (October 4, 1972). McGovern's poor showing. *The New York Times Magazine* p. 15.

Robinson, J. P., and W. Swinehart (1968). World affairs and the TV audience. *Television Quarterly* 7:47–54.

Rogers, E. M., and D. K. Bhowmik (1970–71). 'Homophily-heterophily', relational concepts for communication research. *Public Opinion Quarterly* 34:523–528.

Rokeach, M. (1960). *The Open and Closed Mind.* New York: Basic Books.

———. (1968). *Beliefs, Attitudes and Values.* San Francisco: Jossey-Bass.

———. (1973). *The Nature of Human Values.* New York: Free Press.

Rosenberg, M. J. (1960). An analysis of affective-cognitive consistency. In C. I. Hovland and M. J. Rosenberg (eds.), *Attitude Organization and Change.* New Haven: Yale University Press.

Rosenblatt, P. C., and J. M. Hicks (May 1966) *Pretesting, Forewarning and Persuasion.* Paper presented at Midwestern Psychological Association Convention.

Rosenfield, L. B., and V. R. Christie (1974). Sex and persuasibility revisited. *Western Speech.* 38:244–253.

Rosenfield, L. W. (1968a). The anatomy of critical discourse. *Speech Monographs* 35:50–69.

———. (1968b). A case study in speech criticism: The Nixon-Truman analog. *Speech Monographs* 35:435–450.

Roszak, B., and T. Roszak, eds. (1969). *Masculine/Feminine.* New York: Harper and Row.

Roszak, T. (1969). *The Making of a Counter Culture.* Garden City, N.Y.: Anchor.

Roth, R. (May 9, 1971). Violent demonstrations bring sorrow to the capitol. *Philadelphia Sunday Bulletin.*

Schachter, S., and J. E. Singer (1962). Cognitive, social and physiological determinants of emotional state. *Psychological Review* 69:379–399.

Scheffler, I. (1967). *Science and Subjectivity.* Indianapolis: Bobbs-Merrill.

Scheidel, T. M. (1967). *Persuasive Speaking.* Glenview, Ill.: Scott Foresman.

Schelling, T. C. (1960). *The Strategy of Conflict.* Cambridge, Mass.: Harvard University Press.

Schiller, H. (1973). *The Mind Managers.* Boston: Beacon Press.

Schramm, W. (1960). *The Process and Effects of Mass Communication.* Urbana, Ill.: University of Illinois Press.

Scott, R. L. (1968). Black power bends Martin Luther King. *Speaker and Gavel* 5:82–87.

Scott, R. L., and B. L. Brock (1972). *Methods of Rhetorical Criticism: A Twentieth Century Perspective.* New York: Harper and Row.

Scott, R. L., and D. K. Smith (1969). The rhetoric of confrontation. *Quarterly Journal of Speech* 55:1–8.

Sears, D. O. (1969). Political behavior. In E. Aronson and B. Lindzey, (eds.), *Handbook of Social Psychology.* Vol. 5, 2d ed., pp. 315–458. Reading, Mass.: Addison-Wesley.

Sears, D. O., and J. L. Freedman (1967). Selective exposure to information: A critical review. *Public Opinion Quarterly* 31:194–213.

Severo, R. (May 27, 1974). Frustration hits the ranks of young U.S. workers. *Philadelphia Evening Bulletin*.

Shadegg, S. C. (1964). *How to Win an Election: The Art of Political Victory*. New York: Taplinger Publishing Co.

Shannon, L. (1954). The opinions of Little Orphan Annie and her friends. *Public Opinion Quarterly 18:169–179*.

Shaw, M. E., and J. M. Wright (1967). *Scales for the Measurement of Attitudes*. New York: McGraw-Hill.

Sherif, M. (1958). Superordinate goals in the reduction of intergroup conflict. *American Journal of Sociology* 63:349–356.

———. (1965). *The Social Judgment-Involvement Approach vs. the Cognitive Dissonance Approach*. Paper presented at meeting of the American Psychological Association.

Sherif, M., C. Sherif, and R. Nebergall (1965). *Attitude and Attitude Change*. Philadelphia: Saunders.

Sillars, A. L. (1974). Expression and control in human interaction: perspective on humanistic psychology. *Western Speech* 38:269–277.

Simon, H. A. (1947). *Administrative Behavior*. New York: MacMillan.

Simons, H. W. (1966). Authoritarianism and social perceptiveness. *Journal of Social Psychology* 68:291–297.

———. (1969). Confrontation as a pattern of persuasion in university settings. *Central States Speech Journal* 21:81–86.

———. (1970). Requirements, problems and strategies: a theory of persuasion for social movements. *Quarterly Journal of Speech* 56:1–11.

———. (1971). Psychological theories of persuasion: an auditor's report. *Quarterly Journal of Speech* 57:383–392.

———. (1972). Persuasion in social conflicts: a critique of prevailing conceptions and a framework for future research. *Speech Monographs* 39:227–248.

Simons, H. W., R. J. Moyer, and N. W. Berkowitz (1970). Similarity, credibility and attitude change: a review and a theory. *Psychological Bulletin* 73:1–16.

Skolnick, J. H. (1969). *The Politics of Protest. Violent Aspects of Protest and Confrontation. A Staff Report to the National Commission on the Causes and Prevention of Violence*. New York: Simon and Schuster.

Sloan, T. O. (1962). A rhetorical analysis of John Donne's "The Prohibition." *Quarterly Journal of Speech* 48:38–45.

———. (1965). Persona as rhetor: an interpretation of Donne's *Satyre III*. *Quarterly Journal of Speech* 51:14–27.

Smelser, N. J. (1962). *Theory of Collective Behavior*. New York: The Free Press.

Smith, E. E. (1961). The power of dissonance techniques to change attitudes. *Public Opinion Quarterly* 25:626–639.

Smith, M. B., J. S. Bruner, and R. W. White (1956). *Opinions and Personality.* New York: John Wiley and Sons.

Staats, A. W., and C. K. Staats (1963). *Complex Human Behavior.* New York: Holt.

Steinfatt, T. M., and G. R. Miller (1974). Communication in game theoretic models of conflict. In G. R. Miller and H. W. Simons (eds.), *Perspectives on Communication in Social Conflict.* Englewood Cliffs, N.J.: Prentice-Hall.

Stephenson, W. (1967). *The Play Theory of Mass Communication. Chicago:* University of Chicago Press.

Stevenson, C. L. (1945). *Ethics and Language.* New Haven: Yale University Press.

Szasz, T. S. (1970). *Ideology and Insanity: Essays on the Psychiatric Dehumanization of Man.* Garden City, N.Y.: Anchor.

Tagiuri, R. (1969). Person perception. In G. Lindzey and E. Aronson, (eds.), *Handbook of Social Psychology.* Vol. 3. 2d. ed., pp. 395–449. Reading, Mass.: Addison-Wesley.

Tannenbaum, P. H. (1966). Mediated generalization of attitude change via the principle of congruity. *Journal of Personality and Social Psychology* 3:493–499.

Tedeschi, J. T., B. R. Schlenker and T. V. Bonoma (1973). *Conflict, Power and Games: The Experimental Study of Interpersonal Relations.* Chicago: Aldine Publishing Co.

Thibaut, J. W., and H. W. Riecken (1955). Some determinants and consequences of the perception of social causality. *Journal of Personality.* 24:113–133.

Thistlethwaite, D., H. DeHaan and J. Kamenetsky (1955). The effects of "directive" and "non-directive" communication procedures on attitudes. *Journal of Abnormal and Social Psychology* 51:107–113.

Thompson, E. (1967). Some effects of message structure on listener's comprehension. *Speech Monographs* 34:51–57.

Thonssen, L., and A. C. Baird (1948). *Speech Criticism.* New York: The Ronald Press.

Thorndike, E. L. (1935). *The Psychology of Wants, Interests and Attitudes.* New York: Appleton-Century.

Toch, H. (1965). *The Social Psychology of Social Movements.* Indianapolis: Bobbs-Merrill.

Tompkins, P. K. (1968). The rhetoric of James Joyce. *Quarterly Journal of Speech.* 54:107–114.

Tompkins, P. K., and E. V. B. Anderson (1971). *Communication Crisis at Kent State.* New York: Gordon and Breach.

Trautmann, F. (October, 1970). *Political Uses of the Mass Media: A History of*

Rhetorical Technique. Paper presented at Pennsylvania Speech Association Convention.

Tubbs, S. L. (1968). Explicit versus implicit conclusions and audience commitment. *Speech Monographs* 35:14–19.

Tucker, R. K., and P. D. Ware (1971). Persuasion via mere exposure. *Quarterly Journal of Speech* 57:437–443.

Turbayne, C. (1962). *The Myth of Metaphor.* New Haven: Yale University Press.

Turner, R. H., and L. M. Killian (1957). *Collective Behavior.* Englewood Cliffs, N.J.: Prentice-Hall.

Valins, S. (1966). Cognitive effects of false heart-rate feed-back. *Journal of Personality and Social Psychology* 4:400–408.

Vick, C. F., and R. V. Wood (1969). Similarity of past experience and the communication of meaning. *Speech Monographs* 36:159–162.

Vroom, V. H. (1964). *Work and Motivation.* New York.

Walker, D. (1968). *Rights in Conflict.* New York: Bantam Books.

Wallace, K. R., ed. (1954). *History of Speech Education in America.* New York: Appleton-Century-Crofts.

Walster, E., E. Aronson, and D. Abrahams (1966). On increasing the persuasiveness of a low prestige communicator. *Journal of Experimental Social Psychology* 2:325–342.

Walster, E., and L. Festinger (1962). The effectiveness of "overheard" persuasive communications. *Journal of Abnormal and Social Psychology* 65:395–402.

Ware, B. L., and W. A. Linkugel (1973). They spoke in defense of themselves: on the general criticism of apologia. *Quarterly Journal of Speech* 59:273–283.

Watzlawick, P., J. H. Beavin, and D. D. Jackson (1967). *Pragmatics of Human Communication: A Study of Interaction Patterns, Pathologies and Paradoxes.* New York: W. W. Norton.

Weaver, R. (March 2, 1966). *Philadelphia Bulletin.* p. 3.

Weaver, R. M. (1953). *The Ethics of Rhetoric.* Chicago: Henry Regnery.

Webb, E. J., D. T. Campbell, R. D. Schwartz, and L. Sechrest (1966). *Unobtrusive Measures: Nonreactive Research in the Social Sciences.* Chicago: Rand McNally.

Weigert, A. (1970). The immoral rhetoric of scientific sociology. *American Sociologist* 5:111–119.

Weiss, E. H. (1973). Rationality and Rhetoric in Policy Deliberations, with an Emphasis on Public School Budgeting. Ph.D. dissertation, Temple University.

Weiss, R. F. (1968). An extension of Hullian learning theory to persuasive communication. In A. G. Greenwald, T. C. Brock, and T. M. Ostrom, (eds.), *Psychological Foundations of Attitudes.* New York: Academic Press.

Weiss, W. (1966). Emotional arousal and attitude change. *Psychological Reports* 6:267–280.

Weiss, W., and S. Steinback (1965). The influence on communication effectiveness of explicitly urging action and policy consequences. *Journal of Experimental Social Psychology* 1:396–406.

White, D. M. (1957). Mass culture in America: another point of view. In B. Rosenberg, and D. M. White, (eds.), *Mass Culture: The Popular Arts in America*, pp. 13–21. New York: The Free Press.

White, R. W. (1959). Motivation reconsidered: the concept of competence. *Psychological Review*, 66:297–333.

White, T. H. (1973). *The Making of the President: 1972.* New York: Atheneum Publishers.

Whittaker, J. O. (1965). Attitude change and communication-attitude discrepancy. *Journal of Social Psychology* 65:141–147.

Wicker, A. W. (1969). Attitudes vs. actions: the relationship of verbal and overt behavioral responses to attitude objects. *Journal of Social Issues* 25:47–66.

Wilkins, R. (August 16, 1964). "What now"—one Negro leader's answer. *The New York Times Magazine* p. 11.

Wills, G. (November 5, 1972). Four more years? Learning to live with Nixon. *The New York Times Magazine* p. 37.

———. (August 8, 1974). The big week in Washington. *The New York Review of Books* 21:17–22.

Winans, A. (1917). *Public Speaking.* New York: The Century Co.

Windt, T. O., Jr. (1972). The diatribe: last resort for protest. *Quarterly Journal of Speech* 58:1–14.

Wise, D. (1973). *The Politics of Lying.* New York: Vintage.

Wolfe, T. (1970). Radical Chic and Mau-Mauing the Flak Catchers. New York: Farrar, Strauss and Giroux.

Wolfe, T. (1975). *The Printed Word.* New York: Farrar, Straus and Giroux.

Wolin, S. (1975). Looking for "reality." *New York Review of Books* 22:15–21.

Woolbert, C. H. (1916). A problem in pragmatism. *Quarterly Journal of Public Speaking* 2:264–274.

Wooten, C. W. (1973). The ambassador's speech: a particularly hellenistic genre of oratory. *Quarterly Journal of Speech* 59:209–212.

Wrage, E. J., and B. Baskerville, eds. (1960). *American Forum: Speeches on Historic Issués, 1788–1900.* New York: Harper and Row.

———. (1962). *Contemporary Forum: American Speeches on Twentieth-Century Issues.* New York: Harper and Row.

Zajonc, R. B. (1968). Attitudinal effects of mere exposure. *Journal of Personality and Social Psychology,* Monograph Supplement 9:1–32.

Zimbardo, P. G. (1960). Involvement and communication discrepancy as determinants of opinion change. *Journal of Abnormal and Social Psychology* 60:86–94.

————. (1965). The effect of effort and improvisation on self-persuasion produced by role-playing. *Journal of Experimental Social Psychology* 1:103–120.

————. (1972). The tactics and ethics of persuasion. In B. T. King and E. McGinnies (eds.), *Attitudes, Conflict, and Social Change*, pp. 84–102. New York: Academic Press.

Zimbardo, P. G., and E. Ebeson (1969). *Influencing Attitudes and Changing Behavior*. Reading, Mass.: Addison-Wesley.

Zimbardo, P. G., M. Weisenberg, I. Firestone, and B. Levy (1965). Communicator effectiveness in producing public conformity and private attitude change. *Journal of Personality* 33:233–255.

Zinn, H. (1968). *Disobedience and Democracy*. New York: Vintage.

Author Index

Note: Index lists first authors only of articles and books with multiple authors.

Subject Index